STATE OF
AMBIGUITY

STATE OF AMBIGUITY

CIVIC LIFE *and*
CULTURE *in* CUBA'S
FIRST REPUBLIC

STEVEN PALMER, JOSÉ ANTONIO PIQUERAS,
and AMPARO SÁNCHEZ COBOS, editors

DUKE UNIVERSITY PRESS
2014

© 2014 Duke University Press
All rights reserved
Designed by Heather Hensley
Typeset in Minion Pro by Tseng Information Systems, Inc.

Library of Congress Cataloging-in-Publication Data
State of ambiguity : civic life and culture in Cuba's
first republic / Steven Palmer, José Antonio Piqueras,
and Amparo Sánchez Cobos, editors.
pages cm
Includes bibliographical references and index.
ISBN 978-0-8223-5630-1 (cloth)
ISBN 978-0-8223-5638-7 (pbk.)
1. Cuba—History—19th century. 2. Cuba—History—20th
century. 3. Cuba—Politics and government—19th century.
4. Cuba—Politics and government—20th century. 5. Cuba—
Civilization—19th century. 6. Cuba—Civilization—20th century.

I. Palmer, Steven Paul. II. Piqueras Arenas, José A. (José Antonio).
III. Sánchez Cobos, Amparo.
F1784.S73 2014
972.91′05—dc23
2013048700

CONTENTS

Introduction: Revisiting Cuba's First Republic | 1
Steven Palmer, José Antonio Piqueras, and Amparo Sánchez Cobos

1. A Sunken Ship, a Bronze Eagle, and the Politics of Memory: The "Social Life" of the USS *Maine* in Cuba (1898–1961) | 22
Marial Iglesias Utset

2. Shifting Sands of Cuban Science, 1875–1933 | 54
Steven Palmer

3. Race, Labor, and Citizenship in Cuba: A View from the Sugar District of Cienfuegos, 1886–1909 | 82
Rebecca J. Scott

4. Slaughterhouses and Milk Consumption in the "Sick Republic": Socio-Environmental Change and Sanitary Technology in Havana, 1890–1925 | 121
Reinaldo Funes Monzote

5. Attributes for the Capital of an Austere Republic | 148
José Antonio Piqueras

6. Transcending Borders: *¡Tierra!* and the Expansion of Anarchism in Cuba after Independence | 181
Amparo Sánchez Cobos

7. Steeds, Cocks, and Guayaberas: The Social Impact of Agrarian Reorganization in the Republic | 208
Imilcy Balboa Navarro

8. District 25: Rotary Clubs and Regional Civic Power in Cuba, 1916–1940 | 231
Maikel Fariñas Borrego

9. *El naciente público oyente*: Toward a Genealogy of the Audience in Early Republican Cuba | 251
Alejandra Bronfman

10. New Knowledge for New Times: The Sociedad del Folklore Cubano during the "Critical Decade" (1923–1930) | 269
Ricardo Quiza Moreno

11. Nation, State, and the Making of the Cuban Working Class, 1920–1940 | 292
Robert Whitney

Bibliography | 323
Contributors | 349
Index | 353

INTRODUCTION

Revisiting Cuba's First Republic

Steven Palmer, José Antonio Piqueras,
and Amparo Sánchez Cobos

On May 20, 1902, the Republic of Cuba was proclaimed in an act transmitting sovereignty from the U.S. occupation authorities to the Cuban people's elected representatives. A new state was born in the family of American nations. The republic came after three wars of independence in the space of thirty years that had served to express the Cuban will to self-government and erode Spanish colonial dominion, though they had not been sufficient to provide liberty to the island directly. The intervention of the United States in the conflict in 1898 had precipitated the defeat of Spain and reserved for the United States a special role in determining the future of the "Pearl of the Antilles." Despite the subordination to a new empire implicit in this relationship, the new state of Cuba enjoyed a democratic constitution that had been written by an elected constituent assembly a year earlier. It could build, moreover, on a series of measures adopted by the U.S. occupation government between 1899 and 1902 intended to address the main problems of reconstruction, even if these had also been designed to constrain and channel the country's political orientation. Cubans had been able to elect new municipal governments in June 1901, and they had gone to the polls on New Year's Eve that same year to choose congressmen, governors, and provincial councilors as well as the electors who would vote for president, vice president, and senators. On February 24, after the only other candidate for the country's highest office withdrew from the race, Tomás Estrada Palma was acclaimed president of Cuba. The outcome was popular and legitimate: Estrada Palma had been president of the Republic in

Arms in 1876–77, and during the independence struggle of the late 1890s he had acted as José Martí's delegate to the Partido Revolucionario Cubano.

That is to say, the Republic of Cuba was born democratic in 1902. It possessed a founding charter that organized political life and enshrined the rights of its citizens, among them freedom of assembly and association, freedom of speech and the press, the right to make petition, habeas corpus, the inviolability of correspondence and dwelling, and freedom of worship. Education was declared obligatory, and while the state was unable to provide it, the burden would fall on the municipalities and the provinces. Political equality was guaranteed, as was universal suffrage for men over twenty-one years of age. Following the U.S. model, the constitution adopted a representative system that authorized wide powers to the presidency even as it promoted administrative decentralization to the provinces, a compromise solution to avoid the frictions of federalism while giving continuity and honoring the federal spirit of the constitutional charters issued by independence forces in 1869 and 1895.[1]

At the moment it came into the world the Republic of Cuba enjoyed political and economic conditions much more favorable than those that the great majority of Latin American nations had worked through eighty or ninety years earlier at the beginning of their respective republican lives. It is true that the U.S. occupation apparatus and a Cuban creole elite that had devoted itself, between 1878 and 1895, to the cause of Autonomism rather than outright independence were both interested in a conservative regime that denied agency to popular forces.[2] To that end they brokered a transitional pact that pulled the rug out from under the more radical democratic impulses of the Cuban independence struggle. And it is true that the highest officers of the independence armies would opt to join in that pact to further their own material and political interests in the republic.[3] Nevertheless, the country enjoyed a much more fortuitous and truly democratic basis for independent national politics than what had been achieved almost anywhere else in Latin America to that point. This was due to the later era in which Cuban independence was proclaimed, which occurred after the entrée of the masses into institutional politics. It was also, of course, due to the long struggle to achieve national liberation in which the protagonism of Cubans of African ancestry was widely acknowledged as key to the popular mobilization that had taken place and during which the ideals of Martí had united the dispersed national forces.[4] These formative experiences also proved an immovable impediment to Cuban and U.S. elite designs to engineer annexation of the island to the United States. Perhaps most important, they ensured that the formal embrace of meaningful democratic politics would not be sacrificed to the doctrinaire and authoritarian liberal formulas that dominated the political panorama in the nineteenth century and that persisted in most countries in Latin America and Europe.

Yet neither democracy nor independence would flourish in the first Cuban republic. After a mere four years, amidst a crippling revolt of rival factions opposed to the (constitutionally quite permissible) reelection of Estrada Palma, the threatened president took the fateful step of requesting that the United States intervene to prevent civil war. Cuba would endure a second U.S. military occupation government from 1906 to 1909. Then, starting with the presidency of William H. Taft—ex-secretary of war and interim governor of Cuba in 1906—the United States would regularly practice "preventive intervention" in the island's affairs. In 1912 the Independent Party of Color (PIC) would revolt, claiming that Afro-Cubans, after playing a predominant role in the independence armies, had been thoroughly marginalized from the political process. Prickly diplomatic statements from the North raised the possibility that the unrest might provoke yet another U.S. intervention. The PIC challenge was met by a savage racist backlash from the state and civil militias that left some gaping new wounds in the Cuban body politic, even as it reopened barely healed ones left by a slave society still very much part of living memory, emancipation having only finally become a reality in 1886.[5] Another liberal rebellion erupted in 1917 in the wake of electoral fraud perpetrated to keep the Conservative Mario García Menocal regime in power, and again the United States intervened to broker results favorable to "stability" (for U.S. investors in particular).

By 1920, despite rivers of gold flowing from Cuba's sugar plantations thanks to unprecedented prices on the world market, a wide variety of voices began pronouncing Cuba's republican experiment a failure.[6] They decried a political culture rotten with clientelism and misappropriation of funds at every level and a sovereignty grossly mocked by the island nation's acute economic and foreign policy dependence on the United States. By that point the cancer of the Platt Amendment had been diagnosed. When the amendment was passed into U.S. law in 1901 under the direction of Senator Orville Platt, its acceptance by Cuba became the condition for ending the U.S. occupation. The Platt Amendment prevented Cuba from entering into many kinds of international agreements and gave the United States specific rights on the island. These included the right of intervention under certain circumstances and the right to establish a naval "coaling station" on the island (eventually built in Guantánamo Bay as something substantially more than a fuel depot).

Much has been written about the folly and perfidy of the Platt Amendment.[7] Suffice it to say that, although in 1901 the constituent assembly had been offended by the heavy-handed substance and style of the legal imposition, the eventual acquiescence to insertion of the clause in the Cuban constitution was not seen at the time as a fatal blow to the republic's sovereignty. It was the growing tendency of increasingly interventionist U.S. administrations to adopt the most interventionist reading of the amendment that turned it into a symbol of neocolonial affront to sovereignty and international law in an emerging world system of nation-states. And it was the political elites of republican Cuba—important leaders of the independence movement among them—who first invoked the Platt Amendment in order to seek U.S. arbitration of conflicts over political succession. Once the door was opened by Estrada Palma in 1906, the United States began to get a feel for Platt leverage, and so did subsequent Cuban leaders: José Miguel Gómez would use the threat of further U.S. intervention to suppress the PIC revolt in 1912, and Mario García Menocal would use it to keep his faction in power in 1917.

The commercial reciprocity agreement signed with the United States in 1903 was embraced by the majority of Cuba's principal economic actors and quickly proved a boon for the Cuban sugar industry. Sugar exports, almost all to the United States, grew 40 percent within five years, and Cuba quickly amassed a favorable balance of payments with the United States. Imports and investment from the United States also grew dramatically, with results that did not necessarily favor Cuban sovereignty. The emergence or resurgence of many local industries was curtailed by the presence of cheap manufactured goods from the United States. By 1927 the country was, after Mexico, the second most important destination for U.S. investment in Latin America, and this rapid expansion of U.S. capital in the Cuban economy paved the way for the transfer of an unhealthy proportion of the island's productive assets into the hands of U.S. financial concerns following the crash of 1920.[8]

As the sweet cycle went sour after that year, so went the republic. The total collapse of international sugar prices led to economic ruin for many Cuban companies and sugar concerns. U.S. banks were the main beneficiaries, rapidly achieving majority ownership over the island's agricultural sector. During the shockingly corrupt presidency of Alfredo Zayas in the first half of the 1920s, Enoch H. Crowder, "special envoy" of the president of the United States, exercised unofficial rule over island politics and fiscal policy, first as a sinister proconsul who lived on a U.S. battleship in Havana harbor and later as ambassador.[9] In the midst of widespread disenchantment, the demand for the revitalization of Cuban republican democracy was taken up by a new generation. Intellectuals, professionals, workers, and university students confronted the persistent abuses of the political class and the presidency of Gerardo Machado, whose co-optive populist regime slid inexorably into a bloody dictatorship. If this cycle ended in 1933 with a cathartic nationalist revolution that rid the people of one dictator, it only proved that the republic could not shrug off the shackles it had been born into. Another U.S. ambassador was waiting in the wings to turn the screws; another strongman, Fulgencio Batista, was not long in showing himself capable of keeping the house of cards in order. The revolution of 1933 would soon become just another republican opportunity lost, ultimately going down in history as a prologue to the "real" revolution of 1959.[10]

It is easy to see why the Cuban republic has become "el tiempo omitido" (the "time that is left out"), as Marial Iglesias has put it. The fact that the current Cuban state let the centenary of independence pass by without notice in 2002—unprecedented in the history of modern statehood—reveals the derision with which the first republic is dismissed in official Cuban historical culture. In this version, the U.S. intervention of 1898 and subsequent occupation kidnapped Cuba's history just as the insuperable contradictions of the late colonial period and the patriot blood spilled in the war of independence had put the people on the brink of revolutionary sovereignty. The Platt Amendment is the smoking gun that proves the United States cheated Cuba of its true nation-statehood, replacing it with a "protectorate," a "pseudo-republic," or a "neo-colony" where U.S. power was mediated, in thinly disguised fashion, by a former colonial ruling class turned into flunkies of U.S. financial and corporate power.[11] Seen this way, the entire republican experience prior to 1959 is merely the antithesis of the Cuban revolution. It is a fifty-seven-year period of U.S. proxy rule studded with villains and martyrs and punctuated by political upheavals that prefigure the historical absolution of 1959. A main task for revolutionary scholarship has been to recuperate the radical, popular, and epic nationalist character of the independence struggles in the face of the uncomfortable fact that a good proportion of its revolutionary leaders defected, during the occupation and the republic, to the service of a bourgeoisie dependent on U.S. capital.[12]

In U.S. historical culture the Spanish-American War and the occupation of Cuba pack a kind of "shock and awe" punch—1898—a watershed moment for a country en route to its place as preeminent world power. Whether approving or disapproving, a great deal of the historical work done within the U.S. fold picks up the story on the twentieth-century side of the great wall of 1898. The year marks the beginnings of the country's exercise of imperial power over foreign peoples, the unleashing of the foreign policy controversy leading to the Platt Amendment, the start of repeated U.S. military, diplomatic, and economic intervention in Cuban affairs, and of U.S. support for sun-drenched, mob-backed dictatorships that would come back to haunt them after 1959.[13] A third strong historical culture—that of Spain—takes a proprietary interest in Cuba's past as well and is also fixated on 1898. It is notable that studies of Cuba done in the Spanish scholarly context almost always end abruptly in 1898, mirroring the way that studies done in the United States so often begin there.[14]

There is no doubt that, as Louis A. Pérez puts it, 1898 "changed everything": the U.S. occupation and the early republic *were* times of dramatic interruptions, reorientations, truncations, and inertia. Wars are cataclysms, and wars that result in the death of 10 percent of the population, bring to an end four centuries of rule by the same colonial master, and usher in a fundamentally distinct (and in many ways even more potent) type of foreign oversight must be ruptures marking a "before" and an "after." There are also a number of studies that range across the divide of 1898 and work to incorporate the republic into the logic of Cuban historical evolution. Principal among them are works by Pérez himself, beautifully crafted studies that stand out for their synthetic vision, ability to convey the perspectives of the United States, Spain, and Cuba in the momentous changes of the independence era, and fresh and provocative location of social and political continuities.[15] Notably, however, Pérez's vision of Cuba is often framed in terms of an essential liminality. Cuba seems always in the process of becoming something through contradictions that negate that becoming—eternally "between" (reform and revolution, independence and colonialism, being American and being Cuban). The island is ceaselessly entering moments in which things will never be the same even as hopes will remain unrealized, its ruling class always already reduced to an empty shell. Even his boldly original and erudite ventures into long-term patterns in Cuban climate and social behavior focus on the extreme, catastrophic, and self-negating—hurricanes and suicide.

These three nationally based historical views of Cuba show a strong tendency to frame events in terms of what did *not* happen. Spain failed to find a reformist solution to the colonial question. The United States stopped Cuba from finding a route to national independence and social revolution. Cubans failed to attain clear independence or build a robust, sovereign, and democratic nation-state and national economy. Little wonder that republican Cuba is predominantly portrayed as constrained and truncated and that we are frequently asked to understand this period principally in terms of failure, discontinuity, deformation, and illegitimacy. The main premise of this collection is that there is a need to revisit the Cuban republic on its own terms, in its own time, and with an eye to all segments of society, and to do so in a way that bridges the three historiographical solitudes discussed above. This is in no way to question the integrity or the value of the historical scholarship that has been done on the republic to date, much of which stands out as among the very finest work accomplished on the history of Latin America and on the history of Spanish and U.S. foreign policy and imperialism. Nevertheless, there is a certain narrowing of vision that comes from seeing periods of history as failures, or as adjuncts to grander historical processes whose subjects lie elsewhere, or in teleological terms as simply anticipations of other more authentic and significant periods.

The historical experiences of the republic were as real as any others, as authentically Cuban as any others. Deserving of infamy as some of its signature episodes are, the republic was also made by a broad spectrum of Cubans who embraced a political and civic culture of national self-realization through citizenship, though they may have remained ambiguous about how precisely to achieve it. In revisiting republican Cuba, our collection shows how this period in Cuban history can be recast as one of deep continuity in processes of liberal state- and nation-building that were periodically upset—but also reinvigorated—by foreign intervention and profound uncertainty. Its contributors explore how Cubans at all levels were urgently involved in the creation of liberal national political communities—imagined and real—and in defining the meaning and practice of a democratic modernity, though times and conditions did not remain long in their favor.

In this sense, we might see republican Cuba as a "tropical Weimar," for it shared certain important traits with its later and more notorious German sibling. The Cuban republic, too, was born of (and in) military stalemate; it, too, saw the United States enter the fray at that point of stalemate and determine the outcome. In terms of net effect, the Platt Amendment and the Versailles Treaty were also surprisingly congruent. Imposed in the context of postwar occupation, each crippled sovereignty and inserted a wedge that ultimately prevented patriotic people from identifying their sense of national selfhood with the state. Both Weimar Germany and postcolonial Cuba constructed a republican politics in the shadow of foreign intervention legitimized in treaties that were the price of assuming statehood, and both did so in a context of constant political instability that was in good measure a product of that "legitimate" shadow. Each political experiment was pitched about by volatile economic extremes while vital sectors of national industry suffered domination by foreign capital backed by military occupation or the threat thereof. All the while society was consumed by fits of violent racist paranoia carefully cultivated by political elites and in each case drifted toward political dysfunctionality, inflated nationalism, and dictatorship.

To adopt the perspective of a recent book on Weimar Germany, Cuba's first republic still speaks to us as a "warning sign"—among other things of what havoc is wrought by opportunistic interventions and occupations that disguise imperial designs behind hollow commitments to democracy-building. Yet both Weimar and Cuban republican political cultures were also transformed by irrepressible boundary crossing, especially in urban spaces associated with cultural and intellectual flowering. And as with the case of Weimar Germany, republican Cuba's serious political and cultural conflicts and disasters should not erase its significant political and cultural achievements. In Cuba, too, the "destruction of the old imperial order in war and revolution unleashed the political and social imagination."[16]

A similar comparative point can be made without leaving the hemisphere. In essential ways, late colonial and early republican Cuba fit nicely into what Latin American scholars call the Liberal period, typically understood as running from roughly 1870 to 1930. Curiously, almost without exception, Cuban scholarship eschews this periodization.[17] For many Latin American countries Liberal state-building was based on primary product exports benefiting an alliance of foreign capital and a local ruling class, and it was characterized by autocratic regimes capable of maintaining stability. Cuban historians have tended to avoid the "Liberal era" classification, concentrating on what they see as the uniqueness of the island's brutal wars of independence and their aftermath, the U.S. intervention and occupation, the torturous experiment with democratic government that was crippled by corruption, patronage, electoral fraud, and gangsterism, and the precious sectors of the economy swallowed up by U.S.-based banks and super-corporations like United Fruit that created an acute agro-export dependency. Yet even a casual student of Latin American history will have noted how readily all these "uniquely Cuban" structuring experiences apply to Latin American states of the era, particularly to Mexico, Central America, and northern South America, all of which shared a geopolitical proximity to the new imperial United States. Cuba's first war of independence is in many ways analogous to Central America's struggles against William Walker in the 1850s, and Mexico's against European reconquest in the 1860s. The strong regional inflection and social yearnings of Cuba's second war of independence and the interventionist arbitration of the United States are comparable to the experience of revolutionary Mexico, with its northern insurrectionism, its populist nationalism, and U.S. military intervention in Veracruz in an effort to broker a political outcome palatable to U.S. interests. There is also an enormous, and almost entirely unploughed, field of potential comparative study between this era in Cuban history and Brazil's late emancipation of slaves (both coming only at the end of the 1880s) and tardy and curtailed republican experience (in the Brazilian case, the "old republic" of 1889–1930).

Historians of Latin America are acutely aware of the anti-democratic, economically dependent, and militarist polities of the Liberal era. Yet they have not shied away from exploring them as authentic expressions of political cultures and foundational processes of nation-building. Indeed, recent studies tend to take the political cultures of the Liberal period much more seriously and fully than in the past. They are treated with much greater nuance as important for the imagining of national political community, for the constitution of modes of gendered and racialized citizenship, for the launching of modern urban identities, and for the structuring of central-regional dynamics in the modern state, to name just a few areas of current focus. There is no question that the Platt Amendment undermined aspects of state sovereignty and called into question Cuba's degree of national independence in a peculiarly explicit way. However, the main thing separating the Cuban plight from that of most Latin American countries who were also in the United States' sphere of influence may have been its unique (and uniquely awkward) status in international law. The republic became neither a protectorate nor a colony in the formal sense, nor was it a colony of a new kind whose typology had yet to be defined. It is true that an external power limited in some ways the ability of the island's representatives to make decisions about some issues. At the same time, this limitation did not erase the existence of a new juridical framework that provided a normal domestic government with complete powers of rule legitimated through participative mechanisms of citizenship.

Placing Cuba in the Latin American context is revealing and not simply because U.S. expansionism and its voracious Caribbean appetite were visible elsewhere. The Cuban republic had a rocky life, but if it was not the best of political regimes, for a long time it was far from the worst. The country freed itself from its former colonial master, and Cubans were able to provide themselves with their own institutions. The ideals of the revolutionary struggle were partially put into practice, if in some measure sacrificed in the interests of pluralism and the opposition of interests, and for the most part they suffered a rapid decay. Cuban citizens were able to associate freely and elect their representatives, even if the processes for doing so showed marked deficiencies. Over the first three decades of the twentieth century a very small minority of American nations enjoyed constitutional systems that were respected and authorities who were subject to periodic electoral renewal, and even more rare were those that accepted universal male suffrage and a secret and direct vote. Cuba's representative democracy quickly showed defects in its machinery. Different from virtually all its Latin American sister states, however, the Republic of Cuba was born democratic and endowed with representative institutions that stood in marked opposition to the arbitrary authoritarian rule and political exclusion that the people had been subjected to during the Spanish colonial era.

The Puerto Rican nationalist Pedro Albizu Campos contributed to promoting the expression "república mediatizada" [mediated republic] by using it for the title of a pamphlet on the Cuban situation. The adjective *mediated* fits nicely with the "republic of generals and doctors" that provided the title to Carlos Loveira's famous novel: a state that was nominally free but actually dependent, conditioned less by external dictate than by the threat of intrusion into national life and the imposition of a transitory administration that would reorient politics in a direction conducive to the occupier. The example of the U.S. occupation government of 1899–1902 was ever present. By not establishing with precision the unbreachable limits of Cuban sovereignty, a mirrored conditionality was created in the country's domestic life. On the one hand, this imposed self-limitation and even surreptitious submission to signs and suggestions emanating from Washington and, on the other, it gave different factions the option of going to the American Protector (or threatening to) to resolve internal disputes. This was a double perversion, based on the threat of invoking an international treaty.

Still, the task remains to define precisely the margins of action of Cuba's republican government and the real degree of interference by U.S. diplomatic agents versus the threat of foreign intervention as a domestic political tool. Just as important would be to deepen our knowledge of the effective space of sovereignty that was developed during the republic, one that seems to have had a greater impact on the future of Cubans during the first three decades of the twentieth century than did those limits imposed from outside, no matter how important these latter were. Exploring the evolution of a republican society that it is impossible to reduce to the shrunken figure of dysfunctional politics is a task of considerable historical urgency that we turn to in the following pages. As editors we have chosen to characterize the main patterns of republican civic life and public culture in terms of ambiguity rather than betrayal, failure, deformation, or liminality.[18] By doing so we mean to acknowledge the hesitation, doubt, and uncertainty of different individual and collective Cuban actors as to the course republican political culture should take. We also acknowledge the dubious and sham qualities the republic all too often exhibited. At the same time, we wish to emphasize that this historical experience must be understood in multiple ways, in terms of many levels of significance, and as the result of choices made and not made by Cuban actors themselves.

The following pages present contemporary work by leading scholars of Cuban history from all three of the "national" historiographical networks mentioned above—the Spanish, the Cuban, and the North American. Many of the authors are based in Canada or Valencia, and the Cuban contributors are distinguished by their contemporary training in historical methods. The ensemble expresses new ways of thinking about the late colonial and early republican period, developed over the past decade or so in overlapping networks that have come together, in varying combinations and with different objectives, in Havana, Trinidad, Matanzas, Cienfuegos, Cárdenas, Ann Arbor, Windsor, Montréal, Toronto, Castellón, Valencia, and Madrid. Whether presenting panels on specific themes, reading documents together in methodological workshops, or building bridges between different tendencies in Cuban historiography at ecumenical seminars, the authors in this collection have coalesced on the basis of a shared historical sensibility and a sense of complementarity in their approach to the Cuban past.

Marial Iglesias begins the collection by exploding 1898. She takes us past the contentious domains of diplomatic, military, and economic history that have focused discussion of the United States' most egregious acts of imperial excess (which are sovereign Cuba's most painful episodes of violation).[19] Iglesias instead explores the political and popular culture of the successive exhumations of the "cadaver" of the USS *Maine* from its resting place in Havana harbor where, in 1898, it sank after a mysterious explosion—a blast that ostensibly triggered the U.S. intervention in the Cuban war of independence. Republican Cuba had a forensic obsession, one displayed early in the submission of the exhumed skeleton of Antonio Maceo for anthropometric examination in a racially anxious attempt to de-Africanize a hero of the new Cuba in the interests of creole hegemony.[20] Iglesias draws our attention to this culture of unsettled republican remains: if the United States took possession of certain sacred portions of Cuba's sovereign history when it brokered and restricted Cuban independence, Cuba also came to possess sacred

Introduction | 11

"American" relics. The monumentalization of the *Maine*'s remains would take a volatile course throughout the history of the republic. It showed itself capable of signifying a wide variety of public feelings about the fusion of U.S. and Cuban experience, from catharsis and love to hatred for the U.S.-backed dictatorial manipulation of public space. The rupture of relations between the two countries in 1961 at the beginning of the socialist revolution meant that the remains of the ship that stayed in Cuba would fall into oblivion in a corner of Havana's Malecón, but not before being the object of a wave of anti-imperialist ire unleashed by the new regime. The United States did not simply impose itself on republican Cuba; its material presence circulated symbolically around the country, becoming part of Cuban popular culture in the process, vulnerable to expropriation, possession, and public and private violence and rejection.

Iglesias's magisterial redeployment of the *Maine* sets up four studies that explore important continuities connecting the late colonial period to the republican era. In many respects, and in good measure because of the essential conservatism of the U.S. occupation government, the republic was more reformulation of an agenda sketched out under Spanish sway by Cuba's creole elites than a radical break with the past. As the important liberal intellectual José Enrique Varona noted in 1915 (when he was vice president of the republic!), "republican Cuban looks like the sister of colonial Cuba."[21] Yet it was far from a twin, identical or fraternal. The radical break with the past dreamed of by many in the independence armies was frustrated by U.S. occupation and the room it gave the old creole elites to reestablish themselves in positions of strength in the new republic. At the same time, the reformulation of a late colonial agenda allowed for considerable maneuvering and the launching of novel programs and processes.

Deep continuities linking colonial to republican Cuba can be discerned in the domain of scientific research and debate. Steven Palmer explores the way that research in medicine, health, and the natural sciences were reconfigured in the republic following a creole renaissance in the late colonial era focusing principally on laboratory medicine. The principal players in Cuban science remained practically the same between the 1870s and the 1920s. What changed was their position of power relative to one another and to the state. The U.S. occupation acted as a prism, refracting concentrated scientific energies into a more eclectic dispersal that tended to work within networks defined by U.S. scientific and political needs. The search for scientific sovereignty that had characterized the program of the strongest actors in the late colonial research milieu gave way to scientific pursuits that could be of service to the attenuated sovereignty of the Cuban state and creole political society. In this context, laboratory-based medical research was supplanted as the mainstay of original Cuban science by eugenics and agronomy. At the same time, the role of foreign scientists, especially from the United States, increasingly influenced the national research agenda. This did not, however, make science in the republic "less Cuban" or less important in the making of a cosmopolitan and original intellectual culture. Nor did it exclude those who had been the powerbrokers of scientific research in the colonial era from staging a comeback in the republic by regaining control of a wider spectrum of scientific and professional associations.

Among recent historians of Cuba, those who have studied problems of gender and racial emancipation have been most likely to take republican political practices seriously and to explore them as nuanced and profoundly consequential. Lynn Stoner has drawn attention to the formation during the Cuban republic of one of Latin America's most successful movements for women's suffrage and legal reform.[22] In a provocative reconsideration of race politics in the republic, Alejandro de la Fuente showed how the dominant political parties engaged Cubans of color as a significant electoral constituency. He revealed the dimensions of the material and political resources that were at stake in this dynamic, as well as the fact that, during periods when democratic politics were severely eroded in the republic, as under Menocal especially, Afro-Cubans had less access to employment, political representation, and other rewards.[23] The nature and meaning of those spaces of freedom for those who fought to open them—the "degrees of freedom" available to people of color in late colonial and republican Cuba for pressing claims on citizenship, stature, and property—are the subject of groundbreaking work by scholars led by Rebecca Scott.[24] Scott's contribution to this collection is a classic consideration of these "dynamics of the search for political voice"—the emancipatory possibilities that the wars of independence opened up for former slaves and their children in republican Cuba.

Scott, too, locates deep continuities in struggles for political voice among former slaves that date from the era of emancipation itself, through the claims made by societies of colored people for desegregation and for electoral rights during the periods of Spanish flirtation with political opening. Full citizenship, meanwhile, was put squarely on the agenda of the independence armies. The U.S. military occupiers were imbued with the experience of reconstruction after the U.S. Civil War, accepting of segregation and the mechanisms developed to deny the franchise to African Americans. Flying in the face of this, the "tenacity of the claims advanced by ordinary Cubans,"

Scott writes, was such that the battle for full franchise rights for Afro-Cuban males was won. Such claims-making dovetailed with labor activism in Cienfuegos during the U.S. occupation and later in solidarity with striking Havana workers in the early days of the republic in 1902, while former slaves and their descendants emerged as combative and dissenting figures during the second U.S. occupation of 1906–9. The electoral system fell short of true democracy in many ways. Nevertheless, constructed within a framework of Cuban *caudillismo*, it still had to acknowledge many midlevel black and mulatto leaders—a pattern also visible at the level of municipal politics, trade unionism, and police forces. Among its many foibles, the republic also had spaces of vigorous struggles for "expanded citizenship."

Reinaldo Funes offers an environmentally considered take on new health and production technologies that transformed Cuban life in the latter years of the colony and first three decades of the republic. His study delves into the applied scientific guts of milk and meat processing, inspection, and distribution. Funes focuses on a forgotten but key social group in the changing relationship with animals and animal products that defines modern urban civilization—veterinarians and their politically and economically sensitive tours of the slaughterhouses, stables, and milk factories of the capital city. The implementation of these processing and distribution systems made possible dramatic gains in life expectancy and decreased infant mortality in the first two decades after independence, but by the late 1910s these systems were degenerating alongside the political culture of the republic.

As José Antonio Piqueras argues in his meditation on the urban material and symbolic culture of late colonial and republican Havana, there was more continuity than rupture in the periodic reinvention of the capital. If the "Americanization" of Havana's architecture and spatial layout after 1900 is often pointed to as evidence of the U.S. "takeover" of Cuba, Piqueras shows that similar processes were visible as early as the 1850s. Colonial Havana was readily becoming "American" even as it tasted its first moments of sugar splendor, while republican Havana readily reembraced Spanish colonial styles—whether real, imagined, or newly popular in the United States (for example, the missionary style that rapidly took over in early twentieth-century California and Florida). Piqueras paints a transitory, ephemeral capital city for an "austere republic." Havana was always undergoing demolition and reconstruction, ceaselessly reproducing an emergent modernity in a second city arising beside the old "colonial" one and *against* a "vast third city that was neither modern nor traditional, but simply deprived." Neither the colonial nor the republican incarnation of Havana had much time for public planning or grand edifications of statehood. The social contours and architectural expressions of urban development were for the most part left for the market to determine—even if these sometimes needed a helpful nudge from the forces of order to empty out sectors of the city targeted for building. What type of city did the capital of a new republic require? And what type of city was it possible to make or construct in accordance with the state of public funds, the island's political status, and the idiosyncrasies of the ruling class?

There are a number of excellent studies of radical worker organizations in Cuba, most of them concerning the 1920s and 1930s when working-class organizations were led by the Cuban Communist Party (organized in 1925 and a member of the Third International). In these studies, the culmination of working radicalism and combativeness is the revolution of 1933, the maximum expression of class and national ideals that led all workers to struggle together independently of nationality or skin color and under communist leadership.[25] Amparo Sánchez Cobos shifts attention to an earlier phase of working-class struggle during which anarchist currents were among the most dynamic. The anarchist newspaper *¡Tierra!* was a staple of the radical press during the first two decades of republican life, spreading news and interpretation different from the "bourgeois press" and serving as a network in its own right bringing together contributors, editors, and readers. Sánchez Cobos looks at the newspaper as a nexus of anarchist discourse that linked reader-workers throughout Cuba with an Atlantic community of anarchist thought, news, subscription, and solidarity. This community was concentrated in certain parts of the United States and Spain, but understood as a transnational network free of divisions based on nationality, skin color, and other markers. Such an analysis views the reorganization of workers after independence in terms of a different internationalist and ideological tradition from that of the later communist stage. Ironically, the new blood of the new republic was drawn in large measure from massive immigration from Spain, an immigration wave promoted by a creole elite eager to dilute the Afro-descended makeup of the population. This massive influx of almost a million Spaniards between 1900 and 1930 also reestablished and developed "old" Atlantic networks of popular solidarity. It was a process in which migrant worker intellectuals, many of them from Spain, played a significant role, and the meshing of Cuban and Spanish anarchist energies in the production of *¡Tierra!* serves as an example of the originality and cosmopolitan horizons of working-class culture in the early republic.

Imilcy Balboa takes us into the island's agrarian history and to the heart of one of the great debates over the fate of Cuban republicanism—namely, whether or not the absence of a rural middle class doomed republican democracy. She explores the finer points of the restructuring of the sugar industry that began with the creation of the great *centrales* (large-scale processing factories) at the end of the nineteenth century. In part driven by the arrival of more intense capital investment from the United States, the phenomenon would have profound social consequences after independence. The idea that the expansion of this latifundium system choked off the possibility of the birth of a rural middle class in Cuba that could have been the principal social base for the republic has given rise to a historical explanation of the "failure" of the new political system of the independent country. Without a middle class to support it, politics became a parasitic business for a Cuban elite dispossessed of the economic production that was now in the hands of foreigners.[26] Against such presumptions, Balboa's study focuses on demonstrating the existence of a middling agrarian bourgeoisie during the first decades of the republic, one that allied itself with the upper classes and assumed political offices that, in spite of the apparent contradiction this involved, shared interests and needs with the large centrales and sugar companies and benefited from the policies imposed by their representatives.[27] In the context of the crisis of the 1920s, some notable figures of this agrarian petit bourgeoisie—among them the intellectual and politician Ramiro Guerra—invented the figure of the Cuban *colono* destroyed by the evils of the *latifundio* that should have provided the bases of the new nation and republican system.[28] But according to Balboa, the image of the colono created by Guerra and the other ideologues of the nation is an image of a colono who is white and—dressed in guayabera, mounted on his steed, a regular at the cockfights, and touring about on Sundays—symbolically one with the old colonial *hacendado*, reflecting a colonial past that resists disappearing with the economic crisis.

Maikel Fariñas looks at forms of sociability related to the early arrival of the Rotary club in "District 25" (Cuba). This is a pioneering study that looks at social clubs outside of the capital and during the republican era. Fariñas proposes that the Rotary clubs acted as authentic centers of power and as pressure groups. Though their membership was principally among the white middle classes, it permeated the middle and upper strata of Cuban society.[29] The Rotary club networks in Cuba extended to all the productive lines of the island, and their technical superiority was based on the support given by the national and international networks of the club and also by the important links that they maintained with the press, providing them with the attendant possibility of mobilizing public opinion. This turned them quickly into pressure groups with the capacity to intervene in local, regional, and national issues and even, as Fariñas shows, to exercise influence outside the borders of Cuba in matters under negotiation with the United States.

Alejandra Bronfman tunes our attention to the Cuban ether, asking how a public for broadcasting emerged in the republic and under what conditions. In seeking to identify the first audiences for this novel medium of the public sphere, Bronfman understands the public and the machinery of radio as "artifacts of mutual intervention," in a constitutive moment of great contingency, unevenness, and incompleteness when the seamless selling of hygiene products and romantic radio novelettes was still part of an unimaginable future. The radio had yet to be wrestled into its serviceable shape by those who would make it accessible and profitable, and in its beginning it threw up unruly practices of listening in the street and other public places. Amateur operators constructed equipment and searched for "an esoteric variety of emanations from multiple locations"—among them the 9 P.M. cannon shot over Havana harbor that began the two-hour PWX broadcast each Wednesday and Saturday, followed by a weather forecast. Immediately political—the first official broadcast was an awkward presidential address by Alfredo Zayas—the intromission of foreign signals in Caribbean skies echoed the fragility of Cuba's sovereignty. Inexorably, the audience that came into being was constituted by private capital exhorting listeners to listen from private, domestic, moneyed spaces, but the process, insists Bronfman, was incomplete and left alternative publics in its wake.

One such alternative public was the Cuban Folklore Society, one of many new intellectual coteries and associations that fleetingly flowered in the *década crítica* of the 1920s. Ricardo Quiza explores the society as an articulation of a dynamic civil society and vehicle for the emergence of new social actors. Although propelled by luminaries—in particular Fernando Ortíz—Quiza shows that the society made possible the creation and circulation of novel symbolic goods that expressed the complex racial and gender reformulations of the public sphere. The membership of the society and authorship in its journal included a notable participation by women, while it brought together an eclectic group of mature cultural figures with a star-studded cast from the first generation of intellectuals who grew up entirely in the context of the republic, oriented by a new populist nationalism and, frequently, an embrace of leftist ideologies. From 1923 to its demise in 1927, the Folklore

Society expressed the dialectic between tradition, change, nationalism, and social science that burned brightly during the 1920s in a Cuba in search of national reconstruction. It also explored the margins of tolerance and dissidence within a civil society brushing up against increasing authoritarian moments.

The volume closes with Robert Whitney's work on the way Afro-Antillean migrants were kept from the enjoyment of labor and political rights during the Batista-dominated regimes of the 1930s. It is a fitting end to our consideration of Cuba's ambiguous republican state. Whitney documents an explicit effort by a more sophisticated, if considerably less democratic, Cuban state to bring certainty to bear on the island's population: in a tight labor market, hiring preference had to be given to "Cubans." But shearing Cuban nationality of its many ambiguities—over half the 4 million inhabitants were migrants who had arrived since independence (mostly from Spain, Haiti, and the British Caribbean)—and establishing with certainty who was a worthy Cuban was a process fraught with discrimination. Between 1936 and 1940 Batista oversaw the successful implementation of the nationalization of labor laws passed by the revolutionary government of 1933. Perhaps the most dramatic episode in this process was the mass expulsion of thousands of Haitian and West Indian workers.[30] As Whitney shows, making the labor laws real also involved a deep institutional transformation: establishing civil registries and labor exchanges throughout the country, especially in eastern Cuba where state power had remained weak during the buildup of the enclave economies of the vast sugar estates owned primarily by U.S. corporations. The late republican state was able to "nationalize" a working class that had, until then, retained an eclectic and frequently extra-Cuban repertoire of cultural characteristics, tendencies, and ties.

These eleven chapters propose new approaches to the study of the history of the early twentieth-century Cuban republic. They tackle issues such as the circulation of urban material and symbolic culture in new civic institutions and public practices; modes of sociability and self-representation among an emerging middle class; changes in scientific and technological practices to regulate humans and animals; and the repercussions of slave emancipation, agrarian reform, and labor organizing on struggles over citizenship and the making of social identities. No collection of this nature can be comprehensive. Many crucial themes and episodes certainly remain for future exploration, but there is no doubt that such exploration is overdue. In introducing or reintroducing readers to the political culture broadly conceived of the first

Cuban republic, *State of Ambiguity* reframes central concerns of civic and cultural life and rehangs them in the gallery of history so that the period can be considered on its own terms.

Notes

1. Academia de Historia de Cuba, *Constituciones de la República de Cuba*. One institution that the republic did not have was an army. The U.S. occupation authority disbanded the independence armies, and political elites initially hoped that police forces and a rural guard in conjunction with U.S. protection at the international level would obviate the need for a standing army. The absence of a military had complex consequences and did not seem to promote political stability; an army would be created by the second U.S. occupation authority of 1906–9.

2. Autonomism was the ideology of the main Cuban creole followers of liberalism during the interwar years when Spain had allowed a limited democratic opening in Cuba and toyed with the idea of greater self-government by colonial elites. This model sought to acquire sovereignty slowly from Spain (along the lines of Britain's white settler colonies) in order to attain local self-government without risking social and "racial" upheaval. See García Mora and Naranjo Orovio, "Intelectualidad criolla y nación en Cuba, 1878–1898." In Cuba, *creole* means Cuban-born but tracing lineage exclusively to Spain on both sides of the family (and hence, supposedly, of pure European ancestry).

3. On this point, see Zeuske, "1898: Cuba y el problema de la 'transición pactada,'" and Piqueras, *Sociedad civil y poder en Cuba*, 318–28.

4. The progressive democratic nature of this formative period is the subject of Ferrer, *Insurgent Cuba*.

5. This history is comprehensively captured in Helg, *Our Rightful Share*; see also Fuente, "Myths of Racial Democracy: Cuba, 1900–1912," and for a trenchant Cuban view, Fernández Robaina, *El negro en Cuba, 1902–1958*.

6. Rojas, "Otro gallo cantaría: Ensayo sobre el primer republicanismo cubano." Santí proposes that these intellectuals may have contributed to killing the republic with "an overdose of idealism": "Primera República," 131.

7. Principal among them is Pérez, *Cuba under the Platt Amendment, 1902–1934*. For a detailed view of the understanding of the amendment within the constituent assembly, see López Rivero and Ibarra, "En torno a 1898."

8. See Zanetti Lecuona, *Los cautivos de la reciprocidad*.

9. The era is brilliantly captured in Jenks, *Our Cuban Colony*, though the title is misleading in that Jenks gives considerably more autonomy and responsibility to Cuban actors in the unfolding of politics prior to the 1920s than most scholars have been willing to give them, and he even provides the basis for a revisionist rereading of the Zayas presidency as politically astute and, despite massive corruption, able to provide some forward-looking coherence to republican politics.

10. A fate registered in the title of the superb study of the fall of Machado by Aguilar, *Cuba 1933: Prologue to Revolution*.

11. Riverend, *La República: Dependencia y revolución*; Yglesia, *Cuba, primera república, segunda ocupación*; López Segrera, *Raíces históricas de la revolución cubana*. Pino-Santos, "Lo que fue aquella República: Protectorado y neocolonia," differentiates between the first phase, from 1902 to 1934, which he designates a protectorate, and a second phase from 1934 (after the Cuban abrogation of the Platt Amendment following the overthrow of Machado) to 1959, which was a neocolony with distinct characteristics, but this is not a differentiation apparent elsewhere in this special issue devoted to a discussion of the first republic.

12. Armas, *La revolución pospuesta*; Figarola, *Cuba 1900–1928: la república dividida contra sí misma*; and Ibarra, *Cuba: 1898–1921: Partidos políticos y clases sociales*.

13. A comprehensive consideration of this historiography is Pérez, *The War of 1898*.

14. An excellent discussion of this focus, and an expression of it, can be found in Naranjo Orovio and Opatrny, "Estudios cubanos a fines del milenio," 11–22.

15. Pérez, *Cuba: Between Reform and Revolution*; *On Becoming Cuban*; *To Die in Cuba: Suicide and Society*; and *Winds of Change*.

16. Weitz, *Weimar Germany: Promise and Tragedy*, 2.

17. Notably, though a Liberal era periodization, common for the rest of Latin America, is rarely used for Cuba, when it has been "forced" onto *cubanistas*, the fit is rather comfortable; see, for example, the two superb contributions to volume 5 of *The Cambridge History of Latin America*, Aguilar, "Cuba, 1860–1934," and Moreno Fraginals, "Sugar in the Caribbean, 1870–1930" (with Cuba discussed as part of a regional context).

18. The notion of the wars of independence as an "ambivalent revolution," particularly in terms of the vacillations in imagining the racial equality of republican subjects, is threaded through Ada Ferrer's *Insurgent Cuba*.

19. A new cultural history of this relationship, pioneered by Pérez (see especially *On Becoming Cuban*), is also apparent in recent works such as Iglesias, *A Cultural History of Cuba during the U.S. Occupation, 1898–1902*, and Casimir, "Champion of the *Patria*."

20. The Maceo postmortem would have a ghoulish echo a decade later in the autopsy performed on the body of executed Partido Independiente de Color leader Evaristo Estenoz, the intention apparently to demonstrate a pathological and degenerate negroid constitution.

21. "Cuba republicana parece hermana de Cuba colonial"; Varona, "Recepción en la Academia Nacional," 248.

22. Stoner, *From the House to the Streets*.

23. Fuente, *A Nation for All*.

24. Scott, *Degrees of Freedom*; Scott and Zeuske, "Property in Writing, Property on the Ground"; Bronfman, *Measures of Equality*.

25. See, for example, Carr, "Mill Occupations and Soviets"; Carr, "Identity, Class, and Nation"; and Whitney, *State and Revolution in Cuba*.

26. For example, see Ramos, *Manual del perfecto fulanista*, and Carrión, "El desenvolvimiento social de Cuba en los últimos veinte años," cited in López Segrera, *Raíces históricas de la revolución cubana*, 298–300.

27. One of the first works to tackle this question was Ibarra, *Cuba: 1898–1921*.

28. Guerra, *Un cuarto de siglo de evolución cubana* and *Azúcar y población en las Antillas*. An insightful analysis of this issue is Díaz Quiñones, "El enemigo íntimo." On the reply of Fernando Ortiz to Guerra's criticism of the latifundio during the crisis of the 1920s, see Santí, "Fernando Ortiz, o la crítica de la caña," 138–44.

29. Joaquín Añorga, "El rotarismo en Cuba: Su origen, sus características y sus obras."

30. Mcleod, "Undesirable Aliens: Race, Ethnicity, and Nationalism in the Comparison of Haitian and British West Indian Immigrant Workers in Cuba, 1912–1939."

CHAPTER 1

A Sunken Ship, a Bronze Eagle, and the Politics of Memory
The "Social Life" of the USS *Maine* in Cuba (1898–1961)

Marial Iglesias Utset

In June 1961, at the age of 106, María de la Cruz acquired sudden notoriety. Learning to read and write at such an advanced age, as part of a major literacy campaign, turned this elderly woman into a public celebrity.[1] Born as a slave on a Havana sugar plantation in 1855, María de la Cruz Senmanat witnessed the wars of independence, the emancipation of slaves, and, in 1898, the U.S. intervention that helped put an end to four hundred years of Spanish domination in Cuba. Like so many thousands of other residents of Havana, she probably saw the U.S. flag raised in the Explanada del Morro, only to see it, with exultation, lowered and replaced with the Cuban national flag in 1902. The Cuban Republic, formally inaugurated as an independent state, was nonetheless tied by "bonds of singular intimacy"—seemingly unbreakable—to the new imperial power in the region: the United States of America.[2]

Nearly six decades later, María de la Cruz would witness another exceptional event: the symbolic rupture of those bonds. In January 1961, Cuba and the United States severed diplomatic relations. Three months later, in the early hours of May 1, in accordance with the declaration of the socialist character of the Cuban Revolution, a large crane from the Ministry of Public Works knocked down from its pedestal the bronze eagle that had adorned the monument dedicated to the victims of the explosion of the battleship *Maine*. Soon after, the former slave famed for the extraordinary longevity of her life recalled the event commemorated by the monument. On the night of February 15, 1898, while working as a servant in the house of her former masters—where, like many other ex-slaves in urban areas, she had continued to reside many years after her emancipation—she heard the explosion that sank the ship reverberating from the Bay of Havana. According to her testimony, she knew immediately that "the culprits of the explosion had not been the Spanish but the Yankees themselves."[3] María de la Cruz likely adapted her account of the *Maine* explosion, which had occurred sixty-three years earlier, to accord with the nationalist and anti-imperialist reinterpretations of this event in the context of the Cuban Revolution. The interview took place in April 1961, when ardently anti-U.S. rhetoric permeated all media and public opinion, only days after the unsuccessful invasion of CIA-backed Cuban exiles at the Bay of Pigs.

The story I wish to narrate here takes place precisely at a time that is either omitted or demonized in the version of national history that begins to impose itself at the same moment in which María de la Cruz is called upon to recount episodes from her long life. Somewhere between the two most symbolic caesuras in Cuba's contemporary history—1898: the end of the "time of Spain," and 1959: the "time of revolution"—a republic emerges, flourishes, and perishes, marked from its birth by traces of its ambiguous conception. It was at once the legitimate child of the Wars of Independence and the bastard of U.S. intervention.

The sudden explosion and sinking of the battleship USS *Maine* in the Bay of Havana on February 15, 1898, was the singular event that gave rise to the first of these caesuras. The catastrophe provoked an impassioned reaction against Spain within U.S. public opinion that acted as a catalyst for the intervention of the United States in the war between Cuba and Spain. A few months later, Spain laid down its arms before the overwhelming military superiority of the United States, and the remainder of its once great colonial empire—Cuba, Puerto Rico, and the Philippines—was handed over to form part of the territories then under U.S. control. The U.S. Congress, nonetheless, approved a historic agreement known as the Joint Resolution due to strong sympathies and a sense of solidarity toward Cuba among the public, pressure from anti-imperialist circles, and the influence of Cuban émigré lobbyists. This resolution ultimately obliged the United States to concede to Cuba its much sought after independence in 1902, though it would be an independence circumscribed by the Platt Amendment.

The sinking of the *Maine*, the intervention of the United States in the war, and the birth of the republic have been subject to contradictory political interpretations in the Cuban historical memory. According to one interpretation, a young nation is constituted as a sovereign state by the noble gesture of a powerful state that, by intervening in the war against the old Metropole, lends a helping hand in eliminating the colonial yoke. In another version of these events, the U.S. intervention is condemned: the republic—an aspiration that had motivated more than thirty years of fighting over the course of two independence wars—was born deformed, bound as it was to the United States by neocolonial political ties that de facto prevented the exercise of full sovereignty. In other words, accounts of the factors behind the explosion of the battleship *Maine* are embedded in one or another political hermeneutic—either that of a rhetoric of gratitude for Uncle Sam's generosity or a rhetoric of nationalism denouncing imperialist intervention.[4]

My text, however, is certainly not a historical investigation of the "real" causes of the explosion and sinking of the battleship, an issue that is in dispute even today, despite the sheer quantity of research and superabundance of literature on the catastrophe amassed over the course of a century. Rather than try to establish a history of "what really occurred" with the *Maine*, I am interested in exploring the politics of memory around this event, the ways in which it was remembered, reconstituted, and forgotten in different political contexts. Accordingly, this is a history of a *lieu de mémoire*, to use loosely the expression coined by Pierre Nora, where "place" is not exclusively a physical site, a material enclave, but a space of representation around an artifact (the contorted remains of a ship), the object of powerful remembrance on both sides of the Florida Strait.[5]

The issue I am tackling here is not just a conventional history of a specific site of commemoration: the monument to the victims of the battleship *Maine* inaugurated at the beginning of 1925. What follows is a history of the "social life" of the *Maine*'s remains: the cycles of "death" and "resurrection" of its memory, cycles spanning several decades, and the dynamics of its sanctification as a relic of patriotism or, conversely, of its mutation into a banal object, rendered as merchandise or souvenir. Finally, I tell the story of its integration into the urban landscape—at first half submerged in Havana's bay and later incorporated into a collection of monuments at the city's seafront.

At the same time, as became evident after the mutilation of the monument at the beginning of the Cuban Revolution, the history of the vicissitudes of the sunken battleship and its wreckage is metonymically and inextricably related to the "bonds of singular intimacy" between Cuba and the United States. That is, studying the saga of the multiple political lives of the *Maine*'s "corpse" between 1898 and 1961 is also indirectly a way of contributing to an understanding of the tense, yet fascinating, history of the political and cultural relations between these nations.

Figure 1.1 Destruction of the U.S. battleship *Maine* in Havana Harbor, February 15, 1898. *Source:* Library of Congress. Prints and Photographs Division.

"Remember the *Maine*"

It is quite possible that there is no other event over the long course of Cuban history that so immediately became "immortalized" in countless illustrations, photographs, films, and resurrections by way of a series of invocations and commemorations. Sent to the Cuban coast to protect "American life and property," the USS *Maine*, according to Fitzhugh Lee, the U.S. consul, entered Havana "gliding smoothly" into port on a peaceful winter morning on January 25, 1898. "It was a beautiful sight and one long to be remembered," Lee wrote in a letter to William R. Day, the U.S. assistant secretary of state.[6] The consul was quite satisfied: since his appointment in 1896, he had pressed his superiors on the issue of taking part in the conflict between Cuba and Spain. His contentment, however, was not long lasting. Within a few weeks, the arrival of the *Maine* in Havana became, as Lee had predicted, an object of powerful remembrance. Nevertheless, the *Maine* was less remembered for the spectacle of its graceful entrance into the bay of Havana than for the terrible explosion that sank it and killed 266 members of its crew.

The day after the explosion, although news of the tragedy had only barely reached its destinations by telegraph, myriad accusations were published. The coverage of the *Maine* incident is a paradigmatic example of the kind of sensationalist and aggressive journalism that proliferated in the United States in the last decades of the nineteenth century. The industry fiercely competed for the attention of millions of readers that constituted the new urban public. People who had only recently gained access to the printed word augmented, without precedent, literacy rates: recent immigrants, women, migrants from the countryside, and descendants of slaves newly resident in large cities because of the start of the Great Migration. They seemed to enjoy sensational headlines, simple and emotive language, abundant illustrations, the comics, and numerous commercial advertisements. This new style of journalism also required bold journalists who could immediately mobilize to the site of action and telegraph dramatic accounts that, at times, although plagued by exaggeration or conveniently "fabricated," were nonetheless convincing and compelling. The coverage of the war in Cuba—especially the explosion of the *Maine* and the reactions to it—cannot be understood apart from this era of sensationalist journalism, boosted by the fierce war that sustained the New York press barons, Joseph Pulitzer of *The World* and William Randolph Hearst of the *New York Journal*.[7]

As for the *Maine*, the magnitude of the disaster and the substantial loss of life, in addition to the mystery surrounding the explosion, turned this event into a news story of the first order.[8] The sinking of the battleship raised the print run of newspapers to record numbers. *The World*, which sent divers to Havana to "cover the story" in situ, and the *Journal*, which first coined the slogan "Remember the *Maine*, to hell with Spain," and offered $50,000 to those who found the "perpetrators of this outrage," managed to sell 1.5 million copies in a single day. In turn, the coverage of the catastrophe provided a unique occasion to mobilize public opinion in favor of U.S. intervention. Despite a lack of evidence, most articles accused Spain of being responsible for the explosion. Within days, the headline "Remember the *Maine!*" put the entire country on the warpath. The promptness and enormity of this mobilization of popular opinion in favor of war with Spain, which ultimately developed into a national cause, was most certainly an expression of solidarity with the cause of a small populace confronted with a tenacious colonial power refusing to grant independence. Nevertheless, it revealed the strength of latent expansionist longings of a nascent U.S. imperialism that, with the closing of the western frontier, searched for new horizons to conquer abroad.

The image of the battleship was transformed into a powerful icon, whether accompanied by narratives of solidarity that emphasized Uncle Sam's responsibility to a nation struggling to free itself from the yoke of Spanish imperialism, or employed as an instrument of jingoist propaganda. It was reproduced, until thoroughly exhausted, in drawings, engravings, photo-

Figure I.2 Wm. H. West's Big Minstrel Jubilee (formerly of Primrose & West).
Source: Library of Congress. Prints and Photographs Division.

graphs, and stereoscopic pictures. The scenes of the *Maine*'s catastrophe were represented in theatrical reenactments as well as in the short current-event documentaries with which the film industry made its debut.[9] The silhouette of the USS *Maine* became a kind of *trademark* of the year 1898, permanently marking the memories of those old enough to remember it, both in the United States and, of course, in Cuba.

Perhaps surprisingly to us today, because of its popularity and resonance, the saying "Remember the *Maine*" was almost immediately turned into a slogan used to attract the attention of consumers. Employed so widely in solemn editorials, fiery news reports, and countless patriotic songs, poems, and hymns, it also appeared in enticing advertisements for merchandise as diverse as books, furniture, clothing, jewelry, dishes, and even pianos.[10] The tension between the "sacred" and the "profane" manifested itself in a fascinating conjunction between the sacrificial rhetoric of editorials on the catastrophe, appearing in the first few pages of newspapers, and the references to it featured in the papers' advertisement sections at the back, is a vivid testimony to the complex ways in which nationalism was converted into a mass phenomenon and "consumed." By the end of the nineteenth century the rapid development of industrialization had lowered the prices of manufactured goods and hence broadened the consumer public; new practices of retailing, of advertising, and of extending credit all transformed the consumer landscape. If saving, abstinence, and frugality (associated with puritan creeds) still represented the ideal values of the Victorian generation, at the gates of the twentieth century, advertisement and the growth of a "shopping culture" were turning the increasing capacity to consume into one of the foremost indicators of success within the American Dream.

A profusion of merchandise—including spoons, dishes, buttons, clasps, brooches, ashtrays, paperweights, matchboxes, cards, and children's toys—began to appear stamped with the image of the battleship. Even biscuits were imprinted with the words "Remember the *Maine*." This abundance of representation certainly serves as a testimony to the popularization of a culture of nationalism, one that not only invaded public spaces but also penetrated the interstices of the domestic sphere as well, embodied as it was in the lure to purchase countless objects for daily use.[11]

A Monument to the Memory of the *Maine*: The First Proposals

In contrast to the U.S. public, whose accounts of the sinking of the ship were received entirely through media, residents of Havana had been firsthand witnesses. Within barely half an hour of the explosion, even as desperate rescue measures were in place, the police battled with hundreds of onlookers. Attracted by the roar of the detonation that shattered the windows of neighboring buildings and rumors of the event that quickly traveled across the city, residents of Havana congregated near the bay, conjecturing over the causes of the explosion. When the sun rose, the sheer magnitude of the catastrophe, in all its dimensions, could finally be observed: that which hours before had been an impressive military gunboat was now reduced to a heap of twisted, blackened iron, half-submerged at one side of the city's bay.

Two days later, more than 50,000 residents of Havana, hundreds of *reconcentrados* among them, congregated in the streets to see the funeral procession on its way to the Cementerio de Colón. There the corpses of the first nineteen marines recovered from the bay received provisional burials. Among those present at the ceremony were the Spanish military and civil authorities, the captain of the *Maine*, Charles D. Sigsbee, his chaplain, Father John Chidwick, the surviving sailors, Clara Barton, founder of the American Red Cross, and Fitzhugh Lee, the American consul in Havana.[12] The funeral on February 17 was only the first of a series of interments and disinterments that—accompanied by public ceremonies that were at times modest and at other times spectacular, carried out in various locations in-

Figure I.3 Destruction of the USS *Maine*, Havana Harbor, Cuba, Spanish-American War, 1898. *Source:* Library of Congress. Prints and Photographs Division.

cluding Havana, Key West, and Washington—kept the memory alive for more than a decade.

The remains of the victims were buried in a plot in the Cementerio de Colón, donated and designated for this purpose by the Roman Catholic bishop of Havana, and the idea of building a monument dedicated to the memory of the destruction of the battleship was born, literally, on the tombs of these victims. On March 4, 1898, on the occasion of another interment of sailors belatedly recovered from the bay, one attendee mentioned the idea of inaugurating a monument: "flowers were the only tribute possible at present to the poor fellows who died in the line of duty, but [it is hoped] that someday a shrine would rise there, to which Americans visiting Cuba would come to pay honor to the dead."[13] Nevertheless, for the moment, in the absence of a definitive monument, the modest wooden crosses in the Havana cemetery would stand in place of a tribute.

In the United States, the mobilization to raise funds for a commemorative monument had begun within a day of the sinking. On February 19, one of Hearst's newspapers, the *Journal*, published a call to the generosity of all social classes to support the campaign for the construction of a monument to the *Maine*. "Send a dime, a dollar, a hundred or a thousand or five thousand dollars. Send your tribute, no matter how small, to the memory of the 250 men who typified all that is most admirable in American manhood." The appeal was warmly received and, by June, the "*Maine* Memorial Fund" headed by Hearst had raised over $100,000.[14]

Nevertheless, not all "popular voices" in the United States joined in this patriotic chorus. A meeting of the Central Labor Union, an organization that consolidated labor unions in New York, Brooklyn, and New Jersey, was the scene of a debate. Many delegates from unions with anarchist and socialist leanings voiced their objections to the memorial project. One worker, representing the Cornice and Skylight Makers Union, stressed, "I do not believe in this talk about pride of country and patriotism. The soldiers and marines are not our friends. They are hirelings of monopolies and corporations. I do not believe in a monument to the lost sailors and marines, for they are not producers." His delivery was met with a mixture of applause from among the ranks of anarchist delegates and cries of disapproval from a large majority of those present in the meeting. In the end, nationalist workers won, and a resolution was approved to support the collection of funds for the future construction of a monument to honor the victims of the explosion.[15]

In the meantime, hundreds of residents in Havana, both the curious and the dismayed, watched, over several days, the work of U.S. Navy divers, submerged in the dirty waters of the bay in attempts to recover the bodies trapped in the ship's hull. The work was compelling. The divers, wearing two-hundred-pound suits, dove for hours into the dark waters of the muddy Havana harbor. Charles Morgan, an official of the USS *New York* and also a trained diver, left a stunning account of the experience:

> It was horrible! . . . As I descended into the death-ship the dead rose up to meet me. They floated toward me with outstretched arms, as if to welcome their shipmate. Their faces for the most part were bloated with decay or burned beyond recognition, but here and there the light of my lamp flashed upon a stony face I knew, which when I last saw it had smiled a merry greeting, but now returned my gaze with staring eyes and fallen jaw. The dead choked the hatchways and blocked my passage from stateroom to cabin. I had to elbow my way through them, as you do in a crowd. While I examined twisted iron and broken timbers they brushed against my helmet and touched my shoulders with rigid hands, as if they sought to tell me the tale of the disaster. . . . From every part of the ship came sighs and groans. I knew it was the gurgling of the water through the shattered beams and battered sides of the vessel, but it made me shudder; it sounded so much like echoes of that awful February night of death.[16]

Figure I.4 Stereoscopic photo of American divers at work, exploring the *Maine* wreck, Havana Harbor. *Source:* Library of Congress. Prints and Photographs Division.

While the remains of the sailors were recovered and buried, arms and other personal belongings of the crew, remnants of furnishings and dishes, and fragments of the ship's hull were carefully packed and sent to the United States to begin a new life as "relics" displayed in public exhibitions or hoarded in private collections.

However, in April recovery efforts suddenly ceased. The U.S. flag that had been lowered at half-mast by the captain the day following the explosion was taken away. The rescue fleet of tugboats and barges headed back in the direction of Key West. The official explanation was that, after many days of hard work, there remained nothing left to do, faced with the impossibility of recovering the remains of crew members whose bodies were likely already completely decomposed or were trapped in the sunken hull of the ship out of reach of the rescue boats.[17]

Days before, on March 25, the results from the U.S. investigative commission had been released, concluding that the explosion that destroyed the battleship was provoked by external causes, presumably an explosive mine. This statement confirmed the culpability of the Spanish, an assumption that had already been declared by the press.[18] In consequence, the suspension of the recovery mission and the subsequent retreat of the U.S. consul from Havana was a clear sign to Havana residents of the imminent outbreak of hostilities. They were not mistaken: on April 14, Henry Cabot Lodge, advocating for the declaration of war in the Senate, temporarily closed the debate on the memorial to the victims of the *Maine*. "There is only one monument to raise over that grave, and that is free Cuba and peace in that island. That is a worthy monument, worthy of men who died under the flag they loved, died in the cold language of the law, in the line of duty."[19]

Forgetting the Maine

In the end, as a result of the war's outcome, the withdrawal of Spanish troops from Havana, thereafter in the hands of U.S. military authorities, provided the first opportunity to pay homage to the victims of the *Maine* at the original site of the explosion. With the military occupation barely under way, a group of women—wives of American officials based in the city—initiated the first celebration of "*Maine* day" in Havana. Thus in February 1899 the appropriation of $10,000 for the construction of a granite monument in the Cementerio de Colón was debated and eventually approved.[20] On February 15, the first anniversary, the ship's wreckage was adorned with flowers, a U.S. flag was raised on its mast, and U.S. troops congregated in the cemetery to pay their respects.

Nevertheless, at the request of the victims' families, it was later decided to exhume the bodies of the sailors in order to bury them in the National Cemetery at Arlington, Virginia. The project for a Havana monument was promptly abandoned. After the bodies were transferred to Washington at the end of 1899, all that remained to recall what had happened were the bare remnants of a blackened ship, half sunken in the middle of the city's port. Over time, the "corpse" of the ship integrated into the familiar landscape of the bay and was eventually transformed, as all quotidian things are, into an almost invisible presence for those who lived in Havana. Only flocks of travelers from the United States convened at the site. Colorful postcards, mostly printed for tourists, and stereographs (an early form of three-dimensional photographs) perpetuated the image of the *Maine* in the waters of the bay as one of the first stereotypical images of the city created for the tourist market, a market that began to develop as an industry in the United States. In those years, the emphasis upon the project of memorializing the war of 1898 was moved to Santiago in eastern Cuba. This was the site of the "splendid little war" to which, in 1901, the military occupation government inaugurated a monument on San Juan Hill. Three years later, the "First Landing Monument" was erected in Daiquirí to mark the site in which marines disembarked in July 1898. In 1908, a bronze plaque was mounted in Siboney to commemorate the ten-year anniversary of the taking of Santiago. The space around the enormous tree where the armistice with the Spanish was signed was converted into a public park. At the foot of the tree, in a bronze book, were the names of the U.S. soldiers and sailors who had fallen in battle during the capture of the city.

Thus, in 1906, the eighth anniversary of the sinking of the battleship was not celebrated in Havana but in Santiago with the inauguration of a memorial in El Caney. Speeches exalted the bravery of the U.S. soldiers who seized the city and emphasized the protective role of the "great nation to the north" for a young Cuban republic. According to General Samuel B. M. Young, who traveled to Cuba expressly for this occasion, the United States intervened in 1898 to guarantee Cubans "a fair, square deal and a chance to play their own hand at the game of self-government." "You, my Cuban friends," asserted Young in a paternalistic tone, "have shuffled and dealt the cards and you are happily playing the game well for beginners."[21]

However, the "beginners" soon failed to meet their mentors' expectations in the game of self-government. Riots provoked by a dispute between the liberals and conservatives over fraudulent presidential elections marked by caudillismo set the stage for a new military occupation. The failure of the first attempt to stabilize a Cuban republic made it immediately evident that "the bonds of singular intimacy and force" that united Cuba and the United States, far from a metaphorical expression, held real consequences, certainly with respect to force. It also demonstrated that the controversial Platt Amendment was no dead letter. If there remained any doubt about this, the 5,600 U.S. soldiers that invaded Cuba in order to "pacify" the country in 1906 were proof enough.

"Remember the *Maine* II": The Remake

Charles Magoon, a lawyer from Minnesota, was an official of the Bureau of Insular Affairs in the U.S. Department of War; as the ex-governor of the Panama Canal Zone and an expert in the legal management of "territories under occupation," Magoon was appointed military governor of the island in September 1906.[22] When the second U.S. occupation came to an end and self-government returned to Cuba in 1909, Magoon's activities while military governor became a topic of controversy. Although congratulated by his government for the success of an extensive public works program, as well as the sanitization of Havana and other regions, he was nonetheless unfavorably remembered in Cuba. Magoon was accused of squandering the island's treasury and opening the door to U.S. investors with contracts and unscrupulous tenders that only served to aggravate the dependency of the Cuban economy on U.S. capital.

One of the governor's proposals, included in the 1908 annual report, reopened the polemic surrounding the now "slumbering" memory of the *Maine*. According to the testimony of a U.S. official, a decade after the sinking of the vessel, a sandbank had formed around the ship that was presenting a significant obstacle to the navigation in the bay; the problem was exasperated by an increase in commercial traffic within the harbor. What was worse, affirmed Magoon, was that the public as much as the government had forgotten about the wreckage, despite the fact that it still harbored the bodies of more than sixty sailors. Magoon's report, which recommended proceeding without delay to remove the *Maine*'s frame from the bay and put an end to the "deplorable spectacle" of its abandonment, received ample publicity in the United States. His report was followed by an extensive debate over the fate of the remains of the ship.[23]

As could be expected, the suggestion to flood the vessel so that it might finally meet its definitive end in the coastal waters of Cuba was met by opposition that considered this inappropriate and almost "sacrilege." An engineer from New York proposed building a monument in its place: an artificial island in the bay of Havana, "properly decorated with roses and palm trees, could be arranged so that people could promenade there and rest on settees while they meditated over the fact of the gallant sailors entombed below."[24] Others proposed raising the ship to recover the bodies and inspect the remains one last time. This was nothing new: in 1900, Beach & Co. in Washington had tried to obtain authorization from the navy to undertake a project to extract, reconstruct, and sail the boat from one port to another throughout the United States—a kind of patriotic "pilgrimage" that would keep the (itinerant) memory of the victims alive.[25]

A decade later, some still attempted to take advantage of the wreckage. Engineer John O'Rourke offered his services in retrieving the remains. After a detailed explanation of the technical procedures necessary to accomplish the task, O'Rourke demanded a high price—affirming, however, that no amount of money would be sufficient for the task of retrieving not simply a ship but the very "historical truth" whose secret is guarded by its remains. He added that one could only imagine the patriotic rapture that the very sight of this mythical craft, entering New York harbor, would arouse: "That day of patriotic hysteria will do us a tremendous lot of good."[26]

In Congress, the topic was the subject of lively deliberations. William Sulzer, U.S. representative from New York, advocated the approval of the sum of money necessary to retrieve the ship. "It was a national disgrace to allow the wreck to remain and not take out the 63 bodies still in the hulk," declared the congressman. On the other hand, Albert Douglas, U.S. representative from Ohio, made a call for laying the memory of the *Maine* to rest. "We would better quit remembering the *Maine*," he announced. In the end, he felt, the corpses that could not be recovered in 1898 were no longer bodies but food for fish, so that bringing home the hideous remains would serve only to reopen old wounds.[27] Finally, in early May 1909, both the House of Representatives and the Senate approved the allocation of funds necessary to retrieve the ship, recover the remaining bodies, and give them an honorable burial in Arlington. The principal mast of the ship would be preserved and added to the pantheon of the *Maine* located in the Arlington National Cemetery. The U.S. Army Corps of Engineers, not a private institution, took charge of retrieving the ship while the federal government covered the costs of this complicated task.[28]

The Cuban government immediately stepped forward to collaborate. In a letter to President Taft, José Miguel Gómez conveyed the desire to conserve a part of the ship's wreckage in Cuba in order to preserve its memory. "On the eve of the raising of the remains of the *Maine* whose sad fate is so closely connected with the history of the independence of Cuba, I desire, voicing the general sentiment of the Cuban people, to ask the American people to let us have one part of the ship with which to erect a plain and shining monument that will forever recall the union of love between the great Republic of the United States and the Republic of Cuba."[29] In the meantime, a permanent guard stationed by the authorities of the port of Havana would avoid the potential of "depredations" from souvenir and relic hunters.[30]

The Cadaver of the *Maine*: Exhumation, Autopsy, and Burial in the Waters of the Gulf

Thus in February 1911, on the thirteenth anniversary of the sinking of the battleship, a celebration was organized with a ceremony in the bay, where memorial services were carried out near the remains of the ship. A corps of Spanish-American War veterans and the Havana chapter of the Daughters of the American Revolution organized the event. Cubans were included in the official delegation for the first time. Among those present were Alfredo Zayas, the vice president of the republic, as well as veterans of the Liberating Army and representatives of different associations and political parties.[31] As a result of a year of strenuous work and the construction of an enormous cofferdam around the wreckage, which was itself an extraordinary work of engineering, the hulk of the battleship partially resurfaced. Between November and December 1911, a new investigative commission inspected the remains

Figure I.5 *Maine* in cofferdam, Havana. *Source*: Library of Congress. Prints and Photographs Division.

that were now exposed to the light of day, only to concur with the expert conclusion of 1898, which had determined that an external cause (such as a mine or torpedo) had destroyed the navy ship.[32]

The recovery project in Havana more than ten years later, and the results of the new investigation, revived the memory of the event, provoking as a result a "remake" of the 1898 "Remember the *Maine*." The discovery of the victims' remains and some of their personal belongings, as well as a number of objects in the hull that had formed part of the ship's equipment, aroused once again an emotional reaction that harkened back to the impact of the first news in February 1898. Scores of articles reclaimed the pages of U.S. newspapers with the stories of survivors and nostalgic accounts of the event. The idea of building a commemorative monument resurfaced to enthusiastic support and, in a matter of months, the *Maine* Memorial Committee had collected over $100,000 to construct a monument in New York City's Central Park.[33]

However, just as in 1898, the explosion of nationalist fervor quickly drew commercial interest that manifested itself in a veritable avalanche of "patriotic" merchandise and advertisements, which profited from the kind of public interest the shipwreck aroused. A decade later, the deliberation in Congress over the fate of the *Maine*'s remains would once again provide evidence of the tension between, on the one hand, the impulse toward a "sacred" cult of heroes and nationalist symbols of a "civil religion" and, on the other, the incorporation of this memory and nationalist symbolism into the everyday circuits of mercantile traffic and the entertainment industry.

In December 1911—when the House of Representatives was debating the question of the funds necessary to complete the task of recovering the ship— a sum that in the end reached $900,000—a group of representatives categorically opposed the idea of making an investment of such magnitude in a process that would end "unproductively" by sinking the remains of a ship that had been so costly to recover in the first place. Robert B. Macon, representative from Arkansas, proposed opening up the sale of the *Maine*'s wreckage to auction. "I believe it would be better for the people to get what we can for the ship," he declared before the House. "There are plenty of novelty seekers and Coney Islandites who would gladly take the old carcass where it is and pay a good price for it in order to get it over here and charge so much per look at it, or sell pieces of it to curio hunters at so much per curio."[34] Thomas Sisson, representative from Mississippi, also spoke for a group of investors "who desire to exhibit it at various ports of the United States and charge an admission fee to visitors," and was therefore offering $1 million for the ship's remains.[35] Both proposals provoked indignant reactions from those who believed that the remains of the ship, especially as it embodied a tragic national memory, deserved to be treated with respect and considered venerable relics rather than merchandise or novelties. "I am surprised that this gentleman has not included in his proposition the selling of the bones of the seamen who died in the *Maine*," articulated James R. Mann, one of the leaders of the Republican Party.

In the end, taking a clear stand against the commercialization of the wreckage, John J. Fitzgerald, chairman of the U.S. House of Representatives Committee on Appropriations, promptly put an end to the debate. "In my opinion, the American people would not tolerate making a public show of that old vessel. There are some things that are sacred to the people, and among them are the remains of men or vessels lost in defense of the Nation. I would deplore the American Government attempting to make profit out of this ship, merely to gratify the idle curiosity of any people of the United States."[36] The law authorizing the remaining funds required to recover the ship was approved by a majority vote and commercial offers from businessman looking to profit from the memory of the *Maine* were rejected; these offers were considered "unpatriotic" and any attempt to commercialize the ship's remains was prohibited. As such, this mass of twisted iron attained the status of "patriotic relic," sharing a destiny homologous with the bodies of the crew that had remained trapped in its hull. The crew would later be buried with military honors in Arlington, and it was decided that the carcass of the ship would similarly be given an "appropriate grave," submerged at the bottom of the sea.[37]

On the island, Havana residents had followed the yearlong developments in the construction of the cofferdam with immense curiosity.[38] The "exhumation" of the *Maine*'s "cadaver" together with the publication of the results of the new investigation into the causes of the explosion—a new "autopsy" if you will—succeeded in reopening the public debate over the implications of the U.S. intervention in the conflict between Cuba and Spain, as well as the nature of the relationship of "tutelage" exerted by their northern neighbor. Nevertheless, both the moving tone of the coverage of the "exhumation" of the *Maine* in Cuban newspapers and the emotional reaction of Havana residents—a populace that gathered en masse on the pier and in adjacent streets on the day of the *Maine*'s "funeral" to witness the "farewell" spectacle—speaks to the presence of conflicting feelings with respect to the memory of the *Maine*, experienced as part of a local and rather intimate memory of the city.

It is very likely that, among the thousands of Havana residents who participated in the symbolic funeral of 1912 were many firsthand witnesses to the enormous explosion in the port, such as María de la Cruz Senmanat. Many had also been present at the burial of the first victims in the Cementerio de Colón or seen the impressive spectacle of rescue efforts that, for several days, attempted to recover the corpses of U.S. Marines from the waters of the bay. In contrast to later generations for whom the *Maine* was merely a monument made of marble and bronze in the district of Vedado or a stereotypical narrative in the pages of a textbook, for those who had witnessed the episode it was a highly complicated experience. The sinking of the ship was no doubt associated with memories of the U.S. military intervention and the image of the ominous U.S. flag flying over the fortress of del Morro. But it also undoubtedly evoked a sense of enormous relief provoked by the end of the war and the *reconcentración*. The event was also connected with the modernization of the city on the North American model that started during the U.S. occupation: the expansion of paved streets, electric lighting, and a telephone network, as well as a modern sewage layout and the creation of new public spaces like the Malecón (the seawall along the outer bay), left an indelible physical mark on the landscape of the urban capital.

"The *Maine*, protruding out in the middle of the bay, its mast faded in color, its corroding bow; this mass of blackened ruins has been a permanent detail in our landscape, it has been truly *ours* for the last 14 years. There is a sincere melancholy in seeing it disappear forever from these greenish waters and blazing skies," noted a journalist in the pages of the newspaper *La Discusión*. This was published on February 15, 1912, on the occasion of the last commemorative ceremony, which took place in the port of Havana, on the anniversary of the explosion. "This is to be the last February sun [the vessel] will experience, since, in short, it is to take its final resting place at the bottom of the sea, indeed a suitable grave for the greatness of such a powerful ship."

A sector of the public refused to part with the "cadaver" of a ship that was perceived to be theirs, particularly since it had been so closely tied to the recent history of the republic as well as the memory of the city. "That reddish light of the battleship as it blew into pieces was the resplendency of the dawn of our republic," an editorial poetically proclaimed in *La Discusión*. "The memory of the disaster must not die alongside the generation of Cubans who were alive during this terrible episode." For this reason, suggested the author, in place of sinking the ship, "it would be far more agreeable to patriotic Cubans if the cadaver of the ship that with its death gave the republic life were held by a dense layer of our land and sleeping below a monument erected for our republic." To conclude, the author wrote, "if the miserable remains have for so many years been immovable in the mud of our bay, why not entrust it once again to the genuine earth of this island of tears in whose process of development it has been silently present as a faithful friend?"[39] Beyond its political implications, then, the remains of the ship, with its aura of mystery and tragedy, had for Havana residents become an intimate part of the city's landscape. Indeed, in the days following the final sinking of the *Maine*, a rumor traveled throughout the city: for inexplicable reasons the ship had resurfaced anew, and several people claimed to have seen it floating adrift like a ghostly presence refusing to make its final departure.[40]

A similar reaction occurred in the United States. Patriotic organizations, a handful of senators, and officials from the U.S. Navy made it known that they opposed the decision to sink the ship. Since the government had invested such a considerable sum of money to recover the boat, it seemed almost sacrilege to return it to the sea. Furthermore, it would have looked particularly irreverent if there existed the slightest possibility of returning it to the United States where so many would look on with satisfaction at its conversion into a monument that preserved the memory not only of the victims of the *Maine* but also of all Spanish-American War veterans.[41] Nevertheless, the decision taken by the government and the secretary of the navy was irrevocable, and

Figure I.6 The USS *Maine* going to her final resting place. *Source*: Library of Congress. Prints and Photographs Division.

on March 15, 1912, the official burial of the USS *Maine*'s "cadaver" took place in Havana.

The final "farewell" to its remains was a theatrical spectacle of grand proportions, carefully conceived down to the minutest detail. Although organized in Washington, Cuban authorities had an important role in the script. The *New York Times* described the ceremony as "the most stately naval funeral in the history of the world." According to the Cuban press, the ceremony witnessed the largest public demonstration in the city since May 20, 1902—the day of the republic's inauguration. It was a great mise-en-scène of the "fraternal friendship" of the two nations. The act included the presence of General William Herbert Bixby, chief of the U.S. Army Corps of Engineers, and the president of Cuba himself, José Miguel Gómez, who took part in the ceremony from a Cuban naval ship. Furthermore, diplomatic representatives in the city, members of various associations, U.S. veterans of the war of 1898, and veterans of the Cuban independence army were present. The USS *North Carolina* and the USS *Birmingham* arrived in the port of Havana for two purposes: to accompany the remains of the *Maine*'s "cadaver" to the waters of the Gulf, where it would be sunk, and to later escort the bodies of U.S. sailors to the United States, where they would be buried in Arlington National Cemetery.[42]

Nearly 100,000 people congregated on the seafront to see the departure of the mythical ship, tugged out from the port where it would be sunk at three nautical miles from the coast. According to the *New York Tribune*, around 2 P.M., with her deck "covered deep with flowers and a great American ensign floating from the jurymast, where the main mast formerly stood," the *Maine* put to sea on her last voyage. As the wreck passed the American squadrons, "the Marines presented arms and the scarlet coated bandsmen on the quarterdeck played the national anthem, while minute guns boomed a requiem." A large procession of Cuban and American ships followed the vessel until the three-mile limit was trespassed. At 5 P.M., the valves in the carcass were opened and the wreck started to sink. A few minutes later "there was a flash of blue and white, as the great ensign floating from the mast struck the waves and disappeared. Simultaneously, the decks were blown up by the air pressure, and with incredible velocity the Maine plunged down, leaving no trace save flowers tossing on the surface of the sea."[43] But a series of photographs that immortalized her "final moments" were at first abundantly published in the newspapers and then reproduced in postcards, giving a graphic testimony to the burial of the wreckage in the sea. In Havana, a film about the "burial" was created by Enrique Díaz, a pioneer of Cuban cinematography, and premiered to the great excitement of the public in the Payret cinema on March 19, 1912.[44]

Four days later, the last of the sailors' bodies were buried. President Taft, accompanied by Charles D. Sigsbee and Reverend John P. Chidwick, the captain and chaplain of the *Maine*, were in attendance. The ceremony brought to a conclusion a series of memorial services that had begun in Havana fourteen years earlier when, on February 17, 1898, the first victims were buried in the Cementerio de Colón.[45]

The "Life after Death" of the *Maine*:
The Resurrection as Monumentalization

But the "social life" of the *Maine* did not end the final sinking of its "corpse" in the sea, with the "honors of a soldier who died in combat." On the contrary. As Katherine Verdery has argued in her book, *The Political Lives of Dead Bodies*, often it is just in the moment of "death" that the more significant symbolic life actually begins. Despite an agreement that was passed by Congress in 1911, explicitly preventing the "dismemberment" of the ship for commercial purposes, all that could be detached from the frame was nonetheless taken away: what Havana residents saw submerged in the sea was only the hull of the battleship. Fragments—veritable "relics"—were dispersed and became part of memorials and monuments that preserved the memory of the sunken ship in stone and bronze.[46]

As we have already seen, the "revival" of the memory of the *Maine*—a consequence of a series of campaigns for its "resurrection" from the Havana bay and its subsequent burial—reinvigorated the activities of the *Maine* Memorial Committee. Though the committee was nominally presided over by James Grant Wilson, it was driven and sponsored by William Randolph Hearst from its inception in 1898. On May 30, 1913, a monument to the *Maine*, sponsored by the committee, was inaugurated in Columbus Circle next to Central Park in New York City. The principal sculpture, created by architect Harold Van Buren Magonigle and sculptor Attilio Piccirilli, was

Columbia Triumphant. According to what is said in the description of the project, it was crafted out of bronze cannons taken from the *Maine* itself. A second allegorical sculpture group, named *The Antebellum State of Mind*, featured a female figure representing peace, accompanied by other figures representing courage and fortitude. This sculptural group also included the representation of a young boy who expectantly advances toward the bow of the boat; according to the creators of the memorial, he represented the "new era inaugurated in Cuba through the Spanish War."[47]

The inauguration of the monument was preceded by a large commemorative Memorial Day parade, which, according to the *New York Times*, was one of the major celebrations in the city. The cost of the monument, $170,000, was defrayed by contributions from "among the poor and plain people of almost every State of the Union," which amounted to more than a million donations. Former President Taft was the keynote speaker at the ceremony and succinctly summarized the significance of the memorial: "The monument we dedicate today is an enduring witness of three facts. The first is the gratitude that our country feels towards the men who went down on the *Maine*, in that they gave up their lives in her service. The second is the birth of new people and the founding of a new nation through our disinterested aid and sacrifice. The third is the expansion of this nation into a wider sphere of world usefulness and greater responsibility among the nations than ever before in its history."[48] The association that Taft made in his address—the connection between the sinking of the ship and the birth of the Cuban Republic, and the relationship of both to the beginning of an era of imperial expansion by the United States—would eventually be the subject of ardent debate and reinterpretation in Cuba in the years to follow, in a time when anti-imperialist discourse carried increasingly more force.

Two days after the "burial" of the *Maine*, the Cuban press circulated the news of the government's decision to preserve the memory of the ship with a monument in Havana. The Republic of Cuba obtained its share of the "relics" that were packed and sent to the United States.[49] It was thus that a secondary mast, some chains, and two of the ship's cannons remained on the island with the intention of being incorporated into a monument that would be constructed to fill the memorial void left in the city by the absence of the ship's proper "body."

In fact, receiving notice that the hull was to be submerged at sea, the council of the Asociación de Veteranos de la Independencia de Cuba [Association of Veterans of the Cuban Independence War] agreed to compose a letter to President Taft, requesting that the cofferdam, built to extract the hull of the ship, be preserved once the ship's remains were removed. The intention was to refill the cofferdam so that a monument could be built on it to perpetuate the memory of the ship in the very location of the bay where it had lain for so many years.[50] Days later, in the Cuban House of Representatives, a similar proposal was forwarded. The senator for the province of Oriente, Erasmos Regueiferos, proposed a bill that would supply funds for the erection of a monument on the cofferdam. Its surface would be filled in with earth, creating a small artificial island upon which the monument would be constructed just as the senator in question had imagined it: a lighthouse with a Statue of Liberty carrying a torch and accompanied by two effigies, one of José Martí and the other of George Washington.[51]

Nevertheless, despite the initial enthusiasm of the newspapers and a presidential order signed on December 6, 1913 by Mario García Menocal, which created a committee to design the monument and allocated the initial funds for its construction, the project eventually fell into oblivion. In September 1915, nearly two years later, the newspaper *La Noche* reported that the cannons and the mast of the *Maine*, which had been donated by the United States to be used in a memorial, remained abandoned in the same warehouse on the harbor where they had been left the day the ship was sunk in 1912. This report had repercussions in the U.S. press, and many papers demanded the return of "relics" that were so underappreciated by the Cuban government.[52]

Under the pressure of public opinion, the committee in charge of the creation of the monument decided to hold an international competition for the design of the future memorial to the *Maine*. Engineer and architect Félix Cabarrocas won the contest with a plan in a neoclassical style that combined both the cannons and chains from the ship. However, it was not until 1918 that the Secretaría de Obras Públicas decided to begin construction on the monument in the designated site: the Avenida "Antonio Maceo." The avenue, known as "el Malecón," is located near the headland where the Santa Clara battery was situated, at the gates of Vedado. Despite good intentions, the commencement of construction was once again delayed by problems with the budget and a conflict between Cabarrocas, the designer of the monument, the organizing committee, and the Ministerio de Obras Públicas. In 1924, the government of Alfredo Zayas resolved to execute the project anew and allocated a budget of 116,000 pesos for that purpose.[53]

Finally, on February 15, 1924, on the twenty-sixth anniversary of the catastrophe, the first stone was laid.[54] This monument to the victims of the *Maine*—the work of sculptor Moisés de la Huerta and Cabarrocas—was inaugurated by Zayas a year later on March 8, 1925, when he was nearly at the point of handing over power to the succeeding president, Gerardo Machado. Nevertheless, just as his presidential authority had been consistently put into question by the presence of Enoch Crowder, the U.S. proconsul in Havana, the speaker at the ceremony was not the Cuban president but U.S. General John J. Pershing, who had come explicitly from the United States for the commemoration. More than a quarter century after the catastrophe—a catastrophe that with the intervention of the United States in the war between Cuba and Spain inaugurated the imperialistic expansion of the United States within the Americas—the tone of U.S. discourse had changed slightly. If, with the first commemorations of the *Maine*, the role of tutelage was repeatedly claimed by the United States in relation to the small and emerging Cuban Republic, this time, at the height of pan-Americanism, the "moral obligation" of the United States to watch over the development of democracy went far beyond Cuba and extended to all its "little sisters" in Latin America.[55] An interesting detail about the commemorative inauguration of 1925 was the participation of the Spanish ambassador to Cuba, who rendered homage to the victims, leaving an offering of flowers.[56]

The monument's base, built of granite, was adorned with the cannons and chains procured from the remains of the ship; two twin marble columns emerged from the base to support a bronze eagle with extended wings, an image whose imperial symbolism was poorly received by Cubans from its inception. It seemed born for a tragic fate. Indeed, within a year of its inauguration, a fierce hurricane hit Havana, leaving more than $1 million worth of damage, destroying the columns, and shattering the eagle.

Nevertheless, the memorial was restored. The marble columns were replaced, and the original eagle was substituted for another with a slender and more aerodynamic body in order to better resist the battering of the winds.[57] In 1928, the area was significantly beautified with the building of the Plaza del *Maine* around the monument. A series of esplanades and gardens added not only equilibrium and beauty but also symbolic connotations to the site: the plaza was complemented by the busts of former U.S. presidents William McKinley and Theodore Roosevelt, as well as that of Leonard Wood, who had been the U.S. military governor in Cuba during the first intervention. These busts were the creations of U.S. sculptor Gutzom Borglum.[58] The design of the plaza and the gardens bordering it were the work of the prestigious French architect and landscapist Jean Claude Nicolas Forestier. Forestier had been expressly invited to Cuba to act as a consultant on an urban renewal project for Havana, launched by President Gerardo Machado and his minister of public works, Carlos Miguel de Céspedes.

Figure I.7
Bronze eagle from the monument to the victims of the *Maine*. Photograph unknown. Courtesy of Marial Iglesias Utset.

Forestier designed the plaza as a gateway that connected the old part of the city, across from the Malecón, with Vedado. As previously mentioned, both the Malecón—an avenue built during the first U.S. intervention that, with each new government, stretched out further west along the coastline— along with Vedado—a neighborhood made up of straight tree-lined streets, main avenues, parterres, and public parks, as well as chalets and cottages built in the style of U.S. suburbs—were paradigmatic models of the spatial transformation of the city on a U.S. model.[59] Early in 1928, motivated by both the celebration of the sixth international Conference of American States in Havana and a visit from the president of the United States, Calvin Coolidge, Gerardo Machado ostentatiously inaugurated the plaza.[60] In what largely resulted in an insult to the memory of nationalist patriots, the commemorative ceremony, which took place on October 10, the anniversary of the declaration of the war of independence against Spain, was celebrated in the Plaza del *Maine* with an impressive military parade.

In later years the monument would be strongly associated not only with U.S. presence in Cuba but also with the unfavorably remembered Machado

Figure I.8 Monument to the victims of the *Maine*. Photograph by Marial Iglesias Utset.

dictatorship. In 1930, with the construction of the deluxe Hotel Nacional next door to it, the monument became a site of obligatory pilgrimage for the hundreds of U.S. tourists who came to Cuba each winter. In 1953, the inauguration of a new building for the nearby U.S. embassy, a seven-story modernist building designed by Leland W. King, completed the definitive "Americanization" of the area.[61]

At the same time, police and military parades, organized for the anniversary of the *Maine* in the esplanade facing the plaza during the 1940s and 1950s—particularly during the years of tyranny under President Fulgencio Batista—contributed to endowing the site with repressive and progovernment affiliations. As a result, this site frequently became the scene of nationalist and anti-government protests. In March 1949, the monument to the victims of the *Maine* was vandalized in reprisal for the desecration of the José Martí monument in Parque Central by a group of drunken U.S. Marines who urinated on the statue.[62] Carlos Franqui, a veteran of the revolutionary underground in Havana, relates in his memoirs how July 26 Movement attempted in vain to explode the monument. The structure was so solid that the endeavor was impossible: "more dynamite was needed to knock it down than [to depose] the Batista regime itself."[63]

The Fall of the "Eagle of Imperialism"

It is not surprising that with the triumph of the revolution in 1959, the monument, with its imperialist symbolism and unfavorable memories that associated it with both the Machado and Batista dictatorships, was bound to disappear. As if that were not enough, in March 1960, *La Coubre*, a Belgian commercial freight ship transporting arms, exploded in Havana Harbor, killing more than seventy-five people. The revolutionaries immediately claimed the blast was an act of terrorism, and Fidel Castro blamed the United States and compared the incident to the sinking of the *Maine*, though acknowledging that there was no material evidence for this accusation. So this unfortunate event conjured up the ghost of the *Maine*, which resurrected again to become a symbolic trope in the aggressive anti-U.S. rhetoric of the early 1960s.[64] It was in Castro's speech at the funeral of the victims of the explosion of *La Coubre* where the slogan of the July 26 Movement, "Patria y Libertad," was replaced by "Patria o Muerte," a pivotal point in the process of radicalization of the revolution.

A few months later, in August 1960, the nationalization of U.S. property in Cuba provoked an enormous demonstration by Havana residents in the city streets heading toward the Malecón. They intended to "bury," by throwing into the sea, coffins made of cardboard that symbolically represented the "corpses" of U.S. corporate monopolies. Henceforth, tensions escalated and relations deteriorated between the United States and Cuba until the complete rupture in diplomatic relations in January 1961.

And so, immediately after the defeat of a U.S.-backed invasion of Cuba at the Bay of Pigs, and in the early morning of May 1, 1961, the eagle that topped the monument was pulled down by a Cuban government crane—made to fall once again, only this time by force of the overwhelming gale of the revolution.[65] The initial suggestion to substitute it with a cubist sculpture, a peace dove designed by Picasso ("a picassian symbol of liberty atop the decapitated columns of the old *Maine*," according to Carlos Franqui, the mastermind of the proposal) was never realized.[66] Half a century after the mutilation of the monument, its pinnacle still remains vacant. The marble and bronze structure stands as silent witness to the profound political disagreements between the nations.[67]

This very same marble surface of the monument is today a kind of palimpsest, bearing visible traces of the rewriting of the meaning of the event that the monument commemorates. The simple inscription, "To the victims of the *Maine*. The people of Cuba," that originally appeared on the front of the monument was, in 1961, traded in for an accusatory, "To the victims of the *Maine* who were sacrificed to a voracious imperialism in its eagerness to seize the island of Cuba." The text of the resolution approved by the U.S. Congress in 1898 that affirmed that Cuba is and, by right, ought to be free and independent was preserved on the other side; nevertheless, as a nationalist gesture, the cast text that was originally in English was replaced by a Spanish translation.

The singular destiny of the three-ton imperial eagle that was "overthrown" in 1961 can also be read as a metaphorical rupture of the "bonds of singular intimacy" between both nations. The body and wings of the eagle were exhibited for many years in the Museo de la Ciudad (Museum of the City of Havana) as trophies won in the "defeat of imperialism." Meanwhile, the head of the bird was stolen in 1961 by an anti-Castro group from a warehouse of the Ministry of Public Works where it was stored and later returned to U.S. diplomats as a symbolic gesture of making amends. It now hangs on the wall in a conference room in the United States Interests Section in Havana.[68]

"I have been the faithful custodian of the body," the director of the museum and Havana's city historian, Eusebio Leal, recently told Peter Orsi, the Associated Press correspondent in Cuba. After half a century of abandonment and dilapidation, the monument is now being restored, due to the initiative of Leal, who is also president of the National Commission of Monuments. "Gone are the rusty stains beneath the two 10-inch guns that were salvaged from the *Maine*. The statues are a lustrous bronze again after corrosive salt air turned them bright green," wrote Orsi in a piece published on the occasion of the 115th anniversary of the sinking of the *Maine*. But there seems to be little hope that the body and the head of the bronze eagle will be reunited soon, since the normalization of relations between the two countries is unlikely in the near term.[69]

However, in spite of the fifty years that have transpired since the mutilation of the monument, the "social life" of the remains of the battleship *Maine* is not over. Silent witnesses of the encounters, conflicts, and misunderstandings that have marked the tense relationship between Cuba and the United States, from its granite and marble niche on the Havana's Malecón, the cannons and chains of the warship have resisted the battering and corrosion of the sea and the passage of time, awaiting the next stage of the intimately fraught kinship between the two nations.

Notes

The research for this chapter was made possible by a residency at the Universidad Jaume I de Castellón de la Plana, Spain, part of a project funded by the Spanish Ministerio de Economía y Competitividad (HAR2012-36481). I thank José Antonio Piqueras, Alessandra Lorini, Kenneth Mills, Ronald W. Pruessen, Ada Ferrer, Arcadio Díaz Quiñones and Steve Palmer for their support and intellectual collaboration.

1. *Revolución*, no. 779 (La Habana, June 19, 1961): 1, 6.

2. The phrase, used by President William McKinley, would become the euphemism par excellence to describe Cuba's dependence on the United States during the better part of the twentieth century. It is part of McKinley's Third Annual Message, December 5, 1899: "The new Cuba yet to arise from the ashes of the past must needs be bound to us by ties of singular intimacy and strength if its enduring welfare is to be assured. Whether those ties shall be organic or conventional, the destinies of Cuba are in some rightful form and manner irrevocably linked with our own." http://www.presidency.ucsb.edu/ws/?pid=29540, accessed May 2, 2013.

3. *Instituto Nacional de Reforma Agraria*, no. 7 (July 1961): 16.

4. On the importance of the *Maine* incident as the causal explanation for the U.S. decision to intervene in the war between Cuba and Spain, and on the rhetoric of Cuban gratitude to the United States, see Pérez, "The Meaning of the *Maine*" and "Incurring a Debt of Gratitude." In Cuban historiography the work of Emilio Roig de Leuchsenring offers the most consistent attempt to refute, from a nationalist perspective, the interpretation that attributes to U.S. intervention the merit for having contributed in a disinterested manner to the founding of the Republic of Cuba. See Roig de Leuchsenring, *Por su propio esfuerzo conquistó el pueblo cubano su independencia* and *Cuba no debe su independencia a los Estados*.

5. Nora, "Between Memory and History," 7–24.

6. Fitzhugh Lee to William R. Day, January 26, 1898, cited in Eggert, "Our Man in Havana: Fitzhugh Lee," 481.

7. Wisan, *The Cuban Crisis as Reflected in the New York Press, 1895–1898*, 46–83; Mott, *American Journalism*; Campbell, *Yellow Journalism*; Goldenberg, "Imperial Culture and National Conscience."

8. One month after the sinking, *Collier's Weekly* reported that the photos of the *Maine* were selling "better than those of noted beauties and other celebrities," *Collier's Weekly*, March 12, 1898, 4. On visual coverage of the *Maine* episode see Miller, "The Spectacle of War: A Study of Spanish-American War Visual and Popular Culture."

9. Thomas A. Edison Inc., *Wreck of the Battleship* Maine (1898). The film can be consulted on the Library of Congress website, "Spanish-American War in Motion Pictures," http://memory.loc.gov/ammem/sawhtml/sawsp2.html. The sinking of the *Maine* was also filmed by the pioneering Cuban cinematographer José G. González; while in

France Georges Méliès filmed a shortened version of the episode. See Chanan, *Cuban Cinema*, 41.

10. Only two days after the *Maine* explosion, the *Atlanta Constitution* published moving descriptions of the catastrophe on its front page. In the same edition but in the advertising section, a reproduction of the ship illustrated an ad by the R. S. Crutcher Furniture Company of Atlanta with the text, "The terrible explosion of the U.S. Man of War *Maine* . . . is causing a great deal of excitement among the American people, but for the next 30 days we are going to have an 'explosion of prices' on Furniture, Carpets and Baby Carriages that will startle the entire population of Georgia." *Atlanta Constitution*, February 18, 1898, 6.

11. For the relationship between consumption and nationalism, see Fox and Miller-Idriss, "Everyday Nationhood," 549. A theorization of consumption as a cultural practice can be found in Miller, *Material Culture and Mass Consumption* and *A Theory of Shopping*.

12. *Diario de la Marina*, February 18, 1898. For a detailed description of the ceremony, see also Sigsbee, *The "Maine": An Account of Her Destruction in Havana Harbor*, 110.

13. *New York Times*, March 5, 1898.

14. *New York Evening Journal*, February 19, 1898.

15. "Central Union Patriotic: Resolutions Favoring a Monument to the *Maine* Victims Passed by a Large Majority," *New York Times*, February 28, 1898.

16. *Diario de la Marina*, February 17, 1898; "Naval Divers," *Frank Leslie's Popular Monthly* 47, no. 2 (December 1898): 170.

17. "*Maine* Wreck Abandoned," *New York Times*, April 3, 1898.

18. "The *Maine* Inquiry Report," *New York Times*, March 29, 1898.

19. "Will Be No Delay," *Washington Post*, April 14, 1898.

20. "Maine Day in Havana," *New York Times*, January 24, 1899, and "Maine Monument in Havana," *New York Times*, February 4, 1899.

21. "Dos pueblos y dos banderas unidos para honrar gloriosos hechos: Las fiestas de la loma de San Juan," *La Discusión*, February 15, 1906, 1, 10; and *Society of the Army of Santiago de Cuba: Dedication of the Battle Monument at El Caney* (Baltimore Press of John S. Bridge & Co., 1906), 11; cited in Klein, *Spaniards and the Politics of Memory in Cuba*, 311–12. Note that Young's opinion had changed considerably: on August 7, 1898, he had declared to the *New York Times* that the Cubans "are no more capable of self-government than the savages of Africa."

22. Magoon, *Reports on the Law of Civil Government in Territory Subject to Military Occupation by the Military Forces of the United States*. See also "Civil Government by the Military," *Chicago Daily Tribune*, July 14, 1902, and Gonzalez, "The Cause of Civilization," 206–54.

23. "Magoon Says Raise Wreck of *Maine*," *New York Times*, January 25, 1909, and *Wreck of battle ship Maine. Letter from the Secretary of War, transmitting a letter from the Chief of Engineers relative to the rising or removal of the wreck of the battle ship Maine*

from Havana harbor, May 17, 1910, 61st Cong., 2d sess., House of Representatives, doc. 919, Washington, D.C., 1910, 2.

24. "Would Make an Isle of the Sunken *Maine*," *New York Times*, January 31, 1909.
25. "Would Lift the *Maine*," *Washington Post*, January 8, 1900.
26. "New Plan to Raise *Maine* Would Reveal Famous Secret," *Washington Post*, August 7, 1910; and also "Engineer at *Maine* Wreck," *Beaumont Enterprise and Journal*, December 9, 1910.
27. "Contest in House," *Washington Post*, February 27, 1909.
28. "Maine to Be Raised" *Washington Post*, May 5, 1910; "Removal of Wreck of U.S.S. *Maine* in Havana Harbor, Cuba, March 15, 1910," 61st Cong., 2d sess., House of Representatives, report no. 754, Washington, D.C., 1910.
29. Letter of José Miguel Gómez to W. H. Taft, Havana, December 6, 1910, 61st Cong. 2d sess., House of Representatives, Washington, D.C., 1910.
30. "No Relics from the *Maine*," *St. Albans Messenger*, December 24, 1909.
31. "Services for *Maine*'s Dead," *Washington Post*, February 16, 1911.
32. "To Inspect *Maine* Wreck," *Washington Post*, November 11, 1911; "Board Is Kept at Havana," *Washington Post*, December 2, 1911; "Examine the *Maine* Wreck," *New York Times*, November 23, 1911; "Report on the Wreck of the Battleship *Maine*. Message from the President of the United States Transmitting a Report of Board Convened at Havana Cuba, by Order of the Secretary of the Navy, to Inspect and Report on the Wreck of the *Maine*" (old), December 14, 1911, 62d Congress, 2d sess., House of Representatives, doc. 310, Washington, D.C., 1912.
33. "Raising the *Maine* in Moving Pictures," *New York Times*, November 19, 1911.
34. "Clash over Plan to Sell the *Maine*," *New York Times*, December 17, 1911; "Bill to Sell *Maine* Wreck," *Washington Post*, December 20, 1911; "No Gifts of *Maine* Guns," *New York Tribune*, December 21, 1911.
35. "Would Sell the *Maine* Wreck," *New York Tribune*, December 20, 1911.
36. "Clash over Plan to Sell the *Maine*" *New York Times*, December 17, 1911.
37. "Rules Prevent Fight," *Washington Post*, December 17, 1911; "House Refuses to Sell Maine Wreck," *New York Tribune*, December 17, 1911.
38. "¡El *Maine* flota ya en la bahía!" *La Discusión*, February 14, 1912.
39. *La Discusión*, February 29, 1912.
40. "¿El *Maine* frente a la boca del Morro?" *La Discusión*, March 27, 1912.
41. "Wreck of *Maine* Is Sought as War Relic for Capital," *Washington Post*, March 10, 1912.
42. "Los funerales del *Maine*," *La Discusión*, March 15, 1912, 1; "Últimos tributos a los restos del *Maine*," *La Discusión*, March 17, 1912; "*Maine* to Sink Today to Her Lasting Rest," *New York Tribune*, March 16, 1912.
43. "The *Maine* Sinks to Raise No More," *New York Tribune*, March 17, 1912, 1.
44. "Estreno de la película *El epílogo del Maine*," *La Discusión*, March 19, 1912, 4.
45. "Los funerales de las víctimas del *Maine*," *La Discusión*, March 23, 1912.
46. The ship's main mast is part of the monument to the *Maine*'s victims in Arlington

National Cemetery, while the foremast is preserved in the Annapolis Naval Academy. Different pieces and ornaments that belonged to the ship form part of monuments in Bangor, Maine; Marion, Indiana; South Bend, Indiana; Canton, Ohio; Lewiston, Maine; Pompton Lakes, New Jersey; Woburn, Massachusetts; Key West; Minneapolis; and Pittsburgh. See Mayo, *War Memorials as Political Landscape*, 166.

47. Bogart, "*Maine* Memorial and Pulitzer Fountain," 50.

48. "Unveil Memorial to *Maine* Heroes," *New York Times*, May 31, 1913.

49. "Mast of Battleship *Maine* Landed at Navy Yard Here," *Washington Post*, February 10, 1912.

50. "Plan Monument to *Maine*," *Washington Post*, December 17, 1911.

51. "Monumento a las víctimas del *Maine*," *La Discusión*, February 21, 1912.

52. "Want *Maine*'s Relics Back," *New York Times*, September 4, 1915.

53. Santovenia, *Libro conmemorativo de la inauguración de la Plaza del Maine en la Habana*, 121.

54. "Zayas Tells Gratitude of Cuba to Americans," *Washington Post*, February 16, 1924.

55. "Pershing at Unveiling of *Maine* Monument," *New York Times*, March 9, 1925.

56. Klein, *Spaniards and the Politics of Memory in Cuba*, 335.

57. "*Maine* Monument Gone," *New York Times*, October 21, 1926; "Havana *Maine* Memorial Restored," *New York Times*, November 20, 1926.

58. Santovenia, *Libro conmemorativo de la inauguración de la Plaza del Maine en la Habana*, 123.

59. Lejeune, Beusterien, and Menocal, "The City as Landscape," 174–76.

60. "La apertura de la Sexta Conferencia Internacional Americana," *Carteles*, La Habana, 9, no. 4 (January 22, 1928): 23.

61. "New U.S. Embassy in Cuba," *New York Times*, June 9, 1953.

62. "U.S. Statue in Havana Marred," *New York Times*, March 17, 1949.

63. Franqui, *Retrato de familia con Fidel*, 92.

64. "Castro Makes Issue of the *Maine* Loss," *New York Times*, March 6, 1960, and "Palabras pronunciadas por Fidel Castro en las honras fúnebres de las víctimas de la explosión del barco 'La Coubre,' en el cementerio de Colón 5 de marzo de 1960," http://www.cuba.cu/gobierno/discursos/1960/esp/f050360e.html; Walterio Carbonel, "Las explosiones misteriosas del *Maine y La Coubre*," *Revolución*, March 15, 1960, 2; Pardo Llada, "La voladura del *Maine*," 70.

65. "Cayó el águila del imperialismo," *Revolución*, May 1, 1961, 3. A short take of the toppling of the monument's eagle, filmed at dawn on May 1, 1961, can be seen in the documentary collage that serves as the backdrop to the celebrated film *Memorias del subdesarrollo* (dir. Tomás Gutiérrez Alea, ICAIC, 1968).

66. Franqui, *Retrato de familia con Fidel*, 92. In an interview that Franqui gave to William Luis in 1981, he claims that despite Picasso's willingness to substitute a cubist dove for the *Maine*'s eagle, the project was rejected after "Soviet-style" socialist realism was imposed in Cuba. See Luis, *Lunes de Revolución*, 192–93. See also "Picasso to De-

sign Cuba Dove," *New York Times*, July 6, 1961, and "Cayó el águila del imperialismo," *Revolución*, May 1, 1961, 3.

67. "Cuba to Develop along Red Lines," *New York Times*, May 1, 1961.

68. "Cubans Save the Eagle: Anti-Castro Group Retrieves Part of U.S. Monument," *New York Times*, May 21, 1961. Curiously, the U.S. representatives in Cuba also keep the original eagle, tumbled by the 1926 infamous hurricane. Since 1954 the restored eagle decorates the gardens of the Interests Section chief's official residence in Havana.

69. Peter Orsi, "Havana Restores Monument to Victims of USS *Maine*," Associated Press, February 15, 2013. http://bigstory.ap.org/article/havana-restores-monument-victims-uss-maine-2).

CHAPTER 2

Shifting Sands of Cuban Science, 1875–1933

Steven Palmer

The principal cast in the production and politics of mainstream Cuban science did not change much between 1875, when a dynamic group of young creoles began transforming research practice in Havana in the waning years of the first war of independence, and the 1920s, when their last representatives passed away.[1] The U.S. occupation and the birth of the republic allowed many scientists to return home from exile, but most had only been gone for a year or two to avoid the war or to establish a role for themselves in the independence movement. The new republic harbored few new scientists of note. Of the one hundred Cuban scientists featured in a recent biographical dictionary, only nine began their research careers between 1895 and 1920 (and five of these in the social sciences). Twenty-five of the previous generation—those whose research had begun between 1870 and 1890—made the cut (seventeen of them were in medicine or related fields, and most of the rest in the natural or pure sciences).[2] What the occupation and the republic did transform was the political arrangement of scientific institutions, agendas, and practices: their position of power relative to one another, their relationship to the state, and their significance within creole political culture.

The U.S. occupation acted as a prism. It diffracted Cuban scientific energies that had been relatively concentrated in laboratory-based medical research prior to the outbreak of the war of independence in 1895, generating a spectrum of new projects in the republic that, if at certain points vibrant, was dispersed.[3] Moreover, if in the late colonial period many Cuban scientists enjoyed great proximity to the defining research and debates in their field, the science done in the republic was more parochial. There were a number of reasons for this shift. Before the war of independence and U.S. occupation, Cuban science was structured by a creole anti-colonialism in which cultivating a sovereign research capacity was felt to be key. After 1902, with the Platt Amendment giving the United States the right to intervene in the event that Cubans did not effectively manage epidemic diseases that might threaten the United States, scientists and experimental institutions were enlisted to shore up Cuban political sovereignty in a way that valued the reproduction of existing testing and administrative techniques over research autonomy and innovation. In this context scientific service could bring significant political rewards, including appointment to senior state offices. At the same time, especially among physicians, local commercial opportunities during the first two booming decades distracted energies that might otherwise have gone to research. Over the same period, as the resources required for experimental ventures increased with the complexity of much research, it became harder for individual or institutional Cuban actors to compete with, or to collaborate on even terms with, or to get noticed by U.S.- and European-based scientific initiatives. The two areas of greatest innovation in Cuba's republican science were eugenics and agronomy, both domains of inquiry that promised to provide elements for a new creole hegemony.

Of course, these are only the most visible trends in a changing scientific ecosystem that was extremely rich and variegated both before and after independence. I will try to illustrate them by looking primarily at the shifts in the power, agenda, and institutional involvement of two main actors, both creole men from the world of medicine, running through the late colonial era, the U.S. occupation, and the first two decades of the republic: the ophthalmologist Juan Santos Fernández y Hernández (1847–1922), who was at the epicenter of Cuban scientific life during the late colonial era, and the physician, medical bacteriologist, and tuberculosis expert Diego Tamayo y Figueredo (1852–1926), who played a pivotal role in reconfiguring scientific power during the U.S. occupation and early republic. I will follow this with a look at examples of innovative experimental practice that dotted the intellectual landscape of the republic, in particular that of the primate collector and breeder Rosalía Abreu. Their stories show that science and scientists were at the heart of creole politics, both before and after independence. They also demonstrate the strong continuity in scientific leadership that, incredibly, lasted almost half a century and even continued to condition scientific practice and politics through the Machadato.

Searching for Scientific Sovereignty

From 1875 to 1898, Cuban science was not just clustered in the domain of medicine; it was increasingly concentrated in a vanguard group of creole physicians led by Juan Santos Fernández.[4] Born in 1847 on the Atrevido sugar mill in Bolondrón, Matanzas, Santos Fernández was one of a number of extraordinary scientists spread around the Atlantic world in the second half of the nineteenth century who were children of Matanzas or Cuatro Villas sugar plantation owners. They were at once hugely privileged beneficiaries of the colonial slave-based sugar economy and inherently dissident vehicles of creole desire for political autonomy and nationhood. Indeed, Santos Fernández was not so different in profile from the eight first-year University of Havana medical students sent to the wall for a student prank in November 1871 during the first war of independence. Their mock execution was a symbolic acknowledgment by colonial Spanish society that creole doctors were the emerging leaders of the imagined political community of independent Cuba.[5] Fearing some such trouble, in 1870 Santos Fernández's parents had taken their two boys out of medical studies at the University of Havana after their first year and sent them to Spain.

At Madrid's San Carlos school of surgery, alongside many liberal-thinking medical students from South America, Santos Fernández gravitated toward a famous professor of anatomy, Pedro Velasco, and was later captivated by the surgical acumen of Spain's leading ophthalmologist, Francisco Delgado Jugo, originally from Venezuela. Both maestros were part of the Liberal camp in the turbulent Spanish politics of the 1860s and 1870s, as well as directors of the Spanish Anthropological Society, founded in 1869 in Velasco's home (which doubled as his private museum of anthropology). Santos Fernández became an enthusiastic member. After a period of study in Delgado Jugo's Madrid Ophthalmic Institute, he specialized in Paris under the meteoric Xavier Galezowski before completing his doctorate in medicine at the University of Barcelona.[6] Returning to Cuba in 1875, Santos Fernández set himself up at Prado 3, in the heart of the capital's fashionable new district, and within two years was a leader of the creole intellectual avant-garde.

Within months of his return he founded a medical newspaper, the *Crónica Médico-Quirúrgica de la Habana*, and assembled a de facto medical society of some renown to act as its contributing staff. One of those on the masthead was Luis Montané, who had also just returned from Paris after making a name for himself as a brilliant disciple of the medical anthropologist Pierre Broca. Santos Fernández avoided seeking a place in the university faculty, with its scholastic politics and traditional horizons of teaching, but he did immediately bid on a seat in Havana's Royal Academy of Sciences and was admitted in 1875 on the basis of his doctoral thesis on diseases of the eye (the similarly precocious Montané was admitted the same year). In 1877, with wartime restrictions on creole assembly still in effect, he surprised many by receiving permission from the colonial authorities to establish the Cuban Anthropological Society, whose inaugural session was held in his apartments on the Prado. The society is usually recalled as the creature of Montané, but Santos Fernández was just as significant an agent in its founding: aside from the fact that he had formed a special relationship with Joaquín Jovellar, the captain general of Cuba, after operating successfully on his daughter's eyes, he apparently had accepted a mission from his Madrid mentors to found a Cuban chapter of the Spanish Anthropological Society.[7]

The *Crónica Médico-Quirúrgica* and the coterie of physicians behind the Anthropological Society are two clear expressions of the dynamic medical universe that took shape in Havana in the aftermath of the Ten Years' War. The number of licensed doctors practicing in nineteenth-century Cuba was always large by Latin American standards. Cuba had hosted many skilled medical practitioners since the early nineteenth century, an anomaly produced by the expanding demand for medical and hospital services on ships, in garrisons, and on slave plantations.[8] In 1887 almost one thousand physicians and surgeons practiced in the island, and by 1899 there were five hundred medical doctors in the city of Havana—at one licensed practitioner for every five hundred inhabitants, one of the highest ratios of physicians per capita in the world.[9] Over 80 percent of them were Cuban-born, in many cases homegrown products of the university medical school.[10] Funes has noted the crossing of a threshold of organizational necessity during the 1880s and 1890s, with new associations and organized initiatives springing up with great regularity and variety, though again with leadership clearly exercised by medical doctors.[11] According to Pedro Pruna's history of the Royal Academy of Sciences (1861–98), all but two of the nineteen figures he identifies as the academy's "guiding group" (based on a point-scale evaluation of administrative and academic contributions) were doctors of medicine.[12] The most active in this group over the entire period, in his calculation, was Juan Santos Fernández.

Perhaps because most analysts of the creole intellectual culture and nationalism have literary studies and political history orientations, medical doctors and other scientists have been left out of portraits that emphasize the artistic, social essayistic, and lawyerly constitutional elements that underlay the Autonomist cause. The role of the *Revista de Cuba*, founded in 1877 by the lawyer and leader of the Autonomous Liberal Party, José Antonio Cortina, is often seen as the exemplary expression of this new creole liberalism.[13] Santos Fernández's *Crónica Médico-Quirúrgica* (founded two years earlier) should be read as its pure and applied scientific counterpart. It served an ebullient potential readership that, especially once one considers the rapid expansion in the practice of pharmacy at the time, counted in the thousands. The ambitions of his medico-political project grew apace, especially after 1881 when he married Teresa González de Aguilar, the daughter of the Countess of San Ignacio and heir to the Toca fortune. Now involved in managing sugar capital on both sides of the family, Santos Fernández faced the planter class's conundrum of the 1880s—"threatened with extinction," in the words of Pérez, with the end of slavery in sight, sugar prices low, and the island in the throes of depression. How to reinvent a creole ruling class in a rapidly changing, increasingly capital-intensive and corporate political economy and how to do so in a way that enhanced claims for Cuban autonomy within the Spanish colonial system?[14] His answer was novel and audacious: with echoes of the early nineteenth-century creole reformer Arango y Parreño as described by Moreno Fraginals, Santos Fernández undertook or sponsored a series of voyages to identify new technology and incorporate it into his medical enterprise.[15] He sought a transmutation of the sugar mill into the research laboratory, using sugar capital to build a bacteriology and vaccine research institute according to the model and methods of the Pasteur labs.

Science historian José López Sánchez identifies 1885 as an "eclosion," or coming of age year for Cuban science. Five new scientific periodicals (for the most part medical in nature) saw the light of day, joining the *Crónica Médico-Quirúrgica*, the *Anales* of the academy, and the periodical of the Society for Clinical Studies (founded in 1881).[16] The Instituto Histo-bacteriológico y de vacunación antirrábica de la *Crónica Médico-Quirúrgica de la Habana* also had its origins in 1885. Bacteriology and the hunt for vaccines were the "big things" of the 1880s, promising substantial prestige and power in national as well as scientific politics. The Instituto's first administrator, Eduardo Plá, later recalled that in October 1885 the editorial board and contributors of the *Crónica Médico-Quirúrgica* were sitting around the newspaper office discussing the significance of the recent cable announcing Pasteur's breakthrough in producing an effective rabies vaccine for humans. They began to imagine a radical possibility: "to import the benefits of the Pasteurian method to our *patria*, at the same time bringing it the Glory of being the first country in America to put it into practice." Santos Fernández decided to seize the moment and finance the creation in Havana of a complex medical research facility where "professors and students could familiarize themselves with the discoveries of the modern science of bacteriology, which promises to shed light on many points in the still dim field of intertropical pathology."[17]

The Cubans were instantly on top of the momentous announcements coming from Paris by virtue of the telegraph, but they also had special connections to the inner world of Pasteur's experimental methods. Pasteur's main physician ally in the rabies experiments, Joseph Grancher, was married to the immensely wealthy Cuban sugar heiress Rosa Abreu, and his chief clinician, the eminent Paris urologist Joaquín Albarrán, was also the Cuban-born son of a sugar planter. In 1885 both were corresponding members of the editorial board of the *Crónica Médico-Quirúrgica*.[18] In April 1886, Santos Fernández went to New York to purchase equipment. Again according to Plá, once the installation of the lab had begun, "it became apparent that we needed to send one of the pioneering group to Paris to study the method in its tiniest details at the side of the illustrious maestro."[19] The following month, Santos Fernández sponsored a journey to Paris by two young members of the *Crónica* circle, Diego Tamayo and Francisco Vildósola, to train at Pasteur's laboratories. In August, Albarrán presented the two to Pasteur in his provisional facilities on the rue Vauquelin. After a three-month program of intense study, they returned to Cuba, reproducing strains of rabies vaccines from Pasteur's labs as they traveled.[20]

For the Cubans, Paris was a very practical matter of networks outside of Spanish colonial ones that allowed them direct access to resources: allies, training missions, methods, and living laboratory organisms that could be carried to Cuba and inoculated, magically animating their bacteriological technology with Pasteurian power. Creoles now had quasi-therapeutic powers to prevent a specific and feared disease in stricken Cubans that the Spanish colonizers did not possess; they had scalar powers to see and record and analyze and identify potential pathogens in a vast domain of Cuban microbiological matter that the Spanish colonial regime had no access to; and they had established a technology and a network for publication and dissemination of their new products, to be circulated, evaluated, and reciprocated in a new international network of science in which Spain was far from a dominant player. In May 1887, over three hundred eminent creoles crowded by invitation into the Quinta de Toca, the fabulous mansion on Reina that Santos Fernández had acquired through marriage, to see a modern medical laboratory unveiled and observe the production and inoculation of Pasteur's marvelous new vaccine for rabies. Among the expectant guests were representatives of every instance of Cuban creole cultural power: the

Royal Academy of Sciences, the Sociedad Económica de Amigos del País, the university, the literary and scientific societies of the capital, the Military Sanitary Corps, the militia, the medical-pharmaceutical corps of Havana and Matanzas, and ten newspapers. At the end of Santos Fernández's welcoming address, the luminaries solemnly signed an acta de constancia, constituting themselves in an "extraordinary Junta," a declaration of creole scientific sovereignty.[21]

The Santos Fernández group now made its final ascent on the summit of scientific power and authority in the island. Instituto scientists (a dozen or more of the most accomplished researchers in Cuba could be found at its benches at any given time) took the lead in commissions and expeditions to discover the source of livestock and crop diseases. They also formed the core of the commission appointed by the Spanish governor in 1889 to study what they declared to be an epidemic of glanders (an equine disease transmissible to humans, especially in dense urban concentrations of people and horse-drawn coaches and carts). The Instituto labs were used by both local and foreign luminaries to settle an important international debate over the germ of yellow fever. Diego Tamayo, the Instituto's star bacteriologist who had been on the original training mission to Pasteur's labs, made an international reputation for himself with his cautious lab work and collaboration with high-profile researchers like George Sternberg, a leader in U.S. bacteriology who would become surgeon general of the U.S. Army in 1893.[22]

The First Medical Congress of the Island of 1890 (a "national" medical congress in all but name) was a remarkable expression of the ascendance of the Instituto, with its research associates not only among the principal organizers but also accounting for a plurality of the eighty-seven papers presented.[23] The *Crónica Médico-Quirúrgica* had doubled its production schedule from monthly to biweekly to account for the volume of research being written up for publication under its prestigious brand. The Instituto was awarded the public contract to attend to bromatological and forensic analysis, and by 1893 the Santos Fernández faction had gained control of the Academy of Sciences. Its fortunes tied to the hopes of the Autonomist program, this enterprise was positioned to assume the hoped-for mantle of "national" medical research center and semiautonomous public health advisory unit, a private initiative with an organic connection to a public academic body (the Academy of Sciences).[24] By this time the Santos Fernández group had lost Tamayo, who resigned in anger in early 1891 claiming that the original spirit and group impetus of the Instituto project had been lost.[25] Nevertheless, the lab enjoyed commercial success with its services and biologics, and in February 1895 its researchers triumphantly announced that they had developed an effective diphtheria antitoxin. These triumphs were eclipsed by the outbreak of the 1895 war of independence. Neither the Instituto's science nor its political influence prospered in a context of polarized and populist belligerence, and the lab would find itself sidelined in the reconstruction of Cuban scientific life under the U.S. occupation.

The Return of Diego Tamayo

After the stabilization phase under General John R. Brooke came to an end and General Leonard Wood took over the government in December 1899, the U.S. occupation became peculiarly medical in nature. Wood himself was a physician, and his tenure in Havana began with an extraordinary effort to sanitize the city by dousing its streets and diluting its fetid port waters with oceans of disinfectant.[26] Among the principal targets of this epic sanitizing program was yellow fever, whose source remained a mystery, though it was still strongly believed to be bacterial and likely, then, to be endemic in the putrid organic morass of the capital. The failure of this emblematic effort to reduce the incidence of yellow fever was followed by the splash of a dramatic and entirely novel medical research project in which Cuba's colonial science played a leading role. Through a complex transaction whose dynamics remain the subject of considerable and heated debate among historians of medicine, two of the most important research clusters in the history of tropical medicine—a Cuban one led by Carlos Finlay and a U.S. military one led by Walter Reed—combined their knowledge of mosquitoes and yellow fever epidemiology. The Reed team was able to carry out an elaborate series of experiments at a U.S. military encampment outside Havana to test the proposition, first proposed by Finlay as early as 1881, that yellow fever was transmitted by the *Culex* mosquito.[27]

The famous results showed definitively that the mosquito was the main issue in yellow fever prevention, and this led to a sanitary engineering program in Havana that eradicated yellow fever from the city in the space of one year. Because of the international profile of these experimental findings and their enormous political implications for development in the tropics (demonstrated in short order in the isthmus of Panama), the episode quickly became the basis for a struggle on the part of virtually every influential physician in Cuba, including former rivals of Finlay like Santos Fernández, to ensure that Carlos Finlay was recognized as the key scientist in the unraveling of this research puzzle. The sense that Finlay's role was given short shrift by Reed and in international medical reportage of the scientific triumph became, overnight, the central symbol of Cuban medical nationalism, and it remains so to this day.

The politics and symbolism of the glamorous Finlay-Reed affair were crucial to the shifts in Cuban science during the second half of the U.S. occupation, but a second drama pitting Diego Tamayo against Juan Santos Fernández, one that has gone essentially unnoticed in Cuban history, was just as fundamental in redrawing the landscape. On taking charge in 1899, Wood established a "creole cabinet" to broker the reconstruction of Cuba, and he appointed Santos Fernández's estranged protégé, Diego Tamayo, to the crucial position of Cuban minister of the interior. This was a portfolio that charged him with overseeing the civilian side of health and sanitary matters.[28] Tamayo, originally from an important family from eastern Cuba, had strong connections with creole elites in the capital. He was an internationally respected scientist who had shared laboratory benches with members of Pasteur's famous research team as well as with Sternberg. Tamayo was, moreover, a former Autonomist who had abjured at the proper time, gone into exile, and joined the Revolutionary Junta as soon as war broke out in 1895. Wood encouraged and enabled Tamayo's election to the Constituent Assembly in 1900, where he would play a key role in helping convince the assembly to acquiesce to the Platt Amendment. Wood also appointed Tamayo to the presidency of the Cuban Academy of Sciences when it was refloated in 1900 as a republican institution-in-waiting. Given the history between Tamayo and Santos Fernández, this was a serious affront to the power and honor of the latter who had been president of the academy when it lowered the Spanish flag and relinquished its royal status in 1898.

The response of the Santos Fernández group came during the Third Pan-American Medical Conference, held in Havana in late 1900 and early 1901 with delegates from throughout the Americas in attendance. The announcement that the mystery of yellow fever transmission had been solved caused a sensation, and the Santos Fernández group seized the opportunity to conduct a public relations campaign in a journal of popular hygiene published by one of its researchers. The cover of the January 1901 issue of *La Higiene* sported the caricature of a triumphal Carlos Finlay flying astride a giant mosquito, with an admiring chorus of smaller *Culex* winging along beside (see figure 2.1). Its pages contained a profile of Cuba's premier scientific facility, Santos Fernández's Instituto, a research laboratory still waiting for a sign from the new authorities on its future role. A month later the cover of *La Higiene* featured the Instituto's leading researcher, Juan Dávalos, reverentially and pointedly caricatured as Quijote on a glanders-ridden Rocinante:

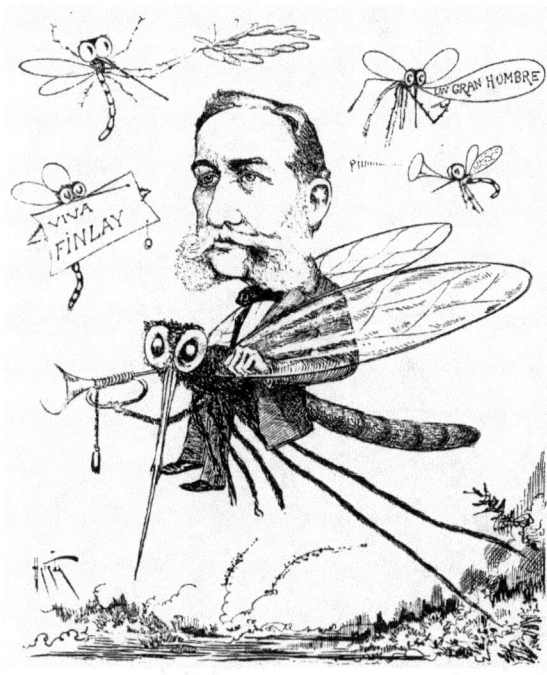

Figure 2.1 Cuban physicians extol Finlay, *La Higiene*, 1901. Courtesy of the Rare Books Library, University of Havana.

here was the heroic figure of the "Cuban bacteriologist" who had been the first person to identify the glanders germ in Cuba and had battled against the disease during the Spanish empire along with others of the Instituto (see figure 2.2). Although the U.S. authorities had introduced regulations to eliminate diseased horses from the capital as early as May 1900, both animal and human glanders were still endemic in the city. The accompanying article, "Glanders and the Intervention" was extremely critical of the U.S. occupation authorities. "The Intervention Government has taken control of city sanitation," and though they found hideous abuses by the owners of stables and horse-drawn transportation concerns, the "Chief of interventionist Sanitation" had not acted. "Glanders continues to take its course, the same with the Americans as with the Spaniards [in the late 1880s]. The truth is that the Intervention Government only cares about yellow fever, as though Cuba must be forever the exclusive patrimony of those foreigners who have no acquired immunity. Neither the TB hitting our children nor the glanders that shames us in the eyes of civilized peoples enter into the calculations of our non-Cuban governors."[29]

The challenge was pointed, but so was Wood's response: Tamayo was named to head a Special Commission for the Extinction of Glanders and

Figure 2.2 A quixotic Juan Dávalos celebrated for his work on glanders, *La Higiene*, 1901. Courtesy of the Rare Books Library, University of Havana.

Animal Tuberculosis. While Gorgas has gone down in history for overseeing the elimination of yellow fever from Havana during 1901, Tamayo's success in eliminating glanders during the same period of time was, for the Cuban audience of professionals, probably more decisive in consolidating the scientific and public health legitimacy of the occupation authorities and their Cuban interlocutors. The creole medical profession had seen the Santos Fernández group make the fight against glanders, during the late 1880s and 1890s, the defining struggle against the irrationality of Spanish colonial control. Tamayo's success, using the tools placed at his disposal by the occupation authorities, showed that the new regime was more than capable of responding to the shortcomings of Spanish colonial public health. Tamayo's strict enforcement of regulations concerning the keeping, reporting, and quarantining of sick animals, complemented with an offer of compensation for each suspicious animal culled, seems to have made the difference in the eradication of glanders from Havana by the end of 1902.[30] This was a significant victory for the U.S. occupation government and for those Cubans in the sanitary world who backed it.

Cuba's best physicians clamored to get on board and participate in the U.S. hygienic mission, seeing it as the practical materialization of the anticolonial scientific agenda.[31] But they soon saw that they were collaborating in something quite distinct. Whereas, under the anticolonial banner of the Santos Fernández group, hygienism had been part of a rationalist discourse that also envisioned a sovereign Cuban scientific capacity for research and innovation, under the banner of the United States and in the context of the republic, it was the organizing principle of a discourse of sanitary administration using established techniques that was explicitly decoupled from any notion that the island would have state-backed centers of original medical research. Indeed, Santos Fernández's power base, the Instituto, was seriously weakened by the occupation regime when, in 1901, Tamayo and Wood promoted the creation of a new official state laboratory, the Laboratory of the Island of Cuba. Renamed the National Laboratory in 1902, it displaced much of the public function and all of the public authority that the Instituto together with the academy had fulfilled in the 1890s. Wood and Tamayo added insult to injury by hiring away Dávalos, the Instituto's senior microbiologist. The very figure the Instituto group had trumpeted on the cover of *Higiene* as a Cuban scientific hero working in their employ now became director of bacteriology at the National Laboratory and brought with him a number of the other specialists who had staffed the Instituto.[32] There is no clear date marking the demise of the Instituto Histo-bacteriológico. It was still the principal private producer of vaccines and sera in the republic in 1915, and it continued to function as a private laboratory, but it never recaptured its centrality to scientific research in the republic.[33] Santos Fernández and his project lost out in the politics of the U.S. intervention, relegated to the margins in the reconstruction of medical and scientific power under the occupation and early republic, stripped of power and personnel, drained of recognition and momentum in each domain of action.

Cuba and the New Tropical Medicine

The Cuban medical community rebounded quickly after 1898: by the census of 1907 there were 1,240 physicians practicing in Cuba (almost equaling the number of lawyers), over 1,000 of them creoles. The national average of one schooled and titled medical doctor for every 1,600 people—quite high in Western terms—was matched by a dense urban concentration in Havana: 511 doctors attended 300,000 residents of the capital (1:600).[34] By 1919 the number of practicing physicians and surgeons in the capital had risen by a third to 684, just ahead of the pace of growth in the city's population, and another 300 were established just outside the city in Havana province.[35] The University of Havana's medical faculty was relaunched in conjunction with the U.S. model of the teaching hospital, and Cuban medicine was soon among the leaders in Latin America in medical specialization, something reflected in the growing numbers of professional associations and journals in specialized fields. The center of Cuban medicine, Havana, experienced a proliferation of medical research actors and spaces, but their focus became much more politico-administrative and commercial, much more oriented toward the application of basic sanitary science and clinical and hospital care, with few "pure" research clusters.

Finlayism had instantly become a symbol of the integrity and promise of Cuban medical science, but the sudden power won by U.S. sanitary discourse and tropical medicine—in good measure due to the yellow fever breakthrough in Cuba—was such that it subsumed the program of medical research in Cuba during the first two decades of the republic. Cuba's most important established medical scientists were motivated to throw themselves into the task of organizing and carrying out basic public health measures, beginning with the enlistment in 1900 of more than a hundred eminent Havana doctors to map and sanitize the streets and slums of the capital. They continued to work on basic sanitary management during the cleansing of the city of mosquito breeding grounds, and then carried on staffing the new apparatuses of sanitary administration in the early republican governments. Symptomatic of this shift from innovative research to basic application was the appointment of Finlay as director of sanitation in 1907, a tradition of appointing the most brilliant of Cuban medical researchers to senior politico-administrative public health posts that carried on through the 1920s. To some degree, this was a factor of age and the logical tendency for mature scientists to move into managerial posts and seek public roles. More than this, however, it came of raising Cuban public health to a vital matter of state sovereignty by virtue of Article 5 of the Platt Amendment. Cuba concentrated its most competent scientific minds—especially those recognized as such in the United States—in keeping the island free of diseases the United States considered matters of its own national security. Ironically, in this sense, maintaining political sovereignty through applied science came at the expense of building up a sovereign science.

By the same token, it became clear to established and emerging Cuban medical researchers that resources and recognition would come most readily in the area of tropical medicine. Between 1898 and 1902 medical research on diseases or conditions in countries located in the tropics radically reconfigured the discourse of tropical medicine. On the British side, the key manifestations of this shift included the creation of a Colonial Medical Service by the British Colonial Office (1898); the publication of the "bible" of tropical medicine, Patrick Manson's *Tropical Diseases: A Manual of the Diseases of Warm Climates* (1898); the announcement of the work of Ronald Ross on the role of mosquitoes in the transmission of malaria (1898); and the creation of the London and the Liverpool Schools of Tropical Medicine (1899). On the United States' side were the medical and health apparatuses established in the country's newly acquired tropical colonies—Puerto Rico, the Canal Zone, the Philippines, and of course occupied Havana.[36]

Within a very short period of time, then, two great empires—one in mid-life, the other declaring itself dramatically for the first time—created institutional circuitries of medicine and sanitation for their imperial spheres of influence and electrified them with a scientific discourse coterminous with imperial dominion. Obviously, the moment did not emerge from nothing. Medical researchers whom we might see as engaged in "tropical medicine" had been active throughout Britain's colonies since the seventeenth century, and if the United States was a new player in this game, French, German, and Spanish scientists had been at it for a very long time. But something fundamental had changed. What had been a multi-polar endeavor, with heterogeneous and individual actors, shifted very suddenly toward an Anglo-American apparatus of network-based and institutionalized research, codification, classification, agenda setting, and application. The work of the Reed Commission and Gorgas's sanitary regime in Havana would be a spectacular confirmation of this shift, and the U.S. ability to tackle successfully the disease obstacles of the Panamanian isthmus through sanitary engineering a spectacular demonstration of the practical power of Anglo-Saxon tropical medicine.

This was the vehicle for two powerful dual-national figures, John/Juan Guiteras and Aristides Agramonte, to reintroduce themselves into Cuba after long absences where they created new nodes of medical research. Of course, neither was a stranger to Cuban scientific life. Originally from Matanzas, while pursuing opportunities in Philadelphia where he had studied medicine, Guiteras had been appointed by the United States as a member of the 1879 joint Spanish-U.S. Yellow Fever Commission, and his connections with Cuban science and society had remained strong; Agramonte was in a sense a younger version of Guiteras, a protégé of U.S. Surgeon General Sternberg who had been sent to Cuba on a special yellow fever research assignment that complemented the work of the Reed team. University reforms enacted by the occupation government led to the creation of a chair in Intertropical Pathology at the University of Havana in 1899, and the position was promptly awarded to Guiteras. Agramonte, a member of the Reed team, also created a power base for himself with a university chair in Bacteriology and Experimental Pathology, and following the spectacular outcome of the yellow fever experiments, he assumed a leading role in the island's scientific life. Both Guiteras and Agramonte would later serve as ministers of public health.

But they did not carry on the previous discourse of Cuban tropical medicine. The shift can be illustrated by looking at Guiteras's *Revista de Medicina Tropical*, which he began publishing in 1900 under a new banner of tropical medicine defined in the metropolises of the Atlantic empire, particularly London and Washington. The network described on the masthead of the first issue is another good expression of the shift in scientific networks in Cuban medicine following 1898. His collaborator in the journal was Emilio Martínez, director of the Clinical Laboratory, a rival to Santos Fernández's Instituto. Carlos Finlay figured as a writer, while the list of collaborators included three men who had been central to the scientific project of the Instituto but who were on their way to new appointments under the occupation government: Juan Dávalos, Eduardo Lainé, and Tomás Coronado.[37] Also figuring in the group were Agramonte as well as Enrique López, Santos Fernández's principal commercial-professional rival as a cutting-edge ophthalmologist in Havana.

In his presentation of the first issue, Guiteras proposed that with the growth of subdivisions in medical science, tropical medicine should become the specialty of "our country, due to its climate, its topographical and ethnic conditions."[38] He specifically inserted this project (emerging "in the last five years") into the Anglo-American ascendancy over a French-based anatomo-clinical and bacteriological tradition that had grounded Cuban medical research in the late nineteenth century and linked the project to the emergence of parasitology as a discipline. Guiteras endorsed the reaping of Cuba's comparative advantage in terms of the interest of the new colonial powers in solving problems relating to the colonization of the tropics. He proposed a move to parasitology over bacteriology because it is more applied, and inserted his tropical medical program into the contemporary race science by suggesting that Cuban researchers pursue the lessons of the most recent Liverpool trips to Africa and the work of Koch showing that the population of "Negros" were actually carriers of malaria.[39]

It is notable that Santos Fernández had already moved away from this essentialist mode of racism characteristic of the new current of tropical medicine. Over his first two and a half decades of practice, Santos Fernández had accumulated clinical data on some 5,531 subjects deemed to be of African descent (3,003 "Negros" and 2,528 "mulattos"). In his summary analysis of the data, *Enfermedades de los Ojos en los Negros y Mulatos* (Diseases of the eye in Negros and mulattos) presented to the 1900 International Medical Congress in Paris, he argued that there were no new or special diseases in determinate races; indeed, his immense database demonstrated the opposite: everyone suffered the same diseases of the eye regardless of race.[40] This Paris paper was an early announcement of the kind of reformulation of categories that would characterize postcolonial Cuban racism—a shift that has been part of a major recent historiographical discussion.[41] Virtually all the works on this subject emphasize the way that Cubans of African ancestry were denied citizenship and scripted into a U.S. and Western European–influenced eugenic narrative that focused on atavism. Yet Santos Fernández was precisely moving away from a notion of pathologies native to different races. Instead, his racial vision of the "vision of race" was more in keeping with the dominant Lamarckian eugenic currents in Latin America—that is, the conjuring of a *cubanidad* that would come from the gradual absorption of those of African ancestry into the general population pool.

His racialized medical research project reminds us that the intellectual process of this reformulation predated independence and was the product of the internal development of Cuban science (including its anthropological vector) using Cuban data.[42] Santos Fernández certainly remained a leading creole voice in favor of immigration from Spain, and he was part of an important faction in Cuban eugenics.[43] His predilection, however, was based more on the logic of a "whitening" mestizaje (race mixture) and a belief that Spaniards were more suited to improving Cuba, having acquired greater "civilization." This was a very different current of racism than the more genetically and tropical medicine–based racist essentialism expressed at this time by Cuban intellectuals such as Fernando Ortíz and Guiteras. As Alejandro de la Fuente has shown, by the second decade of the republic both these latter two would also move away from their early essentialism, in the case of Guiteras to a position almost identical to that of Santos Fernández, and in the case of Ortíz to an ever deeper engagement with Afro-Cuban cultural forms and an embrace of "Afro-cubanidad."[44]

In the two decades following 1898, a handful of private laboratories devoted to clinical diagnostics were created, and five state labs began to operate, all under the wings of different ministries, in particular the two main ones devoting their services to the Department (after 1909, Ministry) of Health. The public labs were overtaxed and burdened with analyzing specimens of direct consequence to public administration to the point that they could not even keep up with routine work.[45] This was a constant complaint of Cuba's leading scientific actors in the early republic. When Agramonte and Guiteras were asked to provide bacteriological confirmation of the existence of plague in 1912, for example, they could not complete their analysis of specimens collected from a cadaver because the official laboratories had had their funds "distracted" and so did not have the proper equipment for the job, "and we were forced to omit this very important detail from our investigation."[46] Indeed, one might say the same thing for the energies of all the titans of Cuban medical research after 1898: their science was "distracted" into government sanitary administration work and into service defined by the agenda of U.S. tropical medicine. Even Guiteras and Agramonte, who cultivated successful international scientific reputations through the 1920s, carried out their most significant work as consultants in yellow fever for the Rockefeller Foundation in other countries. (Ironically, Cuba no longer had any clinical research advantage in yellow fever, having eradicated the disease.)

The shortcomings were not lost on the country's medical elites for long. In 1917, the Academy of Sciences paid homage to Juan Santos Fernández, its long-serving president, on his seventieth birthday. The heart of the affair were speeches by former collaborators at the Instituto Histo-bacteriológico. The master of ceremonies, Jorge Le Roy y Cassá, one of the most important social and political intellectuals in the early republican community of Cuban medical doctors, observed that events had vindicated the medical research model that Santos Fernández had built in the late colonial era and then seen displaced by the war of independence and a republican birth under U.S. tutelage. Le Roy y Cassá noted that whenever the Cuban Department of Health required specialized research on particular problems, its facilities were so overburdened with the mundane matters of sanitary and legal laboratory analysis that they had no capacity to carry out the work, and neither did the new labs at the university. He concluded, "Given the character and tendency of science, today more than thirty years ago it is useful and necessary to have a research center that is free, without the obligations of teaching institutions and official centers, where old and young, maestros and disciples, might find the manner to perfect their knowledge and devote themselves to the good of the nation and of humanity."[47]

New Wine in Old Bottles

Funes has called the first two decades of republican Cuban science a time of "expansion and continuity" of processes begun in the late colonial era, though broadening in scope into new disciplines and specializations. While scientific research had hardly been monochromatic in the last quarter of the nineteenth century, central issues in medicine were at the core of scientific debate: from clinical practice and specialization, to epidemiology, bacteriology, vaccines, and serology. This changed during the U.S. occupation. Cuban scientific research—still overwhelmingly dominated by creole men— became an eclectic affair that generated a number of novel projects, especially in the areas of agronomy, botany, and zoology, with medical research more or less confined to a thoroughly reframed field of tropical medicine.[48] Each of the nine scientists listed in García's biographical dictionary who began their careers after the late 1890s worked in a separate field, and seven of them worked outside the field of medicine. Although the Academy of Sciences was reconstituted in the republic, and medicine retained its dominant role in membership and debates, the institution was neither reinvested with the responsibilities of an official or consultative body for the state, nor given any authority to make scientific policy decisions. These powers were dispersed into different state bodies, many of which developed their own limited research capacity. This dispersal also had an expression in the appearance of new specialized societies and journals, especially in the area of medicine that appeared in the fifteen years after independence.[49]

One of the most significant institutions of republican science was the Estación Experimental Agronómica de Santiago de las Vegas, founded in 1904 to pursue research on Cuban crops in the context of a need to rebuild the Cuban sugar industry following the devastation of the independence wars.[50] It was built through close consultation with the U.S. Department of Agriculture on the model of U.S. agricultural research stations, and its first two directors were from the United States. This did not prevent the station from becoming a crucial node in a growing Cuban network of agronomists and botanists, and staff appointments soon "Cubanized" the station. The highly politicized nature of these appointments disrupted research continuity over the first fifteen years of operation. In the 1920s, however, after the 1917 appointment as director of Mario Calvino (the father of novelist Italo Calvino, who was born on the station), there was both a scientific revival and a program of practical popular outreach to Cuban farmers.[51] The autodidact botanist Juan Tomás Roig y Mesa had a long, if fitful, career at the station, and in 1928 he published under its auspices one of Cuba's classic tomes of popular science, the *Diccionario botánico de nombres vulgares cubanos*.[52] The station also developed links with the Atkins Garden for research on tropical botany and agriculture, established on the Soledad estate outside Cienfuegos as a joint venture between the philanthropic planter and Bostonian Edwin Atkins and Harvard University—another venture that transmuted the sugar plantation into a research station.[53] The Atkins Garden flourished in the late 1910s and 1920s and became accessible in a variety of ways to Cuban researchers, but it was also an expression of how the new scientific institutions of the republic could be dependent on U.S. research institutions and models and even formally subordinate to a U.S. agenda.[54]

Of course, not all new science fit this mold. The scientific universalism to which the academy had always aspired, as Rolando García Blanco has noted, "began to be taken on by the University" according to the new model unveiled by the military government in June 1900.[55] For someone like Santos Fernández, who had always staked out his territory outside—and against— the scientific jurisdiction of the university as a moribund, scholastic space, this cut further into his influence, and he could only stand on the outside looking in as the university was recharged with modernist vigor. But not all of his generation or inclination faced the same fate. His old collaborator in the founding of Cuban anthropology, Luis Montané, was invited inside the university structure. Montané's career path recapitulated an important shift in the nature and purpose of creole scientific practice from the late years of Spanish colonial rule to the second decade of rocky republican politics. Alejandra Bronfman has explored this rebirth of Cuban anthropology in 1900, given impetus by the occupation authorities who created a Department of Anthropology and Anthropometric Exercises as part of their university reform project.[56] Montané devoted himself increasingly to anthropological, botanical, and zoological research in a broadly conceived and vaguely defined "political laboratory." Bronfman looks at Montané's role in the combined process of pathologizing and criminalizing Afro-Cuban physiologies and cultural forms. He played no small role in constituting a scientific discourse that served as a reference point and sounding board for the series of disturbing, racist moral panics in early republican Cuba over the alleged kidnapping and murder of "white" children by practitioners of Afro-Cuban religious ceremonies.

Montané also played a role in a world-historical moment in Cuban zoology during the first republic, one stemming from the eccentric genius, international contacts, and great wealth of Rosalía Abreu. Abreu revived and reconfigured late colonial medical research energies in an entirely novel space of republican science: the Quinta Palatino, an estate housing primates that she built on the outskirts of Havana where she became the first person in the world to breed chimpanzees successfully in captivity. In 1915 Montané was called to Abreu's "finca de los monos" (monkey farm) to witness the birth of Anumá, el "chimpance criollo" (the creole chimpanzee) and the first chimp in the world to be bred and born out of the wild.[57] The paper he presented on the subject to the Cuban Society of Natural History "Felipe Poey" (a new republican space of science founded in 1913) attracted the attention of leading U.S. eugenicist and psychologist Robert Yerkes, who had it translated into English and published in the *Journal of Animal Behavior*.[58] Hoping to establish a primate research facility of his own, Yerkes was acutely interested in Abreu's methods. Notably, Abreu initially made contact with Yerkes, who was at that time a Harvard-based researcher, through Harvard botanists who were in Cuba developing the Atkin Gardens.

Abreu was in many ways an extraordinary figure, not least because she was a rare Cuban woman who was able to carve a niche for herself in national or international science, even if that niche was inevitably cast in terms of the "eccentric amateur."[59] The early republican era was arguably more closed than the late colonial era to women in science. This is evident in the trajectory of Laura Martínez de Carvajal, the first woman to graduate from the University of Havana medical school (1888), who became the scientific collaborator of her husband, the ophthalmologist Enrique López, on the brilliant three-volume *Oftalmológica Clínica*. Yet, following López's 1901 death from tuberculosis, Martínez de Carvajal withdrew completely from medical practice and research, secluding herself on an estate outside Havana where she directed a school for disadvantaged girls.[60] Abreu likewise set up her estate on the outskirts of Havana (and, notably, also ran there a trade school for poor girls), but she was hardly a recluse. Instead she hosted one of the country's most important salons, a coterie aligned with leading factions of Liberalism (Luis Estevez, the first vice president of Cuba was her brother-in-law, and Alfredo Zayas lived for a time at the Quinta Palatino during the Menocal regime). Abreu's interests in animal collecting and the creation of a menagerie during the first few years of the republic transformed gradually into a more systematic focus on collecting and then, quite extraordinarily, breeding primates. While universally recognized for her pioneering feat (one she repeated on many occasions before anyone else had deciphered primate breeding needs), Abreu's status in the history of primatology is problematic due to her reluctance to document her ideas or techniques or publish them in scientific fora. Even so, her work has recently been the subject of close attention by zoologist Clive Wynne, who calls her "the founder of the study of captive apes."[61]

Although she sketched out a highly original agenda on the outskirts of republican science, Abreu was herself typical in having been part of the inner circle of the Atlantic medical research world of late colonial Cuban science. She was the sister-in-law of Grancher and had lived in the Paris house of Grancher and her sister, Rosa. In 1885 she married Domingo Sánchez Toledo, a Cuban expatriate who was a leading Paris physician and close confidant of Grancher.[62] She had been, then, a member of the close-knit Pasteurian family during the heyday of its international medical triumph. While it remains unclear how Rosalía Abreu came to study primates, her ideas about breeding and observing animals in captivity were almost certainly formed, at least in part, by her experience of experimental animals kept at the Pasteur Institute.[63] In this sense, her more formal entrée into the scientific world as wealthy and innovative primate breeder in early republican Cuba was simply another instance of the shift of a creole medical research establishment with sugar riches and strong French networks into a new mode and guise. Like Santos Fernández, she created an urban estate that transmuted sugar wealth into a research station whose concerns overlapped with emerging areas of biosciences, though given the republican context she cultivated contacts with scientific networks in the United States.

More work on Abreu is needed to discover what relationship her program had to Cuban political and intellectual life, although there are evidently a number of possible connections between her project to breed, study, and develop techniques for stable social hierarchies using captive African primates and the creole concern to find a way to contain politically an Afro-Cuban citizenry perceived to be dangerous, volatile, primitive, and not yet fully socialized. Certainly Yerkes's interest in developing a primate research facility as the basis for the new discipline of psychobiology has been read by Donna Haraway as an "intersecting construction of nonhuman primates as pets, surrogate children, endangered species, research animals, colonial subjects, and wild animals."[64] Haraway cites Yerkes's book as a particular expression of this. *Almost Human* documents Yerkes's two-month visit in 1924 to study Abreu's estate and her primate management and breeding practices. After a long exchange of correspondence and visits with Abreu, during which they explored the possibilities of establishing his own primate laboratories as an extension of Abreu's estate, Yerkes finally received a large grant from the Rockefeller Foundation to create the Yale University Laboratories of Primate

Biology and the Anthropoid Breeding and Experiment Station in Florida, though he was fortunate to get the core of Abreu's collection as a donation to the Yale facility following her death in 1929. Thus Abreu's Quinta Palatino combined a multitude of strands in late colonial medical, anthropological, and natural history research, from both sides of the Atlantic, to establish an unlikely satellite of psychobiological modernism in republican Havana.

The Fernández Group (Slight Return)

New patterns of Cuban science took shape in the republic. No longer would medical research rule the roost; no longer would creole enterprise and scientific eminence provide a simultaneously official and unfettered state and sovereign scientific agenda to public power. And no longer would the axes of this scientific network run through Paris, Madrid, and Barcelona. Instead, the more common pattern would see actors institutionally entrenched in the university (and other centers of learning) working with private research initiatives that were linked to U.S. scientific networks. Diego Tamayo's career followed a typical path for the new scientific leadership. His cabinet role came to an end in 1905, but his political aspirations continued, and he was elected to the Senate in 1908, the same year that he launched his journal of national hygiene, *Vida Nueva*—at once a vehicle for disseminating a discourse on the intrinsic connection between fomenting hygiene and maintaining sovereignty, and a means for advertising the Tamayo Clinic and its medical product line. He became Cuba's foremost expert on tuberculosis, and in 1919 he was appointed rector of the University of Havana, receiving his own homage from the Academy of Sciences in 1922. He hastened to send a copy of the brochure made for the occasion to his old friend and colleague Leonard Wood, then occupying the governor's chair in Manila's Malacañan Palace. Wood wrote a warm note of congratulations and thanks in return, saying that it brought back "many pleasant recollections of old days in Cuba and your efficient and loyal service in the great work we did there."[65]

Of course, these were tendencies rather than sudden and total shifts— Luis Montané retired to Paris in the early 1920s to live the final chapter of his life as president of the French Society for Anthropology. Indeed there was a strong residual pull toward France and Spain in these years, itself reflective of the eclecticism of the era. And it was in the context of this eclecticism that the Santos Fernández project reformulated itself, in part by disaggregating and redeploying its energies in a way that mirrored and anticipated the diffracted field of Cuban science in the republic. First, at the dawn of the republic, Santos Fernández reclaimed the presidency of the Academy of Sciences.

Tamayo had likely ceded the space willingly once the retooling process of the occupation had come to an end and with it the need to dominate spaces of scientific leadership—even retrograde ones like the academy—for defensive reasons if nothing else. While the Academy had lost its élan and was even the butt of ridicule among a younger generation of physicians, Santos Fernández retook the position as part of a strategy to embrace associationism for its own sake. During the early republic the medical patriarch became a kind of one-man civil society, organizing national and international conferences in medicine, public health, and medical journalism. He also founded medical associations, including the Colegio de Médicos Cubanos, the first attempt at an island-wide professional association, and other groups like the Cuban Society for the Protection of Animals. He began self-consciously to knit a hispanoamerican network with a society and a periodical focused on hispanoamerican ophthalmology that linked practitioners in Spain, Cuba, Mexico, and Argentina. The same kind of "retreat to specialty" characterized his Cuban professional project, as he transformed the *Crónica Médico-Quirúrgica* into a medical periodical focusing on ophthalmology and expanded his practice by taking on his nephew, Francisco María Fernández, who had completed an ophthalmology specialization in the United States.[66]

While Santos Fernández enjoyed some final years of acclaim and homage, it was his nephew who was able to combine these ingredients to attain political power. Francisco María shared the established practice with his uncle, co-edited the *Crónica*, became an important organizer of medical conferences, was elected to the Academy of Sciences in 1921 while his uncle was in his very last year in the president's chair, and soon became a member of the executive himself—treasurer from 1923 to 1926, vice president from 1926 to 1929, and president from 1929 to 1933. His father had risen to be chief of the Liberal Party in Matanzas, and Francisco María used this regional power base to get himself elected to the Chamber of Deputies in 1925 as a representative for Matanzas.[67] He acquired an international profile as one of Cuba's most outspoken eugenicists, culminating in his role as founder of the Cuban League of Mental Hygiene and principal organizer of the First Pan-American Conference on Eugenics and Homiculture in 1927. By the time he welcomed delegates to Havana, he was Machado's minister of health, which did not stop him from subsequently complementing his ministerial power with a Pan-American diplomatic post stemming from the 1927 congress: he served as president of the Pan-American Office of Eugenics and Homiculture from 1927 until 1933, and housed the agency's office in Havana's Ministry of Health.[68]

Thus it would be a mistake to see the residual institutions and activities pursued by Juan Santos Fernández as insignificant to the constitution of scientific or political power in the republic. Not for nothing was his nephew simultaneously an elite practitioner of ophthalmology, editor of a medical periodical, president of the Academy of Sciences, minister of health, convenor of a Pan-American congress, and president of a Pan-American bureau with considerable international cachet. Nevertheless, with Francisco María Hernández's 1933 flight into Miami exile upon the fall of Machado, we might consider that a long period of creole scientific life, first articulated in the 1870s by a coterie of ambitious young researchers led by his uncle, had finally come to an end. To avoid seeing this legacy of Santos Fernández as purely reactionary, however, it is worth pointing out that the Colegio de Médicos, which he cofounded in 1910–11 as part of his ceaseless associationist impulse, metamorphosed in 1925 into the Cuban Medical Federation (FMC), an association that would become a critical forum of Cuban civil society during the Machado period. Not coincidentally, Francisco María Fernández, who was also president of the FMC in 1929, had to face the challenge of a radical faction, Renovación, formed as a result of the physicians' strikes of 1927–28. Medical students and physicians emerged as one of the most trenchant opposition groups to Machado—what Ross Danielson has called a "medical insurgency"—and their role in the dictator's overthrow culminated in 1933–34 with the tantalizing rise to power of the physician, professor of medicine at the university, and member of the Academy of Sciences, Ramón Grau San Martín.[69]

Notes

1. I use the term *science* to refer to the natural and physical sciences including medicine. While, especially in the area of medicine, Cuba was a land rich in the circulation of practices linking orthodox and unorthodox practitioners, it was also a country with a formally constituted and populated domain of self-styled scientific practice and exchange, and this is the relatively elite and in some sense official domain that concerns me here. Thanks are due to Reinaldo Funes for constant support and great feedback, and to Olga Lidia Pérez Moreno, archivist of the Estación Experimental Agrónomica de Santiago de las Vegas, INIFAT, and Magalys Reyes and Graciela Guevara of the Museo de Historia de las Ciencias "Carlos J. Finlay," Havana.

2. García Blanco, ed., *Cien figuras de la ciencia en Cuba*.

3. A recent overview is Fernández Prieto and García González, "Ciencia."

4. Pedro Pruna describes him as the "promoter and patron of various important scientific enterprises." Pruna, *La Real Academia de Ciencias de la Habana*, 25.

5. Le Roy y Gálvez, "Ubicación social de los ocho estudiantes fusilados en 1871," 3, 11; and Le Roy y Gálvez, *La inocencia de los estudiantes fusilados en 1871*.

6. On Delgado Jugo and Galezowski in the history of ophthalmology, see Gorin, *History of Ophthalmology*, 187–91, 217; and Hirschberg, *The History of Ophthalmology in Eleven Volumes*, 10: 243, and 11, part 1-c: 632–38; on Velasco and Delgado Jugo and their role in Spanish medical and intellectual politics, see Pulido Fernández, "Pedro González Velasco," 35–65; and García del Real, *Historia de la medicina en España*, 1032. On Santos Fernández in Madrid, Santos Fernández, *Recuerdos de mi vida*, 1: 85–134.

7. Pruna and García González, *Darwinismo y sociedad en Cuba, siglo XIX*, 100–101n40.

8. López Denis, "Disease and Society in Colonial Cuba, 1790–1840," 72.

9. Funes, *Despertar del asociacionismo científico en Cuba*, 45.

10. Mena, *Historia de la medicina en Cuba*, 251–56.

11. Funes, *Despertar del asociacionismo científico en Cuba*.

12. Pruna, *La Real Academia*, 24–25.

13. García Mora y Naranjo Orovio, "Intelectualidad criolla y nación en Cuba, 1878–1898," 125.

14. Pérez, *Cuba under the Platt Amendment, 1902–1934*, 5–7.

15. Moreno Fraginals, *El ingenio: Complejo socio-económico cubano*.

16. López Sánchez, *Carlos J. Finlay*, 284.

17. Plá, "Memoria annual de los trabajos del Laboratorio Histo-bacteriológico e Instituto Anti-rábico de la Crónica Médico-Quirúrgica de la Habana," 294.

18. Roussillat, *La vie et l'oeuvre du Professeur Jacques-Joseph Grancher*, 74–75; Gelfand, "11 January 1887, the Day Medicine Changed: Joseph Grancher's Defense of Pasteur's Treatment for Rabies," 698–718; Legout, *La famille pasteurienne*. Albarrán was Pasteur's clinician, observing and caring for those undergoing treatment for rabies at the clinic under his direction at the Enfants malades; see Legueu, *Albarran, Joachin (1860–1912)*, 145–59; and Sanjurio D'Arellano, *Inauguration du Pavillon Albarran a l'Hôpital Cochin*.

19. Plá, "Memoria anual," 294.

20. Tamayo, "Correspondencia de París," 606–9.

21. An Acta de la Sesión Inaugural read, "reunidos, prévia invitación, en la morada del Dr. D. Juan Santos Fernández, los señores que firman á continuación, se constituyeron en Junta extraordinaria para proceder á la solemne inauguración del IH-B de la CMQ"; reproduced in Plá, *Memoria anual*. On the inauguration and early history of the Instituto, see Díaz-Arguelles, *El Laboratorio Histo-bacteriológico e Instituto de Vacunación Antirrábica*.

22. Tamayo, *Les microbes de la fièvre jaune*. On this conjuncture, see Palmer, "Beginnings of Cuban Bacteriology," 445–68.

23. Funes, *Despertar del asociacionismo científico en Cuba*, 124–30; *Actas del Primer Congreso Médico de la Isla de Cuba* (n.p., n.d.).

24. The process is covered in Pruna, "National Science in a Colonial Context," 412–26.

25. His resignation letter is Tamayo to Santos Fernández, March 22, 1891, 101362—DTF C03—Archivo del Museo de las Ciencias Carlos J. Finlay, Havana, ff. 2-3.

26. The sanitary dimensions of the U.S. occupation, including an excellent assessment of the work of the Reed Commission, are re-created thoroughly in Espinosa, *Epidemic Invasions: Yellow Fever and the Limits of Cuban Independence*, 73-95.

27. There is considerable literature on this subject, including Stepan's own iconoclastic intervention, "The Interplay between Socio-Economic Factors and Medical Science," 412. The Cuban point of view is presented most fully in López Sánchez, *Carlos J. Finlay: His Life and Work*, while the best global view of the hunt from a Latin American perspective is Benchimol, *Dos micróbios aos mosquitos*. Delaporte, *The History of Yellow Fever*, is very ungenerous regarding Finlay's role in this process and makes no mention of the Instituto.

28. Based on his May 1902 parting letter of appreciation for Tamayo's work, Wood framed that work in terms of "a great reorganization of municipalities, readjustment of municipal boundaries" and enactment of new municipal regulations (101305 DTF C05 Archivo del Museo Finlay). A measure of the extraordinary historical neglect suffered by Diego Tamayo is a recent encyclopedic history of the occupation that misidentifies him as a lawyer: Rodríguez García, *Cuba, Las Máscaras y las sombras*, 427.

29. *La Higiene* 2, no. 41 (February 20, 1901): 490.

30. "El muermo y su historia," *La Higiene*, November 30, 1901, 839, notes that there had been only three cases since the creation of the commission and gives it high praise. In his memoirs, Santos Fernández states that glanders "continued until the U.S. intervention, which quickly made it disappear" (*Recuerdos de mi vida*, 1: 326).

31. The new enthusiasm is discussed by one from Santos Fernández's inner group who began to work with the U.S. occupation sanitary authority (Delfín, *Treinta años de medico*).

32. Staff listing, Cuba. Laboratorio de la Isla de Cuba, *Informe de los trabajos realizados en la isla de Cuba*, 14.

33. Fernández Benítez, "Instituciones científicas creadas en Cuba con posterioridad a la guerra de independencia," 45. Díaz-Arguelles, *El Laboratorio Histo-bacteriológico*, 17, claims that the lab did not formally cease to exist until 1960 when it was collapsed into el Instituto de Higiene following the Cuban Revolution.

34. *Censo de la República de Cuba bajo la administración provisional de los Estados Unidos: 1907*, 301, 545-46, 575.

35. *Censo de la República de Cuba Año de 1919*, 281, 666, 674.

36. Worboys, "Germs, Malaria, and the Invention of Mansonian Tropical Medicine," 181-207; Farley, *Bilharzia: A History of Imperial Tropical Medicine*; Anderson, *Colonial Pathologies*; Stern, "Yellow Fever Crusade."

37. *Revista de Medicina Tropical* 1, no. 1 (1900): frontispiece.

38. Guiteras, "Prefacio," 1.

39. Guiteras, "Consideraciones generales," 3-4.

40. Santos Fernández, *Enfermedades de los Ojos en los Negros y Mulatos*.

41. Bronfman, *Measures of Equality*; Helg, *Our Rightful Share*; Palmié, *Wizards and Scientists*.

42. Palmié's take on this, in *Wizards and Scientists*, seems to reproduce one imperial trope concerning intellectual transmission by proposing that scientific racist ideas originated in U.S. and European metropolises and later were taken to the periphery, and another related trope by suggesting that technical and intellectual expressions of the native colonial elite are simply mimicry and lack authenticity or originality.

43. Naranjo and García, *Medicina y Racismo en Cuba*, 12.

44. Guiteras, "Estudios demográficos," cited and discussed in Fuente, *A Nation for All*, 179.

45. Fernández Benítez, "Instituciones científicas creadas en Cuba con posterioridad a la guerra de independencia," 43–51.

46. Report to Session of October 25, 1912, Academy of Sciences, p. 2, in Expediente Académico de Aristídes Agramonte, Carpeta 4, Archivo de la Academia de Ciencias, Museo Carlos J. Finlay de las Ciencias, Havana.

47. Le Roy y Cassá, "Homenaje al Dr. Juan Santos Fernández," 194–95.

48. Funes, *Despertar del asociacionismo científico en Cuba*, 215–35.

49. The trend is most evident between 1909 and 1920 when specialty journals appeared in such areas as pediatrics, otolaryngology, internal medicine, obstetrics and gynecology, dentistry, and veterinary science.

50. Martínez Viera, *La Estación Experimental Agronómica de Santiago de las Vegas*.

51. "Informe sobre los labores de la Sección Botánica, 1904–1922," Legajo 368, Expediente 29, Botánica, Archivo de la Estación Experimental Agrónomica de Santiago de las Vegas, Instituto de Investigaciones Fundamentales en Agricultura Tropical "Alejandro Humboldt," Santiago de las Vegas, Cuba; and McCook, *States of Nature*, 50–55.

52. Martínez Viera, *Juan Tomás Roig*, 40–42.

53. On the links between the Estación Experimental and the Atkins Garden, see Fernández Prieto and García González, "Ciencia," 486–87.

54. McCook, *States of Nature*, 56–60.

55. García Blanco, *Cien figuras de la ciencia en Cuba*, 44.

56. Bronfman, *Measures of Equality*, 6–7.

57. In this usage, *creole* simply means born in Cuba.

58. Montané, "A Cuban Chimpanzee," 330–31.

59. Kirrill Rossiianov, for example, describes Abreu as a "wealthy Cuban pet-lover and amateur researcher": "Beyond Species," 277–316. For a more popular culture treatment of early women ape specialists, see Hahn, *Eve and the Apes*.

60. Lara, *Laura Martínez de Carvajal y del Camino*.

61. Wynne, "Rosalía Abreu and the Apes of Havana," 289–302.

62. Estrade, *La colonia cubana de París*, 282.

63. Robert Yerkes's biography of Abreu, based on interviews conducted over two months at the Quinta Palatino in 1924, makes no mention of her Pasteurian connections, nor even of the name or occupation of her former husband. Her entire interest in

breeding chimpanzees and maintaining them in captivity is said to be based on a chance to keep a pet monkey while she was a child. Yerkes, *Almost Human*.

64. Haraway, *Primate Visions*, 42.

65. Wood to Tamayo, April 8, 1922, 101385 CTF C04, Archivo del Museo Finlay.

66. Palmer, "A Cuban Scientist between Empires," 110–17.

67. Information from the Francisco María Fernández Papers, FMF, Archivo del Museo Finlay.

68. De la Fuente, *A Nation for All*, 45; García González and Álvarez Peláez, *En busca de la raza perfecta*, 169–226.

69. Danielson, *Cuban Medicine*, 103–6.

CHAPTER 3

Race, Labor, and Citizenship in Cuba
A View from the Sugar District of Cienfuegos, 1886–1909

Rebecca J. Scott

Writing in 1902, Victor Clark, who had traveled to Cuba to report on labor conditions for the United States Department of Labor, made the following startling observation: "Cuba is one of the most democratic countries in the world. Nowhere else does the least-considered member of a community aspire with more serene confidence to social equality with its most exalted personage."[1] Clark's sweeping statements about national character, with their faintly mocking tone, can hardly be considered definitive evidence. But his remarks do suggest that four centuries of colonial domination and hierarchical authority in Cuba had not left precisely the visible legacy that one might expect. This raises the question: can one in fact document a widespread presumption to social equality and with it, perhaps, some of the practices that might be encompassed in the term *citizenship*?[2]

Scholars of Latin America have long noted the marked absence of full rights of citizenship for rural workers, including former slaves.[3] Stanley Stein, for example, took up this question in a pathbreaking 1957 study, *Vassouras: A Brazilian Coffee County, 1850–1900*. In his introduction to the 1985 reedition, Stein clarified the challenge he had intentionally posed to the arguments of Frank Tannenbaum's influential *Slave and Citizen*. Tannenbaum had argued optimistically that in Catholic Latin America the "moral status of the freed man" was higher than in Protestant North America, thus facilitating a relatively smooth transition from slave to citizen. Stein convincingly demonstrated that whatever the notional Catholic recognition of the moral equality of the slave, the coffee planters of Vassouras emphatically did not wish to see their slaves transformed into citizens.[4] Subsequent scholarship has emphasized continuities of impoverishment, patriarchal control, and patron-client relations in rural Brazil, particularly in the sugar regions of the northeast.[5] Brazilian historians, including João Reis and Hebe Mattos de Castro, have retrieved some evidence of claims to citizenship on the part of slaves and former slaves in Bahia and in rural Rio de Janeiro.[6] But such claims generally met with resolute opposition. The trend toward formal disfranchisement and informal subordination of rural workers was very strong in the late Brazilian empire and the early republic.[7]

It may therefore be particularly interesting to ask where, among Latin American slave plantation societies, there might be some exceptions to this powerful pattern. If in most instances economic transformations—including the shift from slavery to free labor—were accompanied by disfranchisement in the political sphere, perhaps in a few instances they were not. The purpose of such a search for alternatives is not to argue that deeply embedded structures failed to limit social transformations. Rather, it is to ask just what it took to break these patterns. Under what circumstances did some forms of political voice construed in terms of citizenship become a reality for those who had occupied the lowest rungs of plantation society? One can then proceed to ask how deeply embedded structures—or shallow contingent ones, for that matter—operated to shape the space and extent of that citizenship.[8]

On the island of Cuba the tumult of the wars of independence, which accompanied the process of slave emancipation, opened up possibilities that not even the prompt United States military occupation could close down. Moreover, these two phenomena—anticolonial war and foreign military occupation—each generated extensive documentary evidence, providing an unusual richness of detail for the study of a postemancipation society in Latin America. The dynamics of the search for political voice by former slaves and other rural workers can thus be examined on the ground, not only in particular regions, but even in neighborhoods.

From Slavery to Free Labor in Cienfuegos

The district of Cienfuegos on the southern coast of the province of Santa Clara, encompassing both the prosperous port city from which it took its name and an enormously rich hinterland, offers the possibility of a revealing case study.[9] In the 1870s the rapidly developing hinterland of Cienfuegos comprised the *partidos* of Camarones, Cartagena, Cumanayagua, Las Casas, Yaguaramas, and Santa Isabel de las Lajas, which together contained some seventy-seven sugar estates (*ingenios*), most linked by water or rail to the port itself.[10] The incomplete agricultural census of 1877 enumerated 5,396

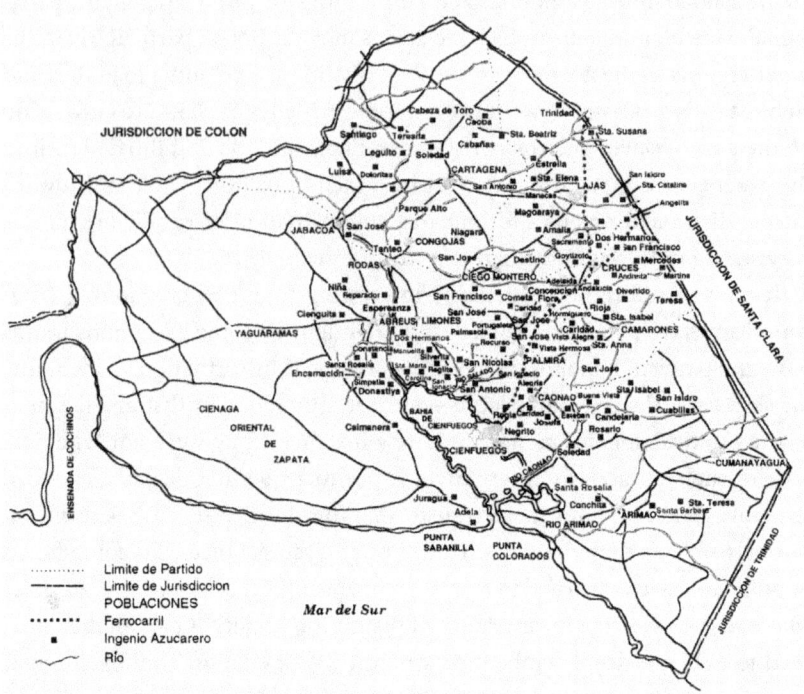

Map 3.1 The jurisdiction of Cienfuegos, with its principal sugar plantations in 1878. Courtesy of Irá Millán.

slave workers on these estates, and the ingenios of Cienfuegos also relied on a smaller number of free wage laborers and Chinese indentured workers.[11] The river valleys of Cienfuegos thus encompassed a large, relatively recently arrived multiracial workforce in sugar, most of whose members were bound by slavery or indenture. At the same time, the hills rising to the east toward the Trinidad Mountains and the interstitial small farms in the valleys continued to be worked by long-free descendants of earlier settlers as well as by former slaves who had recently obtained their freedom.

The planters of Cienfuegos managed to sustain a substantial slave labor force despite the passage of the Moret Law of 1870, which freed children and the elderly, and even through much of the Ten Years' War (1868–78), which raged to the east and undermined the social relations of slavery in those regions that it touched. But Cienfuegos could not hold out indefinitely against the forces undoing slavery in Cuba. The late 1870s brought turmoil as individual slaves traded with, and in some cases joined, the anticolonial insurgents in the hills.[12]

Within the insurgent ranks, a conventional form of address was *ciudadano* (citizen), sometimes abbreviated in rebel records as *c.c.*, for *ciudadano cubano*, and sometimes modified by *de color*. The perceived need to specify that a given citizen was an individual de color hinted at the distinctions that still pervaded the thinking of white rebel officers, and some were reluctant to describe former slaves as ciudadanos at all. But the introduction of *citizen* as a term of description did not go unnoticed by those accustomed to racialized and derogatory forms of address from their social superiors. Rebel nationalists were explicitly proffering the notion of citizenship in an imagined free Cuba, even if some among them subsequently and selectively withheld equal rights from former slaves and other Afro-Cubans in the course of the struggle. As Ada Ferrer argues, the evidence suggests that "free persons of color demonstrated their awareness of the new rebel discourse of freedom and equality and their willingness to make demands on the basis of that discourse."[13]

Challenges within and outside estates multiplied, and rumors of new alliances between slaves and their free neighbors plagued slave owners around Cienfuegos. An informant from the town of San Antón wrote confidentially to the administrator of the Santa Rosalía estate to warn of trouble in July 1879, just before the outbreak in Oriente of the Guerra Chiquita. He reported that word was spreading that "tonight or tomorrow the residents of this district are going to rise up along with the slaves of the plantation."[14]

By 1880 the immediate political threat posed by the Ten Years' War and the Guerra Chiquita had been suppressed militarily, but the breakdown of the social relations that underlay slavery was already well advanced. Moreover, Cuba was now one of only two societies in the hemisphere whose agrarian elite was still attempting to sustain chattel slavery. It had become increasingly evident to the Spanish parliament that to prevent anticolonial rebellion from being nourished by antislavery convictions and slave resistance, the term *slavery* had to be eliminated. Cuban slaveholders, unsurprisingly, hoped that much of its substance could nonetheless be retained. The colonial authorities tried to accommodate the needs of planters by designing a gradual abolition, which provided for an intermediate period of "apprenticeship" during which former slaves were to work for their former masters for token wages. Freedom was scheduled to come in small doses and, finally, by lottery between 1885 and 1888.

After twelve years of war and innumerable challenges from slaves, however, the power relations of a smoothly functioning slave society had become a thing of the past. Apprentices, denominated *patrocinados*, pushed

Figure 3.1 A view across cane fields of Limones, a *colonia* of Soledad (now Pepito Tey), toward Cumanayagua and the Trinidad (now Escombray) mountains. Photograph by Rebecca Scott.

at the limits of their masters' control. Many succeeded in exiting slavery altogether through self-purchase, legal challenge, flight, or negotiation. In the face of an accelerating breakdown, abolition was completed two years early. In the province of Santa Clara, of which Cienfuegos was an important part, the number of patrocinados had fallen from 23,260 in 1883 to 5,648 in 1886, whereupon all were freed by a Spanish decree that ended the *patronato* on the island.[15]

Though they had fought abolition for decades, large-scale planters in Cienfuegos hardly missed a beat, shifting quickly to new structures and new sources of labor. They adopted a three-part strategy, encompassing wage labor, tenantry, and contract farming. Plantations hired Spanish, Cuban, and Chinese workers directly or through labor contractors, they leased out land for the growing of cane, and they purchased cut cane from nearby suppliers. The Spanish government contributed to these strategies, introducing new subsidies for workers and their families who chose to immigrate to Cuba. Innovative planters with capital thus rapidly expanded their operations; others fell behind, and some were simply bought out by their neighbors.[16]

Successful landowners and merchants moved quickly toward modernization of the local infrastructure to facilitate commercialization of the region's expanding production. The most prosperous planters transformed their estates into central sugar mills (*centrales*), grinding cane from multiple suppliers. The most impressive of these was Constancia, owned by the Marqués de Apezteguía, which produced sugar worth a staggering 1 million pesos. By 1890 Constancia's output was larger than that of any other single mill in the world.[17] In an appeal for permission to build new rail lines for private use, Fermín de Solá wrote exuberantly that Cienfuegos was providing a brilliant example of work and of "faith in the future."[18]

A buoyant North American market for sugar, combined with new capital from the United States and from local merchants, made it possible for the most aggressive Cienfuegos planters to expand the scope of their operations and offer wages to old and new workers alike. The sugar plantations of central Cuba had largely escaped the kind of turmoil and open contest over access to resources that marked the occupied areas of the U.S. South during the process of emancipation, where war and Union presence inadvertently opened up the possibilities for cooperative agriculture and hastened the emergence of grassroots "labor companies" and Union Leagues.[19] Nonetheless, labor mobility, the arrival of immigrants, and the continued threat of anticolonial insurgency on the island made an entirely smooth continuity of authority highly unlikely.

The Santa Rosalía estate, tucked in between the Arimao and the Caunao Rivers to the east of the bay of Cienfuegos, provides an example of the pattern of evolution of moderate-sized estates. In 1877 Santa Rosalía held 150 slaves and produced some 32,000 pesos worth of sugar. It had been developed by José Quesada and was later taken over by Manuel Blanco, a politically intransigent Spanish merchant.[20] In 1880 its *dotación* of slaves consisted of eighty-one men, forty-nine women, and sixty-one nominally free children. In 1887, immediately after slave emancipation, its payroll included many of the same names (though surnames now accompanied Christian names), and comprised seventy-four men, thirty-three women, and twenty-four children.[21]

By the early 1890s, the workforce had become significantly more complex. Many of the black laborers bore the surname Quesada, which publicly identified them as former slaves of the estate. Others carried the names of the region's prominent slaveholding families, including Iznaga, Zulueta, Argudín, and Goytisolo. But the estate also listed a series of laborers who had come from Spain and before whose name the honorific *don* was carefully placed. Don Bernardo Villar's pay, for example, was issued in a "letra y giro sobre España," and don Vicente Villar worked nearly every day for fifteen months before leaving the estate "para marchar a la Peninsula." Little racial differ-

Figure 3.2 The livestock-raising settlement of Gavilán, eventually acquired by Soledad. Photograph courtesy of the Massachusetts Historical Society, Atkins Family Papers.

entiation in wages was evident: like the former slaves, the Spanish workers earned about seventeen pesos a month.[22]

Adjacent to Santa Rosalía stood the expanding Soledad central, owned by the energetic Edwin Atkins of Massachusetts. Atkins had acquired the estate from the Sarría family through foreclosure in the mid-1880s, assuming rights over more than a hundred former slaves, now denominated patrocinados.[23] Benefiting from large-scale investments in equipment and a voracious policy of land acquisition, Soledad expanded its production and drew in large numbers of immigrants and other wage workers. Atkins saw the years from 1886 to 1894 as good ones and spoke with some pride of the hundreds of workers who came to labor on his estate. Though it was still overshadowed by giant estates like Constancia and Caracas, Soledad seems to have developed a reputation as something of a model plantation.[24]

The plantation workforce that evolved in Cienfuegos was neither that of an all-male proletariat nor that of a family-based sharecropping system. The names of children and of women loomed less and less large on the plantation payrolls, as women turned to household labor, market gardening, and laundering, but they were not absent. The resident population of Santa Rosalía, for example, still included women. Some planters, however, refused to allow certain former slaves to remain on the estate if their services were no longer needed or if they showed too much independence. Tomás Pérez y

Figure 3.3 Cutting cane on Soledad, early twentieth century. Photograph courtesy of the Massachusetts Historical Society, Atkins Family Papers.

Pérez, born in 1902, remembers that his mother, Bárbara Pérez, a domestic slave who had learned to read from her young mistress, was forced off the Pérez Galdós plantation after emancipation, and she moved to the town of Arimao to work as a laundress. Toward the end of the 1886 grinding season, the administrator at Soledad took pains to expel "a great many negroes who have horses," presumably in an effort to reduce their mobility and their consumption of estate resources.[25]

Managers could not always afford to be quite so particular about the behavior of former slaves. The general expansion of production on the larger estates in Cienfuegos created a strong seasonal demand for fieldworkers and a challenge for employers. In March 1886 the manager of Soledad wrote that all the estates in the district were "short of hands and some have had to stop grinding for a few days." The possible consequences were clear: "I fear if hands continue to be scarce we will have to increase wages and so bring men from other districts."[26] The relatively high wages at harvest time drew not only men but also some women of color, who returned to the cane fields as short-term laborers.[27] There was thus continual mobility of male and female workers, ensuring that workers in the cane would not be isolated from developments in town.

The growth of centrales, which drew in cane from multiple suppliers, brought new opportunities for small renters and landowners. After signing a contract with a nearby central, they could plant their land in cane and reliably plan for the mill to grind it. Smallholders thus gained a foothold in an industry that had previously been largely restricted to those prosperous enough to fund their own milling. These contracts, however, were often draconian. If a *colono* under contract to the Hormiguero estate in the 1890s failed to comply with the terms of the contract, he had just two months to sell out to someone more satisfactory to the estate.[28]

Some colonos tried to resist the terms laid down by the estates, and their obstreperousness placed certain limits on the expansion of large plantations.[29] In 1884 the manager of Soledad wrote with impatience that "the *colonos* are giving us much more trouble than we anticipated; San Pelayo, Roque, and Cantignon all refuse to sign new contracts unless we make them larger advances, for more than their property is worth."[30] In 1891 colonos in the province of Santa Clara organized an attempt to raise the level of compensation beyond the standard rate and seem to have met with some success.[31]

Though sugarcane covered vast swaths of land, it was not the only crop cultivated, nor did large estates monopolize the territory. *Frutos menores*, including sweet potatoes, bananas, and yucca as well as maize, were grown on hundreds of small farms, both for subsistence and for sale. In the property lists of Santa Isabel de las Lajas, in the northern part of Cienfuegos, most of the smallholders seem to have been individuals who could claim the honorific *don* and were probably categorized socially as white. But one can follow through the 1880s a slowly growing group of smallholders listed as *moreno* (black). The *morena* Mercedes Alonso, for example, occupied a *sitio* (small farm) called La Palmita and was taxed about two pesos a year. Her neighbor, the moreno Tomás Mora, occupied the even poorer sitio named Santo Tomás and paid just seventy centavos per year in taxes.[32] From the point of view of former slaves and other rural workers, the hills and unoccupied land on the periphery of sugar estates could provide a kind of refuge. From the point of view of planters, the *monte* yielded wood and a trade in foodstuffs, but it was also suspected of harboring cattle thieves, bandits, and small communities that had escaped the direct supervision of local authorities.

This was not, then, a region of strict monoculture and dichotomous social divisions. At the extremes, of course, class coincided with the prevailing notions of race, and lines were sharply drawn. There was a cosmopolitan and exclusive elite defined as white, some of whom participated in the concerts, "opera, garden parties, sailing parties, or excursions to some country estates" that Edwin Atkins had enjoyed as a youth. And there were former slaves in the *barracón* (barracks) at the Soledad plantation who, according to Atkins's account, "being mostly imported Africans, came from many tribes and kept up their tribal customs for years after slavery was abolished."[33] But both of these groups existed alongside, and of necessity interacted with, administrators, machinists, artisans, and overseers, in the midst of a vast population of Cubans from all racial groups and Spaniards who worked as day laborers, cane farmers, and small-scale cultivators. Moreover, town and country were intimately linked by the *vaporcitos* (little steam-powered boats) and *lanchas* that traveled the river between Soledad and Santa Rosalía and the bay, by the stevedores who loaded and unloaded the sugar, by families who moved back and forth in search of work, and by members of the elite who alternated life in the city of Cienfuegos with residence on their rural estates.

This world was porous and multiracial, but even at its base it revealed some lines of national and racial distinctions. When asked about the private guards on his estate, for example, Edwin Atkins replied that "they were mostly composed of men recruited from Spanish laborers who had nearly all of them served their time in the Spanish army."[34] Though their ostensible purpose was to protect the estate from external threats, it is not difficult to see in them certain echoes of the white militia of the Southern United States. As Spaniards on the lookout for Cuban bandits, or as white men on horseback on the lookout for potential trouble from fieldworkers, they would at times have stood out as distinct from the men and women around them.

Even more starkly, the management of the Soledad estate seems to have moved toward denying employment in the mill to former slaves and their descendants, relegating them to fieldwork. The surname Sarría, taken by many former slaves on Soledad, is rare in the pay lists for mill labor in the 1890s, appearing frequently instead in the agricultural section. Tomás Pérez y Pérez, who worked for most of his life on Soledad, recalls the color consciousness of the administrators of Soledad. Pérez, whose mother, Bárbara Pérez, was a former slave and whose father, Manuel Lago, was a Spanish carpenter, obtained special dispensation in the early years of the twentieth century to work at the mill, from which the administration apparently otherwise excluded workmen of color.[35]

These forms of exclusion coexisted with many forms of cross-racial interaction. On estates and on cane farms, people of all socioracial groups came and went, bought and sold, talked and drank coffee, collected wages and argued about the price of cane. At Soledad, the squalid barracks built during slavery remained, with the same atrocious consequences for public health and personal comfort. But the prison-like control to which their inhabitants had been subjected was now largely gone, though it occasionally reappeared in moments of attack from smallpox or bandits. Partial residential segregation continued alongside growing spaces of integration. For example, the Spanish owner of a *tienda* and a parcel of land near the Caunao River, located behind the Soledad mill, apparently had no objection if families from Santa Rosalía settled there. There soon emerged the small multiracial community of El Palmar, composed of former slaves, some with the surname Quesada, as well as Spanish workers and Cubans of various groups.[36]

The Search for Political Voice

The heterogeneous and mobile working population of rural Cienfuegos did not, by and large, have access to the vote in the early 1890s. The electoral law in force limited suffrage to those paying five pesos annually in taxes—a threshold that easily excluded smallholders like the moreno Tomás Mora.[37] His slightly more prosperous neighbor, Mercedes Alonso, was of course excluded both by her poverty and by her sex. But there were signs that some former slaves and other people of color were pressing for greater participation in the public sphere. The city of Cienfuegos had created a school for children of color, and in several of the district's towns, mutual-aid organizations had been constituted by members of the *clase de color*. As political conflict increased, new voices were raised in public debate, particularly in the towns.[38]

The conservative pro-Spanish and integralist Constitutional Union Party had little electoral use for assertive nonelite Cubans, and few would have been drawn to its intransigent stance in any event. It was primarily the more oppositional Liberal Autonomists, supporters of electoral reform and limited self-government, who potentially stood to gain from wider mobilization. Their task, however, was a difficult one. They had come to an abolitionist position relatively late in the day, and their leaders at the national level were socially very distant from the agriculturalists and urban workers who constituted the majority of the population. Locally, they did develop their own networks of clientage and support, but they were increasingly reviled by Cuban separatists, who supported independence for the island and saw reforms as delusions for the gullible.[39]

All of the Autonomists' difficulties came together in an ill-fated meeting in Cienfuegos in October 1886. Autonomist deputy J. Fernández de Castro was scheduled to speak in the Teatro Zorrilla, the only meeting place his party had been able to secure, located in a section of town largely populated by people of color. As the speakers made their way to the theater, several people of color accompanying them hurled corn kernels at the houses of suspected Constitutional Unionists. The theater was packed, with many of those in attendance described by the authorities as "people of little education, people of color in the majority." When Fernández de Castro first criticized the Spanish government, the audience divided into those who applauded and those who hissed. When he claimed that the Autonomists could take credit for the abolition of the patronato and thus the definitive end of slavery, he was met with shouts of "¡mentira!" (a lie!). The hall broke out in disorder as some cheered for Spain and others for autonomy, while chairs began to crash.[40]

The events in the Teatro Zorilla are not easy to interpret. Some of the "people of little education" present seem to have come in support of the Autonomists; others may have been recruited by pro-Spanish forces for the purposes of intimidation. Indignation at the Autonomists' attempt to take credit for abolition could originate from several quarters: from supporters of the Spanish government who wished credit for the belated emancipation to go to the metropolitan lawmakers who formally promulgated the law, or from others who considered that popular pressure by slaves and rebels, not legislative steps in Spain, had accelerated the end of slavery. Whatever the precise mix of prior allegiances in the crowd, the meeting seems to have reflected the eruption into the field of public debate of a large number of people who did not have access to the vote but did claim the right to political voice.[41]

From the point of view of the forces of order, such mobilization was by its nature problematic. The police chief noted that Fernández de Castro could have avoided these troubles if he had taken into account "la clase de público a quien se dirigía" (the kind of public whom he was addressing).[42] But it was not possible for politicians to entirely overlook the potential of such groups. The Autonomists were fighting a genteel but uphill battle, and they tried the weapons of debate, parliamentary boycott, and, in extremis, popular mobilization.[43]

Despite the generally reactionary tone of much elite life in Cienfuegos, urban activists of color undertook various efforts to achieve racial integration, negotiating with Spanish authorities while consulting with the future *independentista* Juan Gualberto Gómez. Among these Cienfuegos organizers was Gabriel Quesada, a noted baseball player and later cofounder of the Sociedad Minerva, a mutual-aid and educational society for people of color.[44] The colonial government had formally ruled in favor of equality of access to public places, and on January 4, 1894, a group of men of color attempted to integrate the elegant Teatro Terry by attending a performance of *Los Hugonotes*. The ensuing fracas precipitated ferocious debate in the press, denunciation of the activists from various quarters, and criticism of the colonial authorities for having failed to respect the opposition of the white majority to the idea of "decreeing social equality."[45]

As the Autonomists dithered on the question of race and failed miserably to achieve electoral reform from Spain, initiative was already shifting to the separatists in exile, who had long advocated full independence from Spain. At the same time, the financial panic of 1893 was followed by the expiration of the Foster-Cánovas agreement and a disastrous reconfiguration of trade relations between Spain and the United States. The 1891 commercial treaty between these two countries had facilitated the export of Cuban sugars to the U.S. market, but the Wilson Tariff of 1894 took raw sugar off the "free list" and undermined the entire structure of Cuban trade with the United States. In the vivid phrase of Louis A. Pérez Jr., "An impenetrable protectionist wall reappeared around the island in mid-1894, reviving memories of the worst features of Spanish exclusivism."[46]

From Edwin Atkins's vantage point at Soledad, the effects were swift and deadly: As "the cost of living in Cuba advanced and the price of sugar dropped, credit became impaired." By January 1895, wages and cane prices had fallen, and Atkins reported that he had to contend not only with rains and "customs house complications" but also with "strikes owing to low wages." At Soledad the "poor laborers with their thin clothes were suffering from cold and an epidemic very like intestinal influenza."[47]

To many on the island, Spain increasingly looked to be not only an authoritarian colonial power but an incompetent one as well.[48] Cuban planters railed loudly and indignantly at the commercial crisis that threatened to engulf them.[49] For the nationalist movement in exile, the moment was fast approaching to unleash what they anticipated would be a brief but necessary war of liberation from Spain. In the Cienfuegos region, workers discharged at the end of the 1894–95 crop season faced a very uncertain future and might be expected to be receptive to such a call.

The story of the beginning of the final war of independence has been told so many times that it has taken on the character of an epic, marked by drama and a certain sense of inevitability. On February 24, 1895, in the eastern part of the island, insurrection against Spanish rule was proclaimed in the "grito de Baire," and a short-lived "grito de Ibarra" in Matanzas echoed the call. Long-standing separatists in the east left the cities for the countryside when word of the revolt reached them. Lino Sánchez y Murillo, for example, a young white man from a family of conspirators in Santiago de Cuba, reported somewhat boastfully that "since I had use of reason I used to talk about the war of '68 and how the war had been lost by the pact made by Zanjón." On February 23, 1895, the day before the formal uprising began, he took to the woods near a sugar estate in the eastern province, having been alerted by Cuban telegraph operators on the railway line that the police were planning to arrest him.[50]

In April, Antonio Maceo landed near Baracoa, on the north coast of Santiago de Cuba province. One coffee planter later testified: "As he was the soul of the revolution, as soon as we heard that he was there, all of us that had 15 or 10 or 20 men went to join him."[51] Even elderly veterans of the Ten Years' War joined the fight. Gaspar Caballero, an African-born fieldworker from San Luís, in the east, had fought in both previous rebellions. He enlisted with the rebels as a soldier in the first days of the 1895 war and was later transferred to the task of growing crops to provision the troops.[52] Within a month after arriving on the island, Antonio Maceo wrote to his wife that he had six thousand men under his command and much territory under his control. He added an exultant postscript: "No day goes by without people coming to join me, all the youth of Santiago de Cuba have gone to the countryside; we have doctors and lawyers with us."[53]

In Santa Clara and in its core region of Cienfuegos, however, rebellion seemed less epic and certainly less inevitable. The nationalist movement, initially operating from exile, was calling on Cubans to take enormous risks in pursuit of a great gamble: a gamble that Cubans could win against Spain and that winning would make a real difference to the lives of those who suffered from unemployment, humiliation, or impoverishment. Some people from the central region took to the hills; others waited and watched. Already in mid-February, a group of insurgents was reported to be meeting at Los Guaos, near Soledad, and telephone lines were cut. But the anticipated local uprising did not follow.[54]

On the surface, the Cienfuegos district remained relatively quiet through the spring of 1895. The landing of a rebel expedition on the coast of Santa Clara in late spring, however, provided a new impetus to revolt.[55] Troubles began by late June near the city of Santa Clara, and Edwin Atkins received reports that a party of a dozen or so rebels was being pursued in the area of Cumanayagua, close to Santa Rosalía and Soledad. By summer there was little work to be had in the area, and in Atkins's view, "many, particularly negroes, joined the insurgents or took to the woods to live by pillage." Companies of pro-government *voluntarios*, meanwhile, were formed from among elements of the Spanish population.⁵⁶

Around Soledad and Santa Rosalía, black and mulatto men, some with the surnames Quesada or Sarría, began to head to the monte to join forces with others, forming the nucleus of what would later become companies of the rebel Ejército Libertador. Claudio Sarría, born a slave on Soledad, quickly emerged as a leader. Two neighbors from Santa Rosalía, Ciriaco and Cayetano Quesada, joined up as well. News was clearly spreading fast.⁵⁷

In the late summer, rebels from Oriente undertook the initiative that seemed essential to victory: they mounted an invasion westward, aimed at projecting their power out of their region of origin and placing the Spanish on the defensive. After gathering their forces, rebel generals Antonio Maceo and Máximo Gómez made their way across the central province of Camagüey (formerly Puerto Príncipe) and reached the economic heartland of the island. When the insurgent army from the east arrived at the edge of the rich, open central sugar zone, Antonio Maceo is said to have looked out over the land and observed, "Our ship has reached the high seas."⁵⁸

The Spanish captain general, Arsenio Martínez Campos, responded by deploying thousands of new Spanish troops to the central sugar regions and transferring his headquarters to the city of Santa Clara. But the insurgent advance was relentless, and the breakout of the eastern rebel forces provided an additional stimulus for local insurgents to take initiatives of their own. In the town of Las Moscas, in the hills across the Arimao River to the east of Cienfuegos, the black rebel veteran and shopkeeper Benigno Najarro had linked up both with Alfredo Rego, a white conspirator from the city of Cienfuegos, and with Juan Ramírez Olivera, known as el mejicano, to form a cadre of leaders for the rebellion. It was less than a day's ride from Las Moscas to Soledad and Santa Rosalía, and by August and September rebels in that area were said to be operating "under a chief named Rego."⁵⁹

By November, Martínez Campos had relocated to Cienfuegos and was fortifying the immediate region. The insurgent forces under Maceo and Gómez confronted the Spanish in the dramatic battle of Mal Tiempo, near the town of Cruces. The rebel victory provided an impressive demonstration of the capacity of the insurgent armies from eastern Cuba, in conjunction with local forces, to defeat the Spanish troops.⁶⁰ The question was now starkly posed to the residents of the central sugar zones: Would the descendants of slaves and the descendants of slaveholders, as well as those who had been free rural dwellers on the margins of the slave system, perceive themselves to have a shared interest in this revolt? And if so, would they and could they mobilize together?

The Dynamics of Recruitment and Warfare

The rank and file of the forces from Oriente were composed in the majority of men defined as black or mulatto, strongly identified in popular perceptions with the dynamic figure of Maceo, son of a family of free people of color. Alongside them fought many Cubans who counted themselves as white and even a few renegade Spaniards. Rebel units from the central province of Santa Clara, also heterogeneous, had joined up as well. The official ideology of the rebels portrayed racism as a legacy of slavery and colonialism, destined to be eliminated in a democratic Cuban republic. Divisions and ambivalence on questions of race were for the moment muted, as a multiracial rebel army under multiracial leadership swept westward.[61]

This, then, was the force that was visibly overpowering the Spanish in the countryside and seeking new allies to assist in the task. Recruitment in Cienfuegos was becoming a personal, face-to-face affair, as friends and neighbors who had joined the insurgent army confronted those who had not. On the Hormiguero plantation, for example, workers watched as virtually the entire invading force rode or tramped across estate lands in their march to the west. Even those who resisted appeals to enlist found it hard to refuse requests for information.[62]

The moment of recruitment itself could be ephemeral. Rural workers were, after all, committed to their homes and to their families and might have second thoughts about abandoning them, particularly if this meant marching out of their home district. One laborer from Cienfuegos, Miguel Angel Abad, had a small farm of his own but also worked on a colonia supplying the Hormiguero mill. He described the passage of Gómez and Maceo through the estate as they torched the cane before moving westward. Local insurgents came out of the woods to join them, though most of the workers on the estate did not. Abad had joined the insurgents after a friend in the invading force had urged him to go with them. But after a few hours, Abad later recounted, "I slowly fell to the rear, and as soon as I found I could separate myself, I started running for my house."[63]

As the main invasion force passed to the north, local insurgents in the *partido* of Cumanayagua consolidated their forces, and in early January 1896 the administrator at Soledad reported a "uniting of [the] small parties into one large party of rebels. Claudio Sarría, Rafael Monte, Torres, and Najarro have united their forces with *el mejicano* for their own safety." The admin-

Figure 3.4 Officers of the rebel Cienfuegos Brigade, including E. Collado Curbelo. Photograph courtesy of the Archivo Nacional de Cuba, Fototeca (ANC, Caja M-II, sobre 101, reg. 105).

istrators of Soledad had no clear idea of how many of their workers sympathized with the rebellion, and they could not stop rebels from entering the estate to collect supplies.[64]

In mid-January 1896, the rebel troops of Quintín Bandera paid a visit to Soledad. The administrator, P. M. Beal, was impressed by Bandera's forces from the east. "They were here under trying circumstance, hungry, barefooted and half naked, yet not one of them appropriated the smallest thing without permission." He added that "with exception of the officers, they were all colored." So, too, was Quintín Bandera, whom the rebel high command had ordered to remain behind to guard their flank and consolidate their gains as they continued toward the west.[65]

In the core sugar areas around the bay of Cienfuegos, the Spanish hastened to construct a garrisoned *zona fortificada*, blocking the penetration of insurgents and inhibiting recruitment. Confrontations continued on the margins and around estates like Santa Rosalía in Cumanayagua, but during 1896 and 1897 many of the major Cienfuegos estates were secured against insurgent attack. Soledad moved into a liminal state, guarded and fortified to permit grinding, but always vulnerable at its edges.[66]

Despite Spanish efforts to inhibit recruitment, the multiracial world of sugar plantations and of the small farming sector had given rise to multi-

Figure 3.5 Officers of the Cienfuegos Brigade of the Ejército Libertador, including General Higinio Esquerra. Photograph courtesy of the Archivo Nacional de Cuba, Fototeca (ANC, Caja M-II, sobre 100, reg. 104).

racial insurgent forces, and the experiences of cross-racial collaboration in the insurgency had changed the character of social relations in the countryside. To say this is not to claim that lines were so fluid that racial identities were insignificant. But shared grievances against the authoritarian Spanish state and its local manifestations, combined with popular imaginings of a "free Cuba," provided points of convergence among what may in fact have been quite different visions of a postwar future.[67]

In the central province of Santa Clara (Las Villas), most members of the rebel high command were individuals who were identified as white. For example, General José de Jesús Monteagudo, surrounded by white creole officers, appears to have presented himself as a member of the white creole classes.[68] General Higinio Esquerra, who commanded the Cienfuegos Brigade, was described as a white farmer, though his brigade itself was thoroughly multiracial, with significant numbers of black and mulatto officers. There were, however, notable Afro-Cuban members of the high command: Brigadier José González Planas exercised authority over white subordinate officers (including, early in the war, Esquerra himself) and commanded a large number of white, black, and mulatto troops.[69] Throughout the war, smaller bands under local leadership, often black or mulatto, controlled large sections of the countryside. Claudio Sarría, for example, had joined the rebellion in August 1895 and by November 1896 was captain of Company 3 of the First Battalion of the Infantry Regiment of the Cienfuegos Brigade. His neighbor José Sarría was a sergeant, and Ciriaco Quesada, a former slave from Santa Rosalía, served as one of the soldiers under his command.[70]

As the recent works of Ada Ferrer and of Aline Helg have demonstrated, this multiracial alliance was riven through with tensions and conflicts. These included resentment at the frequent relegation of African-born recruits to menial positions and competition for resources between units under the leadership of white officers and those under the leadership of black and mulatto officers.[71] But despite these conflicts, the insurgency itself represented a massive effort at cross-racial mobilization under the formal aegis of equality and antiracism. It could thus serve as a seedbed for strong claims of citizenship, even when in practice many of its leaders fell far short of observing its egalitarian principles. It also led to the emergence and reinforcement of extensive cross-racial clienteles developed by white officers and to the consolidation of leadership by black and mulatto soldiers at various levels.

With increasing urgency and desperation, the metropolitan government, while denying the very idea of Cuban citizenship, had sought throughout the 1890s to persuade residents of Cuba that they had wide access to a qualified citizenship as *Spanish* subjects. In response to pressure from an urban-based movement for equal rights for Cubans of color, the Spanish government had conceded, at least in theory, that the honorific title of *don* could be claimed by all men, regardless of color. Cubans of African descent had also been formally accorded equal rights to education and to public accommodation.[72]

In 1897, in the midst of war, the colonial government belatedly conceded the basic demands of the political reformists and, under the tutelage of Spain, constituted a new autonomist government for Cuba. In theory, a broader suffrage and a more expansive politics would now be possible. Surviving electoral lists from Santa Clara province in early 1898 highlight both the presence of Cubans of color among those recognized as electors and the persistence of distinctions of status in the lists themselves. The *ayuntamiento* of Sagua la Grande, for example, listed hundreds of electors in each district of the municipality, but accorded the title *don* to some and omitted it from others, generally following the names of the latter with the color terms *pardo* or *moreno*. The printed lists from Cienfuegos were more discreet, eschewing these distinctions. Those of the town of San Fernando included hundreds of fieldworkers, half a dozen of them with the surname Sarría, and were equally silent on color. Actual practice at election time, of course, cannot be inferred

Figure 3.6 Officers of the Cienfuegos Brigade of the Ejército Libertador. Photograph courtesy of the Archivo Nacional de Cuba, Fototeca (ANC, Caja M-II, sobre 101, reg. 105).

from such sources.[73] But though the disruptions of war rendered these late electoral rights largely moot, the establishment of integrated electoral lists in itself established precedents for the postwar period. Both sides, in effect, were proffering citizenship without distinctions of color.

Autonomy under Spanish auspices had come much too late. The armed Cuban separatists had by now fought and harassed the Spanish forces to a standstill, though they could not yet expel them. Losses were mounting and raw recruits from Spain were expected to manage the rigors of irregular warfare in the tropics. Spanish forces could not move safely in most of the countryside; they were largely reduced to garrisoning the towns and trying to protect selected fortified rural zones.

By 1898 the effects of destruction were visible throughout the island. For rural Cubans, physical insecurity and widespread devastation were a harsh reality. Many sugar mills had been destroyed, and many others were unable to grind. José Martí had been quite wrong in imagining that the necessary war would be brief. Nonetheless, it seemed plausible to expect that the rebels' summer campaign of 1898 might extend their control from the countryside into the cities and finally win the war.[74]

If the outbreak of the war is often portrayed as epic, its conclusion might best be depicted as tragic. The standoff between Cuban rebels and Spanish

Figure 3.7 Brigadier José González Planas (labeled #1) and members of the Remedios Brigade of the Ejército Libertador. Photograph courtesy of the Archivo Nacional de Cuba, Fototeca (ANC, Caja M-10, sobre 97, reg. 101).

forces was broken by the intervention of the U.S. military, allied with the most conservative wing of the Cuban separatist coalition. The Cubans who had fought the war for three years were quickly constructed as the insufficiently grateful beneficiaries of American generosity and sacrifice. They were said to be, in the unforgettable words of General William R. Shafter, "no more fit for self-government than gunpowder is for hell."[75] Instead of Cuba Libre, the island would become occupied Cuba, and a U.S. military government would take over the sovereignty relinquished by Spain.

Cienfuegos under U.S. Occupation

The leaders of the U.S. military government had little or no sympathy for the wartime vision of Cuban citizenship in which nationality transcended color and in which service in the Ejército Libertador entitled one to political voice and access to resources. The occupation forces represented a federal government that had itself debated the meanings of free labor and citizenship during its own civil war and afterward. After a period of experimentation, the notion of a right of access by former slaves to productive resources (particularly land) had been put aside, and free labor was defined more simply as the right to sell one's own labor. Moreover, the federal government had all but settled on its own territory the question of race and citizenship: although the Fifteenth Amendment prohibited restrictions on voting rights based on color, no significant effort would be made to halt local attempts at systematic disenfranchisement.[76]

The officers of the U.S. occupation government were strongly disinclined to recommence an experiment in interracial democracy on an island they viewed as temperamentally and constitutionally unsuited for self-rule in the first place. Order was far more important than inclusiveness, and mechanisms for providing order were designed to reinforce the supremacy of the right sort of people. A rural guard, for example, if properly constituted, could help to curb disorder and importunate claims of representation. But the rural guard likely to emerge from the demobilized Ejército Libertador would be altogether too heterogeneous.[77]

There was, however, a notable disjuncture between the larger structures of sovereignty asserted by the United States and the local patterns of power on the ground. In several areas of Cienfuegos, for example, Edwin Atkins reported that insurgents "under negro officers" were still effectively in control, keeping the peace and levying small taxes to support their men. When Máximo Gómez made a visit to Cienfuegos in February 1899, the insurgent force of the region, people of color in the great majority, assembled to greet him, demonstrating their continued capacity to mobilize.[78]

The U.S. presence provided a substantive and symbolic counterweight to earlier visions of Cuba Libre. But this presence could not effectively prevent challenges, small and large, from emerging in the cities and countryside. Military pacification was one thing; social peace was quite another. One incident on the Santa Rosalía estate illuminates the tenacity of the claims advanced by ordinary Cubans, especially former slaves who had fought in the rebellion.

Santa Rosalía had been radically depopulated during the war. Some of its residents had joined the rebellion, others were consigned to the reconcentración villages set up by the Spanish general Weyler, and a few remained on the estate to guard the cattle and the property. Descendants of former slave residents recall that when the war was over, the *reconcentrados* returned to Santa Rosalía, only to find that Manuel Blanco would not let them resettle; the land was to be occupied by others. Women in particular seem to have been unwelcome, but arguments between the administrator and male workers, followed by expulsions, were also common.[79]

The administrator of Santa Rosalía, Constantino Pérez, was accustomed to writing nearly every day to Manuel García Blanco, the agent of the owner,

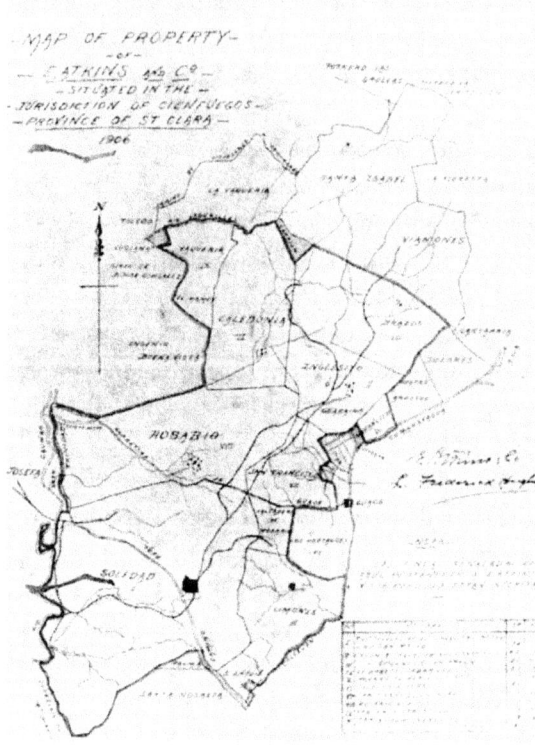

Map 3.2 The various properties constituting Soledad. The Santa Rosalía plantation is its southern neighbor. San Antón, where Ciriaco and Cayetano Quesada settled, is in the southeast corner. Photograph courtesy of the Archivo Principal de Cienfuegos. Photograph by Jack Kenny.

Manuel Blanco. The administrator had many tales of woe, centering on the lack of willing workers and the insolence of those he found. On August 17, 1899, Pérez reported that "un tal Ciriaco y Paulino Quesada," former slaves on Santa Rosalía and sons of "la vieja Francisca," had come to see him about retrieving "la mula ... de Gregoria." Ciriaco Quesada had obtained his legal freedom in January 1886, and he and his brother Paulino had worked seasonally on the estate in the late 1880s and early 1890s. Ciriaco Quesada had enlisted in the rebel Ejército Libertador in August 1895. Now the war was over and he was back. The administrator stood on ceremony: he would not give up the mule without a written order from the owner or his agent. Indeed, Pérez seemed rather pleased with himself for turning away this request from Ciriaco and Paulino Quesada. (He said nothing about Gregoria herself, but other evidence suggests that she had moved to the city of Cienfuegos during the war.)[80]

At seven o'clock the next morning, however, the chief of the Rural Guard appeared on the estate and called for Pérez, presenting him with an order from the mayor of Arimao to turn over the mule to Ciriaco Quesada. Pérez initially refused, but the guardsman threatened to go after the mule himself. Pérez seems to have become a bit flustered. He relinquished the mule, but only in exchange for a receipt, in case Manuel Blanco wanted to collect for the grass the mule had eaten in the meantime. In his next letter, Pérez fumed that any day now Antonico (presumably another former slave) would turn up to look for *his* two mules, since he had come around earlier to get them. Pérez advised Blanco's agent to try to collect from Ciriaco Quesada for the three years the mule had been grazing on estate property, if only to make the point that Ciriaco should not have gone to the mayor.

What is most striking is the speed with which Ciriaco Quesada enlisted the assistance of the *alcalde* of Arimao and of the Rural Guard. He must have had a horse to reach Arimao so quickly, and he must have been received promptly by the mayor. Were these two officials perhaps fellow insurgent veterans, willing to take up the case against the estate's administrator out of friendship with Ciriaco? (Ciriaco Quesada had joined the Ejército Libertador well before the invading rebel army from the east swept through the countryside north of Soledad and Santa Rosalía, and he had served with a local rebel force under Claudio Sarría during 1896.) Was the mayor also moved in part by resentment against Manuel Blanco, an unreconstructed Spanish conservative? The existence of hostility against Blanco is confirmed by Constantino Pérez's later report that an employee on the estate had been mocked at the country store by "un ciudadano de esos Bandidos," who told him that he was "un sinvergüenza" (a person without shame) for guarding the cattle of Manuel Blanco. During these same months, Constantino Pérez feared a strike by Cuban workers. He later concluded that the workers would wait until the terms of peace—and perhaps the fate of Spanish property owners like Manuel Blanco—were settled.[81]

Ciriaco Quesada's decision to take his claim straight to the town of Arimao was an astute one. Arimao, whose population was composed of black, white, Chinese, and mulatto *campesinos*, was a likely spot in which to nourish and reinforce a claim of rights. Home to sugar workers from Soledad and from the Pérez Galdós estates, as well as to many small-scale farmers and tobacco workers, it had a long history of separatist activism. Some of the first rumors of war heard on Soledad had come from "over by Arimao." The 1898 electoral lists of the Arimao district, encompassing the surrounding countryside, accorded everyone the honorific title of *don* and included Francisco Achón, probably a Chinese worker from Soledad; Manuel Lago Tacón, the master carpenter from Vigo, Galicia, who was the father of Tomás Pérez y Pérez; and eight men with the surname Quesada, very likely former slaves

Figure 3.8 Tomás Pérez y Pérez, born 1902 in El Palmar, interviewed in 1998. Photograph by Paul Eiss.

from Santa Rosalía. Twenty-three of the registered voters in Arimao carried the surname Sarría, and many of them were almost certainly former slaves and their descendants from Soledad.[82]

The electoral lists, of course, include only men. But from the memoirs of Tomás Pérez y Pérez we can identify another resident not on the lists and catch a glimpse of the public sphere in this dusty riverfront town. Tomás Pérez's mother, Bárbara Pérez, was born a slave on the Pérez Galdós plantation, where she later attended the owner's young niece as a personal servant. Among her tasks as a slave was to collect the mail when it arrived at the house. One day when she brought the mail back to the main room there was no one around, so she took the liberty of opening up a newspaper to see what she could make of it. Moments later the niece walked in, and Bárbara quickly folded up the paper and lowered her head, expecting punishment. Instead the niece said, "Don't tell anyone I saw you, and I'll teach you to read." Bárbara Pérez seems to have been a ready student, and by the time emancipation came, she could read and write.

In the late 1880s, Bárbara Pérez took her skills with her when she moved to Arimao, after being expelled from the Pérez Galdós estate. Whenever a newspaper arrived in town, her neighbors would each bring a chair from their living rooms out to the sidewalk, and she would read the news aloud to the *pueblo* of Arimao.[83] Bárbara Pérez and her neighbors had, in effect, reinvented that classic symbol of working-class Cuban political consciousness, the *lector* (reader). But instead of a male tobacco worker paid to read to his companions while they worked, this was a *lectora*, a laundress whose direct access to the news made her the central figure in a set of everyday interactions among her neighbors.[84]

In the city of Cienfuegos, this was also a time of formal revindications and collective action. Port workers went on strike in 1899 and obtained a fifty-cent wage increase. On February 19, 1900, the lightermen struck again and were joined by a "sympathetic strike of stevedores, wharfmen, freight handlers on the railroad, cartmen, and etc.," paralyzing business. The union membership and leadership included many workers categorized as black and mulatto.[85] The U.S. occupation forces attempted to set limits to this kind of action. In this instance, the mayor and the leader of the union were promptly "bounced" out of office by General Leonard Wood.[86] But this barely slowed the process of mobilization.

On the larger question of suffrage, the occupation government found itself obliged to back down. Hoping to place power in the hands of the better sort of people, the military government initially imposed property and literacy restrictions that might minimize the voting strength of lower-class Cubans, particularly people of color. Such restrictions, however, flew squarely in the face of the patriotic vision of the liberation army as the force that had won Cuba's freedom from Spain and thus a right to political voice. The occupation government next incorporated a "soldier clause," permitting those who had served in the army to vote. In 1902, when the United States relinquished power and conceded formal sovereignty to the government of Tomás Estrada Palma, the new Cuban constitution went the rest of the way and provided for universal manhood suffrage.[87]

Rural residents of Cienfuegos continued to organize, both in political parties and in unions. In November 1902, "commissions" of workers marched from the town of Cruces to nearby sugar estates to try to obtain the suspension of work in solidarity with strikers in Havana. The U.S. consul at Cienfuegos reported that work had stopped in the municipalities of Lajas and Cruces, including the plantations of Caracas, San Agustín, San Francisco, Andreita, Dos Hermanas, and others. The men in charge of Hormiguero claimed that they "have been threatened by colored men to stop work and laborers have quit work through fear."[88] Anarchists as well as veterans of the Ejército Libertador, including the mulatto officer Evaristo Landa, were conspicuous in these organizing efforts, which encompassed workers from multiple national and racial groups.[89]

The extended suffrage of the early Republic nourished a vigorous local politics, albeit one marked by the proliferation of patron-client relations and corruption. The charismatic Liberal Party leader José Miguel Gómez adroitly sustained linkages of loyalty with former officers and enlisted men from his region. When, in 1906, the Estrada Palma government discredited itself through corrupt manipulation of the electoral law, the Liberal Party rebelled, mounting a military challenge to Estrada Palma's effort to ensure reelection. Loyalties forged during 1895–98 were invoked, and many black and mulatto Cubans became both soldiers and officers in the rebellious Liberal army.[90]

The manifest incapacity of the Estrada Palma government to contain the rebellion brought a reluctant United States back into Cuba in 1906, determined once again to try to create structures of continuity and authority that would protect its interests. A provisional government was set up, and Cienfuegos once again found itself occupied by the U.S. military. Bárbara Pérez, who had done laundry for the Spanish forces in Arimao, would now wash uniforms for the Americans at Soledad.[91]

The occupation forces seemed ill at ease this time. In 1907 the military information officer responsible for Cruces reported that the people of Cruces were "unfriendly toward the Americans." Although some members of the elite welcomed the occupiers, the Military Intelligence Division of the Army of Cuban Pacification could not fail to note that they were surrounded by veterans of the independence struggle, the 1902 strikes, and the 1906 revolution.[92] Even apparently reliable workmen and labor contractors might turn out to have alarming *antecedentes*. One local leader on the Constancia estate was described as follows: "Nicolás Fernández. Black or dark mulatto. Aged about 35. Speaks only Spanish. Soldier in War of 1895–98. Joined insurrection of 1906 as Captain and had company of about 80 blacks, all mounted and said to have been well drilled and under good discipline. Appears to be a strong character. Employed as overseer at Horquita because he has great influence over the negroes and has brought them there to cut cane."[93]

Here, then, was a man with authority over an impressive body of "negroes who have horses," to use the phrase of the Soledad administrator who twenty years earlier had tried to rid his estate of such mobile and assertive workmen.

Automatic deference, one assumes, was not to be expected from Nicolás Fernández.

Some veterans of the 1906 Liberal uprising remained in the hills after formal pacification and the arrival of the U.S. military. One official of the occupation forces reported that "when we first located in Santa Clara in October last, members of detachments of these negroes of the mountain came to camp, some of them remaining all day, in uniform, watching the movements of camp."[94] Each group may have been assessing, uneasily, the strength of the other and wondering how long they would stay.

In Arimao, former slaves from Santa Rosalía and their descendants again emerged as combative figures. Fermín Quesada had appeared on the estate's slave list of 1880 as a seven-year-old. By 1907 he was described by a hostile intelligence officer of the Fifteenth U.S. Cavalry in the following terms: "Quesada, Fermín. Negro. Liberal. Age: About 35 years. A farmer by occupation. Lives near Arimao, Cienfuegos district. Served in the Cuban Army during the 95–98 war reaching the grade of sergeant. Was a soldier in the insurgent ranks during the recent disturbance. Has a very bad reputation. Is said to be a cattle thief operating in the vicinity of Arimao and La Sierra. Is controlled by General Esquerra. Has but little influence, and that among the negro farmers in the country. Is considered a dangerous man in case of trouble."[95]

In addition to enumerating the "dangerous men" in their neighborhood, intelligence officers also filed alarmed reports of contentious gatherings of various kinds. Some of these gatherings reflected party rivalries between Liberals and Conservatives, but others were provoked by conflict over such issues as the presence of U.S. troops or the legality of cockfighting. Observers often noted that the gatherings included blacks, whites, and mulattos.[96]

The Politics of Leadership and Voice

Cuban politics, like Brazilian politics in a comparable period, can accurately be characterized as clientelistic. Its patterns of patronage bear considerable resemblance to familiar forms of Latin American *caciquismo*. But there is a distinctive feature: beginning in 1902 Cuba's electoral system functioned with universal male suffrage in the midst of a politicized population, many of whose poorest members had recently participated in an armed struggle. This was an electoral system in which the construction of alliances involved acknowledging numerous midlevel leaders drawn from among black and mulatto veterans. In the small towns of central Cuba there were mulatto mayors as well as mulatto and black police chiefs and policemen. Overall, men of color made up more than 20 percent of the soldiers and policemen in the province of Santa Clara—not a proportional representation, but a visible armed presence as part of civil authority in the countryside.[97]

Black and mulatto leadership was exercised in the countryside in communities identified as predominantly black, such as Congojas and Parque Alto. It emerged in the cane fields and on the docks as part of the working-class movement. It was demonstrated in the towns at the intermediate levels of the system of clientelism. Some of these leaders suspected, on good grounds, that the most powerful members of the existing parties would not permit them to rise beyond a certain point, and a few undertook to organize an "agrupación de color" that could defend their interests.[98] Over the next few years, the national counterpart of this "agrupación" would give rise to the Partido Independiente de Color, which met with fierce repression.[99] The emergence of an "independent party of color," however, was but one of several forms of assertion and organization at the local as well as the national level.[100]

Certain features of turn-of-the-century Cienfuegos seem to have converged to make possible such vigorous contests over voice and space, along with associated claims to various kinds of rights. First, an expanding and multiracial rural workforce, marked by mobility and a certain fluidity of roles, underlay the multiracial organizing that occurred in the war of 1895–98, in the strikes of 1899–1902, and in the intermittent protest of 1906–9. Second, a recent and powerful experience of armed conflict, in which black and mulatto officers often assumed command over troops from all socioracial groups, provided experienced leaders and multiple patterns of leadership. Third, the wartime ideal of transracial national identity and citizenship, however often violated in practice, constituted a powerful ideological framework within which to claim rights to political voice and representation.[101]

These circumstances permitted a struggle for expanded citizenship to emerge; they by no means guaranteed that it would be successful. Recognizing the dimensions of that struggle, however, may help us to situate Cuba's history among other postemancipation experiences. In this light, the multiracial organizing that characterized the Cuban war of 1895–98 may usefully be compared to the parallel experiment in interracial democracy carried out during Reconstruction in the United States and to the mobilizations in the cane fields of Louisiana that outlived Reconstruction itself. The fracturing of lines of authority on Cuban sugar plantations may also be contrasted to the relative continuity of authority on sugar plantations in the Brazilian northeast, although the settlement of families with the surnames Quesada, Pérez, and Sarría behind the Soledad mill, in the community of El Palmar, echoes the fragile but decisive access of some former slaves in the Brazilian northeast to a *roça* (plot of land) inside or outside the sugar plantation.[102]

Victor Clark's impressions of democracy and social equality in Cuba, with which we began, may by now make a certain amount of sense. Ciriaco Quesada's demand that Manuel Blanco, a wealthy merchant and former president of the Casino Español de Cienfuegos, defer to him in the matter of a mule was issued forcefully and with immediate and successful recourse to the civil authorities. This was precisely the sort of act that might cause a North American to marvel that "nowhere else does the least-considered member of a community aspire with more serene confidence to social equality with its most exalted personage." Though their assertions could not suffice to make Cuba a fully democratic polity, rural former slaves like Ciriaco Quesada and his neighbor Bárbara Pérez exercised rights of public voice in a context in which the concept of citizenship was widely available and vigorously debated. We need not assume that when Cubans chose to address or refer to each other as ciudadanos they used this term with precisely the presumptions attached to it by those who spoke it at other times or in other languages. Citizenship, like freedom itself, could be built up from the ground, even as occupiers and legislators debated its meanings from above.

Notes

I would like to thank Jeremy Adelman, Alejandra Bronfman, Sueann Caulfield, Fernando Coronil, Ada Ferrer, Alejandro de la Fuente, Richard Graham, Josep María Fradera, Orlando García Martínez, Sarah Hirschman, Irán Millán Cuétara, Sidney Mintz, Louis A. Pérez Jr., Javier Pérez Royo, Lara Putnam, Peter Railton, Leslie Rowland, David Sartorius, Stanley Stein, and Michael Zeuske for ongoing discussions of the questions raised in this essay and for their generous sharing of editorial comments and unpublished work. I would also like to thank Leonardo Alomá, Leopoldo Beltrán, Sebastián Asla Cires, Daniel Ponvert, Domingo Cruz Díaz, Modesto Hernández, José M. Iznaga, Santiago Pelayo Díaz, Blas Pelayo Díaz, Tomás Pérez y Pérez, Araceli Quesada y Quesada, Caridad Quesada, Félix Tellería, and Fermín Tellería for oral historical testimony on life in the Cienfuegos region, and Aims McGuinness, Larry Gutman, and Jeffrey Voris for assistance with photocopying and data analysis. Special thanks are due to Orlando García Martínez and the staff of the Archivo Provincial de Cienfuegos; to Peter Drummey and the staff of the Massachusetts Historical Society; to Mayra Mena, Marlene Ortega, Jorge Macle, and the staff of the Archivo Nacional de Cuba; and to Araceli García Carranza and the staff of the Colección Cubana of the Biblioteca Nacional de Cuba.

1. Clark, "Labor Conditions in Cuba," 780. Victor Seldon Clark (1868–1946) wrote for the Labor Department in the early twentieth century and later for the Carnegie Institution and the Brookings Institution.

2. An early draft of this essay was prepared for the conference "Empire and Underdevelopment: The Colonial Heritage of Latin America Revisited," in honor of Stanley and Barbara Stein, Princeton University, December 2, 1995. The current text forms part of the larger project that later yielded the book *Degrees of Freedom*. It first appeared in the *Hispanic American Historical Review* 78 (November 1998) and is reproduced here with some bibliographical and stylistic revisions.

3. For an emphatic early statement, see Stein and Stein, *The Colonial Heritage of Latin America*, esp. 174–85.

4. Stein, *Vassouras*, xi–xviii, 160. See also Tannenbaum, *Slave and Citizen*, esp. 88–92.

5. See, among other works, Viotti da Costa, *Da Monarquia à República*. Graham, in *Patronage and Politics in Nineteenth-Century Brazil*, provides a subtle portrait of relations of clientelism and emphasizes their implicit reciprocities. A compelling picture of social relations in the sugar regions in the twentieth century, but one that presumes rather than demonstrates the historical roots of dependency, is García, *Libres et assujettis*. Fraga Filho, *Encruzilhadas da Liberdade*, provides an analysis of the historical continuities, discontinuities, and challenges to patriarchal control at the local level.

6. See Reis, *Slave Rebellion in Brazil*, 39, for an incident in 1831. See also Mattos de Castro, "El color inexistente," on the apparent use of the term *cidadão* by rural former slaves to refer to themselves. She develops the evidence further in *Das cores do silêncio*, chaps. 15–18.

7. See Graham, *Patronage and Politics*, chap. 7.

8. I do not presume to engage here the vast literature on the meanings of the term *citizenship*, its presumed Enlightenment and French Revolutionary roots, or its continuing traps and snares. I simply aim to denote a set of practices of political voice that were at times accompanied by a self-conscious invocation of rights possessed as a member of the nation, or earned through service to the nation, or claimed in explicit terms of *ciudadanía*. On the larger concept of voice, see Hirschman, *Exit, Voice, and Loyalty*, esp. chap. 3, and Hirschman, *A Propensity to Self-Subversion*, chap. 1. On citizenship, see Cooper, Holt, and Scott, *Beyond Slavery*.

9. The best published overviews of the early development of Cienfuegos are García Martínez, "Estudio de la economía cienfueguera desde la fundación de la colonia Fernandina de Jagua hasta mediados del siglo XIX," and the discussion on pp. 103–21 of Bergad, Iglesias García, and Barcia, *The Cuban Slave Market, 1790–1880*.

10. For the purposes of continuity in discussion, I am using "the Cienfuegos region" to refer to the extended agricultural zone around the bay of Cienfuegos, conforming in its general lines to the "judicial district" of Cienfuegos as defined in the 1877–78 agricultural census. By 1906 the judicial district of Cienfuegos had been expanded and redivided into five municipalities: Cienfuegos, Rodas, Palmira, Cruces, and Santa Isabel de las Lajas. (The *partido* of Rodas encompassed part of the old Cartagena, Palmira encompassed parts of Las Casas, and Cruces incorporated parts of the old Camarones.) See "Memorandum for Intelligence Officers," United States National Archives, Record Group 395, Records of the United States Army Overseas Operations and Commands,

1898–1942, Series 1008, Army of Cuban Pacification, General Correspondence of the Military Intelligence Division (hereafter USNA, RG 395, ACP, series 1008), file 71, item 2. See also the appendix titled "Nombres antiguos y modernos de los centrales azucareros de Cuba," in Rojas, *Las luchas obreras en el central "Tacajo,"* as well as Gobierno Civil de Santa Clara, *Memoria: Año 1901* (Villaclara, 1902), table "Ingenios que muelen en esta provincia en la Zafra de 1901 a 1902."

11. Quite a few owners, however, filed no returns, and the categories themselves are ambiguous. See "Noticia de las fincas azucareras en producción que existían en toda la isla de Cuba al comenzar el presupuesto de 1877–78," *Revista Económica* (Havana), June 7, 1878, 7–24. The counts of "free and rented workers" (1,526) and Chinese laborers (380) seem particularly unreliable.

12. For evidence of the disruption of order on estates, see the correspondence concerning the Santa Rosalía ingenio in January 1877 in "Cartas diversas dirigidas en su mayoría a Manuel Blanco," Biblioteca Nacional de Cuba, Colección Cubana, Colección Manuscrita Julio Lobo (hereafter BNC, CC, CMJL), no. 46.

13. On the use of the term *ciudadano*, see Ferrer, *Insurgent Cuba*, chap. 1. On slavery and the insurgency, see Scott, *Slave Emancipation in Cuba*, chap. 2.

14. See Rosendo Gutiérrez to D. José M. Pérez, July 25, 1879, in "Cartas de varias personas dirigidas a Manuel Blanco propietario del ingenio Santa Rosalía," BNC, CC, CMJL, no. 9A. The text reads: "en esta se corre la noticia que esta noche o mañana se ban a alzar con las dotaciones de los ingenios los vecinos de esta Jurisdiccion."

15. Scott, *Slave Emancipation*, chaps. 6–8. Figures for Santa Clara are on p. 194.

16. These patterns are reflected in the correspondence between the administrator and the owner of the Soledad plantation, located east of the bay of Cienfuegos. See the letters of J. S. Murray to E. F. Atkins and Co., Massachusetts Historical Society, Boston, Atkins Family Papers, Atkins-Soledad Letters (hereafter MHS, AFP, ASL). On Spanish immigration, see Maluquer de Motes, *Nación e inmigración*.

17. See Edo, *Memoria histórica de Cienfuegos y su jurisdicción*, 663, and Iglesias García, "La concentración azucarera y la comarca de Cienfuegos." See also García Martínez and Millán Cuétara, "Testimonios del quehacer constructivo en la industria azucarera cienfueguera."

18. "Construcción de un ferrocarril para el servicio particular del Ingenio Cieneguita . . . 1890," Archivo Histórico Nacional, Madrid, Sección de Ultramar (hereafter AHN, Ultramar), leg. 201, exp. 5. Iglesias García portrays the Cienfuegos region as a pioneer in la centralization of sugar processing. Iglesias, "Concentración azucarera."

19. For a powerful analysis of this phenomenon in South Carolina, see Saville, *The Work of Reconstruction*. On the sugar regions of Louisiana, see Rodrigue, *Reconstruction in the Cane Fields*; Eiss, "A Share in the Land"; and Scott, "'Stubborn and Disposed to Stand Their Ground,'" 103–26.

20. See Rebello, *Estados relativos a la producción azucarera de la Isla de Cuba*, 14, and "Noticia de las fincas azucareras . . . 1877–78."

21. See "Listas de la dotación del ingenio Santa Rosalía, 1879–1887," BNC, CC, CMJL, no. 173.

22. See "Libro mayor no. 3 perteneciente al ingenio Sta Rosalía propiedad de Dn. Manuel Blanco y Ramos," Archivo Provincial de Cienfuegos (hereafter APC).

23. Atkins, a Unitarian from Boston, refrained from acknowledging that he had become an owner of patrocinados, though one can infer their presence from earlier records of the estate and subsequent correspondence from the manager. In 1877 Soledad had held about 180 slaves. See "Noticia de las fincas azucareras . . . 1877–78." In a letter from J. S. Murray to E. F. Atkins, May 24, 1886, the manager refers to "the fiew [sic] patrocinados that remain." See MHS, AFP, ASL box 2.

24. See Atkins, *Sixty Years in Cuba*, 108–10. There are also many manuscript sources for the study of Soledad, including the testimony in Case 387 of the U.S./Spain Treaty Claims Commission, United States National Archives, Washington, D.C., Record Group 76 (hereafter USNA, RG 76, Treaty Claims); the papers of Soledad in the Fondo ICEA of the Archivo Nacional de Cuba, Havana (hereafter ANC, ICEA); the records in the Archivo Provincial de Cienfuegos, Cienfuegos, Cuba; and the Atkins Family Papers in the Massachusetts Historical Society. I am particularly grateful to Leonardo Alomá of Pepito Tey (formerly Soledad), to Modesto Hernández of Santa Rosalía, and to Tomás Pérez y Pérez of Cienfuegos, for sharing information about the estate. For a detailed case study of the Arimao and Caunao valleys and working conditions on the estates, see Scott, "Reclaiming Gregoria's Mule."

25. Interview with Tomás Pérez y Pérez, Cienfuegos, March 1998. On Santa Rosalía, see also "Libro no. 1 de los negros" and "Libro mayor no. 3," APC. On Soledad, see J. S. Murray to E. F. Atkins, May 24, 1886, MHS, AFP, ASL box 2; and Scott, "Reclaiming Gregoria's Mule." Murray seems to have planned to take the workmen back if they got rid of their horses.

26. J. S. Murray to E. F. Atkins, March 9, 1886, MHS, AFP, ASL, box 1.

27. In the "Libro mayor no. 3 perteneciente al ingenio Sta Rosalía," APC, pp. 103–10, one can see the pattern of employment of women workers with the surnames Quesada, Zulueta, and Argudín for the months of January, February, March, April, and sometimes into May or June, of 1892 and 1893. I have found no evidence of women other than former slaves and their descendants working in the cane on Santa Rosalía.

28. See deposition of Elias Ponvert, beginning January 25, 1904, USNA, RG 76, Treaty Claims, claim 293 (Hormiguero), pt. 1.

29. On the relationship between colonos and estate owners, see Dye, *Cuban Sugar in the Age of Mass Production*, chap. 6.

30. J. S. Murray to E. F. Atkins, May 14, 1884, MHS, AFP, ASL, box 1.

31. Juan Bautista Jiménez, *Los esclavos blancos por un colono de Las Villas*.

32. See the "Listas cobratorias de los recibos de fincas rústicas," Archivo Nacional de Cuba, Havana, Miscelánea de Expedientes, leg. 1431, exp. BH; leg. 872, exp. B; and leg. 1370, exp. X.

33. Atkins, *Sixty Years*, 45, 97.

34. See deposition of Edwin F. Atkins, USNA, RG 76, Treaty Claims, claim 387 (Atkins), pt. 1, p. 90.

35. See the pay lists for 1890 and 1891 in ANC, ICEA, Soledad, libro 707. Tomás Pérez

y Pérez was interviewed in Cienfuegos in March 1998 at the age of ninety-six. Manuel Moreno Fraginals, in personal communications in the 1970s, first called my attention to this kind of racial exclusion within plantations. Published accounts and testimony by E. Atkins and L. F. Hughes were so discreet as initially to obscure the phenomenon at Soledad. My later research in the unpublished Atkins papers, however, supports Moreno's general observations about the mill workforce, though it is clear that the field workforce remained quite heterogeneous. Cf. Scott, *Slave Emancipation*, 232–33.

36. On the unhealthy conditions of the barracks, see P. M. Beal to E. F. Atkins, July 23, 1887, ANC, ICEA, Soledad, libro 974. On smallpox, see J. N. S. Williams to Edwin Atkins, February 24, 1896, USNA, RG 76, Treaty Claims, claim 387 (Atkins), pt. 1. On the presence of former slaves from Santa Rosalía in El Palmar, see the letters of Constantino Pérez to Manuel García Blanco, 1899, in Correspondencia, Santa Rosalía, in the private collection of Orlando García Martínez (hereafter OGM, CSR). Manuel Lago built a house at El Palmar, and Bárbara Pérez had moved there from Arimao by 1902, when she gave birth to Tomás Pérez. Tomás Pérez recalls that residents of El Palmar entered each other's houses freely and that color differences were no barrier to neighborliness. Interview with Tomás Pérez y Pérez, March 1998.

37. Spain, Ministerio de Ultramar, *Spanish Rule in Cuba*, 20–22. On electoral reform, see Roldán de Montaud, "Cuba entre Romero Robledo y Maura (1891–1894)."

38. A key source on organizations in the city of Cienfuegos, and in towns such as Lajas and Cruces, is the Fondo Registro de Asociaciones, held in the Archivo Provincial de Cienfuegos.

39. For discussions of the Autonomists and Cuban politics during this period, see Thomas, *Cuba: The Pursuit of Freedom*, 268, 300–304; Roldán de Montaud, "Cuba"; and Casanovas Codina, "El movimiento obrero y la política colonial española en la Cuba de finales del XIX."

40. See the accounts in "Reunión autonomista en Cienfuegos, 1886," AHN, Ultramar, leg. 4896, pt. 1, exp. 174. I am very grateful to Ada Ferrer for sharing with me her transcription of portions of this file.

41. On the complicated question of the relationship between vote and voice, see Barkley Brown, "Negotiating and Transforming the Public Sphere."

42. "Reunión autonomista en Cienfuegos, 1886," AHN, Ultramar, leg. 4896, pt. 1, exp. 174.

43. This phenomenon was even more apparent in the eastern province of Santiago de Cuba. In August 1893, a proposal for colonial reform was on the table in Spain, and Autonomists and other reformers in the region of Holguín tried to rally support for it. An estimated three thousand men on foot and on horseback gathered to protest the naming of a new mayor known to be opposed to reforms. The organizers protested that official repression had prevented additional supporters located in the countryside from attending. See the telegrams of August 1893 from Holguín, collected in AHN, Ultramar, leg. 3899, pt. 1.

44. I am grateful to Alejandra Bronfman for sharing her transcription of the correspondence from Gabriel Quesada to Juan Gualberto Gómez, found in ANC, Fondo

Adquisiciones, caja 40, no. 3103. Gabriel Quesada's role in the Sociedad Minerva was conveyed to me by Santiago Pelayo in a personal communication in March 1998. On the colonial government's stance on integration, see Scott, *Slave Emancipation*, 272–75.

45. See the accounts in newspaper clippings from *El Día, Diario Nuevo, La Verdad, La Evolución*, and *Las Villas*, January 5, 1894, in Fundación Antonio Maura, Madrid, leg. 358, carp. 14. I am very grateful to Ada Ferrer for sharing her photocopies of these clippings.

46. Pérez, *Cuba between Empires*, 31.

47. Atkins, *Sixty Years*, 152–54. It is not clear whether the strikes to which Atkins refers extended beyond the cooks, whose work stoppage he mentions.

48. On the long-standing militarized character of Spanish rule, see Fradera, "Quiebra imperial y reorganización política en las Antillas españolas, 1810–1868."

49. See the *Revista de Agricultura* (Havana), special number, 1894.

50. He and a group of companions quickly joined up with the forces of Guillermo Moncada. Following Moncada's death, command of the group was taken over by Garzón and then by Antonio Maceo. Sánchez served as a second lieutenant on Maceo's staff until September 1895. See depositions of Lino Sánchez, January 27 and 29, 1909, USNA, RG 76, Treaty Claims, claim 475 (Whiting), pt. 2.

51. Deposition of Lorenzo Gonzalez, February 9, 1909, USNA, RG 76, Treaty Claims, claim 475 (Whiting), pt. 2.

52. See the file of Gaspar Caballero, ANC, Fondo Ejército Libertador, 1-2-38 Rechazado.

53. See Maceo, *Antonio Maceo*, 2: 31–33.

54. Atkins, *Sixty Years*, chap. 12.

55. This expedition was under the command of Generals Carlos Roloff, Serafín Sánchez, and José María Rodríguez. See Pérez, *Cuba between Empires*, 45.

56. Atkins, *Sixty Years*, chap. 12; quotation is from p. 162. On the recruitment to the Ejército Libertador of former slaves from Soledad and Santa Rosalía, see Scott, "Reclaiming Gregoria's Mule."

57. See "Documentos relativos a la inspección general del ejército: Expediente que contiene la relación de jefes, oficiales, clases y soldados y el estado de las armas y animales de la brigada de Cienfuegos," November 27, 1896, Archivo Provincial de Santa Clara, Cuba, Colección de Documentos del Ejército Libertador Cubano (hereafter APSC, EL), exp. 60, inventario 1. I am grateful to Michael Zeuske and Orlando García for sharing their photocopies of these documents.

58. Maceo is quoted in Miró Argenter, *Cuba: Crónicas de la guerra*, 1: 170. For a discussion of the invasion westward, see chap. 7 of Ferrer, *Insurgent Cuba*.

59. For a careful analysis of the war in the Cienfuegos region, see García Martínez, "La Brigada de Cienfuegos." The view from the administration at Soledad appears in Atkins, *Sixty Years*, 162–67.

60. See Pérez, *Cuba between Empires*, 50, 52. A classic account of the battle of Mal Tiempo is to be found in Miró Argenter, *Cuba: Crónicas de la guerra*, 1: chaps. 18, 19.

61. Scholars have differed on the question of the degree of commitment of the Cuban

rebel leadership to racial equality and on the relationship between verbal commitment and daily practice. See, for example, the contrasting perspectives of Ibarra Cuesta, *Ideología mambisa*, and Helg, *Our Rightful Share*. Ada Ferrer's *Insurgent Cuba* represents a major breakthrough in this debate. By reading insurgent texts and practices with close attention to nuance, distinguishing among different voices and moments in the development of the rebellion, and tracking the reception and resonance of distinct elements in rebel discourse, she is able to portray a movement that contained elements of racism and antiracism and an ideology that was both liberating and confining. See also Fuente, *A Nation for All*.

62. One Canary Islander who managed cane farms on Hormiguero ended up giving information to a friend who was an insurgent; the Spanish soldiers, by contrast, were strangers to him, and he did not speak with them. Deposition of Emiliano Silva y Placeres, beginning February 15, 1904, USNA, RG 76, Treaty Claims, claim 293 (Hormiguero), pt. 3.

63. He ended up spending much of the war in a *reconcentración* village at Hormiguero. Deposition of Miguel Angel Abad, USNA, RG 76, Treaty Claims, claim 293 (Hormiguero), pt. 1.

64. Atkins, *Sixty Years*, 192, 196. See also the Atkins depositions in his claim before the Treaty Claims hearings, cited in n34.

65. Atkins, *Sixty Years*, 196. For a discussion of Quintín Bandera and the controversies that swirled around him, see Ada Ferrer's examination of his court-martial in "Rustic Men, Civilized Nation."

66. See García Martínez, "Brigada de Cienfuegos," and Zeuske, "Movilización afrocubana y clientelas en un hinterland cubano." See also Zeuske, "Die diskrete Macht der Sklaven." Wartime conditions on Soledad are reflected in the correspondence of Edwin Atkins, MHS, AFP.

67. On the differing visions of a free Cuba, see Ferrer, *Insurgent Cuba*.

68. In 1994, the distinguished Cuban historian Pedro Deschamps Chapeaux suggested that José de Jesús Monteagudo was perceived by some as a mulatto and that aspect of his conduct should be understood in the light of his desire to make himself acceptable to the white elite. I have been unable, however, to confirm this hypothesis. Pedro Deschamps Chapeaux, personal communication, spring 1994.

69. The analysis of racial categories using lists of members of the Ejército Libertador is fraught with difficulties. First there is the obvious constraint that "racial" categories are social constructs, capable of shifting with time and context and not necessarily discernible or interpretable through memoirs, photographs, and biographies. Second is the silence in most of the historiography on this subject—a silence now being broken by the pioneering work of Ada Ferrer, Orlando García Martínez, Michael Zeuske, and others. I am indebted to several colleagues for their assistance in my effort to understand the racial composition of the Ejército Libertador, including Francisco Gómez Balboa of the Fuerzas Armadas Revolucionarias and Pedro Deschamps Chapeaux, who shortly before his death shared with me his thoughts on 1912 and the complexities of racial identity. I have also used, with caution, some of the holdings of the Fototeca in

the Archivo Nacional de Cuba, particularly reg. 104, sobre 100, caja M-11; reg. 105, sobre 101, caja M-11 (H. Esquerra and others); and reg. 102, sobre 98, caja M-11 (General José Monteagudo and others). See García Martínez, "Brigada de Cienfuegos," and Zeuske, "Movilización afrocubana," for careful analyses of the changes in the composition of the insurgent forces from 1895 to 1898.

70. See the records of Company 3, Second Division, Fourth Corps, in "Documentos relativos... Brigada de Cienfuegos," November 27, 1896, APSC, EL, exp. 60, inventario 1.

71. See Ferrer, *Insurgent Cuba*, and Helg, *Our Rightful Share*.

72. See Helg, *Our Rightful Share*, chap. 1. For a study of this activist movement, see Hevia Lanier, *El directorio central de las sociedades negras de Cuba, 1886–1894*.

73. See *Suplemento al Boletín Oficial de la Provincia de Santa Clara*, no. 63, March 15, 1898, Provincia de Santa Clara. I am very grateful to Michael Zeuske and Larry Gutman for their collaboration in the filming and printing of these lists, the originals of which are in the Archivo Nacional de Cuba. On the Autonomist government, see Mena Múgica and Hernández Vicente, *Fuentes documentales de la administración española en el Archivo Nacional de Cuba*.

74. The question of the state of the countryside in early 1898 is a complex one, and it is difficult to establish with any certainty the physical conditions and popular expectations prevalent in Cienfuegos during the months prior to U.S. intervention. I thank Louis A. Pérez Jr. for alerting me to the possibility that 1898 may in fact have brought elements of de facto peace to the countryside, as the area of rebel control expanded, and that most participants expected the rebels' summer campaign to be successful. Louis A. Pérez, personal communication, April 8, 1997. See also Pérez's very provocative essay, "Approaching Martí: Text and Context." The research of Orlando García Martínez suggests that there was a last-minute wave of recruitment to the rebel forces in Cienfuegos in the summer of 1898, which suggests a high expectation of victory. See García Martínez, "Brigada de Cienfuegos."

75. Quoted in Pérez, *Cuba between Empires*, 218.

76. There is, of course, an immense monographic literature on this subject. Foner, *Reconstruction: America's Unfinished Revolution*, provides a magisterial overview. For a penetrating general interpretation, see Berlin et al., *Slaves No More*.

77. The classic work on the occupation is Pérez, *Cuba between Empires*.

78. Atkins describes both the gathering at Cienfuegos and a similar gathering further up the railway line. Atkins, *Sixty Years*, 300–301.

79. Caridad Quesada, born in 1921, whose mother, María Cirila Quesada, grew up on Santa Rosalía, spoke of expulsions in an interview in March 1998. Her recollection of the family history as she was told it seems consistent with the 1899 correspondence of the administrator, Constantino Pérez, located in OGM, CSR. On the protection of the estate during the 1895–98 war, see also Sartorius, "Conucos y subsistencia."

80. The 1880s lists of *libertos* and patrocinados for Santa Rosalía include Francisca, criolla, in her fifties; Ciriaco, age eighteen in 1880; Paulino; and two Gregorias, one of them age twenty in 1883. In 1889, Ciriaco Quesada appears as a worker on the estate, as

do Paulino Quesada and Antonico Apezteguía. See "Listas de la dotación del ingenio Santa Rosalía, 1879–1887," BNC, CC, CML, no. 173; and "Individuos y los días que tienen trabajados en el transcurso del presente mes de Octubre del 1889," as well as a similar document for April 1889, BNC, CC, CML, vol. 1, no. 159. The incidents surrounding Gregoria's mule are recounted in the letters of Constantino Pérez to Manuel García Blanco, August 17, 18, and 19, 1899, OGM, CSR. A detailed discussion of the event and the evidence appears in Scott, "Reclaiming Gregoria's Mule." I am grateful to Orlando García Martínez, who located a land purchase by Gregoria Quesada in the notarial records.

81. See the correspondence of Constantino Pérez and Manuel García Blanco for August through December 1899, esp. the letter of December 27, 1899, OGM, CSR.

82. *Suplemento al Boletín Oficial de la Provincia de Santa Clara*, no. 63, Provincia de Santa Clara, March 15, 1898, Barrio de Arimao, sección única con La Sierra.

83. The details of these episodes are from an interview with Tomás Pérez y Pérez, Cienfuegos, March 1998.

84. On the institution of the lector, see Pérez, "Reminiscences of a *Lector*"; Ortiz, *Cuban Counterpoint*, 89–90; and Stubbs, *Tobacco on the Periphery*, chap. 10.

85. See Edwin Atkins to Gen. Leonard Wood, February 21, 1900, in USNA, RG 140, entry 3, file 1900, 504. Participants included 250 lightermen, 200 stevedores, 110 longshoremen, and 75 cartmen. See also Major Bowman to Adjutant, Rowell Barracks, Pasa Caballos, March 9, 1900, in the same file.

86. See the sources cited above on the strike and particularly Atkins's opinion, in Atkins, *Sixty Years*, 315–16. These events can also be traced in the manuscript "Actas Capitulares" of the city of Cienfuegos, APC.

87. See Pérez, *Cuba between Empires*, chap. 16. For a discussion of questions of race, suffrage, and electoral politics, see Fuente, "Los mitos de la democracia racial."

88. For information on the strike, see the telegrams of Baehr to Squiers, November 29 and 30, 1902, and the draft dispatch of Squiers to Hays, December 2, 1902, in USNA, RG 59, Dispatches from U.S. Ministers to Cuba (available as microfilm publication T158, roll 4); the reports in the Spanish-language pages of *La Lucha* during the period November–December 1902; and the essay by Dumoulin, "El primer desarrollo del movimiento obrero y la formación del proletariado en el sector azucarero."

89. For a more detailed discussion of the strike, see Scott, "Raza, clase y acción colectiva en Cuba."

90. The importance of 1906 in reinforcing patterns of patronage, while facilitating advancement by black and mulatto Cubans, is clear in the profiles of local political leaders prepared by the Military Intelligence Division (sometimes referred to as the Military Information Division) of the Army of Cuban Pacification. For Cienfuegos, see USNA, RG 395, ACP, series 1008, file 79.

91. Interviews with Tomás Pérez y Pérez, 1998.

92. See Ross Rowell to Supervising Intelligence Officer, Cienfuegos, September 10, 1907, USNA, RG 395, ACP, series 1008, file 68, item 33. Jorge Ibarra has recently carried out a systematic analysis of the profiles of public figures in Santa Clara province com-

piled by the Military Intelligence Division. See his "Caciquismo, racismos y actitudes con relación al status político de la República."

93. Report no. 6, paragraph 14, 20 January 1907, Constancia, USNA, RG 395, ACP, series 1008, file 72, item 11.

94. See first endorsement on letter of Blanchester to Adjutant, Post of Santa Clara, January 19, 1907, USNA, RG 395, ACP, series 1008, file 46, item 51.

95. On Fermín Quesada, see the "Listas de la dotación del ingenio Santa Rosalía, 1879–1887," BNC, CC, CMJL, no. 173; and Report no. 95, April 13, 1907, USNA, RG 395, ACP, series 1008, file 79, item 107.

96. For a detailed discussion of this evidence, see Scott, "'The Lower Class of Whites' and 'the Negro Element.'"

97. In the category "policías y soldados," the 1907 census counted 1,130 native white men, 343 men of color, and 177 foreign white men in the province. See U.S. Census Department, *Censo de la República de Cuba . . . 1907*, 549. See also de la Fuente, "Mitos de la democracia racial."

98. For early evidence of initiatives aimed at forming an Afro-Cuban caucus or an incipient party, see Weekly Report of G. W. Kirkpatrick, September 28, 1907, Santa Clara, USNA, RG 395, ACP, series 1008, file 46, item 508. See also Confidential Report, October 4, 1908, Hormiguero, USNA, RG 395, ACP, series 1008, file 68, item 53.

99. See Helg, *Our Rightful Share*.

100. On the events of 1912 in Cienfuegos, see Bronfman, "Clientelismo y represión."

101. Other features of Cuba might be added to complement these preconditions, including the tradition of mutual aid organizations and a vigorous pursuit of educational opportunities by Afro-Cubans. Alejandro de la Fuente calls attention to the role of education in his article "Negros y electores."

102. On the strikes in the Louisiana cane fields in 1887, see Scott, "'Stubborn and Disposed to Stand Their Ground.'" The literature on smallholding and tenancy in Brazil is extensive. See the discussions and references in Schwartz, *Slaves, Peasants, and Rebels*; Barickman, *Bahian Counterpoint*; Scott, "Defining the Boundaries of Freedom in the World of Cane"; and Fraga, *Encruzilhadas*.

CHAPTER 4

Slaughterhouses and Milk Consumption in the "Sick Republic"
Socio-Environmental Change and Sanitary Technology in Havana, 1890–1925

Reinaldo Funes Monzote

"I think of our republic as a sick patient who has to be led by the hand along an endless path overlooking an abyss into which we might fall at the slightest inattention."
—MIGUEL DEL CARRIÓN, 1921

In August 1924, in its "Palpitations of National Life" section, the magazine *Cuba Contemporánea* dedicated one of its entries to the appearance of a serious epidemic of typhoid fever in Havana.[1] The heading, "The Sick Republic," was also the title of one of the permanent sections of the Havana medical journal *Vida Nueva* (*New Life*). The diagnosis in this particular case was that the Republic of Cuba, "mistreated by the ineptitude and avarice of its governors," displaying the general breakdown of its vital organs, had been seized by certain illnesses "whose destructive power was growing within the exhausted organs." Among the conjunctural causes cited were the economic crisis and a deficient official protection of sanitation. The latter was particularly evident in the contamination and insufficiency of drinking water in the capital that came from an aqueduct built originally for a population of 150,000 to 200,000 inhabitants that had now topped 400,000.[2]

While the allegory of the polity as sick organism was common in the Latin American social essay and novel of the era, its appearance in Cuba was surprising, contrasting as it did with two decades of positive evaluations of the island's progress in hygiene and public health starting with the first U.S. occupation.[3] Even during the national crisis years at the beginning of the 1920s there was no lack of voices extolling those advances in hygiene and health and noting how they differed from the state of things in other administrative domains. In 1923, discussing indicators of Cuba's regression since 1906, bibliographer and historian Carlos Trelles noted that there was "little to criticize" about the Department of Sanitation.[4] Whether to certify the decadence of the republic inaugurated in 1902 or to show one successful side of it, medico-sanitary activity and science in general became protagonists of the first order in narratives of the country's social transformation.

The birth of industrial society came with growing urbanization, which in turn demanded a search for solutions to serious sanitary problems that large cities created. Yet there are few works on the Cuban capital that emphasize the role of science and technology on the changes that took place between the last years of Spanish rule and the first decades of the republic.[5] Most of those that touch on the question focus on urban expansion, architecture, political conflict, and the lifestyles of distinct social sectors.[6] To use a current metaphor, we know more about the "software" than about the "hardware" of the transformations during this period, though of course any such separation is arbitrary, since both dimensions are reciprocally determining.[7]

Science and technology were vital in modifying living conditions in Havana in the late nineteenth and early twentieth centuries. We start by making reference to the general question of sanitation and public hygiene according to evaluations made by leading scientific actors of the day. Initially they emphasized the positive changes that were reflected in statistics on, for example, the reduction in mortality and the standard of living of the poorest social sectors. Nevertheless, in the 1920s new criticism emerged among scientists concerning the state of health and hygiene, and it became an important part of the enumeration of symptoms of republican decadence. The valuations using medical symptomatology to demonstrate the sickness of the republican organism centered principally on Havana, its sanitary regression seen as the most obvious symbol of a capital city that had been unable to maintain the "civilizing" impulse after the island acquired sovereignty. From this perspective, the degeneration was a consequence as much of biological and social heritage or the influence of climate as it was of political corruption, bad public administration, and control over national resources by foreign interests. It was frequently asserted that the colony remained alive in the republic—an analogy that was congruent with the evolutionary and social Darwinist conceptions of many scientists and other intellectuals.

Regardless of how the urban transformation of Havana was read at the beginning of the twentieth century, the replacement of animals by automotive vehicles and the simultaneous mechanization and industrialization of products of animal origin destined for public consumption played central roles. Science and technology were determinant in promoting and implanting practices and habits that came to symbolize the life of modern cities, marked by new urbanistic conceptions, the advance of electrification, improvements in the supply of water, and new means of transport and communication. What happened with slaughterhouses and milk consumption are excellent examples of socio-environmental change in modern societies.[8] The need to feed growing urban populations not connected to the direct production of food arose alongside greater productivity facilitated by mechanization as well as the greater need and ability to extend and perfect sanitary vigilance over growing consumption.

In this context, public administrators, physicians, and veterinarians pondered the public health and hygiene implications of slaughterhouses and dairies. Veterinarians in particular were members of a profession that began to have greater presence in Cuba starting with the founding in 1907 of the Free Veterinary School, which shortly afterward became part of the University of Havana.[9] As Stefania Gallini shows for the case of Colombia, the study of veterinarians proves to be fundamental to writing a cultural and environmental history of the production and consumption of meat—a criterion that could be equally well applied to diverse aspects related to milk.[10] Both issues are addressed in the following analysis of public debates on Cuban decadence and are shown to be indicators of the complexity of a society in motion and influenced by rapid transformations made possible by the application of techno-scientific innovations. While the discussion of meat and milk production coincided in some ways with the politicized narrative of the sick-to-healthy-to-sick republic, the chapter proposes that these were more concrete issues within the overall problematic of hygiene and health, in which objective transformations and their limits can be observed beside great discourses about the advancement and regress of the republic or conjunctural statistics. As one of the symbols of the lack of hygiene during the colonial period, slaughterhouse reform and the increase in consumption of sanitary milk became without a doubt emblems of a new era.

Hygienic Modern Capital

In the late nineteenth century, physicians and scientists exercised greater protagonism in their areas of expertise, in the capital as well as in other cities.

The Royal Academy of Medical, Physical, and Natural Sciences of Havana, founded in 1861, and other scientific societies created after 1879, took on the principal problems of health and hygiene that affected colonial society.[11] The most alarming issue was yellow fever. In 1893 the physician Diego Tamayo estimated that yellow fever had killed more than forty thousand in Havana over the previous thirty years, not to mention the great mortality from other diseases like tuberculosis, typhoid fever, diphtheria, enteritis, and tetanus. He also concluded that 60 percent of these deaths could have been prevented had it not been for a lack of urban planning, deficient drainage, the accumulation of waste, and the adulteration of food. Above all, though, was the lack of initiative to achieve change and the absence of "a general plan of sanitary reform that would tend to guarantee the health of the land in which we live."[12]

Tamayo was joined by others such as the engineer Herminio Leyva, who blamed the poor initiative and scarce resources of Havana's city authorities for problems like the presence of stables in populated areas, the state of the plazas near markets and slaughterhouses, the contamination of the harbor (a major cause of disease in the opinion of many sanitary experts of the day), and the "reckless, near criminal, lack of concern" about quarantine.[13] Spanish military doctors added their voice to the clamor over the capital's hygiene, including Cesáreo Fernández, who addressed the Royal Academy of Sciences in 1896 on the subject.[14] The growing number of medico-scientific journals became platforms for specialized debate, including *La Higiene*, the flagship journal of Havana's Society of Hygiene between 1891 and 1895.[15] These efforts, of course, have to be understood against the backdrop of the great advances in hygiene, medicine, science, and technology that characterized the second half of the nineteenth century in Europe and the United States. This was a context that promoted, for example, the creation in 1887 of the Histobacteriological and Anti-rabies Vaccine Institute of the *Crónica Médico-Quirúrgica de la Habana* at approximately the same time that the Pasteur Institute was established in Paris. The institute became a local reference point for complaints over sanitary deficiencies. In the opinion of creole *higienistas*, desires to reproduce such sanitary progress were blocked by the interference of the colonial authorities, adverse socioeconomic conditions, a lack of backing by wealthy creoles, and scarce general concern about hygiene. The outbreak of the 1895 war of independence and, after 1896, Spanish General Valeriano Weyler's military strategy of *Reconcentración* (forced removal of the rural population to urban concentration camps) caused mortality rates in Havana to soar from 32.4 per 1,000 in 1895 to 89.2 per 1,000 in 1898.[16]

U.S. military intervention came in the midst of this crisis. The hygiene and sanitary improvement work during the four years the island was occupied are considered one of the most successful facets of the intervention. Ever since the participation of a U.S. delegation in an 1879 study of Havana's yellow fever problem, U.S. sanitary experts had been convinced that the insalubrious nature of the port city was a major local and international public health concern. They outlined a number of necessary reforms, among them provision of safe drinking water to all social sectors, elimination of swamps, the replacement of existing sewerage with modern systems, widening and maintaining the cleanliness of streets, covering toilets, removing stables from the urban areas, cleaning up the harbor shore, and modifying the customs of the "lower orders." Many local sanitarians agreed, although some like Herminio Leyva were critical of proposals to tear down the majority of houses or widen the streets.[17]

True to form, one of the first measures of the U.S. military occupation government was to form a corps of medical inspectors, as well as clean streets and public places. Regulations were promulgated on quarantine, obligatory vaccination, immigration, prostitution, glanders, infectious diseases, slaughterhouses, markets, veterinary measures, pavement of the streets, construction of a seawall (the famous *malecón*), and provision of water. The assistance of the local medical community was key in making these initiatives work, and many of their representatives occupied high public posts. The most significant of these was Tamayo, who became minister of the interior.

The most notable breakthrough, of course, was the eradication of yellow fever, which the United States was able to achieve, after a number of fruitless initial attempts concentrating on disinfecting streets and water supplies, by applying the theory and method that the Cuban physician Carlos Finlay had been working with since 1881. Proof that a biological vector, the mosquito, was responsible for transmitting the disease meant that effective prophylactic measures could be carried out. General Leonard Wood, the U.S. military governor and a physician by training, maintained that "the confirmation of Finlay's doctrines is the greatest step taken in medical science since the discovery of the smallpox vaccine by Jenner and by itself makes the war with Spain worth it."[18] It has been proposed that the struggle against yellow fever in Havana gave birth to a colonial U.S. public health apparatus oriented to safeguarding its commercial interests, protecting its troops and labor force, and justifying domination.[19]

Sanitation became a kind of guarantee of the island's ability to acquire independent statehood. In fact, among the restrictions on national sovereignty codified in the Platt Amendment, appended to the Cuban constitution by fiat of the U.S. occupying power, was Article 5: "The government of Cuba will execute, and as far as necessary extend, the plans already devised or other plans to be mutually agreed upon, for the sanitation of the cities of the island, to the end that a recurrence of epidemic and infectious diseases may be prevented, thereby assuring protection to the people and commerce of Cuba, as well as to the commerce of the southern ports of the United States and the people residing therein." Failure to do so would be legal justification for further intervention by the United States, something that Cuban sanitary leaders were immediately attuned to. Juan Santos Fernández, in his capacity as president of the Academy of Sciences of Havana, referred to the obligation in the first session of the body that followed Cuban independence in May 1902, with Wood and the president-elect of Cuba, Tomás Estrada Palma, in the audience. "The exigencies of sanitation in the Island of Cuba are an issue of international interest and have to be placed above all political questions . . . because one would have to be blind not to comprehend that we will not have a *patria* if we do not maintain public health at the level established by the United States government during its military occupation, to the astonishment of locals and foreigners."[20]

The warning did not go unheard, if one is to judge by the progress in the area of public health over the following years. Of particular note were the sanitary ordinances; the improvement of the quarantine service; health inspection in the area of immigration; the building of leper asylums, sanitariums, and hospitals; and the laying of modern sewerage and paving of roads in Havana and other cities.[21] One striking event was the creation in 1909 of the Ministry of Health and Welfare, the first of its kind in the world.[22] The physician and public hygiene specialist Enrique Barnet reiterated before the academy in 1913 the favorable image of Cuba's sanitary state. In his judgment, as a small people spinning "like a satellite in the orbit of a star of the first magnitude," the republic could not tolerate "quarantinable diseases" that would compromise health in other territories. Fortunately, however, the situation in the island was so satisfactory that its mortality index placed it "beside the most privileged nations." In 1912 the country had 12.89 deaths per 1,000 inhabitants, and Havana 16.97, while in Washington the figure was 17.4 per 1,000. There was still work to be done on a number of fronts: alongside the usual suspects was a need to build sanitary housing for the lower classes as well as public bathing and washing facilities. Public parks were needed to serve as the city's "lungs." Once in place, according to Barnet, Havana would stand alongside the world's healthiest cities, "and its astonishing and rapid growth and spread, far from being a motive of sanitary alarm, will be more like those of a healthy and vigorous organism that is developing without setback or stumble." The same advances were being made in other areas of the island, thanks to the "centralization and nationalization of sanitary services."[23]

The Sick Republic

In the 1920s, in contrast to these optimistic appreciations and in keeping with a growing unease about "Cuban decadence," the republic's sanitary state also became the object of criticism.[24] The principal points of reference were increases in the general mortality rate and in the incidence of diseases that had seemed under control. In the case of Havana, the theme of the harbor came up again, with Antonio González Curquejo characterizing it in 1921 as "a petrie dish of pathological microbes, and because of its stink a true pigsty."[25] After praising the gains made during the U.S. intervention and the work of the Ministry of Health, he argued that since 1916 the country had "moved backward in hygiene." Part of the explanation he attributed to immigration from the Antilles, seen negatively by many scientists who argued that it introduced diseases that had been eliminated from Cuba, like smallpox and malaria.[26] Among the internal causes, González Curquejo underlined scarce and contaminated drinking water as well as deficient street cleaning, rat infestations, and potholes and breaks in streets, especially those in the outlying barrios, that were sites of infection. Troubling was the fact that public health had regressed most rapidly at the very time during the First World War when the national treasury was in good shape and individual salaries were high. The decadence, in other words, was occurring despite the Ministry of Health's efforts, which were colliding with the established system and the administrative mechanisms in place.

More exhaustive was a 1925 study read at the University of Havana by Juan Antonio Cosculluela, a professor of hydraulics in the School of Engineering.[27] It was predicated on the idea that the modern city was distinct from the old city because it was "a product of steam and electricity." Its growth had been contributed to, moreover, by the great discoveries of biology, which along with progress in science and technical knowledge had allowed for improvement in urban health. The fundamental characteristic of the modern city was its "continuous, incessant, violent growth" and the intense influx from rural areas, which created the grave problem of depopulation in the countryside.[28]

Cosculluela underlined that civilization came with an irremediable consequence: the complete contamination of the environment, such that even the most modern and progressive cities claimed more victims than would be found on a battlefield. He gave the example of New York where, despite the efficiency of the public services, one in every seven inhabitants suffered from tuberculosis and 25 percent of infants died before the age of five. In the case of Havana, statistics showed an alarming increase in mortality from infectious disease, to the point that it was on the road to becoming one of the least healthy cities in the Americas. Its mortality index was 20 per 1,000, while Montevideo's stood at 12 per 1,000, Buenos Aires at 16 per 1,000, and Rio de Janeiro at 19 per 1,000. Havana's sanitary decadence was manifest in a natural population growth that was essentially zero, with natality dropping from 4.16 between 1905 and 1910 to only 1.13 between 1920 and 1924. The growth of almost 45 percent in population in the previous twenty-four years was due to immigration from rural areas and foreign countries. In the first instance, the influx from the interior to the capital meant that the Cuban peasant could no longer be found in the fields but rather in the populated centers, especially Havana, "where he is found working as a peon for a bricklayer or in modest clerical posts." On top of this was the allowing of Antillean immigration, which he qualified as undesirable and dangerous due to the reintroduction of diseases that had been extirpated from Cuba.

According to Cosculluela, the contagious diseases that best demonstrated this decadent sanitary state were tuberculosis, malaria, and typhoid fever. The first was linked to street cleaning, the accumulation of waste, and empty lots that had been converted into dumps. Malaria, in frank resurgence, had to do with the lack of "petrolization" of stagnant waters and the abandonment of the war on the mosquito. But it was typhoid fever that represented the greatest evidence of the sanitary crisis, since mortality from this cause had a determinant role on health indicators for the city. The statistics for Havana showed that mortality had dropped dramatically from 1900 to 1910, from 30.6 to 20.3 per 100,000, before beginning to rise alarmingly and steadily, reaching 51.92 per 100,000 in 1924. This last constituted without doubt an epidemic of hydrological origin, "provoked by the contamination of the public water supply, by its direct mixing with the untreated water of the Rio Almendares." This, in turn, was due to the state of abandonment of the aqueduct, "a fecund fount of fraud and irregularity." So, among modern capitals, Havana occupied an inferior position "due to the complete relaxation of hygiene and sanitary practices in necessary public services." One of the most alarming indicators of this was infant mortality, which had surpassed 15,000 age 0 to 1 between 1919 and 1923.

Cosculluela saw two phases in the urban health indicators of Havana, one of improvement between 1900 and 1915 and one of decline from that point onward. Modern life was not possible without efficient public services like potable water and proper sewerage, "services that must be controlled by competent hygiene and sanitary engineers." Nevertheless, Havana was subject to a degree of fraud and corruption "more intense than any country has ever suffered." This decadence in urban salubriousness was part of a context of "general regress suffered by the country in every area of life, since everything is contaminated, everything is infected, to the point that the purest and most honest souls are sick with it." Meanwhile, the sanitary bureaucrats tried to demonstrate, as a consolation, the efficiency of public hygiene by comparing the mortality statistics of Havana with statistics from the colonial period. For Cosculluela this meant that "if the indices of health measure the degree of progress and civilization in the cities, the fact that Havana's are so poor ... is related very closely with the certain and demonstrated cultural regression that all of Cuban society is suffering at present, in each and every one of its cultural manifestations."[29] In this pessimistic evaluation, Cubans had always remained behind civilized peoples until external factors allowed them to overcome inertia. He cited the taking of Havana by the English in 1762 and the French immigration to the island following the revolution in Haiti as examples, and ended with the U.S. intervention that "provided the greatest and most efficient civilizing impulse." But within ten or twelve years of that impulse, given over once again to its own forces, "the decadence in all our institutions" commenced anew. Not coincidentally Cosculluela invoked the specter of the Platt Amendment, by showing his hopes in new changes: "The geographic fatality of Cuba's proximity to the United States means that we must take care of urban health if we want to maintain our mistreated sovereignty and leave behind these embarrassing periods of pillage and corruption in hopes of better times. . . . That will have to come quickly."

This summation of Havana's state of health was part of a broad national debate that took shape as the republic neared its first quarter century of existence. The most radical analyses pointed to the interference of U.S. imperialism and its growing control of economic and political interests to explain the country's ills. But other visions concentrated more on determining symptoms than deep causes. In the latter cases, biological, climatic, and medical metaphors were commonly used. One example of such a reading was that of the physician and writer Miguel del Carrión, whose analysis broached issues like the lack of "ethnic unity" and the absence of a spirit of association (organizations of civil society), of discipline, and of hierarchical order. He was particularly concerned with the poverty experienced by Cubans in their own land, in contrast to the opulent living of foreigners, leaving nationals only the option of cultivating a political career to garner resources and influence. He blamed the forming of the people's character "in the narrow confines of a colonial regime; lulled into the inactive sleep of an easy life in an enervating climate."[30]

In spite of this, for Carrión the republican slate was not all negative. Despite its deficiencies, Cuban society had progressed in part thanks to the effect of sanitary policies. "Our compatriots have learned to live better, more hygienically, with an order of comfort in their houses and their towns." There were isolated areas and even important towns where the peasantry remained on the margins of "the new cultural currents introduced into the country," but from every town there radiated "beneficent waves" that would permit a metamorphosis. There remained great challenges, like that of "fabricating" citizens in order to change an evolutionary trajectory "strictly controlled by the laws of biology" and to awaken public interest. The Cuban state, in his estimation, was an essentially hypothetical entity, since Cuban society itself did not exist per se. The "de facto" governments of the republic, therefore, had exercised over the country "a doctor's oversight at the bedside of patients attacked by a long illness." This was not something that could be achieved in a single generation. It was only possible through the reconquest of economic wealth. Carrión warned that those in government could not afford to lose sight of the fact that "peoples who do not control the sources of wealth in their own land sooner or later must become slaves." A simple program of government was required to guarantee public hygiene, easy communication, access to schools for all, and a treasury without deficit.

Using terminology familiar to all his colleagues, habituated to the language of science and technology, the writer spoke of the need to establish solid supports for the dangerous bridge connecting this era with the future. Cuba was a republic in its infancy, and it could not be corrected only with laws, since these did not serve "as orthopedic apparatuses on the malformed limbs of the collective body." This was the personified nation as unsteady and immature convalescent that Carrión saw himself leading along the edge of an abyss. "Let us pray to the god of children, and of countries that are beginning to venture their first steps on the slippery slope of Liberty, to preserve us from an untimely fall."[31]

Slaughterhouses of Havana

The great narrative of sanitation, health, and hygiene in the young nation was conjured metaphorically to imagine the state of political independence, institutional integrity, biological destiny, and cultural potency. To what degree was it echoed by evaluations of the state of health and hygiene in everyday life, especially in mundane areas like meat and milk production that were beneath the limelight of epidemics and gross statistics at the heart of debates over the island's health? The two levels did coincide, as for example in Barnet's 1913 address to the academy, where he insisted that, along with a litany of other sanitary measures, the island's well-being required guaranteeing the purity of milk and impeding the adulteration of its food supply. And yet, if we look more closely at the concrete attempts to guarantee that purity and impede that adulteration, we will find a different set of actors and narratives with distinct arcs.

Havana's scientific community had long been concerned with the condition of the capital city's slaughterhouses, and it was a common topic in the discourses and practices related to the modernization of urban life in the process of industrialization.[32] Without going back too far, we might start with physician Ambrosio González del Valle's 1870 demand that they be transferred to the edges of the Rio Almendares. In his judgment this was the most appropriate place because of its topography and the abundance of water for eliminating waste, which could also be used to produce fertilizer if the proper precautions were taken.[33] Ten years later, another physician, Eduardo Plá, reiterated the need to move slaughterhouses, which he saw as true foci of physical and moral infection, to the city's outskirts.[34] Among a number of problems, he mentioned their location in more populous and impoverished barrios to the south, which meant that the bad odors covered the city when the wind blew in a certain direction, as well as the absence of water to carry off the detritus and the contamination of the harbor. The buildings were of primitive construction, without the space they needed and in a state of ruin, with scenes like the washing of intestines in the principal entryway being common. Other criticisms were directed to the lack of a veterinarian to inspect the cattle before their slaughter and the barbarous manner in which the killing was carried out.[35]

In 1889 the Spanish governor, Manuel Salamanca, tried to promote a packet of sanitary measures. The *Crónica Médico-Quirúrgica de La Habana* identified the most important one as the project to build a new slaughterhouse, given that the existing ones were permanent concentrations of infection so bad they kept the necessary influx of immigrants from the island. The banks of the Almendares were considered more appropriate because the river course would permit the cleaning of the enclosure and the washing out to sea of all matter that could not be used for fertilizer and other industrial ends.³⁶ It was noted that such establishments had attained a maximum state of perfection in more advanced nations, and the Havana municipal government asked the Academy of Sciences to evaluate the project. In 1894 the new municipal slaughterhouse was finally inaugurated, with the financial backing of thirty meat wholesalers.

The slaughterhouse question was one of the first to be addressed as part of the sanitary measures for the city undertaken during the U.S. intervention. On July 24, 1899, the municipal government passed the Regulation of Slaughterhouses, followed later on August 31 by rules governing markets and another on October 10 regarding stables.³⁷ At the end of the same year Tomás Mederos wrote a report on his efforts for the year while filling the office of slaughterhouse deputy. In his opinion, these were establishments that gave the city "a great deal of unwanted notoriety and its most repulsive aspect" because they stood out for their absence of hygiene and morality. In the one dedicated to larger livestock (cows, horses, and mules), the refuse could be seen strewn about in every direction and the heaps of manure and other residual products were an affront to the environment. Many sorts of waste were tossed into the river, which was covered with organic matter as it flowed into the harbor. The picture was even worse in the abattoir for lesser livestock (pigs, sheep, and goats)—an old and broken-down building, "a true pigsty" where meat was mixed ceaselessly with the garbage covering the ground. In each place, the slaughtermen, "drunk with such disorder," were prone to forget all social consideration and humanitarianism and show themselves "cruel to the animals and shameless with one another."

Mederos claimed that from the first he understood that the situation required enormous remedial transformation that "could not be the work of a single day or a single man." For this reason he required the assistance of two physicians on a commission charged with evaluating the slaughterhouses and their implications for health, hygiene, morality, and popular consumption. They had been able to show the poor state of the buildings in some cases and in others the way in which the waste clogged up a pipe from which water was taken to clean hooves and intestines. The adjacent river was grotesque and nauseating, with "heaping amounts of intestinal bits" and the water colored greenish black from putrefaction and thick layers of flies. Inspection of the cattle was deplorable, with the veterinarian responsible barred from doing his job scientifically, "to the point of being forced to declare healthy and fat the majority of those cows who were banged up, skinny, and sick."

The work undertaken according to the recommendations of the commission quickly transformed this panorama. In the site for larger livestock the central pavilion was covered with planks and flumes, and basins were installed to manage the water. Solid waste and excrement were deposited in iron tanks and taken to a disposal site in metal vehicles, part of a business run by two men from the United States. According to Mederos, the site soon became the best-run establishment of those under municipal administration. "The pestilent and repulsive buildings, the mountains of garbage, the sludge, the small trench filled with the area's drainage—all have disappeared and the site has been converted into clean and manageable terrain ready for setting up gardens that will provide a certain poesy to a place that used to be famously sinister." Moreover, the river was dredged and its banks disinfected, to the great benefit of those who lived on its course.[38]

Despite these improvements, much was still required to leave the large cattle abattoir in perfect condition. In order to achieve that, the privileges inherited from the colonial era would have to disappear, and for the same to be achieved for the abattoir for pigs, sheep, and goats, which was an affront to "all sense of hygiene and progress," the solution was its complete demolition and combination with the slaughterhouse for larger cattle where a crematory oven needed to be installed to process the waste. Some of the city government's dispositions allowed a glimpse of new horizons, like the suppression of some of the rights and privileges to slaughter animals unimpeded that were enjoyed by the heirs of a Havana aristocrat, Count O'Reilly, or those acquired by the wholesalers who had founded the abattoir for large livestock. Mederos concluded that all such prerogatives should be eliminated, "converting those establishments into property of the municipality which would put them at the disposition of the public," showing neither the favoritism nor the arbitrariness that undermines public order and raises the price of meat. He also requested limits on the activities of the numerous intermediaries in the meat business.

Another of the changes had to do with the reform of the slaughtermen themselves who, once "stripped of vices and bad customs," would carry out their work with good order and economy. The new administrator of abattoirs, Miguel Zaldivar, promised to dedicate himself to this and other improvements. In the meantime, the veterinarians Valdivielso and Etchetgoyen deserved the credit for the fact that meat was clean and nutritious. Their work demonstrated that the fall in the city's mortality rate was due in great part to the rigorous and scientific inspection of slaughterhouse meat. Mederos's report ended with a reference to three deaths from anthrax in the corrals of the slaughterhouse for large livestock. The blood of the cows was sent to the Histobacteriological Laboratory, where the experienced microbiologists and physicians Juan Dávalos and Enrique Acosta confirmed the diagnosis. In response, the municipality decided immediately to establish a laboratory in the abattoir to assess the cattle and to purchase a "splendid microscope." Among other measures, it was determined to take the temperature and blood samples of suspect beasts, as well as from 10 percent of the healthy ones.

In 1909 one of the expert professionals who worked in Havana's municipal slaughterhouse, the physician Manuel Ruiz Casabó, presented a study to the Academy of Sciences.[39] Aside from assessing the facility in which he had worked for ten years, the study also looked at the other two facilities in the city, the Luyanó Slaughterhouse and the Industrial Abattoir. In regard to the Luyanó Slaughterhouse, Ruiz Casabó mentioned that due to complaints from the Cuban Humanitarian Society, two holding apparatuses to avoid mistreatment of the cattle prior to slaughter were built for the corral, and the method of killing was modified. Basically operations relied on the strength of five hundred workers, though the end result was an improvement on the former situation, which had been the subject of "mockery and ridicule around Havana at the time." The facility at Luyanó, founded in 1907, had an electric motor and steam machinery to move the equipment for hanging the beef and weighing or transporting the meat. Electricity allowed the complete service to operate with only twenty-four workers. On the other hand, its corrals left much to be desired. A purpose-built pipe eliminated water after traveling a great distance to the inlet at Guanabacoa, while the waste products were used by industrial entrepreneurs who maintained crematoria nearby to transform them into fertilizer.

The industrial abattoir was the most recent and important for its magnificence, extension, machinery, processes, elegance, and investment. It was the property of a private company, located at the back of the harbor on the edge of the Atarés inlet. Ruiz Casabó regretted the choice of the site, since he felt it was likely the place where Havana's notoriously fetid bay showed the greatest concentration of "microbial fermentations." The plant possessed an enormous refrigerated room and floors for different derivatives of the slaughter, areas for worker hygiene including showers and toilets, as well as metal and wood shops. Huge Westinghouse dynamos generated power for the machines in each department. In sum, everything there was "grand and magnificent." The killing methods were very advanced, especially those for pigs, done by an "original and ingenious machine." All derivatives were used at this slaughterhouse, yet it still had difficulties due to the lack of sufficient water for its operations.

Figure 4.1 Industrial abbatoir, area for slaughtering pigs. *El Fígaro*, no. 39 (September 26, 1909): 491.

An article published in the magazine *El Fígaro*, also in 1909, stressed that the industrial abattoir satisfied a need in the city deeply felt for over half a century, since meat processing had been quite deficient in comparison with progressive capital cities. In terms of sanitation and hygiene, the new installation—a veritable "industrial palace"—was in keeping with the new standards being realized in the country. Moreover, they noted the potential it had to make Havana the meat supplier for the entire republic, the way Chicago was in the United States, and even allow exports to the United States at certain times of the year. The abattoir was, in sum, one of the activities that could consolidate Cuban nationality and a symbol of work, strength, and civilization.[40]

Despite these advances, Ruíz Casadó denounced the fact that the three slaughterhouses were poor in terms of the sanitary inspection of cattle destined for public consumption. In the municipal facility, there were daily protests from merchants who felt disadvantaged by the sanitary regulations. Of the 150 cows that died in its corrals during the ten years he worked there, 115 had had anthrax, and many other cases might have been detected had their slaughter been delayed slightly. The situation was worsened by the naming of unqualified personnel to the inspector positions—for example, a medical doctor who had no knowledge of bacteriological work with a microscope. The author likewise decried the fact that the machinery in the municipal

Figure 4.2 Drawing of the Industrial Abbatoir, Havana. *Source:* Carlos de la Torre y Alfredo Aguayo, *Geografía de Cuba* (Havana: Cultural S.A., 1928).

abattoir for transforming organic residuals did not do their job and that much waste was thrown into the harbor or mixed into the earth of a neighboring piece of land. In its favor, the facility had one professional inspector for large livestock and another for small, whereas in the rest a single veterinarian was in change of inspecting live animals, meat, and viscera. Nevertheless, no facility really guaranteed the quality of meat consumed in the city.

A critical perspective on the inspection of slaughterhouses was reiterated in 1925 by a veterinarian, Ricardo Gómez Murillo, in his inaugural discourse as a member of the Academy of Sciences. In his opinion, the peculiar organization of these facilities and of the markets was a serious danger for those charged with inspecting the animals and the meats at the moment they tried to gain compliance based on the inspection outcome. One veterinarian, Lutgardo de la Torre, was assassinated upon leaving the industrial abattoir after such an incident. Gómez Murillo denounced the fact that "it seems that science in the markets and slaughterhouses of Havana has turned back the clock fifty years and today, as then, all that is needed to guarantee the cleanliness of food of animal origin is a quick and summary examination with the naked eye."[41] He attributed this "inexplicable" backwardness in food inspection, in part, to the fact that it was a municipal jurisdiction, and he advocated nationalizing the service and transferring it to the Ministry of Health.

Milk Production and Consumption

The gradual expansion and perfecting of the dairy industry is another of the great symbols of urbanized industrial society, thanks to the advances in bacteriology, refrigeration, and transport. In this context, milk began to assume the category of the most perfect of foods, as Melanie Dupuis has nicely illustrated in her study of the U.S. experience with this product.[42] Toward the end of the nineteenth century, the distribution and consumption of milk in Havana occurred on a reduced scale and in rudimentary conditions. At

Figure 4.3 System for milk delivery in Cuba, beginning of the twentieth century. *Cuba Review & Bulletin*, April 1906.

the time, the Spanish military physician Fernández Losada noted the high indexes of infant deaths in Havana from the consumption of contaminated milk, given the lack of real organization of a municipal hygiene laboratory to perform services like the analysis of adulterated foods.[43]

At the outset of the twentieth century, the consumption of milk in Havana was constantly climbing. A coachman of the era, Luis Adrián Betancourt, relates how many stables were dedicated to cows, and the city filled up with dairies. Between 4 and 5 A.M., people would head to the milking sites with jars in search of fresh milk, or the milk was sold from horses carrying containers. According to the coachman, around 1910 the health authorities made war on the milk producers on the grounds that the presence of cows in the city caused diseases and huge quantities of flies. Because of this they ordered the creation of carts made of galvanized zinc and painted yellow, a color that identified the milk vendors, and they began to inspect milking sites and bottling the milk with seals from the Ministry of Health to avoid the watering down or adulteration of the product.[44]

The growing importance of milk as a foodstuff was related to progress in bacteriology and its effect on the improvement of public health, as well as with the appearance of new techniques for dairy production, processing, and distribution. More than thirty-five articles in the Sanitary Ordinances of 1906 were dedicated to different aspects linked to the consumption of milk, and in 1913 new norms were added following proposals by a commission made up of academicians Alonso Cuadrado, Barnet, and Coronado. Among their stipulations was that to be distributed milk had to be duly bottled, covered, and sealed; that its sale from stables was prohibited; that licenses for dairies had to be renewed annually or be rescinded indefinitely for those in contravention; that certificates of health had to be secured every six months; and that the milkers had to have well-washed hands. They also recommended fixing the proportions of sugar in condensed milk and that the tins come with dates of manufacture and expiration.[45]

The milk question was relevant not only in terms of food but also in terms of its close connection to distinct diseases. A 1923 article in the *Bulletin of the Panamerican Union* made reference to both dimensions.[46] The departure point was that it was one of the cheapest foods in proportion to the energy supplied in its production and one of the most desirable for rich and poor alike. But despite these qualities it was also a dangerous foodstuff because each year thousands of children died from diseases transmitted in impure milk like typhoid, Malta fever, scarlet fever, tuberculosis, diarrhea and enteritis, diphtheria, and diseases of the throat.

To prevent such disease, the entry of harmful bacteria into the milk had to be avoided by ensuring cleanliness, healthy animals, careful milkers, special covered vessels, sterilized receptacles, and refrigeration. One advantage was that modern vehicles were faster, but the product containers had to be well covered and not left in the sun. To be sold, milk had to be bottled, as was demanded in "progressive" cities. In a number of such cities a dairy inspection service had been created under the departments of health that covered the entire process from the farms to the consumer. The article particularly exhorted pasteurizing the milk, a procedure that was most extensive in the United States and through which a healthier and sanitized product was secured, though it did not discount other measures such as boiling the milk, a method more widely used in Europe and Latin America.

Cuban physicians and sanitary authorities were aware of these calls to increase milk consumption without converting it into a route for disease transmission. In 1914 the eminent medical scientist Arístides Agramonte presented a study to the Academy of Sciences in which he recounted his visits to pasteurization plants in Europe and the United States. His departure point was that milk was the basis for the artificial feeding of infants, so its production and distribution required the oversight of sanitary institutions in civilized countries. One way to achieve this objective was pasteurized milk, which was the kind most consumed in populous cities of the United States and Germany (Berlin, for example). Years earlier Agramonte had been able to visit Berlin's Bolle dairy and facilities in New York. In the latter city, two large companies dominated the market and "in heated and tireless but peaceful competition" extended and improved their installations to the benefit of the public and their shareholders. The Sheffield Farms–Slawson Decker Co. plant in Manhattan could produce sixty thousand liters in four hours thanks to its semiautomatic bottling machinery. The employees, dressed in sterilized, white work clothes, had only to supervise operations to remove cracked bottles while others were taken out for random bacteriological analysis. In sum, with a workforce of only fifty-eight, one thousand liters per worker could be pasteurized. In accord with this experience he recommended that Cuba "get our health authorities to set up something of this nature, since it is still impossible to hope for anything from private initiative." If milk treated in this way could be sold at a normal price, "and given out free to the poor, setting up for this purpose many depots in such neighborhoods throughout the city," Agramonte was "sure that the results would not be long in showing themselves, and we would feel immediate benefits in lower infant morbidity, which more than mortality is what should be concerning us."[47]

Agramonte's comments encouraged another academician, Leonel Plasencia, to present a more extensive study to show that Havana's milk was of good quality but was bacteriologically unclean due to deficient handling.[48] In his estimation, the idea that the milk from Cuban cows was poor had its origins in national pessimism, the tendency "to consider that everything we have is bad and that we are less capable than any other inhabitants of the globe." The problem was in the milking and in the washing of vessels in rural dairies and urban stables where little attention was given to dairy cattle and neither the udders nor the hands of the milkers (who in many cases were children) were washed. Likewise transport was beset by delays and other obstacles. Urban stables were relatively cleaner due to the direct oversight of the health authorities, but they still had sources of infection like "the crowding around the milking by those who want to drink pure milk straight from the cow, who go even in the clothes they've been using to take care of sick people." They also got a lot of germs from the streets, and it was only due to the immunity acquired when the cows "ate papers" ("pastaban papeles") in the streets or the safeguarding habit of many families of boiling the milk that more damage was not done. Another grave danger was the watering down of milk without taking care that the diluting water was sterilized.[49]

The veterinarian José Simpson took up the topic of milk in the academy in 1922.[50] He claimed that it was the food of greatest importance to humanity and of greatest rank from the point of view of physiology, as well as a product that constituted the principal wealth of a number of countries that had dedicated their industrial and agricultural energy and initiative to its production. Nevertheless, despite the fact that Cuba had propitious climate and soil conditions to become one of the most important producer countries, its dairy industry did not have adequate hygienic or industrial methods. In tours of the rural areas of the province of Havana, as chief of the Dairy Supply Inspection Service, he had observed that a primitive system was still in effect. Milking was done beneath a leafy tree, on filthy and foul-smelling soil, by a Cuban *guajiro* who rarely felt the "refreshing splash" of clear, clean water on his hands, making it impossible to apply the milk regulations in the ranches of the interior.

Simpson himself and Domingo Ramos, a university professor, shared the work of channeling the supply of milk to Havana and proposed setting up a school on the El Dique farm, which was the property of the state, to show ranchhands how to milk properly (the farm in question was in an area that could be called "dairy alley," on the road to Güines). Moreover, agronomy experts should visit the dairy farms or groups of dairy workers in their places of work, programs that should not wait for the initiative of foreigners. Just as in England, Holland, and the United States, schools should be set up for adult and child dairy workers. One example invoked was the school in Guelph, Canada, whose fame was such that thousands of interested people with interests in the industry visited annually.

Simpson estimated that Havana needed some 200,000 liters of milk per day, a figure distant from what was then being produced. England's inhabitants had access to 650 cc each per day, Switzerland's 700, those in Brussels 800, in Paris 460, in Canada 450, and in Munich 600 cc. By contrast, those in the Cuban capital barely had access to 150 cc per day, despite the fact that its inhabitants not only ate dairy with breakfast, but also had milk products in their afternoon snacks and meals. Having mentioned statistics on consumption in cities like New York, Paris, and Berlin and the number of cows that produced it, the author intoned: "The rivers of milk produced in these countries that stand at the head of civilization still are not enough, however, to satisfy the feeding of the poor in the great cities, where the weak children of the proletariat cannot get enough to eat proper portions. What can we say about the poor of Havana, whose milk sells at the fantastic price of a luxury good?"[51] The Ministry of Agriculture should devote preferential attention to the dairy industry. Along with special schools and conferences in dairy regions, fairs and competitions could be promoted. The guajiros would have to be taught how to make silos for dried products, how to select cows to create new creole breeds, how to establish a good feeding system based on pasturage and other feed supplements, and how to prepare stables with abundant water for proper milking. Cows as well as milkers had to be clean, the former with tests for tuberculosis and the latter with white clothing and caps, disinfected hands, and training in using the milking machines.

Like other authors, Simpson underlined the importance of pasteurization and refrigeration. Fortunately, the regulations on dairy supply in Havana had produced results in terms of the adulteration of products. Based on his experience he affirmed that the ranchers of Havana did not add substances like flakes of yucca or yam, which he considered a popular myth. But they did become "unconscious criminals by producing an impure food of poor nutritional value," and he criticized their poor techniques—for example, the custom of choosing the best cow in the stable for constant milking. Simpson proposed collaboration with the university, the faculties of medicine and pharmacy, and its professors of medical chemistry and special analysis in an effort to intensify studies on the chemistry of milk. He also proposed that every pharmacy should be ready to provide the public with milk for formula as well as for medicinal purposes, meaning that they would be "equipped to satisfy the need and facilitate the scientific artificial feeding of babies, which is not widespread in our country."[52]

In spite of the limitations outlined in these studies, the nascent dairy industry showed progress over the first decades of the republic. The pages of *The Book of Cuba* (*El Libro de Cuba*), published in 1925, feature four businesses devoted to dairy commerce.[53] The largest of these was the Havana Dairy Supply Company (Compañía abastecedora de la leche de La Habana), founded in 1908. Among the novelties it introduced was the substitution of animal hauling from the countryside with specialized trucks, which allowed for better hygiene and more regular distribution. The system of direct boiling with wood fires was replaced by an expensive steam machine which, along with refrigeration and machines for the rinsing and sterilization of receptacles (the only one in the city), put this factory "at the level of the most perfect in Europe and the United States." The company had acquired properties with large dairy ranches and purchased an ice factory with a capacity of forty tons per day that was later expanded to a hundred tons, a fundamental element for conserving milk over long distances and distributing it via a deluxe truck service.

These improvements raised sales from 5,000 to 30,000 liters a day, alongside the raising of an ice cream factory with the most modern machinery. Sanitary regulations were scrupulously followed during the entire process,

Figure 4.4
Machine for filling and capping milk jugs in a model dairy facility, Havana. *Revista de Agricultura, Comercio y Trabajo*, March 1918.

with constant inspections by the Department of Health and without use of artificial coloring, which produced milk "of an admirable purity and hygienic character," preferred in the majority of cafés, both private and state-run. By 1925 the company had become a commercial and industrial force of the first order, with thirty-five dairy outlets around the city. It was followed in importance by the Palacio de la Leche (Milk Palace), founded in 1900, and by 1925 with an electrified refrigeration plant with the capacity to preserve twenty thousand liters of milk per day and ice cream. Milk was received by rail and transported in eight large trucks for distribution in the city, with four more for ice cream. The company had twenty-four outlets, and its daily sales reached fourteen thousand liters.[54] Two other dairy merchants were Modesto Suárez y Hno (Modesto Suarez & Bro.) and Sixto Abreu. The first was established in 1907 as a business specializing in milk transport, receiving it from the train and transporting it in ten-ton trucks. Its fleet of large and small trucks distributed six thousand liters per day of a milk described as pure and supremely hygienic. By 1925 the company had inaugurated a building that conformed to the most modern methods of hygiene. Abreu's business, for

Figure 4.5 Milk delivery vans of the firm Modesto Suárez y Hno. *Libro de Cuba*, 1925.

its part, was a stable in Vedado for the distribution of milk "according to the strictest sanitary observance."[55]

The sales of all four businesses put together did not surpass fifty thousand liters per day. Though an indeterminate quantity from other smaller establishments could be added to the total, they did not come close to supplying half the potential demand of the city. Together with the criticism on the deficiencies that persisted in the production, distribution, and inspection of milk, this shows that the system was far from meeting the degree of development aspired to by physicians and veterinarians. The wide margin that existed for criticism allowed for calls to solve the problems of hygiene and public health in an era in which techno-industrial advances in relation to food and successes in the control of diseases accompanied the quick rise of big cities.

Years later, in 1938, the veterinarian Idelfonso Pérez Vigueras regretted that the services his profession could add to the dairy sector had been dispensed with. The only assistance vets supplied the industry had to do with the deficient inspection of ranches. He noted that there remained diverse problems that required veterinary science. Pasteurization was insufficient, since there was a large underground sale of untreated milk, and the technique did not apply to milk that went to the smaller towns. There was also a large consumption of fresh cheese made with raw milk and therefore prone to contamination. Even with pasteurized milk there remained the problem of whether or not it came from healthy cows, which could only be determined by competent veterinarians. Moreover, the large companies that did pasteurize their milk were able to impose a very low purchasing price on producers and resell the milk at prices prohibitive to the poor.[56]

Meat, Milk, and the Sick Republic

In Cuba's transition from colony to republic, the theme of hygiene and public health occupied a place of great relevance. Various factors made this the case, from the prior tradition of a solid medical community that had been capable of producing notable science—the supreme example being Finlay's work on the existence of a biological vector of yellow fever transmission—to the interest of the U.S. military occupation government in showing rapid results in this domain that would cement its economic and political influence as well as its superiority over the old Spanish colonial regime. It is not an accident that the defense of sanitary policies became essential to the discourse on the viability of the republic and the independence of Cuba.

As seen at the outset of this chapter, there was initially strong agreement on the positive march of the country in the area of sanitation, but this image was quickly turned upside down when the signs of "Cuban decadence" began to appear in other domains of national life. In that context, scientists, physicians, and other intellectuals used their arsenal of scientific terms to describe the pathologies of the republic in the political, economic, and social arenas, as though it were a sick patient that required urgent treatment, which itself depended to a great extent on the intervention of technocrats and scientific experts. This rise and fall narrative was not reproduced in the area of discourses on meat and dairy production. Instead, scientific assessments of each industry remained relatively optimistic, centered on the need for improvement (and especially the incorporation of more competent experts) while insisting that core sanitary objectives had been reached or were within reach.

Nevertheless, it would be inexact to attribute the relative success in each endeavor to a change in sovereign status or political system. Although these were not without effect, in reality such changes corresponded to wider transformations like the rise of bacteriology at the end of the nineteenth century and its practical application to areas like the quality of food, the beginnings of automotive transportation, the improvements in industrial technique and assembly line production, the development of veterinary science, and incipient types of mass consumption as the great urban centers expanded. In all these areas the role of science and technology would be ever more influential.

In closing we might make reference to the meaning that Fernando Ortiz gave to the consumption of milk in modern society in the middle of the twentieth century, in a 1947 essay on the Good Neighbor Policy, U.S. imperialism, and pan-Americanism. In his opinion, in the realm of the possible created by science there had appeared the metaphorical ideal of Henry A. Wallace, "to distribute each morning a ration of sterilized and nutritious milk to each inhabitant of the globe." In advocating the need for an Inter-American New Deal—a "Renew Deal"—that would bring to all peoples of the Americas a plethora of food, mines, machinery, laboratories, schools, universities, and civic and cultural institutions, he could think of no better allegory than the following: "Ah! And jugs of good milk at the dawn of each day."[57]

Notes

This chapter was produced as part of the research project HAR2012-36481 funded by the Spanish Ministerio de Economía y Competitividad and was initially conceived while I was a visiting researcher at the Universidad Jaume I in 2010. My thanks to the editors of this volume for their useful suggestions.

1. Carrión, "Desenvolvimiento social de Cuba en los últimos veinte años," 27.

2. "Palpitaciones de la vida nacional: La República enferma," *Cuba Contemporánea* 35, no. 140 (August 1924): 349–52.

3. On the use of this metaphor by intellectuals in the region, see Guerra Vilaboy, *Cinco siglos de historiografía latinoamericana*, esp. chap. 3, "La historiografía latinoamericana de fines del siglo XIX y principios del XX," 111–43. Some well-known examples are Zúmeta, *El continente enfermo*, and Arguedas, *Pueblo enfermo* (on Bolivia).

4. Trelles, "El progreso y el retroceso de la República de Cuba," 352–53.

5. Among studies that tackle the issue are Altshuler y González, *Una luz que llegó para quedarse*, and García et al., *Una obra maestra*. For an evaluation of the problem of Havana's urban environment, see the essays in Segre, *Lectura crítica del entorno cubano*.

6. Some recent works are Scarpaci, Segre, and Coyula, *Havana*, and Gómez Díaz, *De Forestier a Sert*.

7. Toledo y González de Molina, "El metabolismo social," 101.

8. On both these antecedents prior to 1868, see Sarmiento, *Cuba: Entre la opulencia y la pobreza*.

9. Mohar, *La escuela de medicina veterinaria de La Habana*. Sources on the evolution of Cuban veterinary science can be found in the electronic journal REDVET, http://www.veterinaria.org/revistas/redvet.

10. Gallini, "De razas y de carne," 291–337. A recent article about the beginnings of veterinary services in a Caribbean country is Pemberton, "Animal Disease and Veterinary Administration in Trinidad and Tobago, 1879–1962," 163–79.

11. Pruna, *La Real Academia de Ciencias de La Habana*; Funes, *El despertar del Asociacionismo Científico en Cuba*.

12. Tamayo, *Reflexiones sociológicas sobre las causas de la mortalidad en La Habana*, 8–11.

13. Leyva, *Saneamiento de la ciudad de La Habana*, 8–9. With 1 death for every 34 in-

habitants, Havana was below London (1:38), Lisbon (1:42), and Paris (1:35), but above Brussels (1:27), Madrid and Berlín (1:25), and St. Petersburg and Vienna (1:24). Paradela, "Examen de los orígenes de insalubridad que se atribuyen al puerto de La Habana e influencia de aquellos en la salud pública," no. 27: 713–36 and no. 28: 108–37, 242–48. Wilson, *El problema urgente*.

14. Fernández, *Consideraciones higiénicas sobre la ciudad de La Habana*.

15. González Curquejo, *Datos para la Historia*.

16. Le Roy y Cassá, *Desenvolvimiento de la sanidad en Cuba durante los últimos 50 años*, 72–77.

17. Leyva, *Saneamiento de la ciudad de La Habana*, 46–49.

18. The citation is from the discourse of Juan Santos Fernández in the session of December 3, 1908 in homage to Carlos J. Finlay, *Anales* 45 (1908): 350.

19. Espinosa, *Epidemic Invasions*, 10.

20. Santos Fernández, "Discurso leído en la sesión solemne celebrada el día 15 de mayo de 1902," 10.

21. República de Cuba, Secretaría de Gobernación, *Ordenanzas sanitarias para el régimen de los ayuntamientos de la República*.

22. Rodríguez Expósito, "La primera secretaría de sanidad del mundo se creó en Cuba," 13. This was "exclusively Cuban" and "a radical innovation for its time."

23. Barnet, "Consideraciones sobre el estado sanitario de Cuba," 7. The favorable views on Cuba's sanitary state did not come only from local physicians. Charles Berchon, from the Society of Geography of Paris, wrote after a 1910 visit that the island enjoyed a healthy atmosphere "due to preventive hygiene measures." As a result, yellow fever had disappeared and tuberculosis was "each day closer to abdicating its devastator role." In his opinion, the wise measures taken were due to a "notable administration" and to great fiscal sacrifices by the Cuban state. He noted that the country had ever lesser need of its thirty hospitals and that its powerful private mutualist societies and their *casas de salud* (health clinics) had also played a positive role. Berchon, *A través de Cuba*, 23–26.

24. See the 1924 text by Ortiz, "La decadencia cubana," 69–80.

25. González Curquejo, *La insalubridad de la bahía de La Habana*.

26. On the scientific debates concerning immigration and racism, see García y Álvarez, *En busca de la raza perfecta*, 466–84, and *Las trampas del poder*, 189–204. Also see Mcleod, "Undesirable Aliens," 599–623.

27. Cosculluela, *La Salubridad Urbana*.

28. An example given was the United States, where inhabitants of cities had gone from 3.35 percent of the population in 1790 to 58 percent in 1924. At the time the urban population of Germany and England were 80 percent and 90 percent, respectively.

29. Cosculluela, *La Salubridad Urbana*, 17.

30. Carrión, "Desenvolvimiento social de Cuba en los últimos veinte años," 5–27.

31. Carrión, "Desenvolvimiento social de Cuba en los últimos veinte años," 27.

32. Lee, *Meat, Modernity, and the Rise of the Slaughterhouse*. A Latin American case study is Pilcher, *The Sausage Rebellion*.

33. González del Valle, *Rastros*.

34. Plá, "Mataderos de La Habana," 199–202.

35. Plá, "Mataderos de La Habana," 201.

36. "El nuevo matadero de La Habana," *CMQH* 15 (1889): 213–15.

37. López del Valle, *Desenvolvimiento de la Sanidad y la Beneficencia en Cuba durante los últimos diez y seis años (1899–1914)*.

38. Mederos, *La gestión municipal en los mataderos de La Habana*, 10.

39. Ruiz Casabó, "Los mataderos de La Habana," 300–329.

40. "Los progresos de Cuba: Compañía anónima Matadero Industrial," *El Fígaro*, no. 39 (September 26, 1909): 483–92. References to the Chicago slaughterhouses were usual in Cuba starting in the nineteenth century. Dominic A. Pacyga, "Chicago: Slaughterhouse to the World," 153–66.

41. Gómez Murillo, "La medicina veterinaria cubana," 621.

42. DuPuis, *Nature's Perfect Food*.

43. Fernández, *Consideraciones higiénicas sobre la ciudad de La Habana*, 58.

44. Betancourt, *Cochero*, 89–91.

45. "Reparos a las ordenanzas sanitarias," *Anales*, no. 50 (1913–14): 236–38. En sesión del 29 de agosto de 1913.

46. "Leche pura: importante problema en la alimentación," *Boletín de la Unión Panamericana* (July 1923): 43–56.

47. Agramonte, "Notas acerca de la pasteurización de la leche," 906.

48. Plasencia, "Le leche que se consume en La Habana, por su composición es buena," 921–57.

49. Plasencia undertook the bacterial counting in three types of stables. The first had frequent cleaning, including of the udders and the hands of the milkers; the second had regular cleanings that did not include udders and hands; and the others had deficient cleaning. The evidence gathered allowed him to argue that infectious material in milk increased in the absence of cleanliness during milking. In the first group he obtained an average of eight bacterial colonies per cm^2, in the second twenty bacterial colonies per cm^2, and in the third fifty-two colonies per cm^2.

50. Simpson, "La leche en Cuba," 34–73.

51. Simpson, "La leche en Cuba," 42.

52. Simpson, "La leche en Cuba," 73.

53. República de Cuba, *El libro de Cuba*, 1925, 797.

54. República de Cuba, *El libro de Cuba*, 1925, 800.

55. República de Cuba, *El libro de Cuba*, 1925, 828, 834.

56. Pérez Vigueras, "Funciones del veterinario en la higiene pública y en la industria pecuaria y nacional," 528–36.

57. "¡Ah! Y jarros de buena leche al alba de cada día." Ortiz, "Imperialismo y buena vecindad," 314, 318.

CHAPTER 5

Attributes for the Capital of an Austere Republic

José Antonio Piqueras

In the new city growing next to the old city of Havana, the traces of Spanish civilization were slowly and relentlessly disappearing. According to notes made by a foreign traveler, they were being replaced by "modern American civilization, which callously invades everything." The narrow streets with elevated sidewalks and large, old houses "built in the pure Spanish style" were things of the past in the urban area that was expanding to the west of the city. Of course, the past had not disappeared, and numerous observers declared that it was still alive, displaying the idiosyncrasies to which Havana owed its fame as a major Atlantic metropolis of Caribbean vocation. The city was a large street theater with a multicolored cast of hawkers and shopkeepers, artisans and wholesalers, public functionaries and animals pulling carts laden with goods from the docks. Atop filthy cobblestones, breathing a thousand city smells, they were all mixed together in a city radiating out from the large inner bay that, in the classic conception of the artists and historians fascinated by the great urban markets of the nineteenth century, was both "the belly and the lungs" of a commercial metropolis. Havana, however, was changing. Modernity was rising alongside it, in a second city that the traveler went on to describe as having "beautiful" roads—wide, spacious, straight, and well designed—with "buildings constructed in the style of the United States" on tree-lined avenues with parks nearby, markedly different from the older buildings. The new city housed modern cafés, theaters, the railway station, industrial establishments, and the "most reputable" schools. Travelers, then, were presented with two opposing cities: one modern, one traditional. The modern city displayed the clear influence of the Anglo-American North. The old city, apparently unmistakably "Hispanic," was in fact a mixture of Spanish and creole—indeed, almost entirely creole, with little real originality beyond its syncretism, its humbler homes built in interstitial spaces and in outlying neighborhoods next to the docks and warehouses. This old city inherited the legacy of large public buildings, fortresses and palaces, convents, churches, and large stone houses.

The image we have just evoked could apply to the dawn of the twentieth century, to the first years of the republic when a paradigm of American modernity began to take shape that contrasted itself with a supposedly traditional Spanish colonial order. The birth of a national state provided the perfect opportunity to open the city to other influences—especially given the decisive defeat of an enemy, Spain, that surrendered once on the battlefield and again in the Treaty of Paris—and to introduce the latest advances from one of the most economically advanced nations of the age, the United States. The United States was the country closest to the New Cuba in practical and functional terms because of the tight commercial links that had already been established, because it was the main destination for Cuban political and industrial emigration, and because it was where the majority of the heirs of Havana's elite received their higher education. Marial Iglesias has elegantly explored discourses and symbols that reveal a desire for change and an identification with a certain imaginary of modernity among ordinary people during the limbo years of the U.S. occupation when the past was dead, the future still to be constructed.[1] The most advanced sectors of society had idealized images and models of this future that they hoped to introduce, as if it were possible to disregard the reality of the existing society and ignore its natural impulses and inertias.

But let us return to our traveler and his tale of a city being ruthlessly invaded by "modern American civilization," an urban image characterized by its duality. The account actually refers to a visit made in 1853 by the Colombian Nicolás Tanco. The author, who shortly afterward began to import indentured Asian workers for work on the main sugar plantations (a new modality in an ancient form of exploitation), contrasted traditional Havana with the new Havana growing outside the city, on the other side of the Paseo del Prado and the Paseo Isabel II, together constituting the main thoroughfare beginning at Castillo de la Punto and ending at the Campo de Marte (see map 5.1). Two different styles of life were gradually taking shape, even in terms of the physical appearance of a city which was, in the words of Tanco, suffering from the ambiguous nature of two civilizations (Spanish and North American) competing with each other.[2]

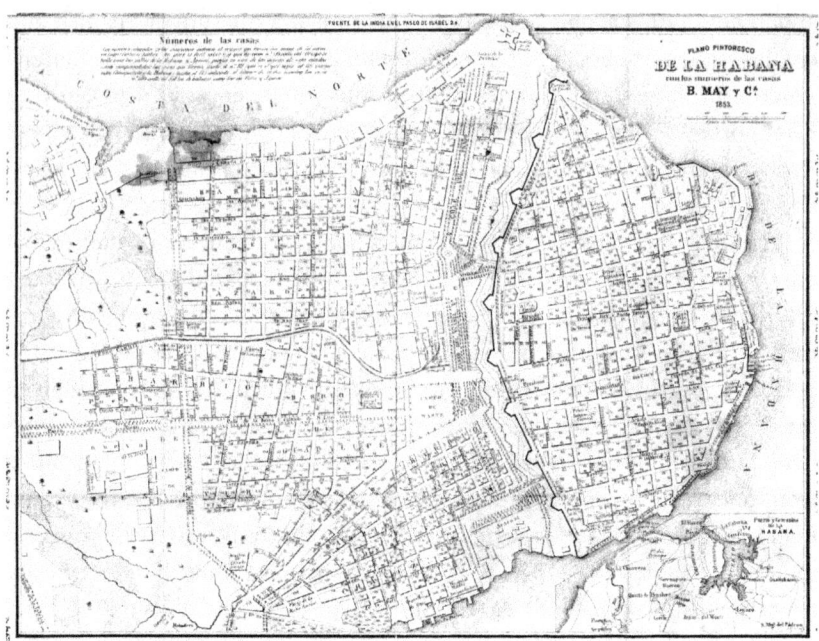

Map 5.1 Havana, 1853. Courtesy of the Archivo Nacional de Cuba, Mapoteca.

Yet these changes were themselves prefigured by the urban expansion plan of 1819 and the reforms promoted by General Tacón (the most important of the reforms carried out during the colony), though they still conformed to the "European style." The sewer system was developed, the main arterial roads were created, and the construction of new emblematic buildings in the area outside the city walls was promoted. This could be seen in the construction of the Teatro Pancho Marty (later the Teatro Tacón), built in the style of the Teatros Principales found in Spanish cities, and in the way avenues were designed and decorated in the European style. The Palacio Aldama was the first major building constructed outside the city walls. It was a splendid residence in the style of the neoclassical aristocratic palaces of the early nineteenth century and before (that is, "in the old style"). It was an accurate reflection of the pathos of an old Spanish American slave trader, the Basque Domingo Aldama, who found inspiration in the homes of the *aristocracia hatera* (livestock owning aristocracy) and the *sacarocracia criolla* (creole sugar barons) of the previous century.[3] The finishing touches were baroque features that forged a link with the more refined mansions of the day.

In contrast to the above, the creole middle classes, who were not involved in the sugar industry, had specific channels of prosperity. These channels were by no means exclusive to creoles, given that the mixing of Spaniards and creoles was a permanent affair that Cubanized the second generation of immigrants from mainland Spain and the Canary Islands. With military careers relegated to a secondary position and high-level administration ruled out, the cultivation of a professional culture became one of the safest means of achieving social mobility. In Cuba, there was a certain model of specialization that provided income and status through higher education and enabled professions to be practiced in several very specific areas: medicine, agriculture, and the law. Some technical professions such as land surveying and construction were also acceptable, with engineering restricted to a large extent to the colonial military corps. Yet in no way did these classes cease to have a hand in commerce and particularly in property speculation.

The conflict between a new city that looked to the north and an archaic city trapped by its physical walls (which began to be demolished in 1863) and by the social and cultural barriers that shackled it to the past and to the colonial administration, as Tanco highlighted in 1853, was more a metaphor than a reality at the time he wrote. From about 1900 on, things would be different, but let us note that it was a question of degree more than one of tendency or essence. What type of city did the capital of a new republic require and what type of city was it possible to make or construct in accordance with the status, the state of public funds, and the idiosyncrasies of the ruling class? There was more continuity than there were ruptures in the periodic reinvention of Havana. Indeed, the only real exceptions to this were the Master Plan commissioned from Jean-Claude Forestier in 1925 (although never fully implemented, it included landscaping the city, creating scenic views, and designing the Capitólio in the image of the Capitol building in Washington) and the *proyecto batistiano* (Batista's urban reform project).[4] In spite of the overwhelming consensus against such a claim, there is evidence to support it.

The Second Hispanicization of Havana's Urban Landscape

Havana emerged from the war of independence in 1898 as the city that best symbolized Cuba's colonial era. The premises of political moderation, social control, and adapting the conditions of the country to democracy faced an acid test in a capital that was almost ten times bigger than the country's next largest city. In 1899, the census registered 235,981 inhabitants, almost one in five of the island's residents. By 1907, the figure had risen to 300,000. The following decade witnessed a more modest increase, with 363,000 inhabitants in 1919, one out of every six residents of Cuba, while from that date on the city population grew considerably until reaching 520,504 inhabitants in

1931. Home to the new institutions and to cultural life, as it had been during the colony, during the first decades of the republic Havana had to create and accommodate various cities: the political, intellectual, financial, working-class, marginal, and speculative cities, but above all the city which housed the middle classes who demanded progress and moderation. The physical creation of the "new Havana" was an accurate reflection of this trend, in which residential neighborhoods stood out more than the emblematic buildings characteristic of a big city, whose construction had to wait until the 1920s. Starting with the U.S. occupation, an image of immediate modernity spread, but took a long time to become a reality and often did not coincide with the political times. Modernity was closely related, on the one hand, to a feeling of fervent hope, and on the other hand to a mirage, an image that never became a tangible reality.

When beginning to organize the Constituent Assembly, General Wood had attempted to lay the foundations for a "stable, well-organized, free government." Stable and well organized, not subject to another foreign sovereignty but instead under the tutelage of the United States—this was a situation that obviously challenged full sovereignty. Stable and well organized, following the natural chaos of the war, with the active participation of social and ethnic actors who had to be included in the new democracy since, even though it was the subject of debate, the republic could not adopt a system that restricted people's rights and freedoms.[5] It was at this point that the middle and upper classes looked forward not to a modernist North American style but rather to the tastes of the past in order to establish once again visual differences marking the social hierarchy, in opposition to the inevitable democratization, to the theoretical dominance of the masses—the people—most of whom were from rural communities, small villages, and the tenement buildings of the Havana slums.

Let us take a look at some examples. Construction work on the Palacio de la Asociación de Dependientes began in 1903. It was a four-story building with a concrete structure, but the style chosen for the building was Venetian Renaissance.[6] Such historicism was all the rage, and the style, inspired in Old Europe, soon became a permanent feature of the cityscape. Whatever was not built in an eclectic style could be classed as Italianized academicism. Large mansions and corporate buildings went even further or looked even further back and drew upon neo-Spanish styles: neo-Mudéjar, so-called Andalusian architecture and decoration, Herrerian Renaissance, and plateresque neobaroque.[7] The stylistic influence after 1900 was of Spanish origin and even more so during the 1910s and 1920s when the same international fashion spread to California, Florida, and the Hispanic South of the United States. The influence was therefore twofold. It came directly from Spain, and it was also reinterpreted in the so-called Spanish style, which the illustrated magazines and the cinema made popular; the style was shown on the screen and also used in the villas owned by the stars.

The adoption of these styles in Cuba began almost as soon as the Spanish flag had been lowered over the metropolis. It was first seen in the Cuban pavilions at the World's Fairs in Paris and Buffalo in 1900 and 1901, respectively. And it was used in two of the major constructions of the first republican period: the train station and the port customs office in 1912. Residential houses were built with porticos and plateresque façades. The national style looked for inspiration in the colony and in the eighteenth century, with additional features taken from popular culture. From 1917 onward, the neo-Hispanic, Californian-style bungalow became popular, with the sloping roofs and angled towers found in Vedado (and Nuevo Vedado) and on the sea front in Miramar.

According to Roberto Segre, one of the best contemporary experts on Latin American architectural history, the architecture of the first decades of republican life missed the opportunity to build a creative interpretation of cultural roots and instead became an artificial façade, a decor that replaced the search for a national style.[8] It could be said that the early "Americanization" of Havana's urban design under Spanish colonial rule was followed by a late "Hispanicization" during the first two decades of the Republic.[9] To a large extent these took place simultaneously and, as we shall see below, Americanization returned as a paradigm after 1920 with the avalanche of capital from the United States. This met opposition (just as it had met opposition from Rodó in Uruguay) from a type of Hispanicity that acted as a line of defense while Cubanizing culture.

Did Hispanic elements mix with modern elements? It is important not to confuse techniques, comfort, and architectural style. With regard to buildings, and insofar as decoration was concerned, Hispanic elements became a synonym for modernity during the republic. Scholars of architecture in Cuba and in other countries classed the group of styles mentioned above as neocolonial, without according them any political connotations because they extended over such varied geographies, from Porfirian Mexico to San Francisco and Los Angeles. The question is why the style was used in Havana. Neocolonial and neo-Hispanic styles became popular in Cuba just when political links with Spain had disappeared and North American influences prevailed over almost everything else, not least the "mediation" of politics. It was not a passing phase: one section of the intellectual movement that opposed the republic promoted or was associated with the flamboyant Institute for Hispano-Cuban Culture.[10]

The first large building constructed in the new era was the Lonja de Víveres or Lonja del Comercio. It was built between 1907 and 1909 in the Plaza de San Francisco and was based on a design by the Spanish architect Tomás Mur. The work was carried out by the Cuban architect José Toraya, who had been educated in the United States, and few changes were made. It was the most grandiose building of the time, five stories high and constructed in a neoclassical style. Toraya soon became the most sought-after architect. He renovated the old building of the Marine Headquarters and converted it into the first building to house the Chamber of Representatives, in Calle Oficios, next to the Convent of San Francisco. He was later involved in the construction of the Banco Nacional de Cuba, in Calle Obispo (1907), and the Hotel Sevilla Biltmore (1908), built in a neo-Moorish style. After leaving the presidency, in 1915 José Miguel Gómez commissioned Toraya to build his home on the Paseo del Prado. Inspired by classical styles, Toraya rejected the baroque style yet still maintained the historicism.

The U.S. construction company Purdy & Henderson was responsible for most of the buildings mentioned and for many others. Modern building techniques were used but, paradoxically, at that time modern styles came under Spanish artistic influence. Again it is worth dispensing with any prejudices that associate U.S. styles with "the modern" and Spanish styles with "the traditional." Around 1900, one of the most innovative and decorative building techniques was the bricked vault, a structure allowing the construction of large arches which represented a modernist retake on classicism. The technique (which was not used in Cuba until the 1960s) appeared prominently in the United States, used in the Boston Library, in Pittsburgh's Union Station, and in New York's Grand Central Station, all works carried out by the Spanish architect and builder Rafael Guastavino, who settled in the United States in the 1880s and patented the system.[11]

Historicism was also a feature of Havana's large public and corporate buildings. The Belgian architect Paul Belau designed the new Centro Gallego in a Hispanic baroque style, and this was annexed to the Teatro Nacional, formerly the Teatro Tacón. It was also symbolic that an immigrant from the old colonial metropolis was responsible for constructing the first national coliseum, the most famous monument in the country (larger and more solemn than the official headquarters of the republican state). As a result of its success, in line with the tastes of the period, the same architect was commissioned to build the Palace of Provincial Government in cooperation with the Cuban architect Rodolfo Maruri. After reappraisal, the project went on to become the Palacio Presidencial, built in a truly varied style, since it included elements of Spanish renaissance and Prussian baroque. The Presidential Palace is possibly, along with the Capitólio, the least Spanish of the official republican buildings. The Centro Asturiano added the finishing touches to the series when it was completed in 1927. It was inspired in the Herrerian renaissance style and had a stone façade with the Spanish coat of arms.

As part of a project to promote tourism, in 1929 Gerardo Machado's government began the restoration of the most emblematic buildings of the colonial period. These included El Templete and the Palacio de Gobierno (Governor's Palace), former seat of the Senate, which had just moved to the Capitólio, thus removing the last symbol of political power from the Plaza de Armas. Restoration work was also carried out on the Plaza de la Catedral. The world of colonial traditionalism was re-created. The work undertaken on the Palacio de los Capitanes Generales was a perfect illustration of the concept of the historic city which the Machado regime was attempting to present: it had everything that a visitor—a modern tourist—could imagine a stately, fortressed city should have, with its defenses and noble buildings. For Segre this was "the beginning of a process to invent a colonial ambience to restore a non-existent classical 'dignity' or a hypothetical environmental coherence" adapted to the image a foreigner required. The first step consisted of removing the buildings' colored plaster (the layer of plaster and lime wash that was considered too ordinary) to reveal the gray stone underneath. This is the appearance we have come to know and which both travelers and residents now believe to be original and characteristic.[12] Shortly afterward, in 1936, Emilio Roig's *Las calles de La Habana* (The streets of Havana) paid homage to the colonial city, and in 1938 Roig persuaded the city council to restore the old colonial names of hundreds of streets in the historic center.

Obviously the "Hispanicizing" style found widespread support among the Spanish immigrant colony and its descendants. The Centro Gallego and Centro Asturiano were the best examples of this, yet the style also caused a sensation among the creole upper middle classes and in official government spheres. These higher social groups and political authorities became "trend setters" whose prestige and privileged position meant that they were soon copied. In addition, they made the "Hispanicizing" tastes of those originally from the old metropolis, Spain, seem more acceptable instead of appearing to be the continuation of a defeated cause. There were undoubtedly exceptions which favored eclectic academicism, such as the residence which the

Pérez de la Riva family built opposite the entrance to the port, now the Palacio de la Música (Palace of Music), but the style was similar to that used in Spanish cities of the period, to which it bore more of a resemblance than to buildings from any other place.

Modernities and Their Expiration Date

Let us agree that urban modernity is but an instant. In 1975, before an audience gathered at the Central University of Venezuela, Alejo Carpentier introduced himself as a member of a peculiar generation. The acclaimed writer, who was born in 1904 and arrived in Havana in 1915, declared that

> Latin Americans of my generation experienced an unusual fate which on its own was enough to distinguish them from European men: they were born, they grew up, and they matured in relation to reinforced concrete.... the city I grew up in was still similar to Humboldt's Havana.... And suddenly, our sleepy capitals become real cities (anarchic in their sudden growth, anarchic in their design, excessive, disrespectful in their urge to demolish in order to replace) and our men, inseparable from the metropolis, become city-men, twentieth-century-city-men, that is to say History-of-the-twentieth-century-men.

Such was the view of this former student of architecture, author of *La ciudad de las columnas* (*The City of Columns*), a declaration of identity within a framework of time standing still.[13]

The notion that people were aware of change and that they were both "bewildered onlookers and the main actors" was repeated once again. When writing about the São Paulo he knew in 1935, Lévi-Strauss maintained that in America, cities "go directly from luxuriance to decrepitude, but they are never ancient," and that part of their essence was that they lacked relics. These words could not be applied to Havana, meaning that its modernization did not conform to the model of the new large American metropolis, so taken with the notion of an essentially vertical avant-garde—or at least that such a modernization was delayed until much later on in the 1950s.

In the New World, continued Lévi-Strauss, cities "are in need of restoration as quickly as they are built, or rather badly built." The anthropologist aimed to highlight the existence of very short evolutionary urban cycles, in comparison with those of the Old World. This "thirst for restoration" of which he spoke was closely related to the cycles of the export economies, in which members of the generation leading the cycle aspired to shape the city and leave their mark on houses, which demonstrated their personal opulence, in other words *social capital* in architecture.[14] On occasion they were also closely related to political cycles, which despite claiming to be reformist, often corresponded to authoritarian formulas, in Havana's case under the aegis of Tacón, Machado, and Batista. David Harvey has provided some valuable reflections on the conflict that underlies the relationship between the imaginative spatial play characteristic of regenerative policies and authoritarianism, and on the nostalgic strain with which the "authenticity" of cities is often established, a combination sought by conservative inertia represented above all by institutional buildings and which is more likely to prevail under authoritarian governments.[15]

Latin American cities periodically reinvented themselves, driven by the price of export commodities and by trade agreements. They presented hints of modernity followed by periods during which they faded away due to cycles of reduced commercial activity—as Lévi-Strauss noted, a permanent "fleeting youth." They were cities that experienced a considerable amount of immigration, attracted by the sparkle of success, and were subjected to the extreme conditions of the tropics, including annual storms and hurricanes. As a result of all these factors, reports by locals and visitors (often the reflections of scholars) continuously bore witness to urban signs of innovation in which modernity was repeated, only to fade away and then reappear once again.

Segre has made Havana the subject of incisive reflections on urbanism, architecture, social hegemony, and political power. He does not hesitate to highlight the *modern* city's rapid transformation after 1899. This modern transformation involved both speculative fervor and the substitution of the symbolic system of the peninsular government—although, as we will see, the same process of speculation could be observed from the 1870s onward in the area of Las Murallas, and the symbolic substitution, which involved moving government buildings to that very area, was a continuation of the same development initiative. It also involved a marked social division, which was perhaps the most unmistakable phenomenon. The bourgeois city (El Vedado, Miramar) was situated in the west, the south was home to the petite bourgeoisie (Santos Suárez, Luyanó, La Vívora), and the poor area of the city was located in the center, in the adjacent suburbs (Jesús María), and in the surrounding areas (Cayo Hueso and the lower part of the bay).[16] However, Segre admits that the division was more a trend than a reality, just as the cited occupation of land and the assigning of symbolic functions were trends, as was the "airborne" republic itself (as Bolívar would have said—without roots or with hidden roots), since the bourgeois and working-class areas were still adjacent to each other. Again, the trend can be detected before 1899.

Map 5.2 View of Cerro and Jesús del Monte, 1875. Courtesy of the Archivo Nacional de Cuba, Mapoteca.

In 1886, three decades after Tanco's comments and after the city walls had been demolished, another traveler (Peris Mencheta, a well-known Spanish journalist) commented on the city's growth since 1878. Of the twenty thousand buildings registered in the census, he said, over three thousand were newly constructed buildings and over two-thirds of the new constructions were for wealthy families. The El Cerro neighborhood, built as a summer resort at the end of the eighteenth century to the southwest of the bay, toward Vueltabajo, had become a residential area with villas and country houses which to the visitor looked similar to those found in the recent extension of the Paseo de la Castellana in Madrid, although in Havana most were one-story houses. The Paseo de la Reina and Paseo de Carlos III, built by the great urban reformer of the nineteenth century, General Tacón (who was so reactionary in politics), gave way to villas set among tree-covered gardens. The place where these came to an end marked the beginning of the new botanical gardens, after the old ones located next to the Teatro Tacón had been demolished and used as the site for the first railway station, the Estación Villanueva (map 5.2).

The city's two modern markets were located outside the city walls (one was the Mercado de Tacón in the Plaza del Vapor and the other was the Mercado de Colón), and these were reconstructed in 1876 and 1884, around the time of Peris Mencheta's visit, using metallic structures imported from Belgium. The new barracks had been built in the area, which also housed the Teatro Tacón, Teatro Albisu, and Teatro Irijoa, among others, together with the modern Nuestra Señora de las Mercedes Hospital (the first of three planned hospitals), finished in 1882, which had beds for two hundred patients. Although the reporter did not mention them, the area also played host to the Teatro Payret (a modern building from 1877 with an iron roof), the Teatro Alhambra, and the Circo-Teatro Jané, which was opened in 1881 and had a roof with an avant-garde cast-iron framework. The Teatro Irijoa, on Calle Dragones and Central (later Calle Zulueta), was opened in 1884. It was renovated in 1897, and in 1900, after being renamed the Teatro Martí, it was used as the venue for the Constitutional Convention.

The *casas de salud*, private clinics providing health care and hospital accommodation through subscription, were located outside the city walls in extensive, tree-covered grounds. The model of *mutuas*, originating in the colonial era, was fully developed by the time of the first republican period, almost always promoted by workers' associations and Spanish regional associations from colonial times. In 1885, the Sociedad Gallega contracted the Quinta del Rey clinic to provide a hospital and sanatorium for its members. In 1894, it bought the grounds on which La Benéfica sanatorium was built, which when finished was able to accommodate five hundred patients in various wards. The Asociación de Dependientes del Comercio (Shop Assistants Association), which was founded in 1880 and consisted mainly of Spaniards, commissioned the Quinta de Salud medical center. In 1912, the association's membership had reached the considerable figure of 27,600 and their health care facilities included sixteen wards able to accommodate 680 patients.[17] Around 1925, they had some eighty thousand members, that is to say, one in six inhabitants of Havana.[18]

Mencheta, who was a keen observer of social and material realities, did not fail to notice the existence of a vast third city that was neither modern nor traditional, but simply deprived. It was made up of tenement buildings (the *solar habanero*) and accounted for approximately one in four homes in which, he said, "Chinese, blacks, and dirty whites (mulattos) all lived crowded together."[19] The modernity of the cities, when visible, was a tiny fragment surrounded by a much wider reality of little interest to occasional visitors, left out of tourist guides and ignored by photographers and the tinted postcards that became fashionable during the third decade of the twentieth century. The history of poor housing, generally occupied by workers, is the history of how the communities living in the areas outside the city walls designated for "modernization," "reform," and "the new" were gradually displaced through the use of brutal methods (as brutal as those used by Haussmann in Paris), and their former residents were subsequently confined in unsanitary ghettos within the old city.

The history of the Jesús María neighborhood provides a telling summary. In 1802, the humble dwellings of 11,370 people (1,332 houses and 1,265 outbuildings and back rooms) were burned down. Rebuilding was prohibited. The residents evicted as a result of the fire were black creoles and "mangrove workers." The fire had broken out simultaneously at various points, an unmistakable sign of arson. In 1828 a second fire destroyed what was left of the neighborhood, which at that time was home to only 3,126 people, two-thirds of them white. The blacks had fled to Horcón and to other outlying neighborhoods. The influx of people into Havana, particularly during the two major anticolonial wars (1868–78 and 1895–98) and as a result of General Weyler's Reconcentration Policy (1896–98), and the fact that a large proportion of that population settled in the city, resulted in overcrowding in the most dilapidated neighborhoods (which the wealthy people gradually abandoned) and the division of houses. Condominiums and apartments were partitioned off, a trend which continued during the hazardous twentieth century in Havana. In 1919, over fifteen hundred *casas de vecindad* (tenement buildings) or *solares*, as they were generally called, were registered in the census. One type had a dozen rooms to rent (the *casa de vecindad* proper), another from 20 to 30 rooms (the *solar*), and a third up to 100 rooms (the *ciudadela*). Juan Manuel Chailloux estimated that there was an average of twenty-eight rooms per solar in 1945 and that their inhabitants represented a third of the population of Havana, which was undoubtedly an increase with regard to the figures for 1886, when the number of poor houses was estimated to be around five thousand.[20]

In 1899, the census indicated that 43 percent of houses in the capital had a cesspit and no drains. It can easily be deduced where those houses were located. In 1904, there were 2,839 solares housing 86,000 inhabitants, in the region of 30 per house.[21] In other words, one in every three inhabitants lived in this kind of "infra-Havana." In 1945, Chailloux explained that several families lived crowded together in old colonial mansions, "divided and subdivided" until they held over 100 people in rooms partitioned off with cardboard and curtains to make poky little rooms reminiscent, in the words of the sociologist, "of the holds of slave ships." In 1910, the first workers' housing estate, named el Redención (or Pogolotti), was distributed and consisted of 950 houses; in 1945, it had as many as fourteen thousand residents, almost fifteen people per house.[22] That meant that overcrowding and insalubrity increased in Havana during the republic, at least for an ever greater proportion of citizens (at least 33 percent and perhaps as much as 40 percent of the populace were generally left out of the general view of urban modernization). The proletarian city and the city in which ordinary people lived were located in the old urban center and overflowed into the suburbs.

At the same time, the centers of production took on a palatial appearance, as could already be seen in the factories of the late nineteenth century—La Meridiana (1880), Gener (1882), Bances y López (1886)—and in factories that other tobacco dealers constructed in "the ring" (the space made available for urban construction by the demolition of the city's walls and moat), quite a long time before the construction of the American Tobacco Co. building in 1902 or the provocative Fábrica Partagás in 1929, right behind the Capitólio.[23] There were previous cases of architecture being used to ennoble manufacturing centers. The Palacio Aldama, having served to augment the grace and style of the family that constructed it and after its use as the seat of the High Court following its confiscation in 1869, was eventually given over to the noble industry of tobacco production ("the only remaining virtue of tobacco is that of the people who work with it," as Martí wrote). It housed the La Corona factory and, from 1898 to 1932, the Havana Cigar and Tobacco Factories, Limited. This was a clear sign that the productive world was devouring the symbols of social prestige, while changing the Spanish trade names for other foreign names. It was certainly true that urban design and social formation bore very little relation to colonial or republican political status.

Commercial life after 1898 was located in the old center and in the center outside the city walls, where buildings were renovated on spaces incorporated more than half a century earlier. The symbolic replacement of the buildings of power, which Segre refers to as a physical reality marking the rhythm of change from a colonial to a republican regime, had to wait quite a long time. The substitution took place during two periods. The first, during the second half of the 1910s, was interrupted by the economic crisis of 1920 and was resumed at the end of that decade and in the early 1930s. The second took place considerably later, in the 1950s, when alongside the establishment of the violent Batista dictatorship, the city underwent its greatest urban renovation. Havana was endowed with public buildings that finally freed themselves from academicism and classicism and experimented with creole functionalism (the Palacio de Justicia and the Palacio de Bellas Artes, the

Biblioteca Nacional and the buildings in Marianao).[24] Meanwhile, planning for the city was based on its new role as the capital of tourism and leisure on a large scale. It was carried out in collusion with inadvisable partners in a similar style to that used in Ciudad Trujillo, in the Dominican Republic, except that more resources were available in Havana and there was a more developed environment that was culturally closer to U.S. customers.[25]

Urban Renovation in the Late Colony

In 1853, Nicolás Tanco could not find a good hotel in Havana. A decade earlier, Salas y Quiroga complained about the city's poor restaurants, while noting that a recently established U.S.-style restaurant offered the highest levels of comfort, elegance, and service aimed at travelers from the United States who had gone to spend the winter there for health reasons.[26] In 1875, in the middle of the Ten Years' War, the Hotel Inglaterra opened next to the Louvre and took its name from one of the most modern and renowned cafés of the city. This period witnessed the beginning of the development of the wide strip of land, referred to as "the ring," created by the demolition of the city walls (decreed in 1863) and the filling in of their wide external moat. It was the most sought after area for construction as it served as a link between the old and the new cities and was close to the axis that had been used during the previous fifty years as a promenade, a leisure area, and a place for the upper classes to show off their wealth. Here the new leisure establishments were situated.[27]

The land became known as the Reparto Las Murallas and was the object of speculative fervor for fifty years, the period between the first transfers made to Julián Zulueta (1870) and the construction of the Palacio Presidencial, the Centro Asturiano, and the Bacardí corporation's building (1930). From 1880 onward, the construction of many of these buildings in the ring made use of the reinforced concrete that Carpentier referred to, mistakenly confusing them with the functional buildings built after 1950 because they left the material exposed. The difference, according to Segre, was that the academicism of the period between 1880 and 1920, spanning the end of the colony and the beginning of the republic, concealed the technical innovations that lay beneath it.[28] In short, technical modernity came before aesthetics and began during the old colonial regime.

Zulueta, the "prince of slave traders," realized the potential of the real estate business and commissioned the Spanish architect Pedro Tomé (who created the Palacio Balboa) to construct a large block of commercial premises. Tomé had arrived in Cuba in the mid-1860s to take up the post of municipal architect. The building, which from 1894 onward was known as La Manzana de Gómez in reference to its new owner, the sugar tycoon Gómez-Mena, was a one-story building with an inner glazed gallery running diagonally through the building in line with Parisian trends. Between 1916 and 1918, four more stories were constructed for apartment accommodation, giving the building the appearance it still has today.

During the last two decades of colonial rule, advertisements for spacious shops selling foreign articles of the type found in the North were often placed in newspapers. It is worth remembering, however, that most shops were of a distinctly popular nature, with the exception of (most of) the most luxurious outlets in Calle Obispo, O'Reilly, San Rafael, and Galiano. They were not like the shops of the Parisian-style boulevards and plazas of the Second Empire, but were instead closer to the model of the bazaar, with large signs traditionally used to capture the attention of pedestrians and large awnings overhanging the sidewalks. This continued at least during the first decade of the republic, as can be seen in the photos taken of the Parque Central at that time, which illustrate a kind of primitivism that was highly idealized by numerous subsequent reports and analyses.

At the same time, the fin de siècle era following the Treaty of Zanjón saw the construction of residential villas to the west, next to the coast, in a new upper-middle-class suburb between El Carmelo and El Vedado. It was completed after 1899 and also given the name El Vedado.[29] The birth of the Vedado residential neighborhood has mistakenly been associated with the republic. This idea was proposed by the geographer and historian Leví Marrero, and he was joined by numerous authors who confused the creation of the neighborhood with its extension toward Marianao and the south (what is known as Nuevo Vedado) into a vast, crowded modern nucleus.[30] The confusion was convenient when all eyes were focused on a foundational, innovative republic that denied or disputed the spontaneity with which civil society, in particular the upper and upper middle classes, designed their own habitat during the colony.

The introduction of an electric tramway improved transport links in the growing city. Distances were measured in traveling time, and the "center" lost its centrality as a result of public transport. However, the greatest impetus to the move toward peripheral areas was when the middle classes renounced the historic city (the old and the new) and turned to the garden-city concept in search of a reflection of harmony, ethnic uniformity, and separation from the lower classes. This was the perfect world to which they aspired; the model inspired the English country cottage, which was transferred to

New England and then suburbanized. Shortly afterward, El Vedado stood out as being the most aristocratic area, with small gardens and unmistakable porticos with Ionic columns a sign of status, a mock classical touch used by the nouveaux rich to pass themselves off as old families while constructing with stucco and limestone.[31] The trend of constructing on a grand scale had been started by Aldama a century earlier when he built his mansion next to the Campo de Marte, then on the outskirts of town.

The early introduction of the automobile to Havana provided freedom of movement to those who could afford it. The phenomenon has been highlighted with regard to other American metropolises, and the experience spread when Fordization allowed the price of cars to drop and made them available to professionals, qualified employees, and traders, but not, for the time being, to those who manufactured them.[32] The city expanded and widened its urban boundaries. The physiognomy of the new outskirts and their exclusivity gave them a select, suburban status that contrasted with the poor, working-class suburban neighborhoods. Transport, both private and public, played a different role for each social group. The introduction of trams in the old city caused countless problems and made traveling difficult for individuals and private vehicles, causing inconvenience and increasing the risk of accidents. In 1945, Chailloux explained that the lack of fuel and spare parts due to the Second World War disconnected the suburbs from the city, leading people to take refuge in urban areas. At the same time, the usual immigration from rural areas continued, giving rise to overcrowding and terribly unhealthy conditions (the same thing occurred half a century later, during the "special period").[33] With regard to the city acting as a magnet and a shelter, the problem was less circumstantial than Chailloux postulated, since the rate of immigration was constant prior to the crisis caused by international shortages: a lot less was built than was needed, which was the fate of the big metropolises and a permanent stigma of Havana.

The traditional interpretation has it that the expansion of Vedado during the first years of the republic was based on the introduction of the electric tramway. In 1929 Martínez Ortiz proposed that "entire neighborhoods, such as El Vedado, grew as if by magic; . . . the value of property rose incredibly quickly and large fortunes were made overnight with the urbanization of agricultural farms and even land which was previously used as a quarry."[34] The explanation has since been repeated again and again. However, the creation of this neighborhood and the tendency of a particular sector of the population (the middle and upper middle classes) to converge went back further. The census of 1899 situated El Vedado as practically the sec-

Map 5.3 Havana, 1900. Courtesy of the Archivo Nacional de Cuba, Mapoteca.

ond neighborhood of Havana in terms of population with almost ten thousand inhabitants, after San Lázaro (twenty thousand) and on a par with El Cerro, Jesús del Monte, and Punta.[35] The difference was that its horizontal, landscaped design meant that it occupied a much larger surface area, with a layout which when finished occupied approximately half the area of the old walled city (map 3).

During the early twentieth century, the Hotel Plaza was constructed in the ring (by redesigning the building previously used as the newspaper offices of *Diario de la Marina*), as was the Hotel Sevilla-Biltmore. On the other side of the Parque Central, the Hotel Telégrafo was built, which was later frequently used as the venue for politicians' celebrations. But before then, in 1876, the Hotel Pasaje was opened next to the Teatro Payret, with its iron and glass-covered gallery, which represented a true innovation. In 1881, the Hotel America was opened, which was later renamed Hotel Roma. In 1908, the Hotel Saratoga was opened behind Teatro Irijoa, opposite the railway station, but the building was actually an apartment block built in 1880, and though remodeled inside, was still modern enough in terms of construction techniques, spatial design, and external decoration to look "modern" three decades later. Trends in fittings, the adoption of new building techniques, and the introduction of aesthetic forms generally associated with the initial decades of the republic actually began around 1875–80.

The surge in construction, the introduction of new techniques, and aesthetic renovation within eclectic academicism (like the era and the social class that were undergoing changes and adapting) coincided with the period of the highest sugar prices on the international market, between 1869 and 1883, and with record levels of exports from 1868 onward, which offset the loss of capital that sought security away from the island starting in 1868 with the first war of independence.[36] Carlos Venegas has highlighted how it fell to the oligarchy of Havana, who had made their fortune from sugar and tobacco, to give social meaning to the Reparto de Las Murallas given that the state was incapable of planning how to use this space for civil purposes, as had initially been intended. Without considering the uncertainty that the war could generate and fully confident in the triumph of the Spanish army, Zulueta, the Marquis of Balboa, Gener, González del Valle, the Marchioness of Villalba, Jané, and others bought land and built luxurious buildings from 1871 onward. They increased their efforts after 1875, when land could be paid for with treasury bonds, whose value was otherwise not liquid.[37] In 1895, a park and a monument in honor of Francisco Albear were opened in the area where the Puerta de Monserrate stood, a remembrance of the military engineer who had built the city's water supply system (the Acueducto de Vento, 1855–93). Albear was a Cuban creole in the Spanish army who had reached the rank of brigadier and who remained loyal to Spain until his death in 1887.

It is important to remember that through these buildings the representatives of the Spanish elite in Cuba "monumentalized" the architecture of Havana referred to by Venegas. To a large extent the following facts provide the key to what happened. There was a state at war which was unable to invest in civil works and a city council which had sought-after land but which was in need of resources, municipal taxes having been committed to the war effort. There were affluent "patriots" who were able to do business having previously purchased bonds that increased their political influence. They were presented with the opportunity of projecting the image of their opulence in what went on to become the center of the city due to the urban redesign process. Against the backdrop of the abolition of slavery, the start of massive peninsular immigration, the final years of high sugar prices, and the feeling of optimism which, in general, took hold of urban social life, the Ten Years' War and the first decade of the postwar period helped to dissolve the old colony and to increase the prospect of material, intellectual, and political improvement.

The building activity that took place between 1875 and 1915 along the axis formed by Fortaleza de la Punta and the Parque de Colón transformed the sleepy city of previous decades. However, the fact that modernity was identified with North American civilization related to an imaginary that had been slowly constructed during the colonial period by one sector of the island's elites. It found inspiration in the progress of the United States, from the education system aimed at the most privileged groups (which attracted their attention from the 1830s onward) to the urban design of the mid-nineteenth century and the extraordinary levels of material growth following the Civil War and Reconstruction, just when commercial links strengthened between Cuba and its natural market. From the last few years of the eighteenth century onward, close economic relations with the most powerful cities of the United States (those situated on the East Coast and in the Northern states, in other words, the most developed cities) had a major influence on the customs, tastes, and pastimes of the most dynamic sectors of Havana's population, a very wealthy, trend-setting minority. This invisible link was strengthened during the second half of the nineteenth century. The greater the prosperity of the United States, to which trade was linked, the greater the desire to emulate that country. Trade is never a simple exchange of goods: it involves a wide variety of influences and a spread of habits that also guarantees a demand for articles. However, the notion of reciprocity cannot be reduced to balancing the value of trade. The export of raw sugar, honey, tobacco, wood, and fruits did not have the same significance in the target market as the importation of machinery, construction materials, books, clothes, and domestic and work equipment. These were accompanied by new sales techniques: a notion of perfectly divided urban space with large, bright shops that invited passersby to enter, thus requiring wide sidewalks, cafés, and leisure establishments next to the stores whose latest goods had been advertised in the press.

From the late nineteenth century onward, graphic publications became more popular and lithography was introduced in the advertising sections of daily newspapers and weekly periodicals. The era of "new journalism" began around 1870, a revolution in social communication during which the newspaper became the intermediary between individuals and the outside world, in which political news and issues of human interest were mixed with advertising promotions and the glorification of modern progress. Printed photographs transformed and renovated the presentation of periodicals and had a major effect on the transmission of images. Then came the invention and expansion of the photogravure process.[38] Seen from the viewpoint of the highly visual culture of the twentieth century, it is difficult to understand the changes that immediate and massive increases in the number of images had on the construction of social imaginaries.

Such imaginaries were brought abruptly up to date in 1899 at the beginning of the occupation government. The United States, that idealized agent of progress, was the leading authority and was in charge of overseeing the birth of the republic. The main measures adopted then were related to health and urban hygiene. Hygiene was associated with the civilization of the Protector State, while squalor and filth were linked to the obscurantism of Spanish domination, as Iglesias reminds us. "American-style" modernization had begun.[39] Or rather, it had begun again, according to Louis Pérez's study, *Ser cubano: Identidad, nacionalidad y cultura*, which details North American influence on Cuba throughout the nineteenth century. However, the elements which in Pérez's opinion contributed to forming the Cuban personality in the image of a modern United States would appear to be exaggerated, regardless of how attractive the model was to a minority of sectors.[40]

"American-style" modernity could already be seen in the urban expansion outside the city walls during the 1830s and 1840s and in Vedado at the end of the century, still during colonial rule. It could also be seen in certain customs. Even so, it did not have a major influence on society. Around 1870, American-style social and sports clubs did exist, but during the 1880s, young wealthy men who had studied in the United States and returned with new pastimes were presented as strange, ironic figures in literature aimed at popular audiences. In Raimundo Cabrera's 1885 comedy for the stage, *Viaje a la luna* (*Trip to the moon*), the author describes the modern dandy as follows: "He is a young man / educated in Pennsylvania. / He can skate very well / he steals the show when he plays baseball; / he's a master at Noké, / but he hardly speaks English." Three years later, in the sequel, *¡Vapor correo!* (*Mail boat!*), one of the characters says that baseball is the most fashionable pastime. Still, even if certain pastimes were beginning to move out of the circles of those who had been educated abroad, they could still be subject to mockery insofar as they had not managed to win over the general public.

Exchanges between the United States and Cuba had been a common occurrence for a long time. They included commercial transactions, financial links, and the heirs of the sugar aristocracy undertaking periods of study in colleges and work experience placements in companies.[41] The best known case was that of Cristóbal Madan in the 1820s, yet it was by no means an exception. Between 1860 and 1895, exchanges also included migrant workers and exiled people, together with people returning to their own country. Emulation became more widespread among the cultured classes after 1878, particularly among pro-independence supporters, the country's self-proclaimed regenerators who were the only ones capable of promoting potentially successful change that would advance society without dragging the country toward another destructive war. These regenerators-*cum*-reformers chose a model of Autonomism: modernization controlled from above which at the same time curbed the signs of social breakup attributed to the prolonged slavery of blacks and the Spanish colonial government's lack of foresight in light of the new reality of a multiethnic society, which they believed suffered from a major gap between civilization and barbarism. Indeed, ¡*Vapor correo!* was dedicated to the Autonomist leader Rafael Montoro. Raimundo Cabrera, the era's most successful writer of light-hearted plays, while describing the chaos and abuses of the colonial administration and criticizing Spanish Americans, reminded audiences how in Havana it was often possible to come across thieves and witness fights among *ñáñigos*—members of the Afro-Cuban men's fraternity, Abakua—which he identified as a "clandestine institution of savages." Such prejudices were also evident in Fernando Ortiz's first major work, *El negro esclavo*, written in 1916, in which he revealed that for a certain cultured section of society, the enemy of civilization (the Afro-Cuban criminal underworld) coexisted in the city and, as a result, occupied certain areas and shared other spaces with exemplary citizens.

The Republican City

If improving hygiene was the most visible measure undertaken by the U.S. occupation government, it was also an efficient propaganda instrument. The census taken in 1899 paid particular attention to this issue—and with good reason, given the conditions found in the city and its renown for insalubrity.[42] Moreover, in addition to the usual unhealthy conditions, ever since the years of the war (1868–78) the public roads had not been cleaned, no investment had been made in sanitation, and there was insufficient urban policing. The situation got worse from 1895 onward with the addition of refugees and the *reconcentrados* (people forced to emigrate to the capital from rural areas). Conditions of hygiene were definitely much worse in 1899 than they had been five years earlier, and in relative terms conditions in 1895 were worse than in 1868. By contrast, in terms of its urban design and buildings, in 1895 the city had a level of modernity which, despite continuing to develop after the end of the war, was not surpassed for a long time. A walk down the Paseo del Prado to Reina and then to the bay along Calle Zulueta is enough to confirm this, since the vast majority of the noncorporate buildings belong to the end of the colonial era and those were the buildings that gave the city its character in 1900.

General Leonard Wood's government was characterized by its ability to draw up balanced budgets during its two years in power (1900–1902). During that time, spending on health represented 20 percent of the budget; spending on hospitals and nursing homes 5.5 percent; primary education 16 percent; higher education 4 percent; and public works 7.8 percent, most of which was assigned to the docks. Health, assistance to the poor, and education accounted for 45.5 percent of spending.[43] Nonepidemic mortality rates in Havana fell from an average of 36 per 1,000 between 1870 and 1899 to 22 per 1,000 during the first decade of the republic, which represents a dramatic decrease.[44] However, in order to obtain the average figure, the census took into account the decades of the wars (when conditions were different for obvious reasons) and periods of peace, without considering how this would distort the figures. For example, the figures ranged from 29 per 1,000 in 1889 to 89.19 per 1,000 in 1898.[45] If yellow fever and smallpox deaths are removed from the equation, in the 1880s the mortality rate in Havana was 28 per 1,000, which is not so different from the figure for 1908.

There is no doubt that the sanitation works undertaken after 1899 were substantial and essential. But in addition to providing an account of the progress made, statistics became a political instrument aimed at partially concealing reality and presenting the best possible image of the protection provided by the United States. The census ordered by Governor Charles E. Magoon in 1906, at the beginning of the second intervention, bore witness to this.

The first investment made in hospitals after 1898 involved renovating buildings and providing them with equipment and medical instruments. According to Martínez Ortiz, the "unsanitary and gloomy hospitals of the old regime became pleasant, hygienic places," and the new wards were equipped with "all the latest advances."[46] The most important building work involved conditioning the Hospital de las Mercedes, which in 1886 (four years after it was opened) was classed as modern and became the clinical hospital of the university, which was built nearby. The biggest building project, the Hospital Calixto García, was carried out between 1914 and 1917 under Menocal's government, which expanded the scope of the project and also built the main buildings of the university. The new 625-bed hospital incorporated the latest technological advances, but it was built on land made available after the demolition of the Alfonso XIII Spanish military hospital (which had only been built in the 1890s during the war) and continued a project which had begun in the early 1860s to build a hospital complex with nine hundred beds. At the end of the period of Spanish rule, the only part of the complex to have been built was the Hospital de las Mercedes. The joint capacity of these two hospitals corresponded approximately to the forecast made half a century earlier, but there was now a much larger urban population to cater for.

Let us concur that modernity was selective and provisional. After some repair work, the Hospital Alfonso XIII was used as a military hospital for North American troops during the intervention, and in mid-1900 it was opened to the public as Hospital No. 1. In 1906, the Cuban Congress authorized the president to spend 650,000 pesos over four years to build the Hospital Nacional on that land.[47] On numerous occasions when referring to hospitals for infectious diseases, hospitals for women, charitable hospitals, and so on (either new or built during the colonial period), the medical historian of the early republic, Jorge Le Roy, repeatedly states that they were "equipped with the most modern facilities."

The occupation government took responsibility for the health service, for education, and for sanitizing Havana, in addition to attending to the hospitals and looking after the maintenance of the city's streets, all areas for which the city council was normally responsible. Under its authority, in 1900 work began on the Malecón (the city's oceanfront esplanade), the Academia de Ciencias (Science Academy), and the Escuela de Artes y Oficios (School of Arts and Crafts). In the meantime, the city council was responsible for policing the city and resorted to expeditious methods that sent offenders to correctional institutions. The deterioration affected not only buildings and roads but also customs as a result of the habits and the extremely rural nature of the inhabitants. This was also a sign of people's voluntary or forced immigration from rural areas. Drastic measures were then taken to "reeducate"— that is, they were forced to urbanize their way of life.

The first governor of the U.S. occupation administration, John R. Brooke (1899), suspended the city council's contract with the Banco Español, freeing it from the debts that the municipal corporation had been burdened with, which were the original reason basic services were no longer provided. Wood began construction of the sewer system and paved the main streets, continuing the projects of his predecessor. It was during this period that the "modern sanitation system transformed the concept of cleaning services through the construction of drainage and sewer systems, regular rubbish collections, and hosing down the streets." Up to 1.5 million pesos per year were spent on such measures.[48] Chroniclers generally pointed out that the city council limited itself to increasing employees' wages without undertaking any

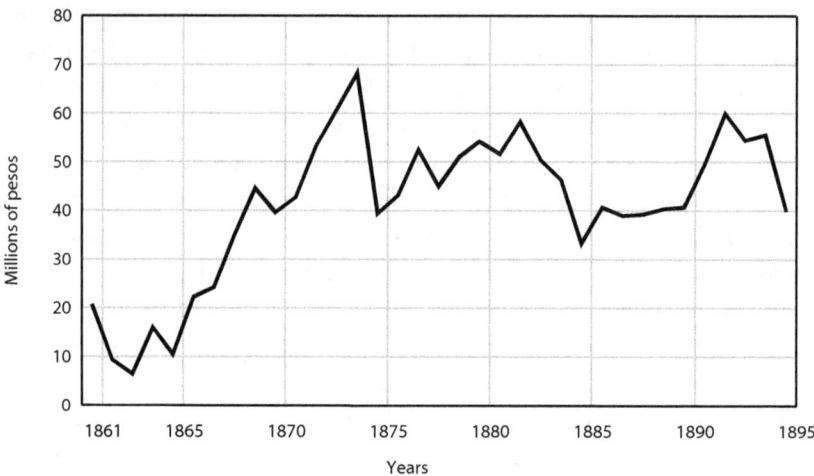

Figure 5.1 Balance in Cuba's favor. *Source*: Author collation of data.

major works. No monumental buildings were constructed, nothing that, in the words of Martínez Ortiz, "demonstrates the sublimity of design, high spirit, broad-mindedness, and breadth of aspirations."[49]

Of course, the person who wrote this also dedicated his book to President Machado (1925–33), the promoter of the Carretera Central (the Central Highway, which had been the object of various projects since the mid-nineteenth century, one of them the work of the military engineer Francisco Albear) and the Capitólio Nacional, among other monumental buildings. According to Martínez Ortiz's compelling analysis, this increased Machado's political stature in contrast with the modest beginnings of the republican regime, though he fails to mention the fact that Machado and his minister of public works, Carlos Miguel de Céspedes, were shareholders in Warren Brothers, the company contracted to build the Carretera Central. Neither was there any mention of the loans taken out with the House of Morgan, which were used to fund some essential infrastructure and other structures that were purely symbolic, in conditions that very soon made it difficult to pay off the debt.

In a letter in 1901 describing the philosophy with which he aspired to preside over the new state, Tomás Estrada Palma wrote the following: *"when setting up* the republic, so to speak . . . it is necessary to bear in mind . . . that we are a new nation with moderate resources; that it will be more dignified to remain within the limits of prudence, as modestly as possible . . . and we must therefore carefully combine the organization of public services and their allocation with the financial capacity of the island, in moderation."[50]

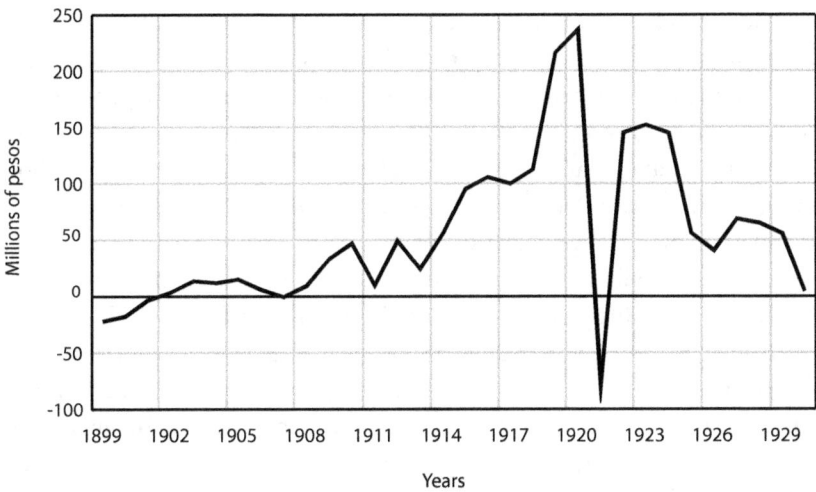

Figure 5.2 Trade balance. *Source:* Author collation of data.

In 1904, when conservative political elements regrouped and attracted the president to their ranks to back his reelection, they took the name of the Partido Moderado, a name which reflected the obsessive concerns of José Martí's former collaborator: moderate resources, prudent and modest limits, services in moderation.

In synch with the profits of the sugar industry and the waves of material accumulation, investments were made in order to make a new city and to construct new and generally privately owned buildings. However, public spending was moderate, in line with the spirit of the presidency (and more importantly the fiscal policy), in particular with regard to public works. A state that collected little revenue could spend little on infrastructure and services. And the republic, because of its opposition to the tax system of the colony and its predisposition to facilitate private investment and the reproduction of capital, adopted a "prudent" (in other words weak) fiscal policy. It was fundamentally based on raising funds through customs duties, thus extending the abusive taxation policies of the colony. Customs duties provided over 50 percent of the money collected, and during the early years these were affected by the drop in trade and by reductions in exportation rights due to the temporary drop in the price of sugar.

The 1907 census acknowledged that prior to 1906, budgetary spending on repairing and extending state buildings was "very small." Between July 1906 and September 1907, a period that included the first twelve months of the second U.S. occupation government (which started in September 1906), double the amount was spent on such things than during the period between 1902 and 1906.[51] In 1913, after calculating the balance of what today would be referred to as capital endowment and calculating the balance by sectors, the head of information of the Department of Agriculture, Trade, and Labour stated that in fifteen years, between 1898 and 1913, 61.5 million pesos had been invested in new buildings, residences, and premises. Government investment in public works had been 57 million pesos. Whereas the second figure could be confirmed in the state budgets, the first was only a low estimate. "In fifteen short years, the island of Cuba has risen like a phoenix from a vast wasteland of ashes and ruins to high levels of prosperity and financial prestige," he concluded, after adding that the value of landownership in Havana had increased by 144 million pesos and that foreign capital invested in Cuba during that time amounted to 112 million, half of which corresponded to British companies.[52]

Analysis of the activities of the legislature reveals that in July 1903 a small loan for the construction of a building for the House of Representatives was approved and then the executive branch was granted authority to use a plot of land belonging to the state for that purpose. No further progress was made in this respect. The legal authorization for the presidency of the republic to acquire the Teatro Nacional in 1905 was put on hold by Estrada Palma.[53] The result was that in the republic, the configuration of the urban area was still dominated by the old city and the adjacent area, as well as by the functions undertaken by administrative centers, commercial hubs, and services. The transition toward republican sovereignty and the formation of a hegemonic social and political bloc under the effective tutelage of the occupation government was clearly correlated to the construction of the new capital and the way in which it was conceived.

The Liberating Army—the Cuban independence forces—never entered Havana; even more symbolically, the House of Representatives of its government-in-waiting had to meet in Cerro, a Havana suburb used by the now modest middle classes, instead of choosing a central location that offered the kind of dignity that the occasion demanded. In symbolic terms, the previous Autonomist government of 1898 (convened by Spain as a last-ditch effort to undercut the independence rebellion) had been equally unfortunate: the Casino Español was chosen as the headquarters of its parliamentary chamber, and the headquarters of the executive branch were situated in the Palacio de los Capitanes Generales (Palace of the Captain General) and in the Palacio del Segundo Cabo (Palace of the Second Lieutenant), the very locus of Spanish colonial power in Cuba. The latter was also the scene of the transfer of powers between the North American commission and the Spanish authorities, which included Autonomist leader Rafael Montoro "as a member of the Cuban Government," a fact that is generally omitted.[54] Special witnesses to the effective transfer of sovereignty, this time in the Palacio del Gobierno (Palace of Government), included the General Staff of the Liberating Army: Generals José Miguel Gómez, Mario García Menocal, and Mayía Rodríguez y Lacret, the future usufructuaries of the republic.

With regard to the new public buildings that were representative of the republic, the austerity of the first Occupation Government and, above all, of Estrada Palma's presidency delayed the creation of buildings that symbolized the new state. The initial decision to house the House of Representatives in the old marine headquarters (a modest building in terms of size and appearance even after it was extended and renovated), the Senate in the Palacio del Segundo Cabo, and the presidency of the republic in the Palacio de los Captianes Generales (where it shared the building with Havana's city council) was a means of reasserting the traditional areas of power, which were now occupied by the institutions of the new nation-state. Not until 1910 did the legislature plan the new Palacio de Gobierno Provincial, and not until the plan was reviewed in 1915 was the building used as the headquarters of the executive branch, fueled by the first multimillion-dollar revenue from the sugar industry and also by large loans taken out by García Menocal (up to $52 million during his term of office, $1 million more than the loans taken out by his two predecessors put together, though $2 million less than the debt run up by Zayas in half the time during his presidency of 1921–25).[55] Only then did the republic finally begin to rid itself of its initial austerity and assert its physical presence through buildings that symbolized power.

The creation of scenographic frameworks that represent the functions of the state (referred to by Segre with regard to the Master Plan that Machado commissioned from Forestier) is as old as the transformation of the palatial court of the Renaissance into a truly complex, bureaucratic state.[56] The same was true of the multiplication of the number of public servants in twentieth-century states: in Cuba the number increased to 25,600 in 1907 and to 51,400 in 1930; over the next twenty years the figure grew to 130,000.[57] The creation of the city of Washington, D.C., was the first republican example of a scenographic framework of power and the first example of the modern era. Emulating the U.S. Capitol, irrespective of the political nature of the regime that promoted it, clearly demonstrated the desire to make the authority and dignity of the institutions visible through their monumentalization. Without doubt this also helped to formalize them, to grant them the appearance of institutions that were above the government of the time and to distract attention from that government's actions.

At that time and afterward, the city was in private hands, partly inherited and partly fostered by private interests. From the very beginning (and with no significant resistance) these prevailed over the general will. The fact that such a public renovation project was never carried out became the basis of successive laments for "the republic which could have been," a powerful myth under permanent construction during the twentieth century. Around the time that Fernando Ortiz wrote about the Afro-Cuban criminal underworld as an enemy within the city (1916), in other Latin American metropolises which were experiencing strong growth, the lumpen, together with workers (to a large extent immigrant workers) and those excluded from society through poverty, tended to be defined as "dangerous classes" and were the target of measures of control, in addition to being pushed out of the city center, confined to working-class suburbs, and subjected to disciplinary rules. This happened during the expansion of São Paulo over the first two decades of the twentieth century, when it became clear that efforts were being made to establish clearly demarcated neighborhoods according to social classes. The aim, in line with the orders of the city's mayor, Washington Luís (1914–16), was "to purify [the city] morally and physically" and to eradicate the "vicious mixture of scum of all nationalities, all ages, all of them dangerous."[58] At the same time that the mansions of the city center were being demolished to make way for offices and commercial areas, laborers were being moved out to working-class colonies. Washington Luís, a lawyer and historian with little sensitivity to urban history, was able to extend the scope of his ideas when he was elected state governor in 1920 and president of the republic in 1926.

The process of confrontation with workers organized in trade union or socio-ethnic groups in the urban environment of Havana progressed at the same time as the businesses and organizational capacity of the subaltern classes also progressed. The economic opportunities ushered in by the First World War, with increases in the price of sugar and the subsequent multiplication of the island's other activities linked to the sugar industry, also led Cuba to stigmatize and marginalize any social sectors that were not integrated and any labor sector that adopted a more aggressive position during Mario García Menocal's first term in office (1913–17). It was this period that witnessed the deportation of unwanted anarchist trade union leaders, claiming that it was due to their status as foreigners.[59] The increase in exports between 1915 and 1917, when the volume doubled that of 1914, was followed by the "boom years" between 1916 and 1919, which attracted North American capital to the sugar industry and made wealthy Cuban businessmen richer than they could have ever imagined. Menocal noticed the rapid urban development of Havana toward the west, beyond Vedado and the barrier that the River Almendares represented, and commissioned the construction of a second bridge (there was a recently constructed but obsolete bridge at Calle 23). The bridge reached the 5ª Avenida in Miramar and was opened in 1921.

The real estate business was at its height. Powerful real estate and urban development companies had just been set up offering exclusive plots at the Playa de Marianao and between Miramar and the Country Club. A newspaper advertisement from 1920 stated that "Traders, landowners, and industrialists who have made their fortune . . . can improve their good luck even more and multiply their capital by investing in land at the Alturas del Country Club, where mansions are being built that are worth over $1,200,000." The ad went on to use the slogan "It's the modern Havana! An elegant, aristocratic Havana!" Once again, as always, there was the claim of a renovated, modern Havana compared with the old one, just as there had been in 1835 and 1853, just as there had been in 1875 and 1900. The developers stated that they were looking to create "a meeting place for elegance" which would welcome those who due to their position and education formed part of an elite, offering them mansions in accordance with their status and with the "insurmountable barriers between different social classes." Social and residential segregation was finally expressed in very clear terms, with suburbs that were inaccessible to groups with less spending power, with special urban designs and styles that partially distanced themselves from the Hispanicizing trends that could nevertheless still be seen in the "tropical-style" mansions. One year after his presidency, García Menocal became a shareholder in the company that developed the Miramar area and together with his family he went on to take control of the Board of Governors.[60] Havana (this time a private, exclusive Havana hidden from public view) began to be reinvented with its sights set, once again, on a modernity that could always be sensed but that remained elusive.

Notes

This paper was prepared as part of the research project HAR2012-36481 funded by the Spanish Ministerio de Economía y Competitividad and P1-1B2012-57, Universitat Jaume I, and also Programa Prometeo 2013/023, Generalitat Valenciana para Grupos de Excelencia. The current version has drawn on comments made during its presentation in the symposium "After the Intervention: Civics, Sociability, and Applied Science in the New Cuba, 1895–1933," Windsor, May 26 and 27, 2010.

1. Iglesias, *Las metáforas del cambio en la vida cotidiana*.

2. Tanco Armero, *Viaje de Nueva Granada a China y de China a Francia*, 110–11.

3. *Hatos* were large areas used for extensive livestock farming, and from the sixteenth century onward they determined the distribution of land on which the island's first oligarchy was founded. The historian Manuel Moreno Fraginals used the term *sacarocracia* (sugarocracy) to refer to the aristocracy whose fortunes came from owning land and selling sugar, mainly from the end of the eighteenth century onward.

4. See Segre, "El sistema monumental en la Ciudad de La Habana, 1900–1930," 187–200. I am grateful to Carlos Venegas for recommending this text to me.

5. This subject was examined in Piqueras, *Sociedad civil y poder en Cuba*, 295ff, in the chapter "La obstinación por gobernar el orden."

6. Venetian Renaissance refers to the style of art and architecture produced in the Venetian republic in the sixteenth century.

7. Neo-Mudéjar refers to the revival of styles characteristic of Muslim architecture; Andalusian to the style characteristic of Muslim Spain; Herrerian Renaissance to a sober style characteristic of late sixteenth-century Spain; plateresque neobaroque to the revival of Spanish architectural styles of the early modern period; and Hispanic baroque to the later Spanish art and architectural styles of the seventeenth and eighteenth centuries.

8. Segre, *Arquitectura antillana del siglo XX*, 128.

9. The synthesis in the form of a paradoxical succession was suggested by Adrián López Denis.

10. La Institución Hispano-Cubana de Cultura. See Puig-Samper and Naranjo, "Fernando Ortiz: Herencias culturales y forja de la nacionalidad," 197–226.

11. On Guastavino's influence, see Collins, "The Transfer of Thin Masonry Vaulting from Spain to America," 176–201. For the effect on Cuba, see p. 200. Pérez Echazábal et al., "Escuelas Nacionales de Arte de Cubanacán: Diagnóstico y proyecto de restauración de artes plásticas," 45–51. Guastavino's technique and style would only be used in Cuba for one of the most original and emblematic constructions of the first period of the revolution: the National Schools of Art were designed in 1961 by the architect Ricardo Porro and are now in a condition of neglect due to construction defects and lack of maintenance.

12. Segre, *Arquitectura antillana del siglo XX*, 130.

13. Carpentier, "Conciencia e identidad de América," 5–6.

14. Lévi-Strauss, *Tristes trópicos*, 81–82.

15. Harvey, *Spaces of Hope*, 163–69.

16. Segre, *Arquitectura antillana del siglo XX*, 77.

17. Lloyd, *Impresiones de la República de Cuba en el siglo XX*, 440.

18. "Habana," *Enciclopedia Universal Ilustrada Europeo-Americana*, 434.

19. The descriptions quoted are translations from Peris Mencheta, *De Madrid a Panamá*, 97–109, 125–26.

20. Chailloux Carmona, *Los horrores del solar habanero*, 96–97 (Jesús María), 112–13 (census of 1919), 116 (typology of the solar).

21. Scarpaci, Segre, and Coyula, *Havana*, 58.

22. Chailloux Carmona, *Los horrores del solar habanero*, 105. The neighborhood was also known as "Pogolotti Lots" soon after the first houses were built, in reference to Dino Pogolotti (father of the Cuban painter Marcelo Pogolotti, who originally owned the land and was one of the housing developers).

23. Chailloux Carmona, *Los horrores del solar habanero*, 46.

24. Academicism denotes the Greco-Roman revival; Classicism Greco-Roman style itself; and creole functionalism refers to local architecture displaying a preference for function over decoration.

25. Santo Domingo, capital of the Dominican Republic, was renamed Ciudad Trujillo during the dictatorship of Rafael Trujillo (1930–61).

26. Salas y Quiroga, *Viages*, 148–51.

27. Venegas Fornias, *La urbanización de las murallas*.

28. Segre, *Arquitectura antillana del siglo xx*, 46.

29. An informative monograph has been written on the neighborhood by Pavez Ojeda, *El Vedado*.

30. Marrero, *Geografía de Cuba*, 472: "El Vedado, the first of the big residential neighborhoods constructed during the republic, stretched over 5 km."

31. *Impresiones de la República de Cuba en el siglo xx*, 413.

32. Wolfe, *Autos and Progress*.

33. Chailloux Carmona, *Los horrores del solar habanero*, 108.

34. Martínez Ortiz, *Cuba. Los primeros años de independencia*, 333.

35. Sanger (dir.), *Informe sobre el Censo de Cuba, 1899*, 192.

36. Sugar prices in Deerr, *The History of Sugar*, 2: 531. Exports in Moreno Fraginals, *El Ingenio*, III: 71. The economic context and the strategy of diversifying assets in Piqueras, *Cuba, emporio y colonia*, 187–214.

37. Venegas Fornias, *La urbanización de las murallas*, 48–53, 62.

38. Following Bordería, Laguna, and Martínez Gallego, *Historia de la comunicación social*, 319–46.

39. Iglesias, *Las metáforas del cambio*, 41–44.

40. Pérez proposes that U.S. culture and life shaped the making of Cuban national identity before 1898, but considers U.S. influence after the occupation practically boundless, calling it a "design without a plan" or "the order of the new." However, the architectural examples that he mentions, and the buildings that he reproduces, though sometimes the product of U.S. builders, correspond to styles that were already present in the island during the colonial period and that were of European and Spanish inspiration.

41. See Ely, *Cuando reinaba su majestad el azúcar*, epigraph 26.b.

42. Sanger (dir.), *Informe sobre el Censo de Cuba, 1899*; Salas y Quiroga, *Viages*, 239–40.

43. Martínez Ortiz, *Cuba: Los primeros años de independencia*, 337–39.

44. Olmsted (dir.), *Censo de la República de Cuba bajo la administración provisional de los Estado Unidos 1907*, 164–66.

45. Le Roy, "Sanidad pública," 139; see pp. 140–41 for deaths due to yellow fever, malaria, typhus, etc.

46. Martínez Ortiz, *Cuba: Los primeros años de independencia*, 337.

47. *Impresiones de la República de Cuba en el siglo xx*, 144.

48. Clark, "Obras públicas," 331. The author was the head of the Department of Public Works.

49. Martínez Ortiz, *Cuba: Los primeros años de independencia*, 340.

50. In Martínez Ortiz, *Cuba: Los primeros años de independencia*, 363.

51. Olmsted (dir.), *Censo de la República de Cuba bajo la administración provisional de los Estado Unidos 1907*, 90.

52. *Impresiones de la República de Cuba en el siglo xx*, 520.

53. Chamber of Representatives, *Compendio legislativo*, 18–47.

54. Martínez Ortiz, *Cuba: Los primeros años de independencia*, 21.

55. Pino-Santos, *El asalto a Cuba por la oligarquía financiera yanqui*, 134.

56. Segre, "El sistema monumental en la Ciudad de La Habana," 189. See also for Machado and Céspedes's participation among the shareholders of the concessionaire.

57. Ibarra Cuesta, *Cuba: 1898–1958*, 90–92, which the author identifies as unproductive, client-based expenditure.

58. Wolfe, *Working Women, Working Men*, 9.

59. Sánchez, *Sembrando ideales*.

60. On the expansion toward the west and the boom of the real estate business, see del Toro, *La alta burguesía cubana*, 15–23. The advertising slogan and the social reasoning can be found on pp. 15–16. On the River Almendares as a barrier, industrial area, and main artery toward urban expansion, see Zardoya, "Ciudad, imagen y memoria," 63–75.

CHAPTER 6

Transcending Borders
¡Tierra! and the Expansion of Anarchism in Cuba after Independence

Amparo Sánchez Cobos

In 1917 the Cuban socialist and writer Carlos Loveira published *From 26 to 35: Lessons from My Time in the Workers' Struggle*. Among his early experiences in Cuba's "workers' struggle," he recounts the harsh impact of the failure of the 1911 railway workers' strike in Sagua la Grande in which he had figured as one of the leaders. Dejected by the way events had developed, he decided to abandon the area and seek better luck in Havana. "I directed my feet to a house at 115 Aguila Street, headquarters of the anarchist weekly *¡Tierra!* a publication widely renowned in the revolutionary workers' movement spanning all languages, races, and countries. . . . I wasn't an anarchist but, not knowing the address of any other workers' centers, and without money, friends, or colleagues who could lend a hand, where better to go than the editorial offices of *¡Tierra!* to get orientation and solidarity in such sad circumstances?"[1]

Loveira's anecdote begs the question, how did *¡Tierra!* come to transform itself into the point of reference for radical labor on the island and transcend its anarchist framework? Loveira knew the anarchists, including the members and distributors of the Havana paper, because he had collaborated with them on a number of occasions, not least during the 1911 strike when he was president of the Sagua la Grande section of the Cuban League of Railway Workers. Nevertheless, the centrality of *¡Tierra!* for radical Cuban intellectuals like Loveira had to do with the paper's capacity to articulate particular international as well as national communities. These were communities that transcended the borders of anarchist ideology. The following pages reconstruct these communities from the pages of ¡Tierra! in an effort to counter the tendency to conceive narrowly of Cuban labor radicalism in the postindependence period only in terms of a struggle between a national working class and U.S. capital in its new imperial sphere of influence in the Caribbean basin.

Cuba's traditional historiography proposed that anarchism during the first years of the republic was associated with a group of Spaniards who only concerned themselves with the defense of their compatriots and, under the influence of a "pernicious" ideology, left island workers ideologically disoriented and backward in their consciousness and organization. According to this vision, the distortion was corrected by the communists starting with the foundation of the Cuban Communist Party in 1925. Together with this interpretation came the idea that Spanish anarchists did not understand Cuba's political and social realities and that by transplanting Spanish practices and ideology to Cuba—the "Spanification" ("españolización") of the Cuban labor movement—they fomented division and confrontation in the island's working-class community.[2] The role of the Spanish press on the island, and that of ¡Tierra! in particular, has received scarce attention, although many studies have used the newspaper to glean information on the Cuban labor movement even as authors have disparaged the paper for its ideological perspective.[3]

Some recent studies have acknowledged the relevance of anarchist activity in reorganizing workers following independence and the important legacy of theory and practice they bequeathed to the Cuban labor movement.[4] Kirwin Shaffer's work regarding ¡Tierra! locates the periodical in the array of radical papers and analyzes its function as the principal nucleus of the transnational anarchist network established in the Caribbean, connecting Havana with Panama, Puerto Rico, and Florida (principally Tampa, St. Augustine, and Key West), and responding, among other things, to North American policies in the region. Shaffer's fine work is representative of current U.S. historiography in that relations established among worker communities in the Caribbean, and particularly in Cuba, are framed and contextualized in terms of the United States and U.S. foreign policy.[5] This context was clearly important, above all in terms of financing. The weekly publication was distributed and had subscriptions throughout the Atlantic world, however, and the relations established by the members of its editorial team transcended the Caribbean region and cannot be fully understood outside of a broader Atlantic context that includes Spain.

The exchanges and connections made through ¡Tierra! refer us to the existence of an organic internationalism in the Atlantic world—that is, to organizations and individuals that transcended national frontiers and that related to one another through a print medium that represented their common interests. ¡Tierra! was in direct and constant contact with what was happening outside of Cuba's borders, while at the same time serving as a forum for discussing ideas and translating from the local to the international domain issues that were common to the broader community of workers. In some cases the paper became the voice of those "libertarian" communities located in places where the local anarchist press did not have any forceful presence.[6] In the process they participated in the creation of an "imagined community" of adherents in the ideological sense—an international community of workers who perceived themselves to be in analogous situations, with similar problems and desires.[7]

This immersion in the libertarian circuits of the Atlantic world had its reflection in the expansion of common experiences inside Cuba. The direct relation with Spain established during the colonial period and continuing after independence in a context that favored immigrants from the Spanish peninsula—anarchists among them—was visible in the type of enterprises implemented. The nearly 900,000 Spaniards who arrived in the island in the three decades following independence explain in part the continuities with the previous century, especially in terms of organizing workers and in the cultural practices spread after independence that had a European orientation. The new conjuncture demanded putting into practice different strategies to ensure the expansion of anarchism throughout the island and, just as in the late nineteenth century, the press would play a key role in this process. In sum, the success and centrality of ¡Tierra! in the first two decades of the Cuban republic forces us to take note of a dynamic network in the island's working-class culture that has been written out of dominant narratives, one that was cosmopolitan, transnational, and nonsectarian, and revolved around a largely Atlantic axis running from Cuba to Spain, and taking in places like Florida, Wales, and France (not to mention California) along the way.

Part-Time "Journalists"

¡Tierra! Periódico Semanal (Land! A weekly paper) was born in early July 1902, only two months after the birth of the Cuban republic itself. Aside from a few suspensions in publication caused by the Cuban authorities and the content of some of its issues, and aside from financing problems that slowed its publication at certain points, the most important anarchist publication in Havana and the island of Cuba in the first years of independence came out with a good deal of regularity until the beginning of 1915, when it was closed by the authorities for having published articles attacking the government. Also contributing to its definitive disappearance were the deficit suffered starting in the final months of 1914, combined with repression directed against anarchists that led to the deportation of some of its most important collaborators.

Two clear periods are distinguishable in the life of the paper, in each case linked directly to the composition of the editorial team: the first runs from its creation to the middle of 1908, and the second from that point until its disappearance in early 1915. The first editorial team was made up principally of native-born Cubans. The founding director was Feliciano Prieto, a tobacco worker. Among the first on the writing staff were the Cubans Juan Aller, Arturo Juvanet, Bernabé Ugarte, Oscar Martínez, Andrés Castillo, and Manuel Martínez Abello and the Spaniards Pedro Soteras and Rafael Cusidó i Baró.[8] The majority of this first team were also tobacco workers, and some were from the Society of Cigarmakers (Sociedad de Torcedores). From its inception the paper enjoyed the collaboration of other Spaniards, among them Domingo Mir Durich and José Guardiola, who were two of its most important distributors in Havana, as well as Adrián del Valle and Luís Barcia, both of whom were well known among the anarchist community in the United States. Barcia had participated along with Feliciano Prieto as a writer on the anarchist paper *El Despertar* (*The Awakening*), published in New York starting at the end of the nineteenth century. Del Valle, commonly known by his pseudonym, Palmiro de Lidia, had emigrated to the United States from Barcelona in the late nineteenth century and quickly distinguished himself by his contribution to the anarchist press. Arriving in Cuba immediately following the war of independence during the years of U.S. occupation of the island, he published *Nuevo Ideal*, the first anarchist paper of the new era that lasted until the beginning of 1902.[9]

This first team carried on with little variation until 1908 when the paper was taken over by the "24th of November" group, whose name referred to the "Apprentices' Strike" of 1902, essentially a general strike that seized the island. According to the editors, personal problems among the original members motivated the change.[10] From that point on more Spaniards could be found among the dedicated staff. A confidential file put together by the Cuban Secret Police around 1912 claimed the director was Sebastián Aguiar, a carpenter originally from the Canary Islands, and the administrator was Domingo Mir Durich, from Lerida city in Catalonia, who worked for the Department of Public Works. The same police report listed among the writers the Majorcan day laborer Juan Tur i Tur; a tobacco worker, Juan Tenorio Fernández; a chemist from La Coruña, Paulino Ferreiro del Monte; and shoemaker Juan Búa Palacios and shopkeeper Gregorio Hernández, both from Spain. The police also found, however, that the paper still had significant contributions from natives of Cuba like Miguel Lozano Ariza, a Havana tobacco worker; the builder Joaquín Lucena; and Marcelo Salinas, a tobacco worker from Batabanó. They also made special note of the Colombian schoolteacher Juan Francisco Moncaleano.[11]

Anarchism had been introduced to Cuba in the 1870s in good measure through the arrival in Cuba of publications, mostly from Spain and particularly from Catalonia. The ideas and principles cohering in Europe following the breakup of the First International found a good seedbed among workers in Havana and surrounds who had formed radical republican groups and guild and reform organizations.[12] According to the Cuban historian José Rivero Muñiz, the links grew after the celebration in 1882 of the Second Congress of the Federation of Workers of the Spanish Region (Segundo Congreso de la Federación de los Trabajadores de la Región Española) where a motion was passed to foment the spread of anarchism in Cuba.[13] The Cuban Enrique Roig San Martín founded the Center for Artisan Instruction and Recreation in Santiago de las Vegas, outside Havana, in the same year, and it soon became the principal propaganda nucleus for anarchist ideology because in conjunction with the Spanish anarchist weekly *La Tramontana* it coordinated the distribution of anarchist publications in Cuba. The first Cuban anarchist periodicals appeared soon after, the most important being Roig San Martín's *El Productor*, which was published between 1887 and 1890. As Joan Casanovas has shown, the ideology and tactics of urban workers were coordinated in these papers over the final decades of the colonial period, led principally by workers linked to the tobacco industry, notable among them the Cubans Roig San Martín, Enrique Ceci, Pedro Rodríguez, and Enrique Mesonier and the Spaniards Gervasio García Purón, Maximino Fernández, and Eduardo González Bobés.[14]

Cuba's final war of independence dismantled worker organizations and led to the exile, repression, or death of many of its most important leaders (Ceci, for example, died in the conflict). At the close of the war, it was common to see former anarchists from the colonial era, especially native-born Cubans, become reformists interested in creating nationalist organizations that might represent workers in the legislature—the most important of these being the League of Cuban Workers (Liga General de Trabajadores Cubanos), created by Messonier in September 1899.[15] These organizations would henceforth rival the efforts of a new anarchist movement, born of postindependence politics and economic conditions, in its efforts to attract workers and others from the popular sectors. Parallel with the gradual growth and expansion of the sugar industry, and likewise stretching eastward across the island, came the growth of the working class. It was a working class with a strong Spanish character due to the collaboration of the U.S. authorities and the first republican governments in promoting policies that favored immigration from Spain as a way of combining two key desires of racist elites: satisfying the insatiable need for labor following the abolition of slavery in the late 1880s, and "whitening" what would now be the "national" population.[16] According to the Spanish Geographical and Statistical Institute, 822,291 immigrants from Spain arrived in Cuba between 1900 and 1929—making up 61 percent of the total immigration of the period and roughly 10 percent of the island's population.[17]

As a result, the end of Spanish colonialism did not mark a clear point of rupture with the workers movement of the late nineteenth century, especially given that this immigration current included many anarchists. Practical experience of anarchism, and the importance given to the press in particular, reinforced links and continuities with both the earlier Cuban movement and the anarchist community in Spain. A novel impulse was added: transcending the frontiers of Havana and environs to reach the new working class. Unless they became naturalized Cubans (the only way they could vote), immigrants were on the margins of the political possibilities being explored by the new reformist organizations. This helps to explain the adherence of many to the anarchist project, as do other factors such as the long-term goals of the native reformists and the extended period of time it might take to gain a foothold in the republican political sphere (of little interest to workers who did not necessarily intend to remain in Cuba forever), and the scant experience of many of the new arrivals from Spain with participation in a democratic political sphere. The pro-Cuban (and thus anti-Spain) discourse of the Cuban reformists also made that option unpalatable to new immigrants.

The anarchists who survived the war and the change in the political character of the island, together with those who arrived as immigrants to participate in the new stage ushered in by independence, focused on the two measures they considered most urgent: the reorganization of their groups and the expansion of anarchist principles. At the same time they spread an "openness and integrationist" discourse that called for the unity of the worker community of the island in defense of its class interests over and above divisions based on nationality, race, skin color, or any other differentiating characteristic. During the first years of the republic, the anarchist press and especially ¡Tierra! would become the voice of that workers community, continuing the integrationist spirit that characterized its late colonial ancestor. It railed against the use of immigration to lower production costs by reducing salaries through an abundant labor supply. At the same time it spread the image of a working class that was expanding throughout the island—one that, if united, had great potential to exert pressure in a context of economic growth. The syndicalist tactics promoted by the Havana weekly—among them the general strike—were an attempt to connect that potential to the main desires of the worker community, which could be summed up in most cases as a reduction in the work day, an increase in the daily wage, and payment in U.S. money.

But as with other prior and contemporary anarchist publications, ¡Tierra! was produced *by* workers, not just for them. A constant characteristic over the more than twelve years ¡Tierra! was in publication was that its editorial team, just as its correspondents and collaborators, were workers of different occupations—tobacco workers, carpenters, agricultural laborers, shoemakers, or shop clerks—who turned themselves into journalists in their "free time." All of them, far from seeking profit or recompense from the sale of the paper, participated altruistically, dedicating the greater part of their off-hours to its production. As its editors noted, they worked from 7 to 11 P.M. six days a week, and from 9 to 11 A.M. on Sundays.[18]

The fact that its promoters and writers were workers of distinct nationalities helps to explain why the paper devoted itself to covering the problems of the island's workers, regardless of their social or political nature. The stance was articulated in the paper's very first editorial, along with its stated intention of becoming the intermediary and unifier of the working-class community. ¡Tierra! would be a "truly workers' paper that without exclusivism or limitations will devote itself to the defense of the working class in general . . . and holding aloft the banner of socialism . . . to foment revolution and the class spirit and rebellious sentiment necessary to achieve the union of all the workers of the island of Cuba."[19] But it also helps to explain why those who produced the paper involved themselves directly in attempts to resolve those problems, participating in strikes and protest movements that had consequences for them as well as for the paper itself.

For example, anarchists—especially members and collaborators of ¡Tierra! like Prieto, Del Valle, Manuel Martínez Abello, Francisco Ros Planas y Arturo Juvanet—played a leading role in the Apprentices' Strike of 1902, organized by Havana tobacco workers, and soon joined by workers from other sectors and organizations of diverse political tendencies in the capital and neighboring provinces. Prieto, the director of the paper, was the main strike leader, and along with Martínez Abello and Ros Planas he was sentenced to six months in jail for the articles they published in favor of the strike.[20] Throughout the wave of labor actions and the main strikes that took place over the first republican decade, a similar pattern is visible: collaboration of workers linked to different political tendencies; involvement and in many cases leadership exercised by anarchists; repression, again principally against anarchists; and the newspaper ¡Tierra! subjected to prosecution and temporary suspension of publication due to its support for the strike and protest movements.

At the same time, as with other anarchist newspapers, the relation between ¡Tierra! and its readers was mutual and reciprocal: in many cases the subscribers and consumers of this type of press were not only readers but also involved in the writing and signed as authors of some of the accounts or news published in its pages. And, though not numerous, some of these occasional correspondents were women. Slowly women began to join the anarchist cause thanks in good measure to the discourse launched by the newspaper, a tendency also visible in the development of anarchist pedagogy and schools in the island.[21] In a majority of cases, there was a direct relationship between the sending of money from different places within and beyond the borders of Cuba, for sales as well as subscriptions, and the sending of chronicles and news from the same places.[22]

Indeed the anarchist press is an excellent resource for illustrating the relations among communities of workers at the national and international levels. As the Spanish jurist Juan Díaz del Moral noted in 1929, beyond their principal function of transmitting messages, anarchist periodicals and publications "served as organs of communication among all the committed and even among all Spanish-language workers. To subscribe to a paper and pay, to announce the creation or orientation of groups, to ascertain the location of a friend or a debtor, to send notice of a change of address—the worker used his newspaper, thanks to its spread through all countries where Spanish was spoken."[23] The editorial team itself addressed the issue of the nature of those who wrote for the paper: "Here every worker who wishes to improve his own condition and that of others by showing the way is the writer of this newspaper, just as every man of generous feelings and who loves real liberty and equality for that part of humanity that is enslaved and overworked can also find a place in our paper as a writer. . . . Some of our writers are in London, others in France, still others in Mexico and sundry countries of this unfortunate planet."[24]

Shaffer emphasizes the Caribbean-U.S. orientation and significance of ¡Tierra! by pointing to the collaborators and correspondents who sent reports to the Havana paper, as well as the network of distribution and subscriptions established in that area between 1903 and 1911 and which made up one of the main sources of external financing.[25] But the newspaper's network exceeded this emerging regional political community. There were essentially two types of foreign writers and collaborators: those who sent news or shared information with the community of readers on an occasional and sporadic basis, and those who sent stories to Havana on a regular basis. Among this latter type of "assiduous correspondent," the Spaniard Vicente García stands out. An anarchist who wrote for the Havana paper first from England and later from France, he was responsible for a time for the sections "Desde Inglaterra" (From England) and "Cosas de España" (Spanish Happenings). Following the first few installments these were joined together and renamed "Things of the World" (the title was in English, apparently a reflection of its point of origin), with the correspondent tackling a variety of themes. After 1909 this became a regular section that was open to other correspondents. With a focus centered on the proletarian community, García fairly regularly sent to Havana the series titled "Workers' Struggle," and between 1908 and 1912 he also sent "Letters from London" and "Letters from Europe"; in 1914 this anarchist, originally from Burgos, was also the one in charge of keeping the Cuban working community up to date on the world war. All his chronicles tended to appear on page 2 of ¡Tierra! García became well known among the worker community of the Atlantic world for these collaborations sent from Dowlais, in the south of Wales. In fact he is a perfect example of the collaborator profile in the anarchist press.[26] But García was much more than a correspondent for ¡Tierra! Through him the weekly paper received money originating with the sale of the paper throughout the European anarchist community, principally that of Britain, as well as the donations that he himself coordinated from this Welsh locale.

While García is an excellent example of the correspondent-subscriber-distributor, he is not the only one. Indeed, this type of figure was common in the provinces of Cuba as well as in foreign lands. The editors, writers, and collaborators of ¡Tierra! were, then, "intellectual workers" converted into transmitters of a particular ideology and practices. Among other roles assumed by these "part-time reporters" was that of selecting what to send, and in this sense they functioned as catalysts of a collective way of thinking: anarchist thought. The selections they made, like the news they disseminated or wrote, were subjected to their value judgments, their prejudices, and their particular ideological representations. They were conscious, as well, of their power of persuasion and of the necessity to reach as many readers as possible in order to attain their principal objective, which was the diffusion of anarchist thought. These were transmitters of an ideology of action, of a way of thinking whose main thrust was about practical acts. And stimulating the impulse toward practical activities was precisely another of the missions of ¡Tierra! If the fact that its promoters were workers explains the orientation of the newspaper and its involvement in workers' issues, the significant presence of Spaniards among those collaborators helps to explain the type of projects they sought to implement.

Subscriptions and Distribution inside and outside Cuba

The expansion in the circulation of ¡Tierra! beyond Havana to the rest of Cuba, related to the intense activities undertaken by its prime movers, is revealed in its sales and subscription data. In its first months it was sold only in the Havana bookshops La Pluma de Oro, La Única, and La Bohemia and could also be purchased directly from Domingo Mir Durich and José Guardiola. Only two years later it was sent to distant points in the island and distributed in all the provinces.[27] A single issue was sold for three cents, while a fifty-issue package cost fifty cents, making subscription the largest method of sale. Subscriptions partially explain the projection outside the capital, as well as outside the island itself. In 1904 subscriptions had also been taken out in Barcelona, Jerez de la Frontera, and La Línea (Spain); in Dowlais (Wales); Veracruz and Mérida (Mexico); as well as some locales in the United States, from Tampa, Key West, and St. Augustine in Florida to Brooklyn, New York; Paterson, New Jersey; and San Francisco. In 1908 ¡Tierra! started to be sold in New York, at the Italian Bookshop of B. Spano on Oath Street; the following year it could be bought at the Librería Española on Vallejo Street in San Francisco and from the "Agencia de Publicaciones de Valdespí" in Ibor City, Tampa.

An overview of subscriptions and distribution inside and outside the island (see figure 6.1) gives us an idea of the rather dynamic network established by anarchists around three corners of the Atlantic world, one made possible no doubt by the mobility characteristic of anarchists and especially those with links to Spain. It is no coincidence that those involved were political émigrés immersed in the general migratory currents established between Europe and the Americas starting in the late nineteenth century. State re-

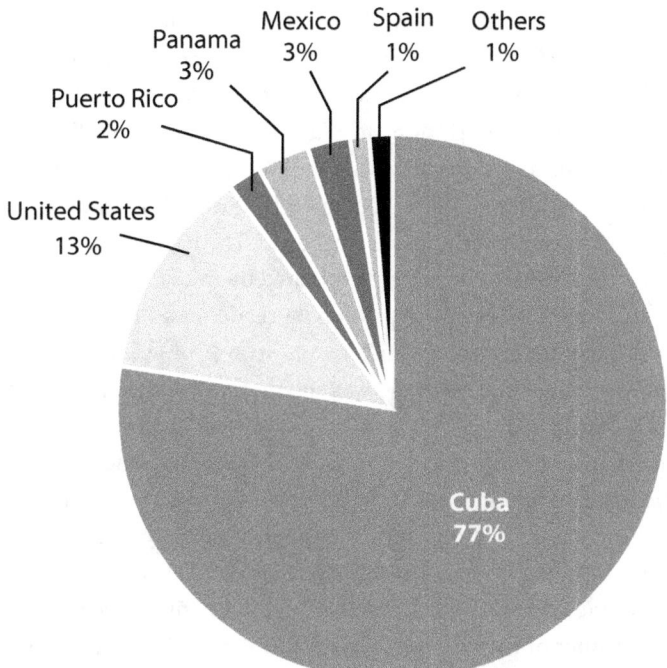

Figure 6.1 Financing and distribution of ¡Tierra! Source: Author's collation of data from available issues of ¡Tierra! Others include the United Kingdom, Canada, Peru, Brazil, Uruguay, and Argentina.

pression against the most radical sectors of labor—among them, obviously, anarchists—or the search for work were two of the most common reasons behind this mobility, though in the specific case of the anarchists we should not forget those who emigrated to plant the "libertarian" seed in other places. Indeed, the independence of Cuba—the new era that began for the island's workers at that point—would compel many anarchists to establish themselves in the island.[28] The advance in communications starting in the second half of the nineteenth century offered them the technical support they needed.

There are multiple examples of this dynamic and of anarchist movements among the foreign subscribers and distributors of ¡Tierra!—for example, the Spaniard Francisco Ros Planas, mentioned above as having participated in the Apprentices' Strike of 1902 and having spent time in jail. After getting out of jail in June 1903 he emigrated to Mexico, where he set up in Mérida. Also following jail time for political activities, the Cuban tobacco worker Marcelo Salinas left Havana in 1912 for Ibor City, Tampa, a place where Cuban and

Spanish tobacco workers had settled in the late nineteenth century. Part of the money collected in Ibor City for subscriptions to ¡Tierra! arrived in Havana via Salinas. For their part, migrants who worked on the Panama Canal explain the connections and subscriptions to ¡Tierra! in Panama. Shaffer explores nicely how the Havana paper filled the void in anarchist publications in the Canal zone, something that also happened in Puerto Rico, where we find an immigrant community of tobacco workers.[29] The figures on sales of ¡Tierra! in the United States can be largely explained by the same reasons.

In some cases the subscribers were passionate readers and collectors of the anarchist press, like the German Max Nettlau, who wrote to the paper's offices in Havana to ask for the issues he was missing, or the Spaniard José Sánchez Rosa, who registered among the most faithful subscribers of ¡Tierra! in the southern Spanish city of Seville. A self-taught teacher, Sánchez Rosa was a perfect incarnation of the anarchist of humble origins converted by his relationship with the anarchist press and its content into an "organic intellectual" of anarchism in the Gramscian sense of the term.[30] Family connections explain the money that arrived occasionally from Brazil, where Nicolás Villamisar lived, brother of the Spanish anarchist Francisco Villamisar, who had resided in Havana since the 1890s.

In many instances the newspaper's relations were woven through support for the great workers' causes. Most notable were the connections with exiled members of the Mexican Liberal Party in the context of the Mexican Revolution. Collections arrived from California sent by Pilar A. Robledo, the pseudonym of the Mexican anarchist and book dealer Rómulo S. Carmona. In 1912 and 1913 Carmona participated in distinct activities with the Colombian Juan Francisco Moncaleano, mentioned above as one of the writing team of the Havana weekly, who had gone from Cuba to Mexico in 1912, though soon after found himself deported to Spain due to his anarchist links. Following a brief stay in the Spanish peninsula, Moncaleano emigrated to Los Angeles, where he played a leading role in the Mexican and anarchist struggle. Carmona and Moncaleano were members of the junta formed to demand the release of the Flores Magón brothers, Ricardo and Enrique, and of Librado Rivera and Anselmo L. Figueroa, imprisoned in the United States on McNeil's Island. María Broussé, the partner of Ricardo Flores Magón, also collaborated by sending money to the Havana offices of the paper. Notable in this regard was the collection taken in the Los Angeles Federal Court during the trial of members of the PLM in June 1912. In many cases, ¡Tierra! subscribers were members of anarchist groups, and the groups were used as a platform for distributing the paper.[31] The role played by the groups in solidarity with the paper is especially visible in the Panamanian case and explains the 3 percent share of money gathered there registered in figure 6.1.[32]

The reception of ¡Tierra! in international anarchist circles can also be observed in the relations established with other like publications, links that in many cases explain the subscriptions and the money sent to the offices in Havana. The money from Spain generally arrived through the anarchist paper, *Tierra y Libertad*; also *La Protesta* of Buenos Aires was responsible for some of the money received from Argentina, just as the money from Costa Rica came via the periodical *Renovación* and from its administrator, Ricardo Falcó Mayor. Likewise, as we have seen, members of the editorial team of the Mexican anarchist paper *Regeneración* account for some of the remittances coming from California between 1912 and 1914.[33] On more than a few occasions these exchanges included a back-and-forth dimension: through *¡Tierra!* remittances to other countries were sent and other foreign publications were sold in Cuba. Already in 1903 the Havana paper announced that it was selling *Tierra y Libertad*, at the time edited in Madrid; *La Revista Blanca*, also published in the Spanish capital; and the Barcelona periodical *Natura*. The following year the repertoire of foreign publications offered for sale had expanded to include Madrid's *El Rebelde*, Barcelona's *El Productor* and *El Boletín de la Escuela Moderna*, and *La Protesta* and *Vida Nueva* from Buenos Aires. These relations continued to grow, and by 1912 a network had been consolidated connecting the newspaper administration in Havana with those papers with which *¡Tierra!* maintained an open account. This involved, as well, acting as an intermediary for the foreign publications in terms of receiving and sending money collected for subscriptions and for different causes. Among the anarchist papers with which *¡Tierra!* maintained open accounts were *Tierra y Libertad* from Barcelona, *Cultura Obrera* from New York, *Regeneración* from Mexico (though published in California), and Costa Rica's *Renovación*, and after 1913 *La Protesta* from Buenos Aires, *Acción Libertaria* from Madrid, and *El Obrero Industrial* from Tampa.[34]

Finally, to continue underlining the reasons that explain the success of the Havana weekly in reaching workers inside and outside the island, and still related to the monetary question, were the solidarity campaigns. Beyond receiving money to keep itself going, *¡Tierra!* relentlessly collected funds to support innumerable struggles that the international anarchist community waged in distinct moments, both inside and outside Cuba. The solidarity funds collected in 1902 "on behalf of those dead, wounded, or imprisoned during the general strike"—the Apprentices' Strike—was one such major cause. The fund-raising campaigns most commonly found in the pages of the newspaper were those in support of people "imprisoned for social questions" and on occasion included the fees of the lawyers contracted for those detained, without whom the workers would not have been able to defend themselves. For example, thanks to appeals in the pages of the newspaper, funds were collected in 1908 to send to a lawyer in Camagüey who had taken on the defense of the four workers imprisoned after the Jagüeyal strike—jailed for demanding the seven months' pay the sugar mill supposedly owed the workers. Other appeals for donations were made to help comrades or their families in difficult situations, as in the case of the Spaniards Abelardo Saavedra and Francisco González Sola, who had been expelled from the island in 1912, or in the same year the family of Moncaleano after he emigrated. Fundraising was also done to maintain anarchist schools or propaganda excursions around the island, two issues I return to below.

With respect to the campaigns to support international causes, again the most notable were those to help anarchists detained for social struggles—among the most popular were in support of those imprisoned in Alcalá del Valle, Spain, in 1904. Also worth mentioning was the intense support work carried out by ¡Tierra! in favor of "the Mexican revolutionaries" thanks to a fund-raising campaign that ran from 1912 to 1914, which finished up with another one specifically on behalf of the PLM members who were in prison. In support of the Mexican anarchists, the Havana team published a protest coupon that was also printed by other anarchist publications of the Atlantic world in 1912 (see figure 6.2).

The reflection of this extensive and consolidated network of distribution and subscription can be seen in the slow growth of the weekly's print run. In 1904 it had already reached 2,000 copies, by the end of 1906 it was 2,500, and in 1912 it surpassed 4,000. In 1913 the run topped 6,000 copies at one point, though the normal print run was about 5,500. Due to funding problems, the final months in the life of ¡Tierra! saw the print run drop to three thousand copies. The deficit dragging it down combined with the drop in subscriptions meant that by the week of December 10, 1914, the paper ceased to come out due to lack of funds. Overall, these print runs were surprisingly large, especially if compared to anarchist periodicals in other countries with a much larger working-class population than that of Cuba. For example, according to Spanish author Ramiro de Maeztu, at the end of the nineteenth century and beginning of the twentieth, the anarchist papers in Spain reached print runs of twelve thousand copies and sold at the very least four thousand copies an issue.[35] In Argentina, another country that had a considerably greater population than Cuba, the anarchist paper of greatest distribution at

> # CARTA DE PROTESTA
> ## AL PRESIDENTE DE LOS ESTADOS UNIDOS
> Mr. Woodrow Wilson,
> White House, Washington D. C.
>
> Yo, el firmante, después de una entera investigación en el caso del encarcelamiento de los miembros de la Junta del Partido Liberal Mexicano, y después de haber quedado convencido de que se cometió perjuria por los testigos del gobierno de los Estados Unidos, demando la libertad de Ricardo Flores Magón, Enrique Flores Magón, Librado Rivera y Anselmo L. Figueroa, que actualmente están en la Penitenciaria de Mc Neil Island, sufriendo una condena injustamente.
>
> Nombre . . . .
> Calle . . . .
> Pueblo . . . .
> Estado . . . .

Figure 6.2 Letter of protest to the president of the United States from a 1912 issue of ¡Tierra!

the beginning of the twentieth century, *La Protesta*, had a print run of between eight thousand and twelve thousand copies, and the rest of like publications oscillated between two thousand and three thousand copies sold.[36] But the *¡Tierra!* numbers are even more surprising if we take into account that, as the historian Lily Litvak has noted, the sales of this type of periodical press were significantly lowered by the fact that the same issue of the paper passed through various hands and might also be read in the workers centers or in the social studies centers (Centros de Estudios Sociales).[37]

Organization—Diffusion—Inspiration: Following the Spanish Model

The first U.S. intervention saw the reorganization of groups and periodicals that had been dismantled during the independence war. No organ was able to consolidate itself to the point that it was powerful enough to promote the growth of anarchism throughout the island, despite the efforts made in this regard by Adrián del Valle through his paper, *Nuevo Ideal*. Starting in 1902 *¡Tierra!* did play this role. In order to do so, its members followed a strategy defined in three steps: organization, spread, and practical education of workers and their families. The organizational model pushed by *¡Tierra!* was intended to overcome the existing divisions at the heart of the island's working-class community and to direct their energies according to common objectives and tending to resolve problems in the short or medium term.

Unlike the guilds and associations defined by trade, typical of the nineteenth century, whose actions in the public sphere only represented affiliated workers, the writing team of the Havana weekly advocated the organization of small groups that were intended to overcome the guild framework and congregate workers independently of their trade; they also sought to include their families, which provided a way into the project for women and children. The model involved small action-oriented cells, not to exceed fifteen members, that were without rules governing their functions. They generally met in different places to prepare tactics for direct action or to choose projects that would serve to direct the propaganda or revolutionary orientation of the workers. These groups had an anarcho-communist base in terms of organizational and economic orientation, though they totally disassociated themselves from the use of violent methods. The ultimate objective was to form a Federation of Anarchist Groups in which each group would maintain its independence—including its capacity to abandon the federation—and would be in charge of coordinating the actions of all its members. This organizational structure echoed what were known in Spain in the last three decades of the nineteenth century as anarchist groups of affinity, *tertulias*, or cells, with which the ideology's pioneers coordinated organization and propaganda in the early days of this current of thought in the peninsula.[38] Their transfer to Cuba can be explained by the presence of Spanish anarchists and also because in the recently emancipated island "the group" showed itself to be the best option to overcome the disarticulation of anarchism during the war of independence.

To ensure support, the editorial team spread an "open" discourse in keeping with the spirit of the paper itself, making clear that among its groups, and so in its centers, every worker and his or her family was welcome independently of skin color, gender, nationality, or political status. *¡Tierra!* put it this way: "In our houses the stupid hatred for color or nationality disappears, substituted by love and fraternity, the bases of a new and close form of social organization resulting from our complete emancipation."[39] The group, and with it the anarchist center, were born in Cuba with an integrating and globalizing intent: they welcomed all workers and extended to all spheres of daily life. "The groups could advantageously supplant mutual aid societies, information agencies or those for placing workers, and even the meeting places, availing themselves of locales where they might pleasantly read, discuss, and even entertain themselves."[40]

During the years when the paper was in print, anarchists organized more than eighty groups dispersed across the island of Cuba, though with greater density in Havana and in Oriente, areas where workers was most numerous.[41] All of their memberships included at least Spanish anarchists together with Cuban-born workers, and in some there were also workers of other nationalities. The so-called Direct Action group, for example, organized in 1912 in Manzanillo, Oriente, was made up of French, Portuguese, and Italian anarchists—notable in that European immigration to Cuba at this time was not numerous except for those from Spain. The growth in the number of groups, according to information published in ¡Tierra!, was especially visible after 1907, coinciding with the end of the first propaganda excursion carried out in almost the entire island (discussed below). So, while between 1902 and 1907 a total of thirteen groups formed around the island, between 1908 and 1914 a further fifty-five were organized—a growth that was also no doubt the result of the expansion of the paper's presence outside Havana.

The 1908 change in the ¡Tierra! editorial team led, on the one hand, to an intensification in the back-and-forth relations with Spain (because the new team was made up in its majority by peninsulars), and on the other hand to a clearer intent on exercising the role of mediator of Cuba's anarchist community. The paper itself announced the change: "In its new epoch, ¡Tierra! will be the organ of Cuba's anarchist groups (*grupos libertarios*) and will be in constant communication with them on issues relating to our ideal, as well as on initiatives that come of either the '24th of November' editorial team or any other group; they will not be implemented without consulting the other groups. . . . This will be a principle of the anarchist federation in Cuba according to the basic points approved in the 1907 Amsterdam Congress."[42]

From this point on, ¡Tierra! would maintain a more direct relationship with the international anarchist community, one that entailed among other things following the doctrinal mandates established in international congresses and meetings. Indeed, starting in 1912 the proposition on organizing promoted in its pages veered toward anarcho-syndicalism, the model prevalent in the Atlantic world and also in Spain. During the first years of the twentieth century, syndicalism—an outgrowth of the French Labor Exchange (Bourse de Travail) created at the end of the nineteenth century—became influential among European and American anarchists due to the influence exercised by the French General Workers Confederation (Confédération Général du Travail—CGT). This integration of anarchists into the labor movement, which connected with the Proudhonist roots of anarchism, became visible in Europe and the United States following the adoption of these principles in the 1906 Charter of Amiens (Carta de Amiens) (1906) and the Amsterdam congress (1907). The U.S.-based Industrial Workers of the

World, organized in Chicago in 1905, and the Argentine Regional Workers Federation (Federación Obrera Regional Argentina), born in 1915, are examples of this influence in the Americas. Anarcho-syndicalism also became dominant among Spanish anarchists following the creation of the National Workers Confederation (Confederación Nacional del Trabajo) in 1910 that adopted the organizing principles of the French CGT and of Workers Solidarity (Solidaridad Obrera), founded in Barcelona four years earlier.

These principles were widely spread in Cuba through the pages of ¡Tierra! due above all to the articles by the Spaniard Pedro Irazoqui, who from 1912 on figured as one of its principal campaigners. For the first time in Cuba words like *revolutionary syndicalism* and *sabotage* became widespread through the efforts of the ¡Tierra! anarchists. Also starting in 1912, other groups were organized to promote anarcho-syndicalism: La Alarma was founded in Havana in 1913 with the main objective "to propagate syndicalism through all means at our disposal."[43] In the same way, the use of peaceful methods of struggle became widespread—the boycott, the general strike, among others—which held sway at the time among workers throughout the Atlantic world, while the organization of industrial unions was being recommended. This reorientation in organizational typology was also related to the growth in the Cuban community of workers which was especially visible during the second decade of the republic. Many unions were born during this period, and between 1917 and 1920 above all. The final stage in this movement was the organization in 1921 of the Havana Workers Federation (Federación Obrera de La Habana) and, four years later, the National Workers Central of Cuba (Central Nacional Obrera de Cuba). ¡Tierra! then laid the bases for the organization of the island's workers in the years following the paper's disappearance.

One of the most important practices in the formation of new groups, or cells, was the "propaganda excursion." The first one, organized at the end of 1906 by the members of ¡Tierra!'s writing team, was carried out between April and August of the following year. It took in almost the entire island, with the exception of Pinar del Río, and had as its main goal extending anarchist ideology and organizing groups of *ácratas* throughout the country.[44] To direct the initiative and the excursion, three leaders were chosen, two of them Cubans—Manuel Martínez Abello and Juan Aller—who were also members of the ¡Tierra! editorial team. The third organizer chosen, Abelardo Saavedra, came after an appeal to Spain for collaboration. Saavedra was from Cádiz, in the south of Spain, who since 1904 was part of Madrid's "4 de mayo" group, at the time in charge of publishing the anarchist paper *Tierra y Libertad*. Saavedra was a very well known anarchist in the Spanish community, in part due to his participation in this type of excursion activity in the peninsula. He was also a friend with other important peninsular leaders, among them Fermín Salvochea, Pedro Vallina, Francisco González Sola, and José Sánchez Rosa, all Andalucians like Saavedra and recognized anarchist speakers and propagandists with experience in all types of locations. Saavedra arrived in Havana in April 1907, only days before the beginning of the excursion.

On top of the participation of Saavedra, the link between Spain and the excursion is also demonstrated by the type of activity proposed. The so-called sociological excursions or propaganda excursions were long-distance sojourns with an itinerary fixed beforehand. Anarchists in the Spanish peninsula had organized such excursions ever since the ideology began to be known there in the 1870s. They were precisely designed as one of the most important methods of ideological expansion. From that point on, the "Apostles of the Ideal" were a common sight, traversing the peninsula with books, pamphlets, and papers as their only baggage. These apostles were most famous in Andalucía. Indeed an excursion of this type was organized in Spain in 1904 as an initiative of *Tierra y Libertad*, and it toured the entire country.[45]

In the Cuban case, the fact that in the final years of the nineteenth century anarchism was only present in and around Havana explains the absence of this type of practice prior to independence. The first that has left any evidence is the one that brought Saavedra to Cuba, but from that point on these outings became common as an indispensable complement to the rest of the proselytizing and propaganda activities and counted on the economic and propagandistic support of *¡Tierra!* Their impact should be measured in relation to the number of new anarchist groups and with expansion in the distribution of the paper itself around the entire island.[46] Again, Carlos Loveira, recalling the 1911 railway workers strike in Sagua la Grande where he had been a leader, provides insight on these activities and concretely on the role played by the *¡Tierra!* collaborators: "The train that came from Cienfuegos to Sagua la Grande every afternoon, and that joined up in Santo Domingo with the one coming from Havana, brought us a group of high-level worker tribunes, among whom the anarchists stood out for their well-deserved fame. They were manual workers who were expert in the art of perfect public speaking and the envy of many political big shots and not a few grand pooh-bahs [*parlaembaldes*] from the lodges and casinos: Abelardo Saavedra and Francisco Sola."

From that point on, Saavedra became one of the best known anarchists among Cuban workers, precisely due to his involvement in practical experiences and strike actions—activities that would eventually lead to his expulsion from the island. His fame was already manifest in Loveira's 1917 work: "The meeting heard the most experienced public speakers. The high note was the speech of Saavedra, about whom I can say, in addition to the praise already penned, that he is the prototype of the worker-orator in terms of his use of a workers' language with simple phrases and concepts and just the right note of sincerity to move and convince the people. An Andalucian of the kind who doesn't need to belabor a joke, Saavedra's oratorical productions contain jokes [*retruécanos*], and anecdotes full of fun and originality come out spontaneously."[47]

Saavedra, then, was the prototypical incarnation of the activist anarchist involved in all types of practical experiments implemented to spread "the Ideal" in Cuba. One of the most important of these experiments took place in the realm of education. The third step in the strategy promoted by those who made up the Havana newspaper circle had to do with activities related to the education of workers and their families, something that anarchists around the Atlantic world considered essential. Spreading the ideology and educating the masses for the future social revolution were two complementary necessities.[48] In principle, in the middle of the organizational vortex initiated after independence, anarchists used the pages of *¡Tierra!* to spread a discourse that was specifically directed in two ways: first against the education provided by the government, since it did not translate, in their eyes, into an increase in the schooling of working-class children, and second toward awakening the consciousness of those workers who did not take care to educate their families or themselves. The other face of this discourse centered on promoting an educational model that was their own and appropriate to the anarchist sensibility. The pedagogical renovation that took place among anarchists also had its inspiration in the so-called rationalist schools or modern schools organized by anarchists in Spain. In Barcelona, the Catalan pedagogue Francisco Ferrer i Guardia had organized the first modern school in 1901, and it spread in short order beyond the borders of Catalonia to other Spanish provinces. In 1908 the International League for the Rational Education of Children (Liga Internacional para la Educación Racional de la Infancia, or LIERI) was founded in Paris by Ferrer i Guardia and would become a fundamental player in the expansion of these centers beyond the borders of Spain. With a clear internationalist orientation, the school model intended to "introduce into the teaching of children in all countries a practical idea of science, freedom, and solidarity."[49]

Again *¡Tierra!* played a decisive role in the spread of this model in Cuba, as did the larger context of Spanish immigration to the island. Starting in 1906, the anarchist paper became one of the principal backers of rationalist ideas, as well as a center for the promotion and financing of "modern schools." In the same year other Spanish anarchists arrived in Cuba and took charge of the effort to give life to the rationalist movement. One of the first was Francisco González Sola, the Granadan comrade of Saavedra who had achieved fame in Spain for his antimilitarist speeches for which he had to go underground and leave the country. A fund-raising drive started the year before by workers in the Cuban community of Regla, just outside Havana, and publicized in ¡Tierra! helped to pay the costs of his travel.[50] Saavedra himself played an essential role in the rationalist propaganda effort in Cuba, carrying on a job he had already begun in Spain, having participated in the founding of secular schools in Andalucía and, in 1905–6, collaborating with Ferrer in Barcelona.

In this first stage of spreading propaganda and rationalism in Cuba, the Center for Social Studies (Centro de Estudios Sociales), organized in Regla, was key. Saavedra belonged to it, as did the Canary Islander Roberto Carballo, helping the center play a decisive role in the development of these modern schools. The Cuban Section of LIERI was founded in Regla in 1908, and the Valencian Miguel Martínez was elected to represent Cuba in the international body. From that point on, the Committee of Directors of the Cuban section of the LIERI was made up of Cuban and Spanish anarchists.[51] Martínez had just arrived in the island in 1908, charged by Ferrer i Guardia himself with setting up the first rationalist school in Cuba, which was built precisely in the Regla Center at the end of that year. The Valencian had also been a close collaborator of the Catalan pedagogue in Spain and a teacher in a Barcelona modern school, as well as in others that were organized in Valencia.[52]

According to information published in ¡Tierra! the years between 1909 and 1913 were those of greatest expansion of rationalism in Cuba, especially once Ferrer's trial and execution in late 1909 became known.[53] Anarchists organized some propaganda excursions, led mainly by Saavedra and González Sola and promoted by ¡Tierra! At the same time some groups were created that had this as their specific objective: the Educación del Porvenir (Educating the Future) group, for example, founded in Regla in 1908, Cienfuego's 13 de Octubre, founded in 1909, Sagua la Grande's Sociedad Racionalista (1910), and Havana's Agrupación racionalista Ferrer (beginning of 1912). New modern schools were set up throughout the island. Beyond Havana, where there were numerous such schools, others could be found in Manzanillo, Cruces,

Matanzas, Sagua la Grande, Pinar del Río, and Cienfuegos. Cuban and Spanish anarchists were among the teachers, and in the one founded in the Havana barrio of Jesús María, the Colombian couple Juan Francisco and Blanca Moncaleano were especially well known.[54] *¡Tierra!* kept fund-raising efforts open to guarantee the maintenance of these centers and insisted that everyone participate to keep them going. The paper also supported the travel costs of Moncaleano when he embarked in 1912 to revolutionary Mexico on a mission to found modern schools there. Despite the efforts to sustain these schools, not one of them survived past 1913. Financial difficulties explain the majority of closures, although they are also partly explained by the expulsion from the island of their main backers, among them Saavedra and Sola,[55] and the departure of Moncaleano. One final external factor, just as significant, was the renewed effort by the Cuban government to bring to life a public and secular schools system, whose relative success must have drained followers of the anarchist project among the popular sectors.[56]

The sales figures of *¡Tierra!* are surprising, as is the duration of its publication, given that one of the very characteristics of the worker press—and the anarchist press in particular—was its difficulty in sustaining itself. Indeed, the rest of Cuba's anarchist periodicals created in the same era had an ephemeral life. The closest in longevity was *La Voz del Dependiente* and its successor, *El Dependiente*, which lasted from 1907 to 1917. Though these papers, too, had an anarcho-syndicalist orientation, it was closer to the model of the worker press based on a particular trade and focused on narrowly worker issues (both were mouthpieces of the Society of Cooks, Clerks, and Workers of the Cafes, Eateries, Restaurants, and Hotels of the Island—the Sociedad de Cocineros, Dependientes de Cafés, Fondas, Restaurantes, Hoteles y Obreros de la isla) and included announcements and advertisements as its principal form of financing.

By contrast, *¡Tierra!* devoted itself to giving voice and representation to that larger Cuban working-class community, one that came to be made up of immigrants. It takes us to questions of identity and political community of wider horizons—that is, of the Cuban workers movement in general during the first years of the republic and of the relations of the workers of the island beyond their immediate environment to an expansive and plastic transnational network. We might see that dynamic network, itself in large measure brought to life as part of a strong Spanish anarchist presence around the Atlantic world, as overlapping with another one predominantly linking many areas around the island of Cuba to Spain. The dynamism is no doubt related also to the mobility characteristic of the anarchist of the nineteenth and twentieth centuries—a type of political immigration that connected the two sides of the Atlantic world. It is also one with a particularly Spanish caste, and it forces us to consider how, far from any lineal "Cubanization" of the workers movement following independence, or discrete emergence of a U.S.-Caribbean anarchist network that reflected the rise of a primordial sphere of U.S. imperial hegemony, Cuban working-class politics experienced an important period of pronounced "Spanification" following independence from Spain, one that intensified after 1908.

¡Tierra! not only transcended Cuba's borders in a way made especially visible in the paper's transnational relations. It also transcended the borders of anarchism. On more than a few occasions and despite deep ideological divisions, the paper fomented collaboration with other leftist tendencies, especially socialist ones, in favor of the working-class community and beyond to the popular sectors of the island. By spreading an integrationist and open spirit, the paper tried to attract the popular sectors independently of their social or political condition, offering them a project that transcended the frontiers of labor questions and broached all manifestations of everyday life. It is also worth stressing the fact that, in this case, anarchists emphasized the forging of groups of affinity and of educational centers over other types of organizing traditions and focused on families, including women and children, in contrast to the typical organizations based on occupation or guild traditions that were still known in Cuba and that were oriented more narrowly toward the defense of a guild membership who were generally male.

Notes

This paper is the product of the research project HAR2012-36481 of the Spanish Ministerio de Economía y Competitividad and P1-1B2012-57, Universitat Jaume I, and also Programa Prometeo 2013/023, Generalitat Valenciana para Grupos de Excelencia. It was made possible thanks to support from the Canada Research Chair in History of International Health at the University of Windsor.

1. Loveira, *De los 26 a los 35*, 78.

2. On this historiographical vision, and on studies of anarchism in Cuba in general, see Sánchez Cobos, *Sembrando ideales*, 36–44.

3. So, for example, Cabrera, *Los que viven por sus manos*, 59–80, is one of the first authors who uses the anarchist newspaper to outline changes in the Cuban workers movement, at the same time offering a first take on the history of ¡Tierra! Shaffer uses the anarchist weekly along with other publications in *Anarchism and Countercultural Politics in Early Twentieth-Century Cuba*. ¡Tierra! has also been a fundamental object of

study for my *Sembrando ideales*, 189–213. Especially critical of the paper's ideological thrust is José Rivero Muñiz, *El movimiento obrero durante la primera intervención*, 119, which refers to *¡Tierra!* as an "insignificant rag" (*periodicucho*).

4. Fernández, *El anarquismo en Cuba*; Shaffer, *Anarchism and Countercultural Politics in Early Twentieth-Century Cuba*; and Sánchez Cobos, *Sembrando ideales*.

5. Shaffer, "Havana Hub." In this sense the work on Italian anarchists in the United States stands out. See Turcato, "Italian Anarchism as a Transnational Movement, 1885–1915" and "European Anarchism in the 1890s"; and Top, "The Transnationalism of the Italian-American Left."

6. While the term *libertarian* is now (in the United States especially) generally equated with right-wing distrust of government, in the early twentieth century it was often used to describe those on the left as well, especially anarchists who were against any alienation of significant public power to states or governments.

7. Anderson, *Imagined Communities* and *Under Three Flags*. E. P. Thompson also underlines the role played by socialist and anarchist newspapers in the creation of an imagined community among workers in *The Making of the English Working Class*.

8. The composition of the writing team can be found in "Insinuaciones estúpidas!" in *¡Tierra!*, September 27, 1902.

9. Sánchez Cobos, *Sembrando ideales*, 148–67.

10. "A los compañeros," *¡Tierra!*, suplemento al no. 277, August 20, 1908.

11. "Informe confidencial de la Policía Secreta de La Habana sobre las personas que componen la redacción del semanario anarquista *¡Tierra!*," Archivo del Ministerio de Asuntos Exteriores, Madrid, Fondo Política Interior, Serie Orden Público, leg. H 2753, 1911–19.

12. On this stage see the excellent work of Casanovas, *¡O pan o plomo!*

13. Rivero Muñiz, "Los orígenes de la prensa obrera en Cuba," 76.

14. Casanovas, "La prensa obrera y la evolución ideológico-táctica del obrerismo cubano del siglo XIX."

15. Also some socialist leaders such as Vicente Tejera and Carlos Baliño tried to organize a Cuban socialist party during the first U.S. intervention and again in the early years of the republic, though neither found sufficient acceptance among workers to drive their parliamentary program, in part because they competed with the new nationalist project that demanded the participation of all Cubans in support of the new nation instead of promoting a union of workers against capital.

16. On the way policies of whitening converged with national ideals, see Naranjo, "En busca de lo nacional." An excellent study that explains the connections between the need for more labor for the sugar economy and racist concepts is Balboa, *Los brazos necesarios*.

17. The figures are from Maluquer de Motes, "La inmigración española en Cuba." The remaining immigrants were Haitians (15 percent), Jamaicans (9 percent), and Europeans (15 percent).

18. "A nuestros simpatizantes," *¡Tierra!*, May 28, 1904.

19. "A los trabajadores de la isla de Cuba," *¡Tierra!*, July 5, 1902.

20. The article, Martínez Abello, "Trabajadores a la huelga general," is from ¡Tierra!, November 22, 1902. The details of his imprisonment are "Martínez Abello," ¡Tierra!, February 28, 1903. On this conflict, see Rivero Muñiz, "La Primera Huelga General Obrera en Cuba Republicana." On the development of strikes in the first years of the republic, see Sánchez Cobos, *Sembrando ideales*, 243–52.

21. For reasons of space, the role of women in anarchist organizations cannot be developed here. A nice study of the subject is Shaffer, "The Radical Muse."

22. A good example of the relation between news and money, for the concrete case of the Caribbean, is Shaffer, *Havana Hub*.

23. Díaz del Moral, *Historia de las agitaciones campesinas andaluzas*, 179.

24. "Notas y comentarios," ¡Tierra!, December 13, 1902.

25. Shaffer, "Havana Hub."

26. More information on the life and work of this Spanish anarchist is "Vicente García ha muerto," *La Revista Blanca*, Barcelona, November 15, 1930, 285–86.

27. So, for example, already in 1904 ¡Tierra! was available in all Cuban provinces: in the towns of Alquízar, San Antonio de los Baños, Güira de Melena, Batabanó, Vereda Nueva, Regla, Guanabacoa, and Artemisa, in Havana province; in the towns of Pinar del Río, Paso Real de Guane, Candelaria, and Babineyes in Pinar del Río; in the towns of Cruces, Colón, Matanzas, Cárdenas, Santa Isabel de las Lajas, and Rodas in Matanzas; in Camajuaní, Cienfuegos, Placetas, Esperanza, Santa Clara, Amarillas, Sancti Spíritus, Manacas, Santo Domingo, and La Quinta, in the province of Las Villas; in Puerto Príncipe and Veracruz, in Camagüey province; and in Holguín, Santiago de Cuba, and Villa del Cobre, in Oriente.

28. On this point, see Sánchez, "La última frontera."

29. Shaffer, "Havana Hub."

30. See Gramsci, *Selection from the Prison Books*, 131–61.

31. An example is the list of subscribers in Texas published in 1913:
    Fernando Martínez, for the Grupo Suárez y Lerdo, of Gatesville
    María L. Quesada, for the Grupo Bandera Roja, of Wasahachie
    Teodoro Velázquez, for Tierra y Libertad, of Guda
    Luisa G. Gato, for the Grupo Juvenil de Señoras y Señoritas Suárez y Lerdo, of Lorma
    Anastasio Galindo for the grupo de Familia Hacheros del trabajo, of Clipton
    Antonio N. Partida, for Tierra y Libertad, of Kyle

32. The subscribers of this zone were Grupo Germinal, of Río Grande; Los Sin Nombre, of Gorgona; Los Nada, of Pedro Miguel; Los Libertarios, of Miraflores; Los Egoístas and El Centro Obrero, of Gatún; Solidaridad, of Toro Point; and Germinal, of Culebra.

33. The aforementioned were the papers with which ¡Tierra! maintained a constant relationship during its more than twelve-year existence. Nevertheless, it maintained less regular exchanges with other anarchist publications in the Atlantic world, for example, the following made in 1902 with *Amigo do Povo* of São Paulo, Brazil; *Heraldo de París*; *La Rivoluzione Sociale* of London; *El Rebelde* and *L'Avenire* of Buenos Aires; *El Corsario* of Valencia; *El Proletario* of Cádiz; *El Federal* of Tampa; *Unión y Trabajo* of Puerto Rico;

El Libre Concurso of Mahón; *El Obrero* of Cárdenas; and *Memorandum Tipográfico* and *El Alerta* of Havana. In a short time this network extended to include *El Proletario* of Córdoba, Argentina; *La Unión Obrera* of Mayagüez, Puerto Rico; *El Internacional* of Tampa; *El Despertar, Germinal*, and *La Question Sociale*, of Paterson, New Jersey; *Les Temps Nouveaux* and *Le Libertaire* of Paris; and *Rebelión, El Porvenir del Obrero*, and *El Proletario*, among other publications from Spain.

34. "Aviso," *¡Tierra!*, July 25, 1913.
35. Tavera, "Revolucionarios, publicistas y bohemios," 377.
36. Suriano, *Anarquistas*.
37. Litvak, "La prensa anarquista."
38. The term *grupos de afinidad* was retrieved in the 1960s. In the broadest sense of the term, it denotes a small group of activists, not exceeding thirty, who are devoted to the defense of a common ideology and who work together in direct action. These became popular in the U.S. antinuclear movement and appeared in the pacifist movement of the 1960s and 1970s. Currently it has become generalized among diverse types of activism: animal rights, environmentalists, anti-war or anti-militarist, and in the anti-globalization movement, to give a few examples. On the organization of the first anarchist groups in Spain, see Lida, *Anarquismo y revolución en la España del xix*. On the concept and significance of grupos de afinidad, see Tavera y Ucelay, "Grupos de afinidad, disciplina bélica y periodismo libertario, 1936-1938."
39. "Centro de estudios sociales," *¡Tierra!*, August 15, 1903.
40. "Los grupos anarquistas," *¡Tierra!*, July 11, 1903.
41. For detailed information on the anarchist groups in Cuba in the first decade of the republic, see Sánchez Cobos, *Sembrando ideales*, 170-82.
42. "A los grupos," *¡Tierra!*, October 24, 1908.
43. "Nuevo grupo," *¡Tierra!*, January 11, 1913.
44. The term *ácrata* (as *democrat* is one for people's government, so *acrat* is one for no government, though the word does not exist in English) was commonly used in Spanish America as a synonym for anarchist.
45. "Una excursión de propaganda," *La Revista Blanca*, suplemento al no. 69, Barcelona, May 15, 1930.
46. For more information on propaganda excursions, see Sánchez Cobos, *Sembrando ideales*, 213-22.
47. Loveira, *De los 26 a los 35*, 44-46. Saavedra's fame was noted later by Felipe Zapata, "Esquema y notas para una historia de la organización obrera en Cuba."
48. For more on this question, see Sánchez Cobos, "Una educación alternativa."
49. On the development of modern schools in Spain, see Solá, *Las escuelas racionalistas en Cataluña (1909-1939)*, and Lázaro, *Las escuelas racionalistas en el País Valenciano (1906-1931)*. For the organization of the league and its statutes, see "Liga Internacional para la Educación Racional de la Infancia," *Boletín de la Escuela Moderna*, Época II, Año I, no. 1, May 1, 1908. On the pedagogical method developed by Ferrer i Guardia, see Delgado, *La escuela moderna de Ferrer i Guardia*, 89-109.
50. "Relación de anarquistas conocidos en Cuba," Archivo del Ministerio de Asun-

tos Exteriores, Madrid, Fondo Política Interior Cuba, Serie Orden Público, leg. H 2753, 1911–19; "Suscripción para sufragar los gastos de un compañero antimilitarista de España," *¡Tierra!*, February 4, 1905.

51. Executive: M. Martínez; Tesorero: J. Vertua; Members: F. González, A. Silva, B. Castro, R. Barberá, F. Mena, J. Núñez, J. Alarcón, B. González, G. Hernández, B. Berenguer, and M. Hermida; Secretary: J. Lucena. "Liga Internacional para la Educación Racional de la Infancia," *¡Tierra!*, March 13, 1909.

52. For more information on Miguel Martínez, see Lázaro, *Prensa racionalista y educación en España (1901–1932)*, 91, 108. For information on the creation of the first Cuban rationalist school, see "Escuela racionalista," *¡Tierra!*, November 28, 1908, and "Notas varias," *¡Tierra!*, March 21, 1913.

53. In 1909 Ferrer was accused by the Spanish ecclesiastical authorities of being behind the disturbances in Barcelona known as the "Semana Trágica," despite the fact that he was not in the city at the time. He was condemned to death following his trial and executed on October 13, 1909. See Cambra, *Anarquismo y positivismo*.

54. For more information on the role of Spanish anarchists in the creation of Cuban rationalist schools, see Sánchez Cobos, "Los anarquistas españoles y la formación de la clase trabajadora cubana."

55. On the expulsions, see Sánchez Cobos, "Extranjeros perniciosos."

56. According to the 1907 census, 36 percent of children in Cuba between the ages of six and eighteen were enrolled in public school—twice the proportion registered in the census of 1899 and greater than enrollment proportions in many other countries, including Spain and the United States. The official backing for education can also be seen in the schooling of the black and mulatto population which in that year equaled in proportion that of the white population. See Piqueras, *Sociedad civil y poder en Cuba*, 341–42.

CHAPTER 7

Steeds, Cocks, and Guayaberas
The Social Impact of Agrarian Reorganization in the Republic

Imilcy Balboa Navarro

The image of the Cuban campesino that was spread and consolidated in the island in the first half of the twentieth century—as much in literature as in painting—promoted the stereotype of mounted men in white guayaberas who frequented the cockfight.[1] But the fact that this was the most common image does not make it accurate, for it confused the peasant farmer (or campesino) with the *colono*—the latter, as we will see, an extremely elastic social category—and the colono with the *colonia* (the agricultural estate). Because it blurred the distinction between large and small colonos, and between landowners and renters, the image obfuscated the real social relations of the countryside.[2] The republic born in 1902 needed new icons, and this conflated image was part of the new symbolic repertoire constructed by the elites in cahoots with the U.S. intervention authorities. It was convenient to represent the rural sectors in terms of a male campesino who was racially white, and who stood midway between the rural worker and the industrial sugar mill owners, with vestigial elements of the old *hacendado*. This fantastical hybrid ended up being identified with the colono. So the classic image of the Cuban campesino was forged, an all-encompassing figure in whom the new nation aspired to recognize its rural roots.

Take, for example, Carlos Loveira's 1922 novel *Los ciegos* (The blind). Introducing the character of Ricardo Calderería, owner of the Dos Ríos sugar mill in La Cidra, the author provided a double description of the external attributes that defined mill owners and colonos and contrasted their appearance. When he appeared in his city guise, Calderería was described as a Cuban from head to toe insofar as he was always dressed to the nines, with a silky-smooth one-hundred-*duro* Panama hat and very tight-fitting, fine yellow ankle boots made to measure (factory-made boots did not have a high enough instep to accommodate such aristocratic Creole feet). He had a great love of good saddle horses, which during the afternoon carnivals allowed him to compete with the "banker" Magriñat himself in terms of how beautiful and well groomed his mount was, how luxurious his silver tack, and how elegant his stylish Creole riding.[3]

When he returned to the countryside and assumed the role of colono, that same well-dressed rider who rivaled the city's bankers changed his "white civilian clothes for a peasant guayabera shirt, high leather gaiters, and a coarse panama hat of Mexican proportions." His stay in the countryside meant "a folding cot, workers' food, a convict's chastity, and sylvan intellectual isolation."[4] He was faced with rural workers prepared to demand their rights. Ricardo's "heroic" life on the colonia, marked by "horrendously early starts to go to the cane fields," was punctuated by daily clashes which forced him to "battle with laborers who were more demanding and more aware of their worth since the revolution had awakened the conscience of the Creole population and goaded their dignity."[5]

Loveira's descriptions in 1922, made in the context of a fall in sugar prices on the world market the previous year and the bank crash that followed, shrouded the agricultural bourgeoisie (the large and medium-sized colonos) with the old ways of the hacendados (mill owners) which they yearned for and were loath to relinquish. His novel dresses the colonos in the attributes of the hacendados of the nineteenth century: their clothing, footwear, visits to the property, and so on. These are external attributes that the owners of the colonias themselves resisted abandoning precisely because they gave them a certain social recognition. It was this agrarian bourgeoisie—colonos disguised as vulnerable farmers—that saw itself as a threatened group during the second decade of the republic. The crisis of the "lean years" of the 1920s brought underlying class contradictions to the surface and with them a discourse in defense of the small-scale farming bourgeoisie whose greatest exponent was Ramiro Guerra y Sánchez, a twentieth-century intellectual who laid the foundations for modern Cuban historiography.[6]

Between May and August 1927, Guerra published a series of articles on the large landed estate system in a leading newspaper, *Diario de la Marina*, and these were eventually compiled in a book, *Azúcar y población en las Antillas* (Sugar and population in the Antilles). Guerra contrasted sugar cultivation by the large estate system—the *latifundia*—with the farming methods of the peasant producer, but not just any peasant farmer. He reduced the sector to the so-called colonos, the sugarcane farmers, thus confusing what he argued was the truly national sector of agricultural production with an agrarian bourgeoisie associated with growing sugarcane and investing it with the folkloric virtues of the campesino. He also added a racial element, insofar as the image of the peasant that Guerra defended was that of the white colono. The workers and day laborers in the background of his agricultural panorama were at best represented as exploited victims in order to attack the latifundia system, at worst used to sustain a race-based classification of rural labor that excluded Afro-Cubans from the category of colono.

In attempting to explain the changes in agrarian structure as the consequence of the rise of the great estate, Guerra was taking up a debate that had begun in previous decades. The agrarian question, especially seen in terms of property relations, had acquired a certain protagonism at the beginning of the twentieth century with the advent of the republic, when the clarification of types of domination over and ownership of the land had been essential in the new economic conjuncture, given the island's dependent relationship with the United States.[7] For the most part agrarian reorganization in the republic had been explained by way of study of the latifundia and its political and economic consequence, not only on agrarian structure but also as an agent of domination.[8] Its social effects, according to Guerra, were felt primarily by one sector, the colono—or at least the type of colono he represented. What is missing in his work is any discussion of the working and living conditions of peasant farmers and agricultural workers that might clarify the social dimensions of the expansion of the latifundia system.

The following pages attempt to provide just such a contextualized examination by taking a deeper look at the elements that determined the structure of agriculture during the initial years of the republic and particularly the expansion of large estates. We also look at the social consequences of this process—the groups that acquired cohesion and those that were finally left out and the means of social and labor control. The objective is to understand how the colonos came to seek redress for their socioeconomic plight in the 1920s by joining the ranks of the nationalists—a process in which Guerra's text and discourse played a key role. Doing so will allow us to go beyond a body of historical work on the Cuban republic that reduces the problem of agrarian social structure—and by extension, of nationality—to the problem of the colono and to consider the significant role of other social actors, whether owners or not, campesinos or colonos, day laborers or other kinds of agricultural workers.⁹

The Foundations of Agricultural Reorganization:
Expansion and Control

Colonos emerge on the agrarian stage in the period after the first war of independence (1868–78) with the beginning of the process leading to the abolition of slavery and the creation of the *central* (a more industrial sugar milling process getting product from a much greater extension of land, often including many different properties, as opposed to the *ingenio*, the old sugar mill). The rise of the central cemented the separation of the agricultural from the industrial phase of production and generated a new social division of labor that would play a shaping role in the island's destiny.[10] The colono cultivated sugarcane and the mill processed it in return for a share of the colono's harvest. At the outset the colonos might be white campesinos or former slaves, though as time wore on they would be understood only as the former. The *colonato*—the colono regime—took on two guises. The first was an administrative version, whereby the colono managed the cultivation by wage laborers of lands belonging to the sugar mill. The second—the "classic" form—involved the transfer of land to the colono-grower through a rental agreement or through sharecropping.[11] What distinguished the colono regime above all was the double game between independence and dependence. Colonos were independent, it is true, but at the same time the majority of them depended on the central. An even more complex situation was faced by those who subleased from other landowners and so faced conditions of double subordination (both to the mill and to the principal leaseholder).

Independence reinforced these mechanisms. From 1899 onward, the agricultural policies introduced by the U.S. occupation governments endeavored first and foremost to further the agricultural transformation which had begun during the previous century.[12] The measures adopted benefited not only investors from the United States but also the island's large landowners who cooperated with the intervention authorities and acted as their partners in government. This last point, which is often ignored, set the interests of certain groups against those of others. However, it must not be forgotten that prominent figures from national political life also participated in the U.S. occupation governments overseen by John R. Brooke (1899) and Leonard Wood (1899–1902), and this line of action was continued by the Department of Agriculture, controlled by Cubans.[13]

The proposals of the authorities and those of the sugar mill owners concurred on one issue: continuity.[14] Large landowners, grouped together in the Círculo de Hacendados, took up the main demands that had already been raised during the colonial period with regard to marketing and production, ensuring a sufficient supply of labor and making changes to the uses and control of the land. To that end, they requested a reduction in restrictions on access to the U.S. sugar market, the introduction of an immigration law that would guarantee the supply of a labor force, and the removal of obstacles that hindered access to landownership.[15] The government did not try to alleviate existing social inequalities in the countryside by forcing the redistribution of property, and neither did it introduce efficient regulations in order to promote the reconstruction of ruined farms or resolve the problem of the lack of credit. However, more efficient mechanisms were put in place to liberalize the land market. Here it is worth highlighting Military Order no. 139 of May 27, 1901, and Military Order no. 62 of March 5, 1902.[16] The first abolished the moratorium on mortgage repayments, thus making it easier to sell or transfer estates, while the second (of greater importance) established rules for the demarcation, division, and sale of *haciendas comuneras*, vast areas of shared cattle range, mostly in central and eastern Cuba, whose common status had, prior to the new edicts, excluded them from the land market.

As a result, large-scale agricultural estates became firmly established. The spread of these large estates occurred through the same basic mechanisms that had promoted the tendency toward bigger plantations in the latter third of the nineteenth century. Property was increasingly concentrated, and less efficient producers were eliminated. The supply of sugarcane to the large sugar mill was decentralized, with the colono system established as an alternative to small sugar properties with their own mills. The means of controlling small growers and laborers (immigration, railways, contracts, and wage labor) was perfected. From a spatial point of view, two major tendencies were clear. The sugar industry resumed its expansion toward the east, and political power became concentrated in the region of Las Villas where the phenomenon of patronage was strongly felt. The newest element in the system was the large injection of capital by U.S. investors that gave it control over the sector.[17]

The majority of the new estates (sevent-five in total), which also had the highest total area of island plantations (between 30,000 and 85,000 hectares),[18] were set up in the provinces of Oriente and Camagüey, regions where elements at the core of the old agricultural structure had survived to the greatest extent (haciendas comuneras, crown lands, and state land). These elements were opened to the land market as a result of Military Order no. 62. Likewise, investors were favored by the low price of land due to the destruction caused by the war or, as a result of this, the ruin of many landowners who were forced to sell all or part of their estates. All the above reasons were conducive to the establishment of large U.S. companies such as United Fruit, which owned the Preston and Boston sugar mills; the American Sugar Refining Company, which owned the Cunagua and Jaronú plants; the Cuban American Sugar Company, with the Mercedita and Tinguaro sugar mills; and the Rionda group, which acquired the Francisco sugar mill.[19]

The expansion of large estates involved not only controlling the surrounding land but also strengthening control over growers and laborers. The sugar mill played a major role in the whole production and commercialization process. It acted not only as the owner but also as moneylender, purchaser, and carrier. For those who worked on land provided by the sugar mill and for those who worked their own land, the central imposed contracts that determined the surface to be used for growing cane, the amount of land that could be used for other crops, the type of seeds to be used, and the method for eradicating pests. It also specified the day on which the cane had to be cut and reserved the "unlimited" right to inspect the colonias and to construct railways or any necessary infrastructure, in addition to having the right to take wood, water, and so on. The sugar mill also set the terms of payment, the interest to be paid, and any sanctions in case of breach of contract.[20]

For colonos and tenant farmers it was difficult to avoid these conditions, since the railway and the land all around them belonged to the sugar mill. In addition, the sugar mill owners ensured their "loyalty" by other means, namely, through *refacción* (usually a short-term loan guaranteed by a portion of future harvest) and by threatening to cancel contracts.[21] The sugar mill advanced the funds required for sowing and prohibited the colonos from requesting or accepting loans from third parties without their authorization. Any failure to comply with these conditions entitled the company to terminate the contract, and the sugar mills reserved the legal authority to cancel or transfer contracts without prior warning. Growing sugarcane in colonias involved a relationship of subjugation that left little margin for farmers to undertake their own initiatives. The fact that they depended on one source of employment (compared with other less lucrative options) placed them in a vulnerable position with regard to the demands of the owner.

Wages and immigration were used to ensure that sugar mills had control over the labor market. With regard to wages, workers were once again paid in vouchers or tokens, amid claims that it was "for the good of the day laborer." This was despite the penalties for such practices introduced by Military Order no. 213 of 1900 (a fine of up to five hundred pesos and up to six months' imprisonment) and the fact that La Ley Arteaga (Arteaga Law) of June 23, 1909, outlawed the practice.[22] Immigration policy was implemented in three stages: measures introduced by the U.S. intervention governments; changes made to the immigration laws according to the needs of the sugar industry, predominantly regarding projects for the introduction of European workers; and regulation of the entry of workers from the Antilles. Initially, the intervention governments attempted to introduce similar restrictions in Cuba to those that had existed in the United States since the 1880s, which limited the entry of convicts, lunatics, destitute people, prostitutes, and other so-called undesirables. Furthermore, section 3 of Military Order no. 155 prohibited drawing up contracts and making advanced payment for the journey to Cuba (which had been the usual method used by plantation owners to obtain labor during the sugar harvest). The order issued on May 15, 1902, shortly before the transfer of power to the republican government of Cuba, was a clear attempt by U.S. producers to safeguard their position, concerned as they were about competition from Cuban sugar, which could be produced using cheap labor, thus reducing costs.[23]

However, immigration policy was soon adapted to the pressing needs of the industry. Just as in the past, the large plantations blamed the situation in agricultural areas on the "shortage or lack of men to do farming work" and on the fact that workers demanded "exorbitant wages."[24] To solve the problem, they requested an increase in the number of workers in order to flood the market and thus reduce wages. Just one month after the immigration of whole families brought in to do agricultural work was authorized by Tomás Estrada Palma on July 11, 1906, La Ley de Inmigración, Colonización y Trabajo (Law on Immigration, Colonization, and Labor) was passed. The state subsequently provided 1 million pesos (80 percent for families and 20 percent for laborers) to meet the costs of traveling from mainland Spain and the Canary Islands, in addition to other European countries ("preferably" Sweden, Norway, Denmark, and northern Italy). Immigrants' applications could be endorsed by individuals or companies. Immigrants were authorized to disembark in Cienfuegos, Nuevitas, and Santiago de Cuba as well as Havana and even in other ports where a large number of applications had been made. The plantation owners, aware of the problems faced by their class, adapted the laws to fulfill two recurring demands, namely, that the state should meet the costs of immigration and that laborers should be allowed to disembark closer to the production areas. And although it shared rhetoric with the discourse used to promote family immigration, just as in the past the conditions contained in contracts left this type of immigration in the hands of the "plantation owners, landowners, and colonos," and no program was introduced specifically to settle families.[25]

The Law on Immigration, Colonization, and Labor was followed by a series of decrees that extended or specified the conditions under which that immigration would occur. In general, however, it can be said that during the first decade of the century immigration policy was left in the hands of the plantation owners. The justifications put forward, the projects presented and above all the fact that plantation owners, bankers, and traders joined together in the Asociación para el Fomento de la Inmigración (Association for the Promotion of Immigration), created in 1912, clearly showed that their aim was to get laborers for agricultural work and mainly for the sugar industry. In 1913, a further step was taken in this direction. In an attempt to solve the problem of the "lack of workers," on January 10 the government of José Miguel Gómez signed Decree no. 23, which authorized the importation of laborers from the Antilles. Specific instructions were given to comply with Military Order no. 155 of 1902, which prohibited immigration under contract or the advance payment of travel expenses, in addition to the Law on Immigration, Colonization, and Labor of 1906, which promoted the entrance of Spanish and European workers. The plantation owners were granted freedom to bring the laborers they so desperately needed for the sugar harvest in exchange for defraying the costs of immigration and freeing the state from having to meet this expense.[26] In 1913, sugar production already exceeded 2.5 million tons. The volume of the island's sugarcane harvest had grown constantly since the beginning of the century, above all after el Tratado de Reciprocidad Comercial (Treaty of Commercial Reciprocity) was signed in 1902. The island provided over half the raw material needed by U.S. sugar mills, which made Cuba their main supplier.[27]

Together with immigration, the *bateyes* (company towns that grew up around the sugar mills) and repression played a role in perfecting the control mechanisms. The sugar mills turned the bateyes into veritable satellite towns that combined privileges (accommodation, wages, electricity, and water) with coercion (the threat of expulsion, security guards, and Rural Guard posts). The highest-ranking administrators were provided with free accommodation or very low rent. The brick or stone houses with tiled roofs, which generally had bathrooms and toilets, were occupied by the supervisors and elite employees. Mid-level workers lived with their families in wooden houses which were nevertheless spacious and had tiled roofs. Day laborers continued to live in bunkhouses divided into small rooms with a door but no windows.[28]

Even when the shops and services set up in the bateyes were nominally independent (typically including grocery stores, drugstores, tailors, barbers, and laundries), payment in vouchers or tokens limited workers' ability to pay for the services. At the same time, a system of private repression was introduced that used security guards (operating under license from the secretary of the interior) who could make arrests and turn over detainees to the courts. There was also the Rural Guard, which was created in 1899 and whose aim, just like other institutions of this type, was to defend property.[29] Neither must we forget the political clientele and hierarchies cemented, which originated during the war due to the chain of command or for affective reasons and were transferred to economic areas after the end of the war.[30]

Expansion and Crisis: Triple Control over Land, Cultivators, and Day Laborers

The model presented here became even more firmly established as a result of international events. The First World War and the destruction of beet sugar fields in Europe increased the demand for cane sugar. As a result, prices shot up and the cane sugar industry increased production. The earnings generated marked the beginning of the period known as La Danza de los Millones (dance of the millions), in other words, the boom years. As had been the case with the sugar boom in the late eighteenth and early nineteenth centuries, the sugar industry was prepared to take the next step. It had land and a well-controlled labor market. Industry leaders also had access to legislative and executive influence beyond what they had during the previous century when Cuba was a colony. The new government understood the problems of the agrarian bourgeoisie and acted accordingly. Just as the revolution in Haiti had provided the island of Cuba with the opportunity to become the world's largest sugar producer, now the war in Europe provided a boost in the same direction, and the island became once again the world's leading producer.

The urgent need to fulfill the needs of a market that offered huge, quick profits gave rise to a new phase of expansion. Once again, it was carried out via the same dynamic: greater concentration of land, the making available of more land through juridical reform and sale of public land, and the expansion of the rail network. North American investment increased in order to fund the whole project: not only to finance the sugar mills, but also to purchase land and build private railways.[31] During these years, over forty sugar mills were built and fields of sugarcane spread across the island until they took over the landscape. Loveira referred to the time as the "period of national diabetes," with a rapid increase in the number of sugar mills and colonias that "invaded and swept away everything in their wake—woodland, groves of fruit trees, fields of livestock and crops, even the outskirts and streets of rural villages—all for the maddening illusion of 23 cents per pound of sugar."[32]

The provinces of Camagüey and Oriente continued to lead the expansion. This was no accident, given that both provinces still had a high proportion of unused land. There was no longer any crown land, that is true, but there were still forests, which were considered public land during the colony and were later inherited by the state and local administrations. At the beginning of the First World War, the two provinces accounted for 35 percent of the island's total sugar production, yet by 1929 the figure had increased to 60 percent.[33] To meet the market demand, gigantic estates were built with enormous new sugar mills that incorporated the latest technology in order to increase production capacity. In addition, private railways were built to guarantee the supply of sugarcane. This private rail network had over nine thousand kilometers of track, double the amount available for public use.[34]

Modern innovations bound the colono even tighter to the sugar mill. Stiffening the control mechanisms did not lead to a drop in the number of colonos. In fact, it would appear that their total number doubled during the first decades of the twentieth century. In 1899, there were some 15,000 colonos whereas by 1914 the figure had risen to over 37,000.[35] The sugar mills did not aim to eliminate the colonos, but rather to incorporate them into the latifundia system, thus reducing the colonos' negotiating power and limiting their freedom of choice. Control of the land was consonant with extensive agriculture and allowed the sugar mill to impose its conditions and offer low prices for the cane. Contracts became "legal fiction," which explains why they were preferred to sugarcane grown by the sugar mills themselves. The fact that it became commonplace to offer to pay a surcharge to obtain a tenancy agreement indicated that it was increasingly difficult to gain access to land. Ramiro Guerra reported that the tenants of small and medium-sized rural farms were unable to cover costs due to high rents and high rates of interest on refacción loans. He concluded that "the latifundia system is gradually strangling independent farmers, ruining and impoverishing them, lowering their standard of living, and creating conditions in which it is impossible for them to survive."[36]

Meanwhile, the working and living conditions of agricultural laborers became increasingly hard. These sectors "had to make the same effort as before the checks with strings of zeros and the sacks of sugar pawned for hundreds of thousands began swirling around them." Laborers still worked between ten and twelve hours per day and many sugar mills still paid wages in vouchers and tokens.[37] Neither did the profits have any effect on immigrants from the Antilles, except for the fact that their numbers increased. On August 3, 1917, a new law was enacted that extended the inflow of foreign "laborers and workers" for two more years.[38] It was no coincidence that the president of the republic at this time, Mario García Menocal, was among the founders of the Chaparra sugar mill and that during his years in the government he was one of the directors of the Cuban American Sugar Company. García Menocal combined political power with an understanding of the needs of his class, and during his eight years in power more than 81,000 Jamaicans and 190,000 Haitians entered the island.[39] This benefited the island's producers, who had a larger number of workers at their disposal whose condition as people of color, speaking a language other than Spanish, and with limited knowledge of the country and its laws made them more vulnerable and easier to oppress. It also benefited those U.S. officials who were with the occupation authority in Haiti from 1915 to 1934 and who acted as agents for the recruitment of workers.[40]

Sugar production doubled between 1914 and 1919 and sugar prices reached almost five cents per pound.[41] The island's wealth and prosperity were directly proportional to the sugar harvest. The model was functioning successfully, so why question the latifundia system, the aspiration and source of such prosperity? But the crisis was not long in coming. During the 1920s, the sugar industry had to contend with a period of prolonged instability. The recovery and increase in production exceeded the market possibilities, and prices began to fall. The situation was heightened by the world economic crisis beginning in 1929, and it did not improve (and then only temporarily and in line with the interests of the major producers) until 1934, when a new commercial agreement was signed with the United States that established a system of quotas and the reduction of tariffs.[42] In the farming sector the crisis brought about changes in the latifundia model that led to a higher degree of perfection (if such a term may be used) by further streamlining the intrinsic elements—again, the trio of land concentration, increase of available land, and worker controls—that had originated at the end of the nineteenth century and become firmly established during the early twentieth.

Just as the war of 1895 had acted as a catalyst for the elimination of less efficient units, the financial crisis of 1921 eliminated the weaker units and acted as a natural selection mechanism. This had a double effect insofar as each year it led to a decrease in the number of sugar mills while strengthening the overall latifundia system. The large estates tended to increase the number of hectares they had under production. Having large areas of land allowed the companies not only to control several colonos but also to withhold a considerable amount of land. This constituted a "reserve" in case other land was overused or expansion was required. As in the past, control of the factors of production played a key role, and as a result, in addition to increasing the amount of land under their aegis, they continued their policy of controlling the workforce.

There was a decrease in the number of independent colonos, those who owned their own land. At the beginning of the century, the land owned by independents made up 36 percent of the total land under sugarcane cultivation, whereas by 1930 this figure had dropped to 16 percent, and in 1933 such land barely represented 10 percent. Meanwhile, the number of colonias controlled by sugar mills increased from 33 to 63 percent in the earlier period and reached 64 percent in 1933.[43] It is precisely at this point that the voice of Guerra and the other defenders of the "colono" made themselves heard.

With regard to immigration, it is worth highlighting that during this period the laws that were enacted not only provided sugar mills with labor reinforcements but also enabled them to control any unruly workers. When the labor market was saturated as a result of the crisis, noneconomic reasons were used to justify the limitations placed on immigration. Thus in 1921, Decree no. 1,404 attempted to force the repatriation of Haitians and Jamaicans. The decree, signed on July 20 during a lull in sectoral activity, acknowledged that immigrant workers from Haiti and Santo Domingo had been "positive for the development of our sugar industry during the period of exceptional growth." However, the drop in production meant that so many cutters were no longer required. So, although nominally the suppression was due to the "current adverse conditions," it disguised the prohibition of immigration following the so-called threat to the nation's health.[44] However, the interests of one group of landowners (above all, the big estates of Camagüey and Oriente) blocked the implementation of the decree. In fact, the entry of workers from the Antilles continued during the 1920s, although Decree no. 1,158 of June 17, 1921, which regulated the arrival of workers at ports in Santiago de Cuba, Manzanillo, Antilla, Nuevitas, and Puerto Padre, did come into effect. The repatriation of workers once milling had finished did not affect the large mills, and they actually benefited from the fact that workers were made to leave when work was scarce.[45]

The immigration laws must also be seen as a response to the increase in worker protests that periodically shook the country between 1917 and 1924. Above all, during the governments of García Menocal and Gerardo Machado, attempts were made to associate immigration with the increase in social unrest. García Menocal ordered the expulsion of "evil foreigners," who were none other than labor leaders who were mainly Spanish anarchists. Machado's policies were aimed at workers who carried out attacks using explosives; spread subversive propaganda; advocated the destruction of property, anarchy, and the overthrow of the state; and urged workers to carry out similar attacks.[46] To close the circle even more, one year later on August 21, Decree no. 1,331 was issued, obliging the sugar mills' security guards to provide the secretary of the interior with all the information they could gather on propaganda distributed by anarchists, communists, and any other "labor agitators." In addition, the sugar mills used detachments of the Rural Guard to keep the peace.[47] The custom of paying workers in vouchers or tokens, which had been banned since 1909 but which was still common practice, was legally sanctioned on December 6, 1929. The report issued by the Foreign Policy Association in 1934 acknowledged that the grocery stores had become a means of exploiting workers on two fronts, since the majority of workers were paid in vouchers that could only be exchanged in these stores, and they charged high prices for the products.[48]

A Nation Tailor-Made for Colonos
The most direct attack on the latifundia system at the beginning of the twentieth century was led by Manuel Sanguily, who focused his denunciation on the foreign-owned portion. Sanguily, who felt that those who owned the land also owned the country, was alarmed by the growing number of foreigners who "are spreading around the island with the intention of taking ownership over the land." He tabled a law in the Senate in March 1903 that would prohibit sale of land to foreigners, but it failed to win approval. One month earlier Emilio Arteaga, the representative for Camagüey (one of the provinces most affected by the phenomenon), proposed a similar law and also saw it defeated.[49] In his 1929 book, *Latifundia and the Cuban Economy*, Raúl Maestri emphasized the debate over large property holdings and its effects on the island. The work analyzed the latifundia system in its dual aspect, both economic and sociopolitical. He defended the benefits of large-scale sugar production, noting that medium-sized and small properties were "anti-economic" because they brought with them "a paralyzing social caste." For Maestri the small and medium-sized owners impeded the introduction of technical advances and production gains because their principal con-

cern was simply to maintain their slice of land and "settle into a routine and humble existence that, due to deep-rooted inclination, resist any alteration or change even when they are inspired by the fairest concepts of equity."[50] He nevertheless criticized the latifundio as a factor in the island's dependence on the United States and blamed it for the structural deformation of the Cuban economy.

For the creole elite that assumed power in 1902 the republican ideal reproduced certain postulates that they had favored in the previous century, ones directed at creating a country with a majority white population that was synonymous with order, civilization, and progress. These intentions were reinforced by concepts that were held, in similar ways, by the U.S. intervention government. The U.S. authorities brought with them a series of rigorous racial distinctions and negative stereotypes that transcribed the island according to their obsession for whiteness and a clear separation of races.[51] In this way, during the first years of the republic, nationalist ideologues found a favorable context in which to elaborate their archetypical colono.

The consequences of the sugar crisis and the reorganization of farming properties following the financial crash reopened the debate regarding large-scale properties and their effects on the island. Guerra and other such ideologues, in defending the colonos, attacked not the Cuban and Spanish hacendados but rather the Afro-Antillean laborers (in this sense their thinking was not so far from nineteenth-century reformers like José Antonio Saco or Ramón de la Sagra, who despite their differences agreed that the island needed to be whitened). They labeled Antillean immigration "undesirable," pointed to Military Decree no. 155, signed by Wood in 1902, as a "sage piece of preventive legislation," and ended up demonizing the latifundio because it relied on the "importing of low-priced labor."[52] Nowhere is this clearer than in Guerra's identification, in *Azúcar y población en las Antillas*, of an "iniquity that affronts heavenly and human justice": the fact that "while in the countryside millions and millions of tons of sugarcane planted by natives are left in the ground, unable to be milled due to limits on the harvest, Antillean workers are imported to perform labor required to cut a large portion of the cane that is milled in certain sugar mills."[53]

In short, the author supported a nationalistic policy. The sugar problem, he felt, was viewed from above and with no regard for the colonos. As a result of the 1926 policy that restricted the sugarcane harvest, the colonos' "freedom" to grind their sugarcane in the mill of their choice was practically eliminated. Even so, ever since the nineteenth century this had been relative, since it depended on how close the sugar mill was and the means of communication. On this occasion it was not entirely due to the latifundia system. The state itself sealed the demise of this option with the decree of February 28, 1931, which obliged colonos to grind their cane in the same sugar mill as they had the previous year. At the same time, sugar mills ensured that recognition was given to the "normal sugarcane zone," which assigned the nearby growers to them in advance. Perhaps this measure, even without intending to, worked in favor of the survival (albeit with limitations) of the figure of the colono in opposition to the option of company-grown cane.

It is important to mention another factor here that is generally ignored, namely, Ramiro Guerra's participation in Machado's government as presidential secretary (1932) and general school supervisor. Perhaps for that reason he trod gently and refused to criticize the state interventionism that characterized the period, while defending the policy of reducing the sugarcane harvest. In the epilogue to his book, he made a point of defending Machado's economic policy and stated that subsequent governments did not bring about significant changes. Inaccuracy or oversight? During Grau San Martín's period in office, sugar mills were required to purchase at least 20 percent of their cane from colonos. And for the 1935 sugarcane harvest, the Caffery-Batista-Mendieta government raised the figure to 30 percent. Furthermore, Grau's government introduced one of the main measures of the period affecting colonos. Decree no. 16 of January 2, 1934, led to the creation of the Asociación de Colonos de Cuba, which included everyone involved in the sugar industry: owners, colonos, tenant farmers, subtenants, and sharecroppers. It also included those working under "any other temporary agreement," and even so, its membership barely exceeded forty thousand.

Guerra's analysis omitted three important factors determining the social dynamic in the sugar sector. First, there was the connection between the growing social instability and the workers' response, in addition to the incorporation of workers from Haiti and Jamaica to the sector's struggles during the period. Second, there was the response of the middle classes, who invested their political energies in educational and sanitary programs. Finally, there were the measures adopted by the state, which resumed the expulsion of "evil foreigners" and the repatriation of immigrants from the Antilles once the sugar harvest had ended. It must also be pointed out that the wage strategy applied by the owners constituted an instrument used to control the labor market that made no distinction between nationalities. In any case, immigrant workers from the Antilles who spoke a different language and who were unprotected by the law were more likely to be cheated when it came to negotiating or receiving payment for their work.[54] Neither should it be forgotten that in 1929, payment in vouchers or tokens was against the law and a punishable offense. On the other hand, the wealthier colonos who used workers from Haiti and Jamaica to cut their sugarcane were exonerated, since (according to Guerra) they were forced into this situation by the contracts imposed by the latifundia system. It is therefore worth asking if the theory of low salaries did not apply to them.

Precisely which colonos was Guerra defending? There were perhaps not so many of them, but they were not without influence at different levels of national political life. For example, on historian Jorge Ibarra's list of forty plantation owners or large-scale colonos who became politicians during the first two decades of the century, twenty-one were colonos, six were sugar mill owners or co-owners, and ten were administrators, shareholders, and lawyers (the others were a plantation owner, a cattle farmer, and another in the business of importing and exporting sugar). Moreover, those classed as colonos produced between 500,000 and 35 million *arrobas* of sugar (between 5.75 million and 402 million kilos), which situated them among the major producers. Within this group there were twelve congressmen and two senators, while the others held the office of mayor in various towns. A further revealing element was that many of them had a past associated with the independence movement and not exactly as foot soldiers. Ibarra registered ninety-six officers in the Ejército Libertador (Liberating Army) linked to the sugar industry: large-scale colonos (seventy-seven), owners, sugar mill co-owners or shareholders (ten), managers (seven), and chairmen of sugar companies (two). Among these there were five generals, four brigadier generals, four major generals, one lieutenant general, twenty colonels, twenty lieutenant colonels, eleven commanders, twelve captains, six lieutenants, four second lieutenants, and one sergeant.[55]

The interests of the sugar industry also reached as far as the president. General José Miguel Gómez was the owner of the La Vega and Algodones sugar mills. Major General Mario García Menocal was the administrator and an important colono of the Chaparra sugar mill, owner of the Palma sugar mill, and co-owner of the Pilar sugar mill. (All the family were involved in the business, and family members had shares in Menocal's sugar mills, appeared as colonos connected with other sugar mills, and held positions as senators and congressmen.) Brigadier General Gerardo Machado was the owner of the Carmita sugar mill together with his brother Carlos. And Colonel Carlos Mendieta, who served as president of the republic in 1934, was a colono of theo Cunagua sugar mill. The group of officers from the Ejército Libertador who became colonos were not in the majority, but they were representative, and they did have influence. These "colonos-libertadores" had close links with power and the possibility of passing legislation in the interest of this sector. Why, then, did they not do so?

According to figures from 1940, between 500,000 and 1 million arrobas of sugar (approximately 5.75 million and 11.5 million kilos, respectively) were produced by only 21 percent of the colonos. This percentage dropped to minimal levels (barely 1.5 percent) for production over and above this figure.[56] These large-scale colonos considered themselves to be plantation owners, given their past and their proximity to power. Throughout the twentieth century, it can be seen how landowners and colonos joined forces in farming associations, which is paradoxical given the apparent differences in interests. The colonos with the greatest resources took over the leadership of the associations (acting paternalistically in some cases but resorting to tyrannical methods in most cases) and eventually represented the entire sector. However, they did so only in the interest of large-scale producers.

This group used the same methods of labor exploitation and control as those used by the large estates. Cuco, the main character in Loveira's novel *Los ciegos*, is surprised to discover the cane cutters working in the neighboring colonia living in "a large *shack* of the type referred to as *sticks in the earth*, with six, eight, and up to ten filthy, discolored hammocks hanging from the supports." Outside the shack, near one of its corners, "two large, blackened iron caldrons boiled on large cooking stoves made using three stones." He concludes by intoning, "Poor people! How they live! Imagine having to endure six months of this life on a sugar plantation in one of these shacks, in such isolation, eating what they eat!"[57]

To return to our point of departure, the widespread images used to portray the campesino during those years—a white guayabera shirt, horses, cockerels—did not match the reality of the peasant farmer at all. The 1934 report of the Foreign Policy Association made a distinction between the living conditions of the colonos who lived on their land and the conditions of those who held other administrative positions such as foremen and field inspectors, who enjoyed better conditions. It later acknowledged that "those well-dressed horsemen who ride along the roads on Sundays and holidays on their way to cockfights and other forms of entertainment come from these classes; they are also the source of social trends which take the sons and daughters of these families to the *batey* or to the village in search of jobs which provide greater social prestige."[58]

The peasant in an immaculate guayabera shirt was an invention of the rural middle classes, who reinvented themselves by establishing a link between the land and the style of the plantation owners. It was an invention of great significance. Despite his poverty, Liborio, the caricatured figure who represented the Cuban peasant par excellence, continued to wear his white guayabera shirt, even if it was threadbare.[59] Guerra and the nation's ideologists used the concept of the colono in a self-serving and confusing way. They associated the colono with farming colonias without making any distinction between large and small producers or between landowners and tenants. They did not make any distinction because it was not in their interests to speak of a farming bourgeoisie, and they ended up hiding away a whole social class. It was not so much a nation of whites as a nation of white middle classes, of white landowners who had existed during the two decades of the republic despite the spread of North American capital. However, during the lean years they saw that their survival in agriculture was in danger more than ever before, hence their reaction and defense of the agricultural colonia and the colono system that proved effective while they managed to join forces with the large Cuban growers who dominated political office. It was a discourse that also benefited them politically. In the so-called republic of generals and doctors, the agricultural leaders were the large landowners and the voters were the owners of small farms.[60]

Notes

This paper is the product of research project HAR2012-36481 of the Spanish Ministerio de Economía y Competitividad, and P1-1B2012-57, Universitat Jaume I, and also Programa Prometeo 2013/023, Generalitat Valenciana para Grupos de Excelencia.

1. The guayabera is a loose-fitting, tunic-style short-sleeve shirt for men made of light fabric and worn untucked. Its origins are not only Cuban, but it has long been associated with the island. While the guayabera is often now worn for semiformal and even formal occasions, it has always been symbolic of rural life.

2. Among those who have tried to give some precision to the social category of "colono," José Antonio Piqueras has proposed a methodological division between the colono as agricultural producer and colonias as agricultural properties. He restricts the definition of a colono to those directly involved in growing sugarcane whose family production was of a medium scale, and so excludes landowners controlling large extensions and using salaried labor whom he classifies as an agrarian bourgeoisie. Piqueras also emphasizes how the colonos themselves, defined in these terms, originally distanced themselves from "los señores hacendados." See Piqueras, *Sociedad civil y poder en Cuba*, 186–90. Others who have tackled this figure are Guerra y Sánchez, *Sugar and Society in the Caribbean*; McGillivray, *Blazing Cane*; Martínez Alier, *Cuba: Economía y sociedad*; Dye, *Cuban Sugar in the Age of Mass Production*; Ayala, *American Sugar Kingdom*; and Santamaría and García Mora, "Colonos: Agricultores cañeros," 131–61.

3. Translated from Loveira, *Los ciegos*, 38.

4. Loveira, *Los ciegos*, 39.

5. Loveira, *Los ciegos*, 40.

6. On Guerra as historian, pedagogue, and economist, see Almodóvar Muñoz, *Antología crítica de la historiografía cubana (período neocolonial)*, 271–315; García Carranza, "Breve Biobibliografía del doctor Ramiro Guerra"; García Blanco et al., "Guerra y Sánchez, Ramiro"; and Instituto de Literatura y Lingüística de la Academia de Ciencias de Cuba, *Diccionario de la Literatura Cubana*, 397–400.

7. The agrarian holding that received most attention was the hacienda comunera–crown land that was used as commons. See Cancio, "Haciendas comuneras"; Gómez, *Historia, deslinde y reparto de haciendas comuneras*; Celorio, *Las haciendas comuneras*. Pichardo, *Agrimensura legal en la Isla de Cuba: Segunda edición corregida y aumentada* [1902], recently reissued, is another example of this tendency. U.S. authors also showed an interest in the island's agrarian issues, among them Whitbeck, "Geographical Relations in the Development of Cuban Agriculture."

8. Pichardo, *Documentos para la Historia de Cuba*, 2: 261–63, 325; Maestri, *El latifundismo en la economía cubana*.

9. This work was done as part of a research project supported by the Spanish Ministerio de Economía y Competitividad (HAR2012-36481).

10. Piqueras, *Sociedad civil y poder en Cuba*, 185.

11. On the colonato, see Guerra y Sánchez, *Azúcar y población*, 62–68. A detailed study is McGillivray, *Blazing Cane*. An analysis on the second half of the twentieth century is Martínez Alier, *Cuba: Economía y sociedad*, 75–108.

12. For an analysis of the patrimonial issues of the period, see Balboa, "La herencia de la tierra," 123–54. With regard to the economic policy introduced by the United States, see Le Riverend, *Historia Económica de Cuba*, 553–61. See also Torre et al., *La sociedad cubana en los albores de la República*.

13. José Antonio Piqueras, in "Ciudadanía y cultura cívica en la construcción de la República," 24–53, highlighted that the survival of the old legislation made space for *caciquismo*, or political patronage, just like in colonial times. This space was occupied by patriots in office, while common pro-independence supporters became the clientele. He defined the period starting in 1902 as one of the "oligarchization of power," in which the decision-making process was concentrated in a reduced sphere of beneficiaries of the anticolonial struggle, above all, civil and military leaders who had no interest in developing a true representative democracy that could deprive them of their recently acquired privileges. These arguments have now been revised in his work *Sociedad civil y poder en Cuba*.

14. For example, the Civil Code of 1889 and the Mortgage Law of 1893 were still in force. See Dorta, *Curso de legislación hipotecaria*; Cantón Blanco, *Conferencias de derecho de propiedad*.

15. *Revista de Agricultura*, no. 3, Havana, October 15, 1900 (special edition).

16. "On the Demarcation and Division of Estates, Ranches, and Corrals," Havana, March 5, 1902, in Pichardo, *Documentos para la Historia de Cuba*, 2: 181–98.

17. According to Julio Le Riverend, *Historia Económica*, 576–77, U.S. capital invested

in the sector increased from $30 million during the period between 1898 and 1902 to $80 million between 1902 and 1906. On caciquism in Las Villas, see Zeuske, "1898: Cuba y el problema de la 'transición pactada,'" 131–47.

18. Zanetti and García, *United Fruit Company*, 79.

19. García Álvarez, "Estructuras de una economía colonial en transición," 195–210.

20. For the conditions of the contracts, see Guerra y Sánchez, *Azúcar y población*, 231–46, and McGillivray, *Blazing Cane*, 279–86.

21. The term *refacción* refers to short-term loans (usually paid in slaves or in kind) that were granted against the guarantee of future sugar harvests and under other specific obligations. See "Glosario de la manufactura esclavista," Moreno Fraginals, *El Ingenio*, 646.

22. *La Lucha*, Havana, February 28, 1901; *La Ley Arteaga* in Pichardo, *Documentos*, 2: 327–29.

23. On the conditions of immigration to the United States, see Jones, *Historia de Estados Unidos, 1607–1992*, 301; Military Order no. 155 in Pichardo, *Documentos*, 2: 199–201.

24. *La Lucha*, Havana, September 13, 1899.

25. See Naranjo and García, *Medicina y racismo en Cuba*, 40.

26. Pichardo, *Documentos*, 2: 199–201, 273–75, 369–70; Pérez de la Riva, "Los recursos humanos de Cuba al comenzar el siglo," 7–44.

27. The United States bought 88 percent of Cuban sugar exports, and England was the second most important market, accounting for 10 percent of the total. Moreno Fraginals, *El ingenio*, 3: 47; statistical appendix, table 9, in Instituto de Historia de Cuba, *Historia de Cuba. La neocolonia*, 3: 397.

28. Water was fundamental not only for human consumption but also for the work of the sugar mill and for watering plantations. The sugar mills took control of the water supply by setting up private systems of pipes and dams. See, for example, Zanetti and García, *United Fruit Company*, 285.

29. On conditions in the bateyes, see Foreign Policy Association, *Problemas de la Nueva Cuba*, in Pichardo, *Documentos*, 3: 477–81. On the Rural Guard and its functions, see Chang, *El Ejército Nacional en la República neocolonial*, 4–12; Uralde, "La Guardia Rural: un instrumento de dominación neocolonial (1898–1902)," 255–82. See also Piqueras, "La individualización de la propiedad agraria en la transición al capitalismo," 7–24.

30. Relations between leaders and peasants were established during the war of 1895 and were strengthened in peace times given the "protective" role that military leaders (associated with the interests of the sugar mills and in many cases large landowners themselves) took on with regard to their former subordinates. Many of these generals provided employment or leased land to men who fought in their ranks. Likewise, middle-ranking officers who were granted lucrative tenant contracts acted as intermediaries and subleased the land to lower ranking soldiers. Zeuske, "Estructuras, movilización afrocubana y clientelas en un hinterland cubano," 93–116.

31. Dye, *Cuban Sugar in the Age of Mass Production*, and Jenks, *Nuestra colonia de Cuba*.

32. Loveira, *Los ciegos*, 430.

33. Forests played a major role, not only in terms of the land which they provided—due to their extent and fertility—but also because of the possibility of making use of the wood to make houses, factories, sleepers, and private jetties. Funes, "El *boom* azucarero durante la Primera Guerra Mundial y su impacto sobre zonas boscosas de Cuba."

34. Republic of Cuba, *Industria azucarera de Cuba, 1912–1914*; *Censo de la República de Cuba, año de 1919*; Zanetti and García, *Caminos para el azúcar*, 251–66.

35. The figures are contradictory, insofar as the *1899 Census* recorded 15,521 colonos whereas the *Civil Report* only registered 892 sugarcane colonias. Ibarra, for his part, reported 1,365 counting the colonias that had been destroyed and those that were already in production. See *Informe sobre el Censo de Cuba, 1899: Cuba Gobernador Militar, 1899–1902 (Civil Report 1899–1900)*, 7: 295; Guerra y Sánchez, *La industria azucarera de Cuba*. Also Ibarra Cuesta, "La Sociedad cubana en las tres primeras décadas del siglo XX," 164–66.

36. Ibarra Cuesta, *Cuba, 1898–1921*, 116–21. See also Celorio, *La refacción*.

37. Ibarra Cuesta, *Cuba, 1898–1921*, 170–73; Zanetti and García, *United Fruit Company*, 441–42; in their respective studies, they highlighted an average decrease in the real wage rate while the cost of food increased. The quotation is translated from Loveira, *Los ciegos*, 430. See also Pichardo, *Documentos*, 3: 481–82.

38. Pichardo, *Documentos*, 2: 421–22; Pérez de la Riva, "Cuba y la inmigración antillana, 1900–1931," 27–31; Álvarez Estévez, *Azúcar e inmigración*.

39. On this subject, see McGillivray, *Blazing Cane*, 86–117.

40. Ibarra Cuesta, *Cuba, 1898–1921*, 156; Pérez de la Riva, "Cuba y la inmigración antillana, 1900–1931," 2: table VIII-I.

41. Moreno Fraginals, *El ingenio*, 3: 47. For the value of the sugar harvest between 1914 and 1920, see Ibarra Cuesta, *Cuba, 1898–1921*, 442; Zanetti, "El comercio exterior de la república neocolonial," 76–78.

42. The Costigan-Jones Law (1934) divided up the U.S. sugar market among its regular suppliers through a system of quotas valid for three years. Cuba was due 29.4 percent of the market, which despite being higher than in previous years was not even half the amount exported during the 1920s. On the crisis, see Pino Santos, *El asalto a Cuba por la oligarquía financiera yanqui*; Santamaría, *Sin azúcar no hay país*; Toro and Collazo, "Primeras manifestaciones de la crisis del sistema colonial"; Chang, "Reajustes para la estabilización del sistema neocolonial," 194–208, 337–38.

43. Ibarra Cuesta, *Cuba, 1898–1921*, 116–21, 448.

44. Decreto no. 1404, 1921, cited in Pichardo, *Documento*, 3: 22–23. See, for example, the analysis on contracting and returning of Antillean laborers during these years by the United Fruit Company in Zanetti and García, *United Fruit Company*, 216–23.

45. On July 17, 1928, the Haitian government prohibited workers from emigrating to Cuba, and although authorization was granted to companies that were given permission by Cuba, external difficulties combined with the new internal economic crisis meant that this option was used less and less until it practically disappeared. Finally in 1933, the government ordered "all foreigners who are out of work and all illegal im-

migrants" to leave the country. The legislation can be seen in Pichardo, *Documentos*, 3: 22–23, 614. See Robert Whitney's chapter in this collection.

46. Decree no. 1601, June 27 and Decree of November 18, 1925, cited in Pichardo, *Documentos*, 3: 280–83 and 314–19, respectively. The anarchists were accused of "disturbing the peace," "causing strikes" (a right which Cuban legislation did not recognize) or "provoking revolts." They were also branded "Germanophiles" in accordance with the 1918 Law on Espionage. However, as Sánchez Cobos points out, the largest number of deportations coincided with periods when work was scarce. On the reorganization of labor and the role of anarchists, see Sánchez Cobos, *Sembrando ideales*; Toro y Collazo, "Primeras manifestaciones de la crisis del sistema colonial," 216–27; Instituto de Historia del Movimiento Comunista y la Revolución Socialista de Cuba, *Historia de movimiento obrero cubano, 1865–1958*, 1: 219–22; and Tellería, *Los Congresos Obreros en Cuba*, 137–42.

47. Foreign Policy Association, *Problemas de la nueva Cuba*, in Pichardo, *Documentos*, 3: 478.

48. Foreign Policy Association, *Problemas de la nueva Cuba*, 3: 433–34, 480–81.

49. Pichardo, *Documentos*, 2: 261–63, 325.

50. Maestri, *El latifundismo en la economía cubana*, 60–64.

51. The whitening of the island was one of the central themes in the debate over the nation, one that had its expression in the polemic between the virtues of the "hispano" versus the "saxon." Spanish immigration was valued while immigration from China or the Antilles was seen as harmful for the cultural development of the nation. See Naranjo and García, *Medicina y racismo*, 34–60. On the spread of racism, see Scott, "Relaciones de clase e ideologías raciales."

52. Guerra y Sánchez, *Azúcar y población en las Antillas*, 15–16, 86–87, 109, 117, 183. For the reformist thought of the nineteenth century, see Saco, *Análisis de don José Antonio Saco de una obra sobre el Brasil intitulada, Notices of Brazil in 1828 and 1829 by Rev. Walsh, author of a Journey from Constantinople, etc.*, 203–4; Saco, *Mi primera pregunta*; and Sagra, *Cuba, 1860*. Military Order no. 155 is cited in Pichardo, *Documentos*, 2: 199–201.

53. Guerra y Sánchez, *Azúcar y población en las Antillas*, 84, 100, 167–74; citation from 174.

54. In this case the difference between Haitians and Jamaicans should be noted, since the Jamaicans had the backing of the British authorities and in a greater culture of collective defense of their interests, which was clearly visible during the expulsions of Antilleans in the 1930s. On this see McLeod, "Undesirable Aliens," and Whitney (chapter 12 of this volume).

55. In eight cases the person's rank could not be determined. Moreover, there is one who appears as a colono and landowner who has been included in the first group and two who appear as colonos and administrators who have been included in the second group.

56. Chang, "Reajustes para la estabilización del sistema neocolonial," 359.

57. Loveira, *Los ciegos*, 441–42.

58. Foreign Policy Association, *Problemas de la Nueva Cuba*, in Pichardo, *Documentos*, 3: 482.

59. According to Ibarra Cuesta, *Nación y cultura nacional*, 175–85, this idyllic representation and the supposed delay in the representation of Cuba in paintings was due to the relationship between the artists and those who bought their pictures and demanded this type of images (white peasants, palm trees, roosters, partygoers, etc.).

60. See Piqueras, *Sociedad civil y poder en Cuba*, 184–90; Martínez Alier and Stolcke, *Cuba: Economía y sociedad*.

CHAPTER 8

District 25

Rotary Clubs and Regional Civic Power in Cuba, 1916–1940

Maikel Fariñas Borrego

Most studies of sociability in Cuba have focused on migratory processes and the transformation into *lo cubano* of various modes of associating, primarily those rooted in Spanish, Chinese, and African traditions. Generally, they converge along an axis of common themes that tackle various specific models of association, including mutualism, religious brotherhoods, unions, and trade organizations, and with a thematic emphasis on the popular sectors, charity, musical groups, and the development of the sciences.[1] Strategies and forms of sociability inherited from contact with U.S. and British cultures have received very little attention, though they had notable influence in the country's political and economic spheres, especially those that sprang up in Cuba after the founding of the republic in 1902.[2] In an effort to address this imbalance, the following chapter provides an overview of the appearance and operations of Rotary clubs in Cuba in order to discern the multiplicity of positions taken by the "regional bourgeoisie." I try to get away from a historiographical trend that understands the bourgeoisie as a unified and homogeneous group and, in the most extreme cases, identifies their interests with that of powerful groups in Havana.

Studying Rotary clubs makes it possible to demonstrate how various associations, acting at a local level, held a particular sway that was of major importance for regional life in Cuba. The work of these associations went far beyond the mere social and organizational into the very political, economic, and symbolic universes of the locales in which they were established. Intriguingly, analysis of organizations like Rotary provide evidence of occasions when regional groups focused their power within civil society in order to modify laws or policies imposed by the central state or to launch, from their remote position, alternative destinies for the nation as a whole. Rotary clubs, in short, offer a nice way to de-center Cuban history and study regional power and civil society, but their character as part of a national and international network helps to avoid falling into the insularism that often limits the scope of local history.

Social groups that act upon and influence public opinion are usually identified as interest groups. Whether they are ephemeral forms of social coalition or well-structured organizations, a study of their actions allows for the identification of an important dimension of the social history of politics. Our study sets out to analyze forms of civic power in a republic that was extremely centralized in an effort to arrive at a far more pluralized vision of the acting interests and struggles within the country. At the same time, these regional civic actions also transcended national boundaries. In the very same way that power and counter-power, action and resistance, contestation and negotiation intersect within national politics, these dynamics are also in play at the international level—in this case in the relations between Cuba and the United States. In studying Rotary, we will also be able to appreciate the process by which certain strategies of domination employed by the United States were subverted with the same tools conceived for the purpose of this subjugation.

The Arrival and Diffusion of *Rotarismo* in Cuba

Even if abundant manifestations of sociability already existed in Cuba, the law of associations (instituted by royal decree on June 13, 1888) considerably expanded the creation and growth of new societies. A great majority of these associations were inherited from a Spanish cultural tradition that fostered cultural centers like secondary schools and intellectual societies (*ateneos*), social clubs (*casinos*), regional centers, and mutualist and charitable organizations. However, the increasing cultural proximity of the United States began to provoke the creation of other types of associations within Cuba. Very little is known about the gradual predominance of certain organizational forms such as the club, a phenomenon that began to appear at the end of the nineteenth century and accelerated at the beginning of the twentieth century, most notably in the activities and level of social interaction of elites in the capital organized by such entities as the Unión Club de La Habana (1880), the Habana Yacht Club (1886), the American Club (1901), the Vedado Tennis Club (1902), the Young Men's Christian Association (1905), the Club Atlético de Cuba (1909), the Círculo Militar y Naval (1911), the Country Club de la Habana (1912), the Lawn Tennis Club (1913), the Club Rotario de La Habana (1916), the Club Atenas (1917), the Miramar Yacht Club (1926), the Club de Leones de La Habana (1927), the Havana Biltmore Yacht & Country Club (1927), and the Lyceum (1928). To this we can certainly add forms of informal sociability also adopted from the United States, such as the bridge party or baby shower, which were all the rage among the elite of this period.[3] Over the years, the modes and manners of the elite in Cuba increasingly seduced important sectors of the middle class; they were even appropriated and reinterpreted by popular culture and transformed in a variety of ways.[4] Research on these forms of associations is scarce, with the exception of freemasonry, the only form of sociability originating from Britain or the United States that has captured the interest of a significant number of researchers.[5]

The rapid spread of Rotary clubs throughout the world after the foundation of the first club in February 1905 under the guiding principles of Paul Harris has been practically ignored by historians. By 1910 fourteen clubs had been founded in the United States, and the celebration of the first Rotary convention took place in Chicago in August of that same year, resulting in the creation of the National Association of Rotary Clubs, headed by Harris. The following year, at the Portland convention, the characteristic slogan, "He profits most who serves best," was adopted and preparations were made for the publication of the monthly *Rotarian*.[6] By this time, the first club outside the United States had already been founded in the Canadian city of Winnipeg. In subsequent years, the movement toward establishing associations expanded and increasingly claimed considerable international force; within ten years, organizations had been established throughout Europe, Latin America, Asia, Africa, and Oceania.[7]

Rotary clubs assumed different characteristics in each country, and although they established specific organizational objectives meant to cater to the club's development in each nation, they nonetheless outlined their proposals as an international entity. With the appearance of the first clubs outside the United States, it became necessary by 1912 to restructure the National Association of Rotary Clubs, and in 1912 the International Association of Rotary Clubs was created.[8] In 1922, at a convention in Los Angeles, the statute was revised and the denomination Rotary International (RI) was adopted, a name that still identifies the organization today.[9]

Generally, Rotary clubs were established in the capital or principal city of a province or region and spread. In Rotarians' incursions into other cities, whether it was within the same country or in other new territories, the same commercial networks already developed by businessmen were used. These businessmen became commissioners for the organization. Needless to say, the different organizational dynamics and the idiosyncrasies of each country resulted in considerable differences among associations established internationally, even if they were governed by the same institutional norms. In fact, the Rotarian Juan Marinello, speaking on the issue of transferring cultural expression from one nation to another, remarked:

> Every institution, fellow Rotarians, although having by their very nature a universal character, adapt themselves to the demands of each country, and each one comes to adopt its own features. This is certainly not a new argument. It is simply a fact that a Catholic priest from the U.S. has much more in common with a Protestant priest from the same country than with a Catholic priest from Spain. This being a universal law, Rotary clubs have been no exception to it and, furthermore, no one can deny that Rotary clubs in the Republic [of Cuba] work with a certain originality. If compared to other countries, our clubs have dedicated themselves with a special focus to political action with a heightened nationalist consciousness. This state—sad as it is to say, though a great deal sadder to keep it quiet through cowardice—has provoked our disorderly public administration. Our wine—as Martí would say—may be sour, but it is our wine. It is necessary that our Clubs persist with this sublime attitude, which is the most beneficial and necessary thing for us.[10]

The statement reveals the process of adaptation to new cultural elements, as well as an awareness of the protagonists of this process. At the same time, it unveils without hesitation a preferred arena of work for Rotary clubs in Cuba: intervention in national politics.

Rotarians first arrived in Cuba from the Rotary Club of Tampa, Florida, which sought to establish the first association of its kind in a non-English-speaking country. The initial efforts to organize the Rotary Club in Havana began in 1914 under Ernest Berger, a member of the Florida club. Following his first visit to the country, the businessman returned in 1916 with his associates Ángel Cuesta and John Turner. On April 26, 1916, Berger, Cuesta, and Turner succeeded in establishing a Rotary chapter in Cuba, making it the fifth country worldwide to have hosted Rotary.[11] Although concrete information is lacking, we can assume that commissioners were sent to Santiago de Cuba and Matanzas and, as a consequence, in the summer of 1918 clubs were founded in both these cities. From these three founding points, clubs spread the length and breadth of Cuba.

This proliferation across the nation permitted the structuring of a solid

Table 8.1
Founding of Rotary Clubs in Cuban Cities, by Year

YEAR	CITY
1916	Havana
1918	Santiago de Cuba, Matanzas
1919	Guantánamo, Sagua la Grande, Cienfuegos
1921	Sancti Spíritus, Trinidad, Camagüey, Caibarién
1923	Santa Clara
1924	Cárdenas
1925	Morón, Ciego de Ávila, Colón, Güines, Manzanillo, and Pinar del Río
1927	Holguín
1928	Santa Cruz del Sur
1931	Bayamo
1934	San Antonio de los Baños, Antilla, and Florida
1935	Placetas, Nuevitas, Victoria de las Tunas, Artemisa, Palma Soriano, Puerto Padre, Jovellanos, Banes, and Yaguajay
1936	Mayarí, Pina, Gibara, Marianao, and Santiago de las Vegas
1937	Jiguaní
1938	Regla y Guanabacoa

Source: René Acevedo Laborde, *Manual Rotario*, Rotary International, *Conferencia del Distrito 25* ..., Rotary International. District 25: *Memoria del año oficial* ..., 39.

network that allowed for the development of each club's proposals with greater facility. By 1939–40, for example, there were bases in each of the country's six provinces: twelve clubs in Oriente, seven in Camagüey, seven in Las Villas, four in Matanzas, seven in Havana, and two in Pinar del Río. To date, it has been impossible to identify a pattern for the establishment of clubs throughout the country beyond a logical administrative-political hierarchy. What remains clear is that clubs spread from the capital to the respective hub of each province and, from there, to each of the municipalities.

Characterizing the Members

It is well known that Rotary developed a system of classification for its members that became increasingly detailed. As a rule, members had to be established in business or in an independent profession. Departing from this latter condition, an influential individual could be nominated as a member if supported by two already existing members. It was necessary to determine the business that best represented the community in order to attempt to enlist the owner or representative of the company into the local club.[12] Among aspiring Rotarians in a city, the most prominent individuals were always preferred, though the lists of members include a great many individuals who had very low social profiles.[13] Nevertheless, membership included some very well-known actors in Cuban history: Eduardo Justo Chibás Guerra (civil engineer, father of Eddie Chibás, one of the presidents of the Partido del Pueblo Cubano, Orthodox); Juan Marinello Vidaurreta (a leading writer who became president of the Partido Socialista Popular and would occupy important political posts after 1959); Gerardo Machado y Morales (leader of the Partido Liberal, elected as president of the republic in 1925), Carlos de la Torre y de la Huerta (distinguished researcher and university professor in natural sciences and zoology), Conrado W. Massaguer (recognized caricature artist and director of the journal *Social*), Aquilino Entrialgo Bolado (owner of the most important department store in the country), Andrés A. Terry Gutiérrez, Julio Blanco Herrera Clavería, and Juan Sabatés Pérez (three important capitalists and industrialists), and Enrique Godoy Sayán and Juan Gelats Botet (two prominent personalities in the world of finance).[14]

To examine the social character of Rotary clubs in various Cuban cities, I will examine three—those of Pinar del Río, Camagüey, and Havana. At the founding meeting of the Rotary Club of Pinar del Río in 1925, a classification system that determined its initial composition of twenty-one members was immediately established.[15] The following professional categories were approved for the members of this new club: lighting merchant, hotel owner, farmer, agronomist, financier, proprietor, professor, civil engineer, banker, tobacco harvester, bacteriologist, farmer, accountant, surgeon, theater producer, journalist, lawyer, general practitioner, dental surgeon, attorney, and private school teacher.[16] Nine professionals appear on this list, including four physicians. To these were added three financiers and three agriculturalists, only one of them explicitly identified with tobacco, the province's most important crop. There are three individuals that appear on the list dedicated to the provision of services: a hotel manager, a theater producer, and a lighting merchant. We also only see one proprietor, without further clarification on his position. Finally, the list includes an attorney and a representative for private schools who is revealed to be a clergyman.

The Rotary Club of Camagüey numbered fifty-one members in 1939 and only had three men representing the ranching and agricultural sector (a rancher, a sugar farmer, and a coffee roaster). Financiers were a little better represented (there were four), two of them specializing in insurance. A dozen professionals were included in the ranks of this club, and half of them were either physicians or involved in the medical sciences. The largest subgroup, numbering fifteen people, was composed of medium-sized and small manufacturers, most of them focused on food production. Businessmen formed the third largest subgroup with eight representatives; five of these members provided the community with services including light and power, railways, streetcars, and activities associated with hotels and bars.[17]

The Rotary Club of Havana was the largest in the country, with 156 members in 1940.[18] The importance of sugar production, and its extensive cultivation in the country, is such that scholars have distinguished it from the rest of Cuba's agricultural production when speaking of the nation's economy. Nonetheless, the number of capitalists associated with this sector in Havana's Rotarian circle was small—only three members declared themselves involved with sugar (one grower, the owner of a mill, and a wholesaler). What is more surprising is that, in a country for the most part dedicated to stock-raising and agricultural production, the lists do not include other agricultural producers of coffee, tobacco, or food destined for the internal market. Not even ranchers received representation in the capital city's club. Nevertheless, we can identify certain individuals involved in industries that are ultimately linked to agriculture or ranching: coffee roasting factories, tobacco factories, rice mills, tobacco plant warehouses, and commercial refrigeration.

On the other hand, twelve Havana Rotarians were from the world of finance (banking and insurance). Importers represented another significant group, as eleven members were classified as such. Professionals from a variety of disciplines had a large representation, numbering thirty-one—with ten doctors and nine lawyers. Small and medium-sized industrialists numbered thirty, and a significant number of these men were involved in manufacturing foods like vegetable oils, condensed milk, ice, beer, yeast, mineral water, soup, ice cream, rum, and soda. Those to follow in importance were members who were involved in the paper industry and whose areas of concentration were mostly in packaging—paper plates, carton containers, envelopes, and paper cups—and textiles such as fabric, stockings, shirts, and towels. Next was a group of individuals engaged in chemical, pharmaceutical, and cosmetic production—cement, perfume, and painkillers—as well as the remaining manufacturers who were involved in various lines of production including tobacco, cigars, furniture, mattresses, and wooden boxes. Finally, we must include in this subgroup those who were involved in public works, roads, and shipyards. Twenty-eight individuals worked in the service sector: eleven worked in transportation and seven worked in communications. Individuals working in the commercial sector also represented a significant portion of the membership, numbering twenty-six.[19] In general, the members were "white" Cuban men; aside from the fact that Afro-Cubans and mestizos had their own organizations, they were usually not permitted to join organizations formed by white Cubans. The presence of English and German surnames on the membership lists of these clubs is also noteworthy.

Interest Groups: Regional, National, and International
The influence that a Rotary club could exercise in a small town was at times disproportionate to its size. The power of these associations, constantly transformed into local interest groups, grew largely as a result of their advantageous recourse to strong national and international networks. In fact, this provided them with a distinct technical superiority that allowed them to trump other social and political actors in the region. There were other factors that facilitated this process. The sociopolitical standing of club members was of great importance; positions of power and leadership within the local community were qualities that the organization most desired to find in its members. Also crucial was the ability of members to publish directly in journals and magazines or maintain connections with local or national publications that would permit a degree of influence over the community. Public opinion could be shaped through these interventions, aimed at prioritizing solutions to the most predominant conflicts within these small communities. Moreover, Rotary clubs increasingly developed a degree of organization that facilitated their function as an interest group. Although Rotary clubs never saw themselves as interest groups per se, the evidence indicates they functioned in this mode. From a series of simple public interventions we can observe mechanisms and dynamics that reveal the intrinsic characteristics of their procedural methods at all levels: from the local to the municipal, provincial, national, and finally international.

The number of motions initiated by each club in their monthly sessions could be considerable, and some of these activities included lobbying or cooperative projects with public entities that suited their interests. However, a significant amount of time was also devoted to notifications, warnings, follow-ups on issues developed in previous weeks, fund-raising, rulings, motions in support of other associations, and multiple solicitations to governmental authorities. For instance, the projects developed by both the Rotary Club of Sagua la Grande in May 1923 and that of Pinar del Río in August 1928 serve as examples of some of these preoccupations. The former organized a theatrical function to collect funds in order to buy a vehicle for the local health department, acquire street lamps, and initiate a project for a children's park.[20] The latter made several appeals that are worth listing in order to distinguish the managerial character of its proceedings: reiterating to the mayor an appeal for the betterment of parks and streets; requesting that the reserve of funds be administered to pay the costs for the construction of a fire station and the acquisition of equipment; soliciting the secretary of public works to send a chemical fire extinguisher and to repair a major road; requesting that the Ministry of Health clean the parks and avenues; expressing interest in the establishment of a central bank; and supporting the Rotary Club of Camagüey in favor of preserving and advancing cattle ranching in Cuba.[21]

Significantly, Rotarians participated in the decision-making process for mapping out the route of Cuba's great central highway, one of the most important projects of the Machado era. The proposal for the design was launched during one of the meetings held by District 25, which, in accordance with the international regulations created by RI for Cuba at the time, corresponded to the whole of Cuba.[22] These clubs made great efforts to contribute, in a coordinated fashion, to the creation of what would be the principal roads in the country. For example, during the third meeting of the district, "[Mario] Macbeath suggested that each municipality and each provincial council should study the stretch of road that corresponded to their respective locale in order to coordinate their own findings with the government's overall plans for the principal highway."[23] Moreover, they understood the necessity of defining the best way in which to accomplish their goals and of identifying which doors needed to be knocked on in order to achieve them. The suggestion to continue in this direction was taken up immediately: "García Vida proposes that . . . these studies, once completed, should be submitted [for discussion] to their respective clubs and subject [thereafter to further discussion] among the Senators and Representatives of each province in similar club sessions so that the project becomes of interest to the nation."[24] The plan was essentially to have legislators who represented the community in congress participating in club meetings; this was to guarantee the success of club tenders, producing roads that would be as amenable as possible to the vision and particular interests of Rotarians. For example, the Rotary Club of Matanzas executed their studies with this objective in mind and invited the engineer from the province's Department of Public Works and other members of the provincial government to sessions, in order to understand what was needed to finish incomplete stretches of highway from Unión to Bolondrón, Cidra to Sabanilla, and Güira to Navajas.[25]

On several occasions, Rotarians from the interior provinces assumed extremely critical stances against public authorities or called in certain connections within their powerful networks to force changes in whatever they believed needed to be modified. For instance, agreements and treaties conducted with foreign powers that would affect the interests of Cuban ranchers greatly alarmed Rotarians from Jiguaní. There were most certainly members in this club whose investments were tied to businesses that were adversely affected by these agreements. In a meeting that took place in 1937, Rotarians declared, "Taking into consideration the importance of the ranching industry in our country, the Rotary Club of Juguaní unanimously opposes the trade agreement with Uruguay by reason that this stated agreement is greatly detrimental to what we consider to be our second largest national industry."[26] Members of this club undertook immediate and multilevel actions to reverse the situation. First, they made the negative implications of this agreement for the country known to the highest national authorities by drafting telegrams that they agreed to send to the presidents of the republic, the chamber of representatives, the senate, and secretaries of agriculture and state.[27] Second, the club notified Rotarians around the province and throughout the nation so as to coordinate collective action, particularly a "campaign that opposes the aforementioned trade agreement" involving the filing of complaints with public support to increase pressure on state administration by "sending a copy of the same telegram, in order to obtain from provincial and national clubs the aid and cooperation necessary to fight against the government."[28]

In contrast to Rotarians from the eastern provinces, who were actively involved in preventing unfavorable international agreements, their counterparts in the west of the country were fighting for a commercial agreement with Spain that would benefit the export of tobacco. To accomplish this, members of the Rotary Club of Pinar del Río produced a memorandum in collaboration with the local house of commerce that explained the necessity and validity of this project. Shortly afterward, the presidential secretary received a letter that outlined the interests of the project and was accompanied by the aforementioned document. The old colonial metropolis was depicted in this study as an excellent market for the exporting of both manufactured and raw tobacco.[29]

> Since the rate of consumption within the nation is very small compared to the [agricultural] production and the production of the tobacco and cigar-making industry within the nation, [factories within the country] do not have the capacity to process all the tobacco [generated in the country-

side of Pinar del Río], it is necessary and indispensable to find [foreign] markets for the surplus produced in tobacco leaves and raw material. At the same time, in order that the tobacco and cigar-making industries are able to augment their productive capacities, it is equally necessary that markets be found [to encourage] this meager production."[30]

The idea of coordinating a trade agreement with Spain had been in process since the 1910s. Rotarians in this region, who were experts in the matter, promoted the achievement of the blocked agreement. It is worth noting that their particular interest in exporting the tobacco plant was itself a direct outcome of the club's commitment to defending the fundamental interests of the agricultural producers in the region. "The Rotary Club of Pinar del Río, always attentive to the nation's problems, [are] even more interested in local matters and especially in those that are related to the province's principal source of wealth . . . tobacco."[31] However, the most important factor in this case is the persistent and systematic character of the efforts this club made to obtain approval for the agreement. In fact, members never ceased inquiring into the state of affairs concerning the agreement. It must be noted that their fundamental interest in this project was the development of the province and not necessarily the country.[32] Under the banner of acting in the best interest of the *patria chica*—the area defined by deeply felt regional loyalties—the club exerted constant pressure on the national government.

A brief chronology of the events that led to the success of their venture allows us to appreciate the level of work deployed to achieve their objectives. The first steps were taken in December 1925 with a call for support in the city's chamber of commerce to negotiate the realization of this project.[33] In May 1926, they agreed to "review the petitions that must be made to Spain as part of the trade agreement . . . in relation to the interests of Pinar del Río." In July the club met with the minister responsible for the agreement after reviewing the matter with the Comisión Revisora de Aranceles (a customs and excise commission) and after having contacted a number of industry groups like the Asociación de Almacenistas y Cosecheros (tobacco harvest and storage), the Unión de Fabricantes de Tabacos y Cigarros (cigar and cigarette makers), the trade journal *El Tabaco*, and the Federación de Sociedades Económicas (a federation of pro-industry associations). Significant headway was made during this meeting, and "the secretary of state accepted a proposal that was included in the agreement, which obligated Spain to buy a fixed amount of raw tobacco annually." The suggestion to "request the support of local associations and the provincial governor in campaigning for the trade agreement" followed immediately afterward.[34] The club announced that they were looking for the support of all civic entities as well as that of the central authorities in charge of regional administration. In March 1927, the club asked the secretary of state "for information as to the state of negotiations concerning the trade agreement with Spain."[35] Later, knowing that there would be a visit from the president of the republic to the capital of the province, club members decided to deliver "a report on the status of tobacco in the region and [the necessity] of the agreement." Nothing deterred members from achieving this objective, and at every opportunity Rotarians were quick to turn to government officials at all levels to reaffirm these interests. The last memo related to this issue is from May 1927, when members decided to "organize a meeting for mayors of the province who support the negotiations aimed at coordinating a trade agreement."[36] Thus the club not only sought to expand the interest group's support base within civil society but it also sought the backing of all local government officials.

Another case demonstrates far more covert mechanisms employed to exercise political pressure. In late 1925 Julio Antonio Mella, a student leader who had recently become the first secretary general of the Cuban Communist Party, was arrested for allegedly having placed a bomb in the Payret Theater. In prison he staged a hunger strike, a strategic act of protest against the Machado regime's authoritarian tactics to eliminate political threats that triggered a massive national solidarity movement. Though it is often remembered as a movement led by a union of progressive actors on the left, in fact Rotarians were centrally involved. Believing the government to be acting in error, Rotarians pulled strings in an effort to effect a reversal. Nine days after the initiation of the hunger strike, the Rotary Club of Camagüey sent a telegram addressed to the acting interior minister: "The Rotary Club of Camagüey respectfully requests of you, Sir, as a fellow Rotarian and Camagüayano, to exert your valuable influence in obtaining the release of Julio Mella."[37] It is interesting to note that the organization, at this moment transformed into an interest group, appealed first to the minister's status as a Rotarian and only secondarily to his local origins when demanding that he carry out the petition of his fellow club members. Given the importance that Mella's liberation had in calming public opinion within the country, the intervention is notable.

If the actions of Rotary clubs in the different provinces could take on such forms, what about those of the Rotary Club of Havana (RCH)? The protectionist leanings of Cuban Rotarians were well known in economic circles. In debates on protectionism and free trade, Rotarians identified themselves with the former and asked for the implementation of tariffs that would serve these interests.[38] The socioeconomic standing of the club's membership necessarily conditioned the political and economic posture of the organization. Since small and medium-sized industrialists constituted an abundant group within the RCH membership, this resulted in the rest of the members declaring their support of protectionism. The club had manifested its strong support of this economic policy since 1922 and did so more ardently when the matter became a subject of debate in the House of Representatives in August 1922. According to one contemporary media chronicler of Cuban politics, "The matter was discussed in the House [of Representatives] . . . Ferrara advocated free trade, and Santiago Rey and Germán López defended protectionism. The Rotary Club [of Havana] continues to be the stronghold of protectionist ideals and in a session, attended by [Orestes] Ferrara, notions of free trade were vehemently fought by Crusellas, Blanco Herrera, Alzugaray, and Dufau."[39]

The RCH was well acquainted with the economic and political stance of members of the House of Representatives. It was also eager to make its own criteria public and shape public opinion in accordance with the club's own interests. The RCH invited Ferrara to a session on September 7, 1922. Ferrara was then obligated to stand before those who were not only the principal champions of protectionism but also the owners and representatives of the most prominent small and medium-sized industries in the country. This seemed to be a debate that addressed the development of a more diversified economy, which defended sectors not involved in sugar production within the national economy. However, it is worth mentioning that this economic positioning of Rotarians resulted in their public recognition as the fundamental center of protectionist ideals to the extent that their voice was represented in public opinion as conflicting with the House of Representatives. More specifically, their public voice was seen as equaling the latter and capable of maintaining a direct and critical debate with these emblematic institutions of the state.

In the early 1920s, the Rotary Club of Havana maintained a critical stance toward the national government. In fact, the RCH was one of the organizations that, beginning in 1923, supported the Veterans and Patriots Movement (Movimiento de Veteranos y Patriotas) in their effort to reform a corrupt political system and raise the moral tone in public affairs.[40] The RCH affirmed that "only an honest public life and perfect honesty in administration will make us prosperous and, considering that the program of legislative reform presented to the Public Powers by the National Association of Veterans and

Patriots embodies in all its parts the aspiration of this Rotary Club, we wish to publicly manifest our sympathies with the moralizing principles of good government that this association sustains in its program." The club also participated in the Cuban Council for National Renovation (Junta Cubana de Renovación Nacional), which exposed in detail all the wrongs that afflicted the country. This is a clear demonstration of the kind of critical thinking that animated Rotarians from Havana, at least during those years.[41] However, in later years, there was considerable convergence between the interests of the Rotary Club of Havana and the presidential campaign of Gerardo Machado. The well-known slogan "Water, roads, and schools" anchored the presidential campaign of the Liberal Party candidate.[42] His political program was in tune with some principal debates initiated by Rotarians over the previous months during the electoral race. It is noteworthy that Rotarians went from criticizing the government of Alfredo Zayas to helping establish the manifesto for a fellow Rotarian in his journey to becoming president of the country.

All incursions into public life by the RCH marked out positions in civil society by the urban middle class of the capital. Members could openly act as an interest group, initiate subtle changes in the tendencies and criteria of public opinion, or continually reaffirm their public position on matters of national importance. When Machado moved away from his early reformism and assumed dictatorial powers, the RCH moved with the urban middle-class tide as it shifted against the strongman. In 1934, a year after the fall of Machado, in a plenary session for the RCH that took place at the Hotel Nacional, members received notice of the abolition of the Platt Amendment. They expressed their collective delight at the news and sent a message to the president of the republic, congratulating him for putting an end to the appendix that used the nation's sovereignty as collateral. The letter to the president stated: "The president [of the RCH] reminds his fellow colleagues of the pleasant and joyous news of the abolition of the Platt Amendment, which signifies our complete independence without any form of limitation. It was agreed on this occasion to send a congratulatory message to the Honorable president of the republic."[43]

In general, Rotarians focused on making the public aware of the importance of the club's active participation in the socioeconomic processes under way in the country. They affirmed that "each populace has the government it deserves. Contribute in creating one that is worthy of your community."[44] This meant joining their political party's neighborhood committees and voting on election days.[45] However, in time, they succeeded in delivering their social and political positions with greater boldness and even designed government programs for political figures who aspired to occupy the highest offices in the country. The contradictions within the organization were evident as Cuban Rotarians were, if only momentarily, more openly political than was expected of Rotarians in any country. One of the ex-governors of District 25, Carlos Gárate Brú, declared that "Rotary clubs do not discuss or challenge ideologies or forms of government."[46] This contradicted the ways in which the Cuban organization proceeded, since Rotarians even came to explicitly formulate a plan of government that would have national reach. In preparation for the 1944 elections, the RCH wrote a memorandum to Ramón Grau San Martín and Raúl de Cárdenas Echarte, both candidates for the Partido Cubano Revolucionario (Auténtico), running respectively for president and vice president of the republic. This document contained a plan for government that was developed by the association.[47]

On countless occasions Cuban Rotary clubs demonstrated their capacity to exercise pressure well beyond the nation's territorial boundaries. Generally, members would further their projects by means of complex negotiations with their counterparts in other countries and would subsequently receive the support they required. The majority of these negotiations were undertaken with the United States, with the clear intention of obtaining benefits for Cuba. These kinds of negotiations were accomplished either through the collective participation of all the clubs within the country, by a distinct group of clubs seeking help with a specific regional issue, or by one single club alone, which was usually the club in Havana. However, according to the latter, the club was "always supported by other clubs in the District."[48]

Cuban Rotarians sought to defend Cuba's image when confronted with nonsense published as yellow journalism in the United States. Soon after the RCH was founded, they were involved in a battle to deny accusations that Cuba was affected by yellow fever and that, furthermore, the country was inhospitable in its treatment of tourists. Members of the club in Havana launched a written campaign, asking various clubs in the United States to rectify the situation in their locale. The campaign received positive results, and clubs in the United States eventually sent their Cuban counterparts clippings from U.S. newspapers where the false information had been retracted. "However, the club of Colorado makes it clear [in their letter] that only the information that concerns the existence of yellow fever in Cuba was rectified. Stories having to do with various abuses committed by the tourist industry were not retracted, since victims of these had been several Rotarians from this area." Members responded to this with shows of pride in the interest of enhancing the country's reputation to ensure that the economy would not be affected, especially tourism. "At the suggestion of Mr. Julio Blanco Herrera, it was agreed upon that we would respond to your club in order to indicate that isolated instances of abuse should not give motivation for generalizations... and to inform you that the Rotary Club of Havana has already established an information bureau with the objective of avoiding further isolated cases."[49]

In other instances, acts of international pressure even extended into U.S. congressional sessions. In April 1924, for example, Cuban Rotarians looked for ways to persuade this legislative body to issue an official recognition of Cuba's sovereignty over the Isla de Pinos through the proposed Hay-Quesada treaty.[50] During debates surrounding the signing of the treaty, the president of the RCH proposed that "since [this] issue of great importance comes nearer to a court ruling, I propose to my fellow Rotarians that, through the mediation of the governor of our district, we ask Rotary International to use their good and diligent means to encourage the United States Congress— adopting the just rulings issued by the corresponding committees—to proceed to a prompt resolution."[51] Cuban Rotarians sought to involve, with much tact, their counterparts in other parts of the world. The path of political action traveled from the Rotary Club of Havana to the governor of the Cuban district; from there, it followed to the governing body of the organization and then to the U.S. Congress. Negotiations in this case were planned at a national level to solicit the participation of the highest-ranking representative of the Rotary Club in Cuba. Although the function of the governor of District 25 was to represent Rotary International within Cuba, it remains very clear that his duties were not to convert himself into the faithful servant of foreign interests (even if, eventually, this too could have occurred). It is important to stress how these structures of domination, generated within the context of U.S. imperial power, could also be subverted to obtain benefits for the country. Instruments of subjection were now employed to obtain the recognition of Cuba's sovereignty over a fragment of the nation's territory, a territory that had been left pending only to later be seized.

More intriguing still, everything seems to indicate that the initiative of the Rotary Club of Havana was an alliance between Cuban Rotarians and the Cuban government to obtain the ratification of the treaty. In a note of April 3, 1924, apparently written by Cosme de la Torriente, Cuban ambassador to Washington, to the Cuban secretary of state for foreign affairs, and marked "confidential," Rotary clubs were encouraged to intervene in the matter. "It would be advisable, without it seeming that I have suggested it, that the Rotary clubs of Cuba obtain assistance within the country so that all come forth and voice their support of the ratification of the treaty concerning Isla de Pinos before the American Senate."[52] This maneuver was an attempt to counter campaigns that were launched from Isla de Pinos by U.S. citizens residing on the island who portrayed themselves as victims of supposed abuses committed by the Cuban government, a strategy aimed at preventing ratification of the agreement. These campaigns led Rotarians to close ranks around government authorities. Finally, Isla de Pinos, the second most important island in the Cuban archipelago, was recognized as an integral part of the nation on March 13, 1925.[53] What is truly important about this case is that the Cuban government decided to rely on these associations to achieve the successful resolution of a matter of state. Cuban government officials understood that Rotarians had access to mechanisms that permitted them to sway U.S. public opinion as well as to influence government authorities in the United States.

Rotary clubs in Cuba were essentially made up of the urban middle class, composed of three subgroups: small industrialists, businessmen, and university professionals. Essentially, clubs formed a small universe with ample space for social sectors spanning the small and medium urban bourgeoisie to distinguished members of the country's elite. The cases presented in this study demonstrate that Rotary clubs became a force capable of influencing the socioeconomic development of the country in general and, more specifically, of the region where they were established. The zealous defense of local production and the local and national image, the impulse to create infrastructure to achieve socioeconomic development and the systematic intervention in all matters of interest to the public constitute irrefutable proof of this.

Although regional civic power in Cuba involved many more actors than can be addressed in a chapter of this scope, Rotarians played a very important role in this sphere. They had an exceptional organizational structure that simultaneously connected them with the most remote villages and the highest echelons of an international hierarchy. Their focus on the public sphere as a central territory for Rotarian intervention made them a pressure group and a powerful network. They intervened regularly at the local, municipal, provincial, national, and even international levels to guarantee the implementation of their projects. That this organization included members with very powerful connections adds an important element to the study of the capacity of their actions. These connections were sometimes invoked in a publicly transparent manner, at other times behind closed doors; a strategic telegram, letter, or private visit might be enough to catalyze a movement, pass a piece of legislation, secure the signing of a treaty, or reshape a policy plan. Cuba's Rotary clubs were social networks that could reach every possible sphere.

Notes

1. Barcia, *Capas populares y modernidad en Cuba*; Guerra López, *El legado social de los españoles en Cuba*; Funes Monzote, *El despertar del asociacionismo científico en Cuba*; Caveda Romaní, *Las sociedades filarmónicas habaneras*.

2. Without being studies of sociability properly speaking, some studies have explored British-American forms of association to one degree or another; for example, Pérez, *On Becoming Cuban*; Reig Romero, YMCA *de La Habana*; Vega Suñol, *Norteamericanos en Cuba*. See also Fariñas Borrego, *Sociabilidad y cultura del ocio*, an earlier study of mine on Havana's elite clubs, for a more in-depth discussion of sociability and forms of association, esp. 7–18.

3. Fariñas Borrego, *Sociabilidad y cultura del ocio*, 20–21.

4. Fariñas Borrego, "El asociacionismo náutico en La Habana," 145–50.

5. This, of course, has occurred due to the fact that freemasonry has been linked to a Latin American movement of independence. In consequence, it has won the favor of historians that largely focus their studies on the process of emerging nation-states and independence struggles. An important work on freemasonry in Cuba is Torres-Cuevas, *Historia de la masonería en Cuba*, who proposes that there was little U.S. influence on the irregular masonic corps founded by Vicente Antonio de Castro y Bermúdez under the name Gran Oriente de Cuba y las Antillas (GOCA); see esp. 113–20.

6. Torres-Cuevas, *Historia de la masonerí en Cuba*.

7. The list of cities around the world where clubs were founded is impressive: Dublin, Belfast, and London (1911); Glasgow (1912); Honolulu (1915); Havana (1916); San Juan and Montevideo (1918); Panama City, Buenos Aires, Calcutta, Shanghai, and Manila (1919); Tokyo and Madrid (1920); and Paris, Copenhagen, Melbourne, St. John's, Johannesburg, Wellington, Lima, and Mexico City (1921). Rotary Internacional, Distrito 25, *Memoria del año oficial*, 30.

8. *Diccionario Enciclopédico* UTEHA, T-IX, 119.

9. Añorga, "El rotarismo en Cuba," 951.

10. Marinello, "Influencia del rotarismo en el progreso de la humanidad," 6.

11. International Association of Rotary Clubs, *Seventh Annual Convention*, 133–34.

12. Acevedo Laborde, *Manual*, 179.

13. This goal meant that each member could be understood as an "ambassador of their profession," according to Acevedo Laborde, *Manual*, 4. In this sense the tireless search to effect leadership was one of the fundamental premises of Rotary, an intention registered even in the statutes of each club that demanded that each associate be a guiding force in his area of work or profession. See Marinello, "Influencia del rotarismo en el progreso de la humanidad," 6.

14. García Blanco, *Cien figuras de la ciencia en Cuba*, 394; Archivo Nacional de Cuba

(hereafter ANC), Fondo Registro de Asociaciones (hereafter FRA), 1–697, E-18104, 20, 52, 57, 100, 121; ANC, FRA, 1–697, E-18105, 34.

15. Rionda, *El Club Rotario de Pinar del Río*, 44. This preliminary structure could be modified at some future point with the admission of new members.

16. Rionda, *El Club Rotario de Pinar del Río*, 44–45.

17. Rotary International, *Conferencia del Distrito 25*. The other three individuals appear to be classified in ways that are incompatible with those that have been presented thus far, or the information provided for them is insufficient.

18. Lista de socios del Club Rotario de la Habana del 23 de febrero de 1940. From ANC, FRA, L-697, E-18105, 17–28.

19. At least six individuals were difficult to classify due to their foreign status or presented information that is difficult to catalog.

20. "Por los clubs del distrito: La labor del rotarismo," *La nota rotaria* 2, no. 9 (June 1923): 21.

21. Rionda, *El Club Rotario*, 68.

22. In 1953, after a reorganization of Rotary International, Cuba's district number was changed to 101, by which point there were fifty-one clubs in the country; Añorga, "El rotarismo en Cuba," 952.

23. "Tercera conferencia del distrito 25 de Rotary Internacional celebrada en Santiago de Cuba los días 2, 3 y 4 de marzo de 1923," *La nota rotaria* 1, no. 7 (April 1923): 9.

24. "Tercera conferencia del distrito 25 de Rotary Internacional."

25. "Por los clubs del distrito: La labor del rotarismo," *La Nota Rotaria* 2, no. 14 (November 1923): 17.

26. Archivo Histórico Provincial de Santiago de Cuba. Fondo Gobierno Provincial, 1–2407, E-5, 9.

27. Fondo Gobierno Provincial, 1–2407, E-5, 10.

28. Fondo Gobierno Provincial, 1–2407, E-5, 10.

29. Rionda, *El Club Rotario*, 141–49.

30. Rionda, *El Club Rotario*, 143.

31. Rionda, *El Club Rotario*, 141.

32. Rionda, *El Club Rotario*, 59.

33. Rionda, *El Club Rotario*, 58.

34. Rionda, *El Club Rotario*, 60.

35. Rionda, *El Club Rotario*, 62.

36. Rionda, *El Club Rotario*, 63.

37. ANC, Fondo Especial (FE), C-6, N-15.

38. Primelles, *Crónica Cubana, 1919–1922*, 544.

39. Primelles, *Crónica Cubana, 1919–1922*, 544.

40. López Civeira, *Cuba entre 1899 y 1959*, 64–65; "Aclaración del Rotary Club de la Habana," *La Nota Rotaria* 2, no. 14 (November 1923): 15.

41. Pichardo, *Documentos para la historia de Cuba*, 3: 140–50.

42. Club Rotario de La Habana, *Haciendo patria y Club Rotario de la Habana, Actividades desarrolladas*.

43. ANC, FRA, 1–697, E-18104, 114.

44. Acevedo Laborde, *Manual*, 434.

45. Acevedo Laborde, *Manual*, 434–35. The manual also quoted from Martí: "A citizen who stops voting is like a soldier who deserts."

46. Rotary Internacional, Distrito 25, *Memoria*, 291.

47. ANC, FE, C-2, no. 134.

48. Acevedo Laborde, *Manual*, 424.

49. "El Club rotario de La Habana," *Diario de la Marina*, January 5, 1917, 1.

50. Álvarez Estévez, *Isla de Pinos y el tratado Hay-Quesada*. To date, there is no evidence as to whether or not members put up money in order to lobby or bribe U.S. legislators. Rather, it seems that U.S. interest and investments in Cuba had far more of a bearing on their decision to ratify the treaty. The contrary would have strained relations between Cuba and the United States, given the degree of public interest the Isla de Pinos affair had generated within Cuban society.

51. Acevedo Laborde, *Manual*, 439.

52. Álvarez Estévez, *Isla de Pinos*, 113.

53. Álvarez Estévez, *Isla de Pinos*, 88.

CHAPTER 9

El naciente público oyente
Toward a Genealogy of the Audience in Early Republican Cuba

Alejandra Bronfman

Histories of the Cuban media dub the 1940s and 1950s the golden age of broadcasting. Rather than echoing broad historiographic currents emphasizing profound corruption or failure to build democratic institutions, they note instead a pervasive soundscape replete with telenovelas, star announcers, music, news, and political commentary. Cubans organized their days so as to catch programs featuring the Chinese detective Chan-Li Po, the charismatic and loquacious spiritist Clavelito, and the beloved, fiery critic of political corruption, Eddy Chíbas.[1] Local programs also regulated leisure hours in smaller cities and towns, as attested to by Sunday afternoons characterized by empty streets and synchronized receivers.[2] Broadcast listening shaped many of the rhythms and practices of sociability in Cuban everyday life.

The success of Cuban broadcasting extended beyond national borders. As Yeidy Rivero observes, Havana came to be the "media capital of Latin America" during this period. Not only were some of the genres such as telenovelas generated in Cuba widely popular all across the region but, as Rivero convincingly argues, the degree of "technical, advertising, and creative" expertise in Cuba's sophisticated broadcasting industry, which by the 1950s included television as well as radio, had been exported and circulated throughout the region.[3] Havana's prominent position in the region as the source of expertise and programming had, argues Rivero, a lasting impact on Latin American mediascapes.

Cuba's informative and entertaining radio histories proceed quickly from the introduction of broadcasting to the ubiquity of soaps, jingles, and stars, pausing only briefly on an array of experiments, practices, and debates that shaped that transformation. By assuming a public, they take for granted what, as Bruno Latour might argue, needs to be explained.[4] This essay poses a central question: how did a public for broadcasting come into being in republican Havana, and what are the conditions by which it emerged? How did an *audience* grow? As actors in the dramatic political processes of the Republican period, the media and its public merit further consideration. When broadcasting was introduced in Cuba in the 1920s, as we shall see, the audience was mostly elsewhere. That the medium and a local public would become two parts of what we identify as "radio" was not a foregone conclusion.

Thinking about media when they were new counters the appearance of inevitability and naturalness that media take on once they have become ubiquitous. Lingering on initial moments of uncertainty and instability allows for a deeper understanding of, as noted by Lisa Gitelman and Geoffrey Pingree, "how interpretive communities are built or destroyed, how normative epistemologies emerge."[5] I argue here that a public attuned to the particularities of early radio in Cuba did not exist prior to broadcasting but rather materialized in the context of economic and political circumstances in the republican era. As proposed by Carolyn Marvin, histories of media must include an array of users. Along with consumers, it is crucial to take into account entrepreneurs and technicians who policed the boundaries of use, meanings, and purpose as systems of communication began to take shape. Marvin argued eloquently for a decentering of technological histories, away from the progression of different machines and toward the discursive contexts in which they were created.[6] Here I draw from Gitelman and Pingree, Marvin, and Latour to get at the question of the composition of a public. I propose that the machines assembled a public at the same time that people assembled machines. The public and the machines can be understood as artifacts of mutual invention. But this was an incomplete, uneven process. The transposition of broadcasting to early Republican Cuba did not call forth a homogeneous "mass" audience. Rather, from its inception, it assembled a fractured, critical, and skeptical public. The excesses and leftovers remained as counterpublics and a variety of noisy machines that disrupted the sound of mainstream broadcasting.[7]

What difference does sound make? The medium in question reproduced and transmitted sound over long distances, extending the range of the voice and of the ear. Contemporary observers expressed wonder at the capacity of wireless to shrink distances and meditated on the possibilities for new communities and the destabilization of seemingly incontrovertible categories like space and time.[8] But if commentators marveled at utopian possibilities, they remained paradoxically silent about the actual sounds emanating from the machines, evincing a problematic distance between the promise of instant and clear communication and the reality of beeps, whistles, rasps, crackles, and blips, along with the occasional tones of human voices or musical instruments. I would suggest, however, that the appeal of clarity and seemingly unmediated sound as eventually proposed by manufacturers of radio sets obscures a much more ecumenical approach by early listeners. The people listening to their machines did not demand smooth, clear reception at the onset of broadcasting. It was only later that the demand for clarity of sound came to shape a public with specific parameters of social status as well as with particular expectations and practices. In so doing it marginalized other kinds of listening practices and relationships with machines. My intention here is to remain attuned to the exigencies and limits of the aural, but the methodological challenge of doing a history of sound with written texts remains. For the moment these and visual representations of the machines themselves are my sources.

New Machines
What apparatus serves as a point of entry for a history of radio in Cuba? Perhaps it was the telephone, introduced in 1859 as a machine that could receive and transmit sound, especially voices. Since the telephone was intended to provide crucial information to commercial enterprises, it fits neatly into broader narratives centered on empire and technology. A second version might begin with the stations assembled and owned by amateur radio operators, who in the early twentieth century used those stations to send or receive shortwave signals. Such a beginning would privilege individuals rather than state or corporate actors and place more emphasis on informal transnational connections rather than national boundaries in the making of radio.

There is a third beginning: October 10, 1922. At 4 P.M. President Zayas spoke into a microphone first in English and then in Spanish. A series of musical performances followed his speech. The program was aimed at the United States, but also at those in Cuba with the technology to receive broadcasts.[9] This beginning might be understood not as a beginning at all but rather as the moment in which the stories of the telephone and the amateurs come together and, in so doing, confound simpler interpretations of communications technologies as either wholly controlled by imperial, capitalist interests or predominantly in the hands of scattered individuals. The radio station from which Zayas spoke, PWX, was built by the Cuban Telephone Company, an offshoot of International Telephone and Telegraph, and it transmitted via telephone line to its sister station, WEAF in New York, which in turn broadcast within its range. Relative to the expense and labor involved in the construction of this station, listeners were few. One hundred manufactured receivers were dispersed throughout Cuba. In the days before the PWX broadcast, General Electric and Westinghouse had distributed another forty receivers to government employees. On October 10, they opened the doors of their store so that passersby could listen.[10] Any remaining listeners would have been those "amateurs" who had acquired or built their own equipment and for the first time would have been able to tune in to a broadcast from the island itself rather than from across the ocean.

It is worth remembering that Cuba was at that moment emerging from a recent economic catastrophe, in which the price of sugar, buoyed by several years of high demand as a result of war in Europe, plummeted dramatically in 1921. During the war, foreign investment, particularly from the United States, had grown substantially. Twenty-five new sugar mills had been built between 1914 and 1920, raising the volume of sugar produced and bolstering wages for workers. After sugar prices crashed, the prosperity in evidence since 1915 was suddenly at risk, as banks failed, businesses closed, and unemployment grew.[11]

As many historians have observed, the economic crisis spurred a political crisis for the Zayas administration, as urban and rural workers mobilized when confronted with sudden deprivation relative to the past decade. At the same time, students, intellectuals, and veterans framed their protests with a critique of the corrupt relationship with the United States and a lack of sovereignty. Revisiting Zayas's opening speech with this in mind suggests that he was at once lauding technological modernity in an effort to bolster fading legitimacy and making explicit the connection to the United States, perhaps against growing criticisms of his administration.

Thus sonic technologies made their appearance in Havana amid uncertain economic conditions and increasingly vocal expressions of discontent with a political system that many saw as corrupt and demeaning. One of the results of this dual crisis was a shift in political practices that entailed, as Gillian McGillivray and Robert Whitney have argued, efforts to incorporate popular mobilizations into electoral politics and in reformulated nationalist discourses. As in other parts of Latin America, the "people" was constituted as a political actor with varying degrees of force and influence.[12]

With the advantages of hindsight, it seems relatively straightforward to make the connection between interlocutors looking for a medium and a medium looking for an audience. As facilitator to a regime looking for ways to harness and control a politicized "people" as well as for an opposition looking to disseminate its messages of dissent, the place of a medium like radio seems clear, especially given what we know of radio's eventual role. But none of it was obvious to people at the time.

El Naciente Público Oyente

Cubans were not strangers to listening. Across socioeconomic status, modes of sociability included gatherings centered around aural communications. As Marial Iglesias has argued, public festivals were integral to the construction of a nationalist sentiment in the aftermath of colonialism. These included civic and religious processions, *mítins*, commemorations, and funerals. In the streets and plazas of urban centers, the collective listening to music, songs, and speeches that took place during these rituals helped Cubans negotiate the complex transitions from Spanish rule to North American tutelage with a modicum of autonomy. Particularly in a context in which illiteracy predominated, collective aural experiences proved significant to any attempts to elaborate nationalist hegemonies. These were produced and consumed by diverse groups, including Afro-Cubans whose drumming sessions came to be a site of contestation over the meaning of civilization and modernity.[13]

Listening publics had also formed in enclosed spaces. Araceli Tinajero has traced the tradition of reading aloud that came to characterize many cigar factories in Cuba, the United States, and other parts of the Caribbean. Stretching back to the nineteenth century, readers became a fixture on factory floors, offering entertainment and information to thousands of workers. They were paid by the workers themselves and most commonly read newspapers and novels for up to four hours a day. The workforce, which Tinajero argues was ethnically diverse and tended to the lower end of the socioeconomic spectrum, became an expectant and informed listening public whose interests ranged, apparently, from news of politics and sports events to canonical authors like Cervantes, Victor Hugo, and Dickens.[14] The elite also had listening spaces, such as the opera house and concert hall. As attested to by the theaters and concert halls built in the late nineteenth and early twentieth centuries, these were popular pastimes among the bourgeoisie seeking the trappings of distinction in a fluid social context. More recently, the phonograph had made an appearance, rendering living room and parlors listening spaces in a few exclusive homes.

But this rich, diverse, and sophisticated culture of listening did not immediately take up the radio as its next object of interest. In the early years, listening to a box played on different desires and expectations than going to a concert, attending a rally, or taking in a novel over the course of a workweek at a cigar factory. Initially, the medium's appeal was more associated with the machines themselves than with its potential to convey sound to large numbers of people. The most prominent machines that transmitted sound were telephones. By 1888, the Spanish colonial regime had created a telephone network with thirty-four kilometers of lines and one thousand five hundred subscribers. In the wake of the U.S. occupations (1898–1902 and 1906–9), U.S. capital, which had provided the initial financing, took greater control and created the Cuban Telephone Company. The brothers Hernand and Sosthenes Behn subsequently bought this and added it to their growing telecommunications empire, International Telephone and Telegraph. By 1916, Havana had 5 telephones per 100 inhabitants, which was half that of New York, but three times that of Madrid. In 1921, Havana and Key West were connected with the first overseas (or undersea) telephone cables, allowing for speedier communications among the growing capitalist enterprises in Cuba and the United States. Because of the financial relationships, Havana and New York were linked via telephone sooner than New York and other parts of the United States.[15] If one were to map access to sonic media, boundaries of wealth, infrastructure, investment patterns, and urban space would matter more than national boundaries.

Wireless radio sets appeared soon after World War I and seem to have taken their place alongside telephones as the most recent development in long-distance communications. The medium worked for two-way or point-to-point communication. It was suited to bits of information at best and, if not entirely reliable, was exciting for the possibilities of communicating electronically over great distances. A series of men—all men as far as I can tell—became fascinated with the equipment and its possibilities and began to build or buy stations to operate privately. This world of amateurs or hobbyists existed as a more diffuse network already engaged with the emergent technologies prior to the Cuban Telephone Company's efforts to expand to broadcasting. In the United States, many amateurs were boys or middle-class men, relegated to their basements, tinkering late at night or on the weekends, forming associations with other amateurs and exchanging messages mostly about the fact that they could exchange messages.[16] But in Cuba and throughout the Caribbean, those who could afford the equipment tended to be wealthy and established. Often they were planters or sponsored by planters who used the ability to communicate to serve their business interests.[17]

These amateurs and their stories have made a scant impression in published texts. Rather, their presence emerges on the Internet, as part of what is becoming an extensive alternative history of radio. Luis Casas Romero is remembered as both a military man who had fought in Cuba's Wars of Independence and as a musician who founded and directed the Banda Infantil de Camaguey. He built station 2LC in Havana in 1920 and transmitted Cuba's first radio signals in August 1922. Casas began his broadcast with the cannon shot fired from La Cabana every night at 9 P.M., followed by a weather report. According to Lázaro David Najarro Pujol, the programming, initially directed at "aficionades radioemisores"—in other words, other amateur broadcasters—was eventually directed at the "naciente público oyente" invoking a recently incarnated entity, the "hearing public."[18]

Other amateurs included Manuel Alvarez, who built a station in Caibaren, Las Villas, and Frank Jones, an electrical engineer employed by the sugar industry who built a station that opened in early 1922, broadcasting from Central Tuinucú.[19] The contemporary press reports that F. W. Morton and Humberto Giquel also operated stations at the opening of PWX.[20] Yet another to lay claim to originating wireless communications was Frank Butler, chief assistant to Lee De Forest, who, at the behest of the U.S. Navy, established a wireless station in Guantánamo as early as 1905. By his own telling, this was a dangerous and unpredictable adventure, complete with panthers, convicted killers hired as assistants, explosions, and an earthquake. But it was also a successful venture that culminated in the completion of one of five stations planned by the navy during this period.[21] It is possible that in this moment there were as many producers of sound as consumers. The traditional narrative that begins with the Cuban Telephone Company's PWX broadcast in 1922 obscures this existing sonic culture fed by machines, people, and knowledge.

Cuba's nascent listening public in all likelihood included those with links to this economy, as interested parties seem to have been more likely to build, rather than purchase, their own receivers. A newspaper column entitled "Radiotelefonía" inaugurated shortly following the October PWX broadcast, and written by J. M. Baquero, announced early on that since General Electric and Westinghouse sold sets at such prohibitive prices, it would dedicate much of its column space to dispensing advice about building receivers.[22] According to Baquero, anyone with access to a cigar box, some tin foil, a telephone, and a few other household items (as well as his informative instructions) could construct a set that would receive broadcasts.[23] The many letters and responses posted in subsequent columns, full of questions about antennae or the merits of different kinds of wire, suggest that many readers became builders, rather than purchasers, of radios.

By December 1922, commentators witnessed listening throughout the city: a walk on a concert night revealed inhabitants attuned to radios in elite and modest residences, grouped in clusters in a bicycle shop or sharing one set of headphones among six people.[24] But what were they listening to? Programs were intermittent and either without clear direction or extremely specific. On Wednesdays and Saturdays, from 8:30 until 10:30 P.M., PWX broadcast "programas musicales, discursos en español." Humberto Giquel's station also began with the 9 P.M. cannon shot and offered Havanans the weather forecast for the following twenty-four hours.[25] If listeners were lucky and particularly adept at tuning their receivers, they might receive programming from the United States, Canada, or even further afield. In November, PWX broadcast the proceedings of the American Medical Congress, which was deemed a success and prompted a reflection about the nature of programming. Why, asked Baquero, were there no broadcasts of the opera, or of religious services, or meetings of other social organizations?[26] The evidence suggests that the nature of broadcasting took shape much more slowly than the dissemination of technical knowledge about these machines. From this perspective, programming seems an afterthought rather than the main attraction. At the onset, radio as a medium lacked a clear purpose regarding the services it might provide, the parameters of time and taste, and the demographics and interests of anticipated audiences. Thus broadcasting did not insert itself into existing listening practices but rather hovered on the margins, seeking ways to make itself relevant despite considerable technical constraints.

Indeed, absent from discussions of early radio is an overwhelming demand to settle on a fixed format. Radio in this early incarnation appealed precisely because it held out the possibility of receiving noise from other parts of the world. Listeners were pleasantly surprised, perhaps, but certainly did not require that what they heard make sense or provide sustained information or entertainment, or that it dispense up-to-date news regarding sports matches, political events, or natural catastrophes. All of that would come later. In the beginning, radio appealed precisely because it could access and sonically represent the fragmented and dispersed nature of the world—this medium, much more than others that preceded it, gave the impression of transparency.[27] The ether, replete with all sorts of noise, could be captured. As commentator Julian Power of *Carteles* put it, radio sounded like this: "Celeste Aida . . . oiga, quitese de la linea . . . ik, ik, ik . . . Celeste Ai . . . brrrr.

... Station KKK? .... Toc-toc-toc ... señores y señoras, va a cantar Sylvia. ... ik, ik, ik ... you, my baby flapper. ... tratachín, tratachín ... jabon de reuter! ... toc, toc ... ese melyto, a la reja ... solo de violín por."[28] If Power evinced exasperation with this as a listening experience, he positioned himself as an outsider and critic of the mainstream. I suggest that the growing appeal of radio drew from its capacity to offer access to far-flung domains of sound. Perhaps, for some, what was exciting and really new was not that they might receive cohesive and easily audible concerts from across town but rather that they might, on some clear evening, find themselves listening to bits of a boxing match or a weather report from hundreds of miles away.

The machines remained the center of attention and drew dispersed groups into association with one another. Cubans spent a great deal of energy trying to figure out which machine to use, which one to build, and how many ways to use it. In newspapers and publications, diagrams mapped out the way bits of wire, coils, cardboard, and metal could be put together in the most efficient fashion. Marked with neat numbers and labels for each of the parts, the bird's-eye and three-quarter views rendered the machines both impressive and accessible, bound to succeed, because of their complexity, and possible to assemble with a modicum of determination. The listener this machine called forth was self-sufficient, competent, and attentive to precision and detail. Having a radio was not so much about entertainment as about being part of a mechanically minded, electrically literate community. The diagrams, the worrying about antennae, and the anxiety about translated manuals suggest that the machines held out an allure perhaps even distinct from their function. Part of the fascination derived from the tactile, palpable connection to this invention.[29]

So an audience was beginning to take shape, interested in making its own equipment and trolling both for regular broadcasts and for random and distant noises captured by their antennae. At the same time, the presence of these machines gave rise to an assortment of other occupations and preoccupations. The vendors, the "radio-doctors," writers, commentators, and instructors formed part of a cluster of people and activities centered on the equipment. Jorge González, of the signal marine corps, found a new market for his skills when he became an instructor at the new Academia de Radiotelefonía. Cuba's Department of Communications opened its own academy, requiring both instructors and students. And translators were busy producing Spanish-language versions of books on radio.[30] The machines spawned a collection of people concerned with how to explain their function, how to keep them working, how to use them in different ways, and how to sell them.

The rise of broadcasters and performers may in fact have been preceded by and depended on the community of mechanics, engineers, publishers, and pedagogues this medium supported.[31]

Receivers, as machines that emitted entertaining or informative programming, were among many apparatuses introduced during this period. Alongside stories about the growing broadcasting industry, magazines like *Carteles* and *Social* featured articles that predicted an array of uses for the transmission and recording of sound. From abroad came the story of linguistic work in progress by John Harrington of the Smithsonian Institute and William Gates, director of the National Museum in Guatemala. Their use of the "palofotófono" to record the speech of a Guatemalan Indian named Cipriano Alvarado, who had been "found in the mountains and completely ignorant of civilization," promised to be the key to unlocking the secrets of Mayan Quiché. This device, recently invented by Charles Hoxie at General Electric, apparently reproduced images of words on film, thus, according to the authors, allowing for a detailed analysis of tone, inflection, and nonverbal sounds. Where previous efforts to record guttural and laryngeal sounds had failed, the palofotófono promised to further the ambitions of linguists in search of pure samples of a disappeared language. The scientists had recorded Alvarado telling the Maya creation story and broadcast it over the radio, giving audiences "an opportunity to listen to a disappearing language."[32] As Jonathan Sterne has pointed out, an initial impetus for the development of recording technology was a developing interest in preservation of bodies. In the wake of the U.S. Civil War, medical and scientific knowledge devoted some attention to preserving dead bodies for scientific research. The possibility of preserving voices, especially of the soon to be dead, spurred experimentation in recording technologies.[33] Anthropologists working in the 1920s made the leap from recording vanishing voices to the desire to record vanishing languages. Linguistic dictionaries enjoyed long-standing status as an indispensable tool for anthropologists. The use of recording devices seemed a logical next step. These machines would assist them in their endeavors to capture dying sounds and allow (skeptical?) listeners to witness their work.[34]

From London came the account of another technological breakthrough. Engineers were working on the "vidoscopo," a device that would allow for the broadcasting of visual as well as sonic material. So, imagined the author, people sitting in the comfort of their homes would be able to view a film simultaneously to its showing in New York or London or anywhere else in the world. When this happened, the "emoción estética de los fanáticos del radio," already giddy with the radio broadcasts of opening nights at the Apollo Theater, would surely expand and send audiences into new ecstatic heights.[35] This and another potential invention, the phonofilm, pursued the possibility of marrying visual and sound recordings. Lee De Forest, responsible for this latest of several attempts, claimed that the best use for this would be for dance numbers, but the journalist reporting on these inventions projected other uses, such as the recording and broadcasting of educational lectures. He also imagined this as a link to the dead, citing De Forest's lament that the technology hadn't been invented in time to record the great speeches of Abraham Lincoln or Theodore Roosevelt.[36] These machines promised the creation of memory and an archive. In their presence, the future was imagined as one that could hold on more precisely to the past. But they remained fantasies from abroad as Cubans continued to fiddle with their homemade equipment and rely on radio in public spaces as their principal source of electronically transmitted sound.

Buy Buy Buy
Such an anti-consumerist engagement with radio proved frustrating to General Electric and Westinghouse executives, whose own projections had included profits from purchases of receivers. Advertising was not yet a major generator of income, and Cuba did not require the licensing of receivers, as in Great Britain.[37] The companies, whose expansion into Latin America had been premised on growing profits in the face of continuing economic difficulties, embarked on a concerted effort to persuade Cubans to buy new receiving sets.[38]

Given the high cost and the unproven nature of the machines themselves, the General Electric and Westinghouse campaigns involved appealing to expectations of gender and class. Marketing strategies included persuading potential buyers that receivers were easy to use, attractive, and would foster sophisticated renewed social relations. Steve Wurtzler's work on marketing of receivers in the United States has demonstrated the ways that manufacturers worked to transform equipment from apparatuses worthy of garages or basements to pieces of furniture appropriate for living rooms and parlors.[39] A similar logic seems to have been at work in Cuba, as demonstrated by the advertisements populating the pages of *Carteles* and *Social*, publications that served as one of Havana's principal arbiters of bourgeois taste. One General Electric ad promises that listeners will "dance with radio," offering the appeal of dancing in one's own home to the best music coming "from Chicago or New York."[40] A drawing of well-dressed couples waltzing on a veranda of

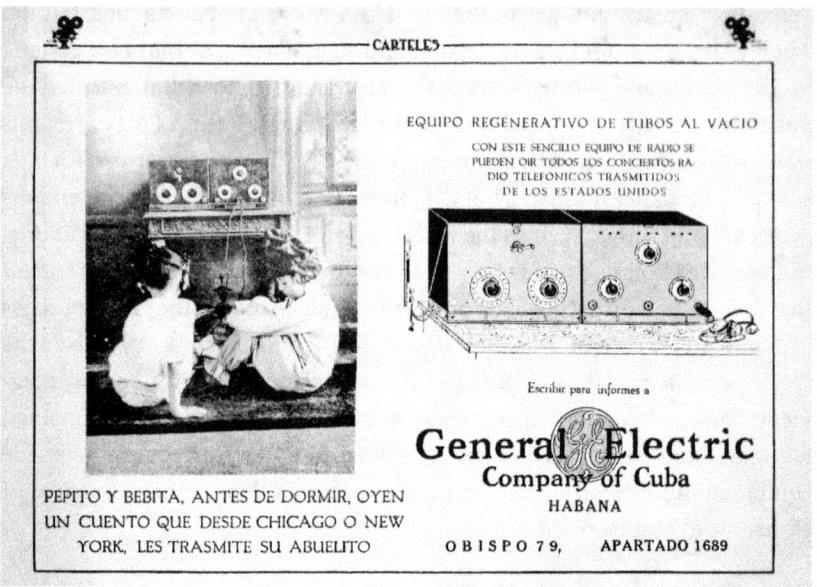

Figure 9.1 General Electric ad: "Before going to sleep, Pepito and Bebita listen to a story transmitted by their grandfather from New York or Chicago." *Carteles*, January 1923.

what seems to be a large house suggests that the receiver's proper place is in the homes and entertainments of the wealthy. The radio could turn a home or a veranda into a privatized version of a concert hall or a dance floor.

Other ads promoted the receivers' simplicity. Itself simple, the ad included a line drawing of a receiver, accompanied by the claim that it would receive all the concerts broadcast from the United States.[41] Continuing with this theme, some ads included images of tuned-in children, simultaneously touting the possibilities of strengthening family ties, fostering cosmopolitan attitudes, and operating accessible technologies: "Pepito y Bebita, antes de dormir, oyen un cuento que desde Chicago o New York, les transmite su abuelito."[42] RCA promoted its receivers in a similar manner. Assurances to potential buyers included clarity of sound and reception from great distances (always the United States, in these ads) without static. They also claimed simplicity and affordability, the latter somewhat undermined by the drawings of elegantly dressed young women gathered around a receiver in a well-appointed parlor. It seemed to matter little that they neglected to explain the array of machines with specialized names: the "Radiola Super-Heterodyne" and "Radiola Regenoflex" were promoted as equally easy to use and effective.[43] The appeal was to be part of a transnational audience. They were selling a relationship with the United States as much as an apparatus.

Figure 9.2 Victrola ad: "To listen to the best music, you need Victrola." *Social*, November 1924.

Against the emerging and existing practices of listening in the street or in public places, or of constructing equipment and searching for an esoteric variety of emanations from multiple locations, RCA and General Electric waged a campaign to promote listening that took place inside homes (particularly those that could afford to buy their apparatuses), by young women, couples, or families, to concerts or other programs broadcast from the United States. The acquisition of manufactured radio sets moved spaces of electronically mediated listening from the street to the home, from a male-occupied nook or closet to a female-dominated shared living space. The public that GE, Westinghouse, and RCA hoped to foster was enclosed in private space and reliant on a commercial company for their entertainment. It was a public that sought cosmopolitan connections in the comfort of their home, enjoyed regular diversions at regular intervals that might move easily from consuming the machines to consuming that which the machines told them to buy, and that would integrate new technologies into traditional rituals of courtship, childrearing, or conviviality.

But street listening persisted, taking on new dimensions. In March 1923,

Figure 9.3 A fifteen-foot loudspeaker. *Carteles*, October 1924.

Humberto Giquel mounted a radio and loudspeaker on a car and presented it at carnaval, during which the car, draped in flags and paper flowers, paraded the streets. Photographs denote the curiosity of onlookers, falling perhaps short of bedazzlement, but certainly indicating the novelty of the "radio-auto."[44] Just as Havana expanded from its older urban core and more cars began to appear in the streets, Giquel linked sound with mobility as a new mode of inhabiting urban space.[45] The loudspeakers themselves were worthy of putting on display, as in the exhibit of a giant loudspeaker with a woman perched on top (see figure 9.3). Underscoring the new commodification of sound, the ad jokingly denied the commodification of women—asserting that though the loudspeaker was for sale, its model was not.[46] As the "magician of the twentieth century," electronically broadcast sound inspired inventors and entrepreneurs to generate an array of uses. It might expand and fuel the entertainment industry, generate and fulfill consumer demands, or fill urban spaces with (more) noise.[47] This pleased some observers and irritated others.

El Octopus Acústico

According to some critics, rather than integrating smoothly into practices of social reproduction or contributing to the pleasures of public space, the radio wrought destruction and disrupted the rhythms of family life. As energetically as it was declared the magician of the twentieth century, radio was condemned on a number of fronts. Critics bemoaned the dangers to both nation and psyches. Julio Power understood radio as science gone awry, taking on a life of its own and producing overwhelming, unbearable quantities of noise: "el monstruo ubicuo . . . perturba la paz del universo." The noise posed multiple dangers, among them that of imperialism—not only were Cubans now condemned to hear more English than they ever wanted, once emissions from Europe or China increased, the cacophony would send Cubans straight to the insane asylum. The apocalypse would come to fruition eventually, with increasing rates of deafness and states battling for airwaves. Only then would a new, sensible silence reign.[48] In the context of rising critiques of imperialism and perceived threats to national autonomy, the radio served as a reminder of the fragility of sonic boundaries. There was no defense against the aural violation of national borders.

Another danger, according to Power, was a radical transformation of daily life, including the enjoyment of other entertainments. No one used cameras or phonographs anymore, and attendance had declined at live performances. The radio had driven everyone inside, he argued, vacating once lively streets and plazas in favor of the ironically described "cajita mágica y radiosa." And public space would be newly filled with the "jinete satanico": advertising. He composed a scenario in which loudspeakers mounted in plazas and street corners would peddle Gillette soap, Bayer aspirin, and El Gaitero cider. Urban centers had already become tremendously noisy, he observed apocalyptically, so much so that those seeking a quiet existence would have to spend their lives in airplanes.[49]

Alberto Guigou also announced the death of traditional social rituals. Drawing a sharper distinction between public and private space, he announced a reign of silence in public accompanying the turn inward to domestic broadcasting. Suffering from the "morbo auditivo," people put on their headphones and neglected cards, chess, conversation, or books in favor of the radio broadcast. This had thrown families into disarray, as children turned away from their grandmothers' bedtime stories or refused to go to bed. But courtship suffered most of all. No more furtive kisses on the sofa, no more lingering conversations, no more kisses blown from windows. Moreover, the radio had introduced conflict, as couples bickered over musical

Figure 9.4 "Radio and Love," by Alberto Guigou. *Carteles*, May 1923.

tastes, or young women worked in vain to wrest their lovers from the tentacles of the "octopus acústico."[50]

If these observers agreed that the radio disrupted and corroded social practices, they disagreed as to how it had affected communal space: while one insisted on an increasingly noisy soundscape in the street, the other emphasized an eerily silent and deserted city. At risk were traditional family structures. And in contention was the use of public space. Newly mobilized political communities had not yet harnessed broadcasting to their purposes. But worries and uncertainties about the capacities of radio to transform space, and the practice of politics along with it, seem to be driving much of this commentary. As R. Murray Schafer observed, there is no ear lid, and the capacity of these new machines to produce sound that could not be shut off or ignored fed these writers' anxieties.[51] Not only were families, couples, and pocketbooks at risk; the radio called into question, and therefore put in danger, the very boundaries of communities and of selves.

An Assembled Audience

Despite their positions on opposite sides of the moral divide with regard to radio, both the critics and the advocates point to a process of what Latour would call a reassembly.[52] Radio reorganized groups of people, bringing them into contact with one another and reconfiguring forms of sociability. Electrical engineers, corporate executives, young women, journalists, advertising agencies, and aspiring broadcasters all came to have a stake in sonic technologies and the process by which they would become part of daily Havanan life. Responding to an initial context of ambulatory listening and consumers that preferred tinkering over buying, private capital worked to create a listening audience in private, domestic, moneyed spaces. Listeners grew accustomed to designing aural schedules, demanding clarity of sound, and regarding emanations from long distances as normal occurrences. Amateurs remained outside and on the margins of the tightening bonds between capital and broadcasting, but they did not disappear. Changing configurations of wires, machines, microphones, transmitters, and receivers conjured people to make, fix, listen to, and buy them. An audience had come into being.

Notes

1. González, *Llorar es un placer*; López, *La radio en Cuba*.
2. "Dos años de un programa radial: *Lo que pasa en Pinar del Río* lo escucha el 97% de oyentes," in *Pinar del Río: El organo official del Comite Todo por Pinar del Río* 1, no. 4 (August 1947).
3. Rivero, "Havana as a 1940s–1950s Latin American Media Capital," 277.
4. Latour, *Reassembling the Social*.
5. Gitelman and Pingree, "Introduction: What's New about New Media?," xv.
6. Marvin, *When Old Technologies Were New*. See also Sterne, *The Audible Past*.
7. Hirschkind, *The Ethical Soundscape*; Warner, *Publics and Counterpublics*.
8. See, for example, Arnheim, *Radio*.
9. *La Discusión*, October 11, 1922, 1, 8. López, *La radio en Cuba*; González, *Llorar es un placer*.
10. González, *Llorar es un placer*, 89–90.
11. McGillivray, *Blazing Cane*; Pérez, *Cuba under the Platt Amendment*; Whitney, *State and Revolution in Cuba*; Commission on Cuban Affairs, *Problems of the New Cuba*; Chapman, *A History of the Cuban Republic*.
12. McGillivray, *Blazing Cane*; Whitney, *State and Revolution in Cuba*.
13. Iglesias Utset, *Las metáforas del cambio*; Rosenthal, "Spectacle, Fear, and Protest"; Bronfman, *Measures of Equality*; Moore, *Nationalizing Blackness*; Palmié, *Wizards and Scientists*.
14. Tinajero, *El Lector*.
15. Altshuler and Díaz, eds., *El teléfono en Cuba*; Pérez Salomón, *Cuba: 125 años de telefonía*; O'Brien, *The Revolutionary Mission*.
16. Haring, *Ham Radio's Technical Culture*.
17. See, for example, McGillivray, *Blazing Cane*, 133–34.
18. Najarro Pujol, "Luis Casas Romero: Iniciador de la era de la radio en Cuba." http://www.upec.cu/baul/27.html, accessed April 21, 2010.
19. Alvarez, "A History of Cuban Broadcasting." http://www.oldradio.com/archives/international/cuban.html, accessed April 20, 2010; McGillivray, *Blazing Cane*.
20. *La Discusión*, November 18, 1922.
21. Butler, "How Radio Came to Cuba," *Radio Broadcast*, March 1925: 916–25. http://earlyradiohistory.us/cuba.htm, accessed April 29, 2010.

22. "Radiotelefonía," *La Discusión*, November 28 and 30, 1922.

23. *La Discusión*, November 21, 1922, 12.

24. *La Discusión*, December 15, 1922, 7.

25. *La Discusión*, November 19, 1922, 2.

26. *La Discusión*, November 24, 1922, 7.

27. Gitelman and Pingree, "Introduction: What's New about New Media?"

28. Power, "Torre de Babel," *Carteles*, April 1923, 38, 43.

29. *La Discusión*, December 5, 1922; December 6, 1922, 12.

30. *La Discusión*, November 28, 1922, 4; December 6, 1922, 12.

31. Marx, "Technology: The Emergence of a Hazardous Concept," 965–88.

32. *Carteles*, September 1923, 56.

33. Sterne, *The Audible Past*, chap. 6.

34. Radick, "R. L. Garner and the Rise of the Edison Phonograph in Evolutionary Philology"; Averill, "Ballad Hunting in the Black Republic," 3–22; Brady, *A Spiral Way*.

35. Moreno, "Tendremos Radiocinematografía?," *Carteles*, November 1922, 17.

36. Moreno, "La Phonofilm De Forest," *Carteles*, April 1923, 17.

37. Hilmes, *Network Nations*.

38. O'Brien, *The Revolutionary Mission*, 227.

39. Wurtzler, *Electric Sounds*.

40. *Social*, January 1923, 52.

41. *Carteles*, December 1922, 26.

42. *Carteles*, January 1923, 21.

43. *Social*, November 1924, 75; December 1924, 57.

44. *Bohemia*, March 18, 1923, 15.

45. Scarpaci, Segre, and Coyula, *Havana: Two Faces of the Antillean Metropolis*.

46. *Carteles*, October 12, 1924, 26.

47. Gutiérrez Lanza, *El mago del siglo veinte*.

48. Power, "Torre de Babel," *Carteles*, April 1923, 38, 43.

49. Power, "Torre de Babel," *Carteles*, April 1923, 38, 43.

50. Guigou, "El radio y el amor," *Carteles*, May 1923, 36, 44. This may have been authored by the same person who wrote "La Torre de Babel."

51. Schafer, *Tuning of the World*.

52. Latour, *Reassembling the Social*.

CHAPTER 10

New Knowledge for New Times
The Sociedad del Folklore Cubano during
the "Critical Decade" (1923–1930)

Ricardo Quiza Moreno

Historians have dubbed Cuba in the 1920s the "critical decade" or the era of a "burgeoning national consciousness." From profound economic crises to the rise of the Machado dictatorship, developments in this period set the tone and shape for the country's subsequent growth. These developments took place within an atmosphere characterized by a dynamic civil society and the emergence of new social actors, including artists and intellectuals with an unprecedented level of awareness of their civic role in subverting the republic of "generals and doctors" and engendering alternative discourses in historiography, music, literature, and the fine arts.[1] The political and economic upheavals of the 1920s pervaded cultural production. This revolution within the aesthetic and academic sphere was enacted through the initiative of artists and intellectuals and supported by the emergence of institutions that facilitated the process of reinvigoration and mediated the implementation of novel political cultures. The Sociedad de Estudios del Folklore Cubano (Society for the Study of Cuban Folklore) was among those institutions that dedicated themselves to researching and promoting nontraditional culture and to developing new scientific standards. This organization aimed at recovering cultural material far removed from the elitist objects of analysis promoted by official academia.

The Sociedad del Folklore emerged within a national and global context that favored the rise of novel focuses and methods in artistic and academic spheres. The end of the First World War brought on a plethora of popular movements—some related to the disruptions provoked by the war itself and others related to the drive of laissez-faire capitalism. Oswald Spengler hastened to proclaim the "decline of the West" due to the incompatibility of a dogma dedicated to individual liberties, the spontaneity of the market, and a mechanical model of progress defined by urban and demographic growth and the expansion of capitalist relations to marginalized sectors. The complex social dynamics following the Belle Époque escaped the normative frameworks of interpretation dictated by Newtonian principles and Darwinism. At their height, psychoanalysis, sociology, and anthropology evinced a "will to know" that grounded its object of study in the Other. Nonetheless, it is important to recognize that these innovative disciplines were frequently used to legitimize regimes cut from a totalitarian cloth; with the growing importance of the masses within the political sphere, such regimes incorporated the popular sectors rather than simply ruling over them coercively. We need only remember the use of Lombrosian anthropology in Mussolini's fascism.

As a dependent country with rigid political stratification, Cuba quickly became acquainted with the paradoxes of the post–World War I era. In fact, the second decade of the republic would witness economic and governmental crises that would discredit the republic endorsed in 1902. In the same period that the Sociedad del Folklore Cubano emerged, a number of groups of intellectuals, women, students, war veterans, workers, and a portion of the petit bourgeoisie manifested their nonconformity to the political project that had been spearheaded by the protagonists of the anticolonial movement at the turn of the century. Notably, the committee that created the Sociedad del Folklore was formed in 1923, the same year that other bellwether organizations appeared: the Federation of University Students, the Communist Committee of Havana, the National Movement of Veterans and Patriots, and the "José Martí" Popular University.[2] During this period, the country celebrated the first congresses for women and students, and two years later the first communist party and first trade union confederation appeared. This decade also saw the manifesto known as the "Protesta de los Trece" (the "Protest of the Thirteen"), a response by intellectuals furious with the reigning state of corruption.[3]

In the academic terrain, especially among historians, confrontation manifested itself as a clash between different modes of reconstructing the nation's past: crisis called for a critical revision of official history. Subjects and theories until then virtually unknown began to compete with more traditional scholarship, and the use of unconventional sources justified these novel interpretations. At the same time, new ideas about the origins and future of the *patria*, or nation, began to flourish and be widely distributed. The historian Ramiro Guerra's well-known text *Azúcar y población en las Antillas* (Sugar and population in the Antilles), for example, a text that questioned the country's sugar production and *latifundista* model was published in the influential, though controversial, newspaper *Diario de la Marina*.

Nevertheless, the public statements of intellectuals and the ideas about Cuba's condition expressed in their works do not tell the full story of the cultural radicalism of this decade. The intellectual rivalries staged in the island's republic of letters displayed particular characteristics derived from specificities in the process of cultural production. An understanding of the dialectic between academic attitudes and their external determinants must recognize not only the quality of a culture to reflect a particular era but also its autonomous character in structuring it. As Pierre Bourdieu puts it, the "specificity of the system of production ... leads to the specificity of the relations which are established within it: the relations between each of the agents of the system and the agents or institutions which are entirely or partly external to the system are always mediated by the relations established within the system itself, that is inside the intellectual field."[4]

It is in this sense that I propose to show how the cultural practices and policies that developed within the Society of Cuban Folklore, an intriguing if short-lived manifestation of the new cultural production of the 1920s, established strategies that contributed to the subversion of the cultural order of the republic while simultaneously creating alternative sensibilities. Beyond an investigation of the decade's cultural products—as the result of a certain mode of expression and aesthetic standard as well as exponents of social conflict—I am interested in specifying the connection between the structure of society and the modes of operation and organization of the institutions that made the creation of symbolic goods possible. I emphasize the practices, rituals, and institutional norms that led to the foundations of a new social imaginary.

Tradition within Rupture: The Sociedad del Folklore Cubano and Its Cultural Debts

The creation of alternative spaces for the social sciences was a distinctive sign of a new phase in Cuba: the debut and subsequent development of the Sociedad del Folklore was a confirmation of this turn of events. Nevertheless, the cultural group was constrained by certain debts—bound as it was to traces of a cultural tradition that mediated its reformist nature. This new cultural project relied on the support of several members of the Academia de la Historia de Cuba (Cuban Academy of History), an organization renowned for its relations with the government and its explicit desire to legitimize an epic discourse saturated with heroes.[5] The inauguration of the Sociedad del Folklore was attended by academic historians and others who endorsed this new organization.[6] Three of six members of the Sociedad's board of directors also served in the Academia de la Historia.[7] In fact, many members of the Academia or similar organizations, such as the Academia Nacional de Artes y Letras (National Academy of Arts and Letters) and the Sociedad Económica Amigos del País (the Economic Society of Friends of the Country, in whose head office the folkloric group was founded), served as committee members of the Sociedad or collaborators of its journal, *Archivos del Folklore Cubano*.[8]

Moreover, the four honorary presidents elected during the organization's first session were prominent individuals in the Academia de la Historia.[9] Although the organization failed to receive the governmental support it required,[10] the Secretaría de Instrucción Pública y Bellas Artes (secretary of public education and fine arts) nonetheless entrusted this new organization with the task of creating and distributing propaganda and documenting popular culture in various cities across the country, cities that would become home to this organization's first folkloric groups.[11]

The Sociedad del Folklore's ties to powerful academic figures and institutions can be explained: beyond the political and conceptual differences visible in the principal cultural projects of the era, there were also affinities that were inherent to the intellectual milieu of Cuba at this time. This convergence stemmed from specific characteristics within the practice of the social sciences, especially historiography, in addition to the historical context. A preoccupation with "the past" permeated the social sciences and remained a strong focus for cultural organizations that emerged in the first years of the republic. There was a certain need to explain the origins of the political regime in Cuba, a necessity that only escalated with the approaching celebrations of a quarter century of independence at the very time that Cuba was experiencing the breakdown of governance and civil consensus. By 1922, the economic model maintained by sugar production was in crisis, which led to General Gerardo Machado's rise to power and the consolidation of the republic's first dictatorship.

The recovery and study of the past pervaded academic production to such an extent that the Sociedad del Folklore understood folklore as "the popular" in historical terms. An editorial in the organization's journal proclaimed: "in Cuba, the moment one cuts through the mental surface of the Pueblo [the People], one discovers the rich veins of ancestral tradition since, in the subsoil of Cuban popular culture, there lies unknown deposits of very different civilizations."[12] This kind of "human geology" proposed by the Sociedad was accompanied by a strong dose of nationalism—a characteristic that made it akin to other intellectual strains in Cuba during the 1920s. Hence the journal *Archivos del Folklore Cubano* was conceived as a "refuge for the Cuban soul under whose shelter we could protect ourselves from the hurricanes raging outside."[13]

The study and recovery of the past and an inclination to focus on national history as well as a similarity in research procedures—examining sources, writing practices, and the defense of the principle of scientific objectivity—made possible a degree of communion between cultural agencies and agents. The model questionnaire for compiling popular Cuban literature, designed by the Society of Folklore and published in its journal, proposed as its premise that "the documenter should not alter what is heard from the narrator: respect his grammar, his logic, and his spirit." In like manner, the institution offered a variety of instructions for researchers: in the event of oral evidence, the researcher was urged to investigate the interviewee and refer to his or her nationality, origin, name, and age as well as the form, moment, and place in which the data was transmitted. In the case of written evidence, the researcher was to record information about the document.[14]

The Sociedad del Folklore established an interesting dialectic between tradition, change, nationalism, and science as a result of its advocacy for "national reconstruction."[15] On the other hand, orthodox institutions were continually affirmed for their significant work and research in culture, demonstrated by the conferring of intellectual distinctions and honors as well as the publication and promotion of individual works. Referring to his election as corresponding member of the Spanish Academy of History (Academia de la Historia de España), Fernando Ortiz accepted that "these Spanish academies retain prestige."[16] Nevertheless, despite its imperfections, the republic's political system possessed a margin of tolerance that allowed for the functioning of civil society and admitted dissident features within its structure even if these were periodically repressed by the emergence of authoritarian governments.

From Heterogeneous to Heterodox:
The Composition of the Sociedad del Folklore Cubano

The variety of individuals directly and indirectly associated with the Sociedad del Folklore was a testament to its innovative and pluralistic character—a quality that affected not only the themes selected for research but the methods of investigation as well. The institution's foundational gathering—a meeting of both female and male intellectuals, some of them affiliated with the artistic and political vanguard of the period—was a sign of what would follow in the seven years of the organization's existence. In contrast to the masculine profile of other cultural centers, the Sociedad del Folklore admitted many women who came to occupy decisive positions in the organization and wrote with regularity in its journal. Carolina Poncet y de Cárdenas, in particular, was a pioneer of folkloric studies; her thesis on ballads in Cuba won the Premio Nacional de Artes y Letras in 1913.[17] Perhaps the most notable contribution made by female members—who were mostly teachers and specialists in pedagogy—was the introduction of childhood as a privileged subject of study. Both "The Folklore of Cuban Children," by Sofía Córdova, and "Superstitions and Cuban Children," by Consuelo Miranda, were doctoral projects from the Escuela de Pedagogía (School of Education) of the Universidad de La Habana that were published in installments in the institution's journal. To these was added "Superstitions and Cuban Schoolchildren," by Manuela Fonseca García.[18]

The folkloric society brought together three generations of scholars: those who had participated in the political and cultural processes during Independence; those who were born in the late nineteenth century; and those born during the republic who, like the preceding generation, achieved recognition in the first three decades of the twentieth century. The latter two generations, recognized as the island's "thirteenth and fourteenth literary generation," forced an air of reform into the organization. They arrived on a scene of cultural production that had long been defined by dogma, a fact that drove them to find other modes of cultural and academic expression and an alternative to institutional legitimization.[19] The majority of those who had not participated in the anticolonial project set forth political ideals that oscillated between a new kind of nationalism and the resolute militancy of the Left. To a certain extent a parallel can be drawn between the organization's academic agenda and the political and generational plurality of its members. In this way, it is significant that the majority of the organization's contributors were scholars who belonged to this aforementioned "thirteenth generation." Among the most prominent were Fernando Ortiz, Carolina Poncet, Juan Marinello, and José María Chacón y Calvo.

Fernando Ortiz was affiliated with the Movimiento Minorista and was a critic of the Machado dictatorship.[20] Ortiz presided over the Sociedad del Folklore, acting as the proprietor of its journal in a moment of crisis and developing the organization's international connections. His works appeared in nearly every issue of *Archivos del Folklore Cubano* and were characterized by their interdisciplinary nature, sheer quantity of data, and extensive use of a comparative approach.[21] Together, Carolina Poncet and Chacón y Calvo applied a philological-historical approach to the study of folklore largely rooted in Spanish traditions, a framework they had acquired through contact with the respected linguist Ramón Menéndez Pidal. Without straying from a descriptive method as prescribed by the Positivists, Poncet and Chacón studied in great depth the etymology of ancestral grammar, mostly originating from Spain, to arrive at the foundations of a national culture. Finally, both approaches can be found in the work of Juan Marinello, an intellectual who would eventually come to embrace Marxism.[22]

In spite of his extended residency in Spain for diplomatic reasons, José M. Chacón never ceased to collaborate with the Sociedad—assisting in its journal as much as in the development of folkloric groups throughout Cuba. It is certainly not by chance that the organization's two most important members, Chacón and Fernando Ortiz, tried to change the logic of tradition and exclusion in the Academia de la Historia. It is perhaps for this reason that both men decided to create a far more open and democratic association with respect to its composition and object of study.

While presiding over the Academia de la Historia, Ortiz advocated for the admittance of new generations of historians while simultaneously denouncing the monopolistic character of the Academia. In 1929 a conflict arose surrounding Chacón's book *Cedulario Cubano*. Chacón had been commissioned by the Academia to procure from Spain a colossal folder of documents on Cuba, which essentially acted as the supporting material to his own volume. Many academics questioned whether Chacón had acted correctly in publishing his text based on the materials he had been entrusted to submit to the Academia or whether he had violated his contract with the Academia. This discussion ultimately highlighted the aristocratic nature of the Academia, a fact that would lead to the resignation of both Ortiz and Chacón years later.[23]

Nevertheless, attitudes toward the generational issue as well as the Sociedad del Folklore's political creed and breadth of academic production were far from univocal. As a result, figures like Emeterio Santovenia and Ramiro Guerra, contemporaries of Ortiz and members of the same folkloric group, held differing positions. Santovenia conducted extensive research that, from a descriptive angle, contributed greatly to local and national history, yet later maintained close political ties to the series of governments that culminated in the authoritarian rule of Fulgencio Batista.[24] Guerra, on the other hand, author of one of the most iconoclastic historical texts of the period, nonetheless embraced the nationalist project of Machado to such an extent that he became his private secretary. The fall of Machado, the "donkey with claws," led to Guerra's self-imposed exile in the United States; when he returned to Cuba, he entirely removed himself from politics with the exception of occasionally participating as an expert in some international events.[25]

In order to carry out its objective of "documenting, classifying, and comparing traditional elements of our popular life," the Sociedad del Folklore relied on specialists from a variety of disciplines.[26] The coexistence of multiple disciplines within the same cultural space signified a breakdown in the predominance held by the disciplines of history, pedagogy, and law within the country. This plurality brought the folkloric organization nearer to the standards for greater disciplinary variety embraced by the Sociedad Económica Amigos del País, although the latter did not count among its collaborators a sufficient number of the new disciplines in Cuba such as sociology, anthropology, archaeology, and ethnography.[27]

Rupture within Tradition: The Structures, Themes, and Objects of Study of the Sociedad de Folklore

In contrast to other cultural institutions, which were quite rigid, the Sociedad del Folklore established a flexible system of organization. One of its most notable features was a spirit of equality among its members, privileging both individual contributions and collective works. Although the organization's membership categories resembled those of other institutions, its requirements for admittance varied substantially. For instance, there was no limit to the number of collaborators allowed and there were no special conditions for admittance; members of this category could be residents of Havana or any other city with folkloric groups. Corresponding members, on the other hand, could be residents of areas abroad or areas with no folklore groups present whatsoever.[28]

The Sociedad's organizational system functioned according to a radial structure unlike the pyramidal structure of the Academia de la Historia and the Academia Nacional de Artes y Letras. The institution had a central organization in Havana with delegations in various parts of the country. Beginning in 1923, branches began to appear in Santiago de Cuba, Pinar del Río, Güines, Camagüey, Cienfuegos, Bayamo, Trinidad, Sancti Spíritus, and Matanzas.[29] The original platform granted its branches "absolute autonomy" in internal management, programs of study, and social activities; furthermore, the right of delegates to participate in the organization's central governing committee was defended.[30]

If traditional organizations grounded their authority in a system of internal hierarchies, other groups like the Academia Cubana de la Lengua (the Cuban Academy of Languages) and the Sociedad del Folklore aspired to make an impact on the academic sphere by using a different intellectual style that held the power to convene. Of course, capturing a following that would enlist itself as equal members in a new cultural project was a recurring and characteristic strategy of this cultural era in Cuba. In this way, there is something revealing about the work developed by Chacón and Ortiz in the Academia Cubana de la Lengua in 1926, motivated by the intention of achieving independence from official and traditional cultural standards. With respect to this, scholars Patricia Motola and Marialys Perdomo, argue:

> One of the most polemical questions concerned the designation of the first members. In his letters to Chacón y Calvo, Fernando Ortiz insisted that this Spanish organization should not immediately appoint longstanding academics. His intention was that the Academia should accurately reflect the intellectual profile of the period. For this reason, among the founders of the Academia there appeared personalities from a range of generations and political postures, all recognized for the merit of their work in the cultural sphere. In every case the designation was motivated by the fulfillment of requirements such as having demonstrated a devotion and competency in philological studies; this was demonstrated not only through prolificacy but also by indicating, in one's publications, an excellent grasp of Castillano. In other words, only Cubans of "high moral standing and good manners" who resided in Havana and were over the age of thirty could aspire to this lifelong post.[31]

In a 1927 statute, the Sociedad changed its parameters of operation and limited the number of full members to thirty. From this point on, in order to be a full member, the individual had to reside in the capital or its surrounding municipalities, be of legal age, and be a published or emerging scholar or author of a completed work relevant to the study of folklore. The same requirements except those related to residency applied to corresponding members.[32] These changes were intended to address logistical issues rather than implement a politics of discrimination, since the most valuable financial and intellectual contributors to the organization were located in Havana. Moreover, the study of folklore was a new discipline, and many of those advocates isolated from the culture of the metropolis were insufficiently prepared to undertake folkloric studies with the professionalism required. These individuals were typically amateurs whose work was limited to collecting information about popular traditions.

However, the editorial politics of the Sociedad del Folklore were particularly democratic, as they accepted contributions to *Archivos del Folklore Cubano* from all over the country; these contributions were granted more or less prominence according to the quality of the work. Even submissions of lesser significance were accepted and published in a collection designated for "various data . . . that due to its brevity or character does not warrant being published separately or in another section." Regular contributors like Fernando Ortiz provided some of the information in this section, but ordinary readers were responsible for the rest. Occasionally, *Archivos del Folklore Cubano* accepted brief notes, commentaries, and observations from readers residing in Pinar del Río, Havana (Marianao and el Cotorro), and Las Villas (Trinidad). At one point the journal even published the notes of a young Cuban boy, Andrés Fernández Estévez.[33]

This academic ingenuity reflects the tensions within an institution that, while avoiding obstructing contributors with valuable information, aspired to innovate within a terrain that was insufficiently explored by the sciences. In fact, nearly 50 percent of the 149 articles initially published in *Archivos del Folklore Cubano* were highly descriptive in tone. The degree of unfamiliarity with folkloric material and sources led Francisco de Paula Coronado, in the organization's second session, to volunteer his services by writing a letter to the major public libraries around the world in order to find groups and publications in other nations that specialized in folkloric studies.[34]

The operational metamorphosis endured by the Sociedad del Folklore was a sign of the existing cultural disparity between the capital—a solid cultural infrastructure maintained by institutions, widely distributed journals, printing presses, publishing houses, schools, and libraries—and the rest of the country. Nonetheless, the modifications did not affect the secular spirit of the organization. On the contrary, the solemnities and exclusivities of other institutions were not implemented in the folkloric organization. The primary sources consulted on the Sociedad reveal neither the existence of any special liturgies upon admittance to the institution nor the conferring of any insignias on its members. There were neither medals nor shields, nor armchairs, nor portraits—at most perhaps a black cat, a symbol of the popular beliefs and traditions that dominated the pages of the organization's journal as a vulgar allegory announcing the displacement of more traditional objects of study (see figure 10.1).[35]

Figure 10.1
Logotype of the Cuban Society of Folklore.
Source: *Archivos del Folklore Cubano*.

Ethnographic questions especially concerning the treatment of black Cubans is a crucial theme when addressing matters that most concerned the Sociedad del Folklore Cubano, given that the country had only abolished slavery thirty-six years earlier, and in 1912 the state had ferociously repressed Afro-Cubans in putting down a rebellion by the Partido Independiente de Color.[36] The Sociedad del Folklore Cubano did not content itself with celebrating pre-Columbian and Spanish traditions. It also recovered a cultural patrimony of African origin. The organization entered the public debate in favor of the importance of Afro-Cubans to the Cuban melting pot and established the contributions of its descendants as a formative part of the nation and Cuban nationality.[37]

Perhaps the most exemplary illustration of their efforts is the constant appearance of articles dedicated to this theme in *Archivos del Folklore Cubano*. Among these articles, appearing under the generic titles of "The Afrocuban Feast Day of the Kings" and "Los negros curros" (roughly translatable as "the Black Dandies") were the works of Ortiz who in this period emphasized connections between Africa and certain Cuban attitudes and celebrations.[38] Ortiz's academic and institutional efforts in the 1920s served as the basis for a cultural movement—expressed primarily through poetry but also through literature, journalism, music, and the visual arts—that acknowledged those of African descent as an essential component to the essence of what is Cuban. Above all, the movement embraced African roots in Cuban music, religion, and language.[39] In contrast to other discourses on race, the Afro-Cuban movement, contemporaneous with the Sociedad del Folklore, emphasized the necessity to integrate *blancos* and *negros* within the same national composite. At the same time, working-class Afro-Cubans championed a similar discourse that spread throughout popular culture.[40]

The catalog of cultural manifestations that were of interest to the Sociedad del Folklore was as vast as the organization's makeup. Work conducted by the institution included documentation of stories, fables, and legends; analyses of ballads, *décimas*, songs, boleros, popular music, and poetry; as well as studies of locutions, idioms, tongue twisters, *cubanismos*, and other popular philological forms. The institution also devoted itself to the recovery of proverbs, refrains, riddles, and diverse modes of expression as well as the compiling of popular knowledge about folk medicine, botany, geography, or agriculture. Finally, the Sociedad del Folklore also dedicated itself to descriptions of superstitions and supernatural beliefs as well as local customs, fiestas, dances, ceremonies, and children's games.

A Change of Scenery: Research Strategies and Institutional Tactics

In order to collect the wealth of folkloric material within the country, the Sociedad turned to techniques that were used infrequently during this period. They used surveys and interviews that led to working relationships with informants and demonstrated the importance accorded oral sources. On January 22, 1923, the Sociedad del Folklore appointed Carolina Poncet and Manuel Pérez Beato to write a questionnaire on Cuban folklore. On February 9 of the same year the Sociedad approved another questionnaire, developed by Chacón y Calvo, relating to popular literature and accepted a proposal by Gaspar Agüero to develop a survey on music. Two months later, both scholars submitted their projects to the Sociedad for further discussion.[41] The questionnaire developed by Chacón y Calvo, who was assisted in the end by Poncet and Pérez Beato, established a series of instructions and regulations for the study of folklore. The authors advised researchers to pay special attention to oral traditions without distorting the information heard.[42] The goals and the nature of the information collected by the Sociedad del Folklore justify the originality of the scientific proposal. Its scientific objective and the use of empirical data and procedures granted this organization—aimed as it was at rebuilding and legitimizing a plebeian history—

a distinctive mark that distinguished it from the heroic and grandiloquent narratives of traditional historiography.

In addition to implementing novel research procedures, the Sociedad del Folklore Cubano engaged in editorial and organizational maneuvers in order to strengthen its cultural project and survive within an adverse environment. The editors of *Archivos del Folklore Cubano* acknowledged antecedents of folkloric research in Cuba to lend to this discipline a certain pedigree. However, this kind of cultural patina that consecrated and certified certain processes of "invention of tradition" was in keeping with academic trends of the period. Reproducing work of this kind served to give scientific value to the institution and supplement its journal, which depended on valuable contributions that were not always readily available.

In order to strengthen the institution's academic excellence, the journal included works written by notable intellectuals of the nineteenth century such as José Martí, the naturalist Felipe Poey, rare book specialist Antonio Bachiller y Morales, and various writers like Gertudis Gómez de Avellaneda, Luis Victoriano Betancourt, and the Puerto Rican *costumbrista* Manuel A. Alonso.[43] Editors also published contributions from distinguished specialists like the North American historian Irene A. Wright's foundational works on early colonialism in Cuba and the works of philologist and lexicographer Antenor Nascentes, an authority on the Portuguese language in Brazil.[44] To these scholars were added Aurelio Espinosa, a renowned Stanford University scholar, Ramón A. Laval, the most prominent Chilean folklorist of his time, and the American anthropologist and sociologist Elsie Clews Parsons. All were united by the influence of Franz Boas, whose works largely shaped the discipline of anthropology in the first half of the twentieth century.[45]

Boas's theory of cultural relativism emphasized the necessity to research without prejudice or discrimination the heritage of so-called peripheral peoples, an approach that fit well in the Cuban setting. Contrary to Spencerian evolution, which dominated universities and research centers in the latter half of the nineteenth century, Boas maintained that there were no superior or inferior forms of culture. He rejected Western ethnocentrism and its assumption of supremacy in relation to other cultures. This concept opened up the potential for close and equitable collaborations between experts of the "First World" and their colleagues in other parts of the world.

Furthermore, sections like "Noticias y comentarios" and "De la Sociedad del Folklore" in *Archivos del Folklore Cubano* served as publicity for the folkloric association and its foreign counterparts. In these sections one could gain a sense of the broad impact of the Sociedad on specialized publications like the British *Journal of African Society*, the German *Volktam und Kultur der Romanan*, and the *Journal of American Folklore*, as well as local papers like *El Mundo* and *Diario de la Marina*.[46] The latter was traditionally a reactionary paper in wide circulation that, thanks to Ramiro Guerra, a member of the Sociedad and one of the paper's principal editors, popularized the institution's work in a permanent section entitled "Cuban Folklore Notes."[47] The voice of the cultural and political vanguard—in addition to members from marginalized sectors like Guerra, Emilio Roig, Nicólas Guillén, and Gustavo Urrutia along with a generation of youth that integrated the Movimiento Minorista—balanced the tone of the *Diario de la Marina*.[48] No less important in communicating the importance of folkloric research was the bibliography section in *Archivos del Folklore Cubano*, which reviewed works about folklore by both Cuban and foreign authors. It became an important tool for transmitting the organization's cultural project in the sense that it suggested to the reader, in a compelling manner, the importance of acquiring new forms of knowledge.

Nevertheless, despite efforts to occupy a relevant place within the academic field, the existence of the Sociedad del Folklore was relatively short-lived, and the organization was plagued by financial worries and the absence of official support. Even at the moment of drafting the first regulations, many members already had a sense of the difficulties the institution would encounter in its trajectory. Article 9 of the bylaws stated that in the event the organization should dissolve, its archives and library would pass to the public library of the Sociedad Económica Amigos del País. This was indeed a brilliant and democratic anticipatory solution of last resorts that ensured that materials conserved by the organization would remain accessible to all.[49] Concerns about the survival of the organization must certainly have peaked when, in its fourth session, the Secretaría de Instrucción Pública y Bellas Artes denied the possibility of financial assistance.[50]

On the other hand, following the logic of enlightenment, the organization's determination to overcome obstacles made it a kind of missionary institution on the verge of new cultural horizons. In fact, the Sociedad del Folklore recognized the advantages of the new scholarship it was producing and insisted on its role as eradicator of "the darkness of our intellectual environment."[51] Yet, unlike other established organizations, it lacked a desire for acclaim.

The organization's financial balance from 1924 to July 15, 1927, showed a deficit of 492 pesos, a sum ultimately defrayed by Fernando Ortiz, who nonetheless conveyed the impossibility of repeating such a "heroic deed."[52]

Monetary problems also placed the institution on unfavorable ground with respect to the publishing houses charged with producing its journal. The terms imposed by the latter, in order to continue publishing *Archivos del Folklore Cubano* without cost, were that Ortiz had to become its owner.[53]

The institution's inability to control the production of its cultural material is indicated by the poor publication quality of its journal—with irregular periodicity and numerous misprints. This was the price to pay for an institution that had attempted to incorporate itself, with new and alternative projects, in the cultural field of the period.[54] A low number of subscribers—at barely thirty-two—and the absence of a large consumer base demonstrate how difficult it was to coin a new cultural project in the midst of a cultural orthodoxy supported by a political model that although decaying still held spiritual force.[55] The difficulty in finding an audience had much to do with the disjoint between tradition and change within the economic, social, and cultural orders.

Archivos del Folklore Cubano attempted to supplement the weak reception of Ortiz's and Chacón's projects with commercial advertisements that ultimately undermined the academic puritanism cultivated by institutions like the Academia de la Historia de Cuba and gave the Sociedad del Folklore the appearance of a pragmatic culture industry.[56] It is noteworthy that advertisements displayed in the folkloric journal came from small and medium-sized businesses with relative preponderance in the Cuban economy. The reason for this is perhaps that this publication was of no interest to large local or foreign sugar-producing industries or perhaps its publishers had either no interest in or simply no access to advertisers with higher purchasing power. What is clear, however, is the confluence between this new cultural project and the aspirations of a sector of the bourgeoisie directed toward an internal market.

At the beginning or end of every issue, nearly always appearing as an entire page, were advertisements from the insurance company El Iris, which had Ortiz as one of its principal shareholders. This was also the place where other businesses would advertise, such as the bookstores Minerva, La Moderna Poesía, and Cervantes, the latter two associated with the publisher Cultural S.A. Other advertisers included Fábrica Nacional de Toallas, the well-known store El Encanto, and the beer La Tropical, which was advertised as the "drink of Liborio . . . folkloric personification of the Cuban people" (see figure 10.2).[57] All these "minor" industries, as they were known in this period, contributed to the precarious sustainability of *Archivos del Folklore Cubano*.[58]

Figure 10.2 Ad for La Tropical beer featuring the Liborio character. From author's collection.

Structured or Structuring? The Legacy of an Academic Institution

The Sociedad del Folklore Cubano was founded on January 6, 1923, a date that coincided with the Afro-Cuban Feast Day of the Kings. On the same date, the *Archivos del Folklore Cubano* published an editorial supporting the institution's mission. The inaugural pages of the publication conveyed premonitions of the uncertain future of the organization, though it nonetheless drew attention to the impoverished state of studies of popular culture and the need to strengthen these kinds of analyses within the nation. The text largely summarized the purpose and character of the folkloric organization detailing the interrelations between its academic and public objectives: "An entire treasure lies hidden beneath layers of modern culture, waiting for Cuban scholars to discover, interpret, classify, and establish it for national civilization."[59]

In this sense, and in accordance with Bourdieu's theory of the conformation of a cultural field with its specificities, it can be affirmed that the actions of the Sociedad del Folkore, even in its routine practices, reveal the characteristics of an entire political and sociocultural sphere undergoing important transformations. The Sociedad del Folklore Cubano constituted an alternative academic forum that, out of the originality of its scientific proposal attempted to carve a space in the nation's cultural sphere. Its dissidence with regard to traditional cultural projects is demonstrated not only by its unorthodox structure and organizational composition but also by its institutional strategies and practices and the novel content of its discourse. Structured and structuring, the Sociedad del Folklore resulted from the demands of an age and, at the same time, conceived of itself as forging national representations far from the dominant ideological standards. Although its domain of activity and capacity to spread its new canon was limited, the Sociedad del Folklore nonetheless constituted a link in the gradual paradigm shift that occurred in Cuba beginning in the 1920s.

The Sociedad del Folklore expressed and enabled transformations in national sensibilities behind other, better known milestones in the offing. In 1937, the Havana-based Teatro Campoamor performed an unusual piece on the sacred music of the Yoruba Africans. For the first time in Cuba, esoteric song, sounds, and dances became a secular spectacle. Fernando Ortiz and the Institución Hispanocubana de Cultura, which succeeded the Sociedad del Folklore, were largely responsible for this project.[60] This artistic representation demonstrated a shift that had occurred in the country's social imaginary—black Cubans had agreed to present their social and sacred values to a public that, although small, opened itself to receive the rich popular culture. Years later, the so-called Constitution of 1940 established, in article 20, that "the republic does not recognize exemptions or privileges and declares all discrimination by motivation of sex, race, color, or class and any other harm to human dignity as illegal and punishable."[61]

Notes

1. The name given to the first republic (1902–33) from the 1920 novel of the same name by Carlos Loveira. The novel describes the atmosphere of corruption and patronage that reigned in an era in which a teacher, three generals, and a lawyer won the presidency.

2. The original Spanish names are the Federación de Estudiantes Universitarios, the Agrupación Comunista de la Habana, the Movimiento Nacional de Veteranos y Patriotas, and the Universidad Popular José Martí.

3. On this event see Pichardo, *Documentos para la Historia de Cuba (Tomo III)*, 119–20.

4. Bourdieu, "Intellectual Field and Creative Project," 92.

5. For a detailed study of the role and place of the Academia de la Historia de Cuba in the country's academic and political landscape, see Quiza Moreno, *El cuento al revés*, 55–69.

6. Among the academic historians who were part of the foundation of the Sociedad del Folklore were Enrique J. Varona, Francisco de Paula Coronado, Joaquín Llaverías, and José A. Cosculluela. Of the academics in solidarity with the new project were Manuel Sanguily, Juan M. Dihígo, Evelio Rodríguez Lendián, and Alfredo M. Aguayo.

7. These were Fernando Ortiz, Alfredo M. Aguayo, and Juan Miguel Dihígo, as well as Manuel Pérez Beato, who was in the Academia until resigning in 1921. "Actas de la Sociedad del Folklore Cubano," *Archivos del Folklore Cubano* (AFC) 1, no. 1 (January 1924): 82.

8. Certain figures stand out in this regard: Fernando Ortiz, who directed three important institutions during this era: the Sociedad Económica Amigos del País (1923–32), the Academia de la Historia (1925–29), and la Sociedad del Folklore Cubano (1924–29); Juan Miguel Dihígo, member of the Academia de la Historia who was on the board of the Sociedad del Folklore as librarian and archivist; and Néstor Carbonell and Ramón Catalá, members at large of the folklore board and members also of the Academia Nacional de Artes y Letras. Catalá was also a member of the Academia Cubana de la Lengua after its foundation in 1927. "Actas de la Sociedad del Folklore Cubano," AFC 1, no. 1 (January 1924): 82; "Fundación de la Sociedad del Folklore Cubano," AFC 1, no. 1 (January 1924): 92.

9. The honorary members of the Academia de la Historia were Enrique J. Varona, Manuel Sanguily, and Raimundo Cabrera. "Fundación de la Sociedad del Folklore Cubano," AFC 1, no. 1 (January 1924): 93.

10. The minister of public education and fine arts, Francisco Zayas y Alfonso, who was recognized as an honorary member of Cuba's first association of folklorists, denied official support to the entity, and this is registered in its minutes. "Actas de la Sociedad del Folklore Cubano," AFC 1, no. 1 (January 1924): 86.

11. "Actas de la Sociedad del Folklore Cubano," AFC 1, no. 1 (January 1924): 77.

12. "Esta revista cubana," AFC 1, no. 1 (January 1924): 5–6.

13. "Esta revista cubana," AFC 1, no. 1 (January 1924): 8.

14. "Cuestionario de literatura popular cubana," AFC 1, no. 1 (January 1924): 9–10.

15. "Actas de la Sociedad del Folklore Cubano," AFC 1, no. 1 (January 1924): 77.

16. Gutiérrez Vega, *José María Chacón y Calvo*, 36.

17. Poncet became the chair in Gramática y Composición in Havana's Escuela Normal de Maestros in 1915 and traveled to Spain in 1920, where she took a course with Menéndez Pidal. Ortiz García, "Cultura popular y construcción nacional," 704.

18. Córdova, "El folklore del niño cubano," AFC 1, nos. 3–4 (May 1925) and "El folklore del niño cubano," AFC 2, no. 1 (January 1926); Miranda, "Las supersticiones de los niños cubanos," AFC 4, no. 1 (January–March 1929); Fonseca, "Las supersticiones del escolar cubano," AFC 5, no. 3 (July–September 1930): 199–221.

19. Portuondo, "Anexo"; Cairo, *La revolución del 30 en la narrativa y el testimonio cubanos*. The thirteenth generation had a concentration of those born between 1880

and 1890, among them Ramiro Guerra, Fernando Ortiz, Emilio Roig, Carolina Poncet, Carlos Loveira, Mariano Brull, Agustín Acosta, José Manuel Poveda, Félix Lizaso, Manuel Navarro Luna, Luis Felipe Rodríguez, José Antonio Ramos, and José María Chacón y Calvo. This group is credited with a series of stylistic, thematic, and conceptual innovations that would be taken up again later and with more radicalism by the subsequent generation. I refer, for example, to the postmodernist movement in poetry and to the social novel and plays. From the social sciences point of view, the work of Ramiro Guerra stands out, sharpened in order to call into question the plantation model of prior history, as well as the work of Emilio Roig, with its frankly anti-imperialist content. Fernando Ortíz's work in the area of ethnology and anthropology would be equally important.

Those born between 1898 and 1910 (Juan Marinello, Rubén Martínez Villena, Pablo de la Torriente Brau, Enrique Serpa, Enrique Labrador Ruiz, Regino Boti, Amelia Peláez, Víctor Manuel, Nicolás Guillén, José Z. Tallet, Dulce María Loynaz, Alejo Carpentier, Elías Entralgo, Jorge Mañach, Raúl Roa, Lino Novás Calvo), along with the preceding generation, led the profound cultural and political renewal of the 1920s, breaking with the academicist canon of traditional plastic arts and choosing Afro-Cuba as the primordial subject of poetry, the novel, and the short story. From the political point of view many of those who belonged to this generation led the historic "Protesta de los Trece" and were part of the Minorista movement, while some swelled the ranks of the Communist Party or fought against Machado.

20. The Minorista movement was made up of a nucleus of the aesthetic avant-garde, most of them against the republican status quo. According to one of their programmatic texts, the Minoristas came together to transform "false values" and struggle for "national culture," for "the economic independence of Cuba and against Yankee imperialism"; they also sought to introduce and propagate the latest artistic and scientific doctrines to the country, while demanding real citizen participation in government, promoting Latin American union and the improvement of the subaltern classes. See Pichardo, "Qué era el Grupo Minorista," 393–95; Roig de Leuchsenring, "El Grupo Minorista de intelectuales y artistas habaneros," 10–12.

21. For the number of texts published by Ortiz in *Archivos del Folklore Cubano*, see García Carranza, *Bio-bibliografía de Don Fernando Ortiz*, 80–91.

22. Marinello's philological work, for example, "Un Guacalito de cubanismos," stands out in his contributions to *Archivos del Folklore Cubano*; see AFC 2, no. 2 (May 1926): 108–19; 2, no. 3 (October 1926): 228–35; 2, no. 4 (June 1927): 363–68; 3, no. 1 (January–March 1928): 21–26.

23. See Quiza Moreno, *El cuento al revés*, 55–69, and *Anales de la Academia de la Historia de Cuba*, 9: 61.

24. Emeterio Santovenia Echaide (Pinar del Río, Cuba, 1889–Miami, United States, 1968) was a historian, journalist, and politician who was affiliated with the anti-Machado organization ABC, and served as secretary to the presidency in the 1934 government of Mendieta, which was strongly backed by the military under Batista and the U.S. ambassador. He was elected senator for Pinar del Río in 1940, and three years later he was in

the cabinet of Batista's constitutional government. In the 1950s he directed the Agricultural and Industrial Development Bank under the Batista dictatorship. Santovenia presided over the Academia de la Historia de Cuba, was a permanent member of the board of the Archivos de la República de Cuba and the Comité Interamericano de Archivos, and a member of the Academia Nacional de Artes y Letras, the Sociedad Económica de Amigos del País, and the Academia Cubana de la Lengua. He was also a member of various Latin American academies and received a Doctor *Honoris Causa* from the University of Florida. Arencibia, "Emeterio Santovenia," 7–8.

25. Curiously, while nearing the end of his career in 1948, Guerra and Santovenia joined the Sociedad Amigos de la República. This organization endeavored to oversee the institutionalization of democracy and moderate between sectors of civil society and the military dictatorship during the state of emergency initiated by Batista in the 1950s. On the participation of Guerra, Santovenia, and other intellectuals of the Sociedad Amigos de la República, see Ibarra Guitart, *Sociedad de Amigos de la República* and *El fracaso de los moderados en Cuba*.

26. "Actas de la Sociedad del Folklore Cubano," AFC 1, no. 1 (January 1924): 77.

27. The emergence and development of these disciplines occurred over the final third of the nineteenth century under the auspices of the Sociedad Económica Amigos del País, the Real Academia de Ciencias Médicas, Físicas y Naturales de La Habana, and the Sociedad Antropológica de Cuba. With respect to sociology, despite the existence of the works of José Antonio Saco, it was not recognized as a discipline until the inauguration of the Chair in Sociology at the University of Havana, occupied by Enrique José Varona, for many years the only professor to teach the subject. See Mestre, "La antropología en Cuba," 9–15; Núñez Jover, "Aproximación a la sociología cubana," 187–203; Dacal and Rivero de la Calle, *Arqueología aborigen en Cuba*; Pruna, *Ciencia y científicos en Cuba colonial*; Hernández Godoy, "Arqueología e historiografía aborigen de Cuba en el siglo XIX," 177–96 and "La primera década del siglo XX y el desarrollo de la Arqueología en la Isla," 2–8.

28. "Actas de la Sociedad del Folklore Cubano," AFC 1, no. 1 (January 1924): 77.

29. "Actas de la Sociedad del Folklore Cubano," AFC 1, no. 1 (January 1924): 83–89.

30. "Actas de la Sociedad del Folklore Cubano," AFC 1, no. 1 (January 1924): 78–79.

31. Motola and Perdomo, "La Academia Cubana de la Lengua," 6–7.

32. "Reorganización de la Sociedad del Folklore Cubano," AFC 3, no. 1 (January–March 1928): 91–93.

33. "Compadres y comadres de papelitos," AFC 4, no. 3 (July–September 1929): 278–83.

34. "Actas de la Sociedad del Folklore Cubano," AFC 1, no. 1 (January 1924): 82.

35. AFC 1, no. 2 (April 1924): 167.

36. Work on the theme of blacks, or Afro-Cubans, is present in all the volumes of the *Archivos* and in almost all the individual editions. On top of the work of Ortiz, other valuable contributions worthy of mention are "Constitución de un cabildo carabalí en 1814," AFC 1, no. 3 (1925): 281–83; Israel Castellanos, "Instrumentos musicales de los afrocubanos," AFC 2, no. 3 (October 1926): 193–208; Israel Castellanos, "Instrumentos musicales de los afrocubanos (continuación)," AFC 2, no. 4 (June 1927): 337–55; Her-

minio Portel Vilá, "Mundamba y Mi Foco," AFC 3, no. 3 (July–September 1928): 242–46; Manuel Martínez Moles, "Cafú o Cafunga," AFC 3, no. 3 (July–September 1928): 281–82; Israel Castellanos, "El diablito ñañigo," AFC 3, no. 4 (October–December 1928): 27–37; V. Pérez Castillo, "¿Mutila sus dientes el afrocubano por estética tradición, o acepta como profilaxis de las caries, los cortes dados sobre las caras mesiales y distales?," AFC 4, no. 1 (January–March 1929): 29–31; Marcelino Weiss, "Comentarios al artículo 'Los afrocubanos dientimellados,'" AFC 4, no. 1 (January–March 1929): 31–33; Herminio Portel Vilá, "Los negritos curros de Cárdenas," AFC 4, no. 2 (April–June 1929): 130–32; Antenor Nacentes, "Glosario de Afronegrismos," AFC 4, no. 2 (April–June 1929): 157–60; "Cinco vocablos Afrocubanos," AFC 4, no. 2 (April–June 1929): 186–87. At the same time, in the section called "Collectanea," there appeared notes and references of interest on Africans and their descendants on the island: "Negros Uancipellos y "Chimbungas," AFC 1, no. 4 (June 24, 1925): 380; Gustavo A. González, "La negra catequista," AFC 4, no. 1 (January–March 1929): 93–94; E. Valdés Rodríguez, "Superstición Afrocatólica," AFC 4, no. 1 (January–March 1929): 95–96; J. Miguel Irisarri, "El Anaquillé," AFC 4, no. 2 (April–June 1929): 186. On the repression of the PIC in 1912, see Helf, *Our Rightful Share*.

37. *Archivos del Folklore Cubano* published a dossier on the contributions "del negro" to Cuban society with opinions from celebrated intellectuals like Ortiz, Ramón Vasconcelos, and the black journalist Gustavo Urrutia, who pronounced on the publication of eight poems by Nicolás Guillén in the "Ideales de una raza" section, edited by Urrutia, of the *Diario de la Marina*. The poems had a big impact in the social and aesthetic domain and were included in a book, *Motivos de son*, a text that has subsequently been recognized as the first great work by Cuba's "national" poet. See AFC 5, no. 3 (1930). On this topic, see the important work of Robin Moore, *Nationalizing Blackness: Afro-Cubanismo and Artistic Revolution in Havana, 1920–1940*.

38. Fernando Ortiz, "La fiesta afrocubana del Día de Reyes," AFC 1, no. 2 (April 1924): 146–65; 1, no. 3 (May 1925): 228–43; no. 4 (June 1925): 340–55; and "Los negros curros," AFC 2, no. 3 (October 1926): 209–22; 3, no. 1 (January–March 1928): 27–50; 3, no. 2 (April–June 1928): 160–75; 3, no. 3 (July–September 1928): 250–56; 3, no. 4 (October–December 1928): 51–53. To these we could add Fernando Ortiz, "Personajes del Folklore afrocubano," AFC 1, no. 1 (January 1924): 62–75; "Personajes del Folklore afrocubano," AFC 1, no. 2 (April 1924): 116–19; "La repatriación postmortem de los afrocubanos" (Collectanea), AFC 2, no. 3 (October 1926): 271–73; "Folklore religioso del cubano: Los Matiabos," AFC 2, no. 4 (June 1927): 387–89; "El baile negro" (Collectanea), AFC 3, no. 1 (January–March 1928): 86–89; "Los afrocubanos dientimellados," AFC 4, no. 1 (January–March 1929): 16–29; "Cuentos Afrocubanos," AFC 4, no. 2 (April–June 1929): 97–112; "El cocorícamo y otros conceptos teoplasmicos del folklore afrocubano," AFC 4, no. 4 (October–December 1929): 289–312; "Motivos de son por Nicolás Guillén," AFC 5, no. 3 (July–September 1930): 222–38.

39. The most solid expressions of this movement originated in poetry through intellectuals like Ramón Guirao, José Zacarías Tallet, and most important, Guillén. Nevertheless there were others who cultivated the theme, like Alejo Carpentier in his novel

Ecue Yamba-O and Lydia Cabrera with her cycle of folkloric short stories of African origin. Another important contribution was that of the musician Alejandro García Caturla, who incorporated certain rhythms and instruments from Afro-Cuban music into classical compositions. See Ortiz, "La poesía mulata," 209-10.

40. See the paradigmatic text of Moore, *Nationalizing Blackness*, esp. the introduction and chapters 1, 5, and 7. Given what I have outlined here, however, I evidently do not agree with the author's perception (126) of a supposed absence of black culture in the early years of the Sociedad del Folklore Cubano and in the pages of their review. Of course, the Sociedad del Folklore dedicated a good share of its efforts to reflect the contributions of Spanish popular culture in Cuba, but rather than a preference for white culture as Moore suggests, this was because the topic had been little addressed up to that point, precisely a time in which many poor Spaniards were arriving in Cuba and facing a harsh future of exploitation in commerce and agriculture; on that process, see González, *La Fiesta de los Tiburones*, and Naranjo, *Del campo a la bodega*.

41. "Actas de la Sociedad del Folklore Cubano," AFC 1, no. 1 (1924): 82-83, 85.

42. José María Chacón y Calvo, "Cuestionario de literatura popular cubana," AFC 1, no. 1 (1924): 9.

43. José Martí, "Los chinos en Nueva York," AFC 5, no. 2 (April-June 1930): 97-104; Felipe Poey, "La avispa de Jia," AFC 3, no. 2 (April-June 1928): 115-20; and "El jején," AFC 3, no. 3 (July-September 1928): 200-206; Antonio Bachiller y Morales, "Los ojos de Cucubá," AFC 1, no. 1 (January 1924): 43-46; and "Jigües, tradición cubana," AFC 2, no. 2 (May 1926): 169-72; "El babujal," AFC 2, no. 3 (October 1926): 244-46; "Las siguapas," AFC 2, no. 4 (June 1927): 356-58; Gertrudis Gómez de Avellaneda, "El aura blanca," AFC 4, no. 4 (October-December 1929): 313-18; Luis Victoriano Betancourt, "La luz de Yara," AFC 1, no. 3 (1925): 222-24; and "Una rumba," AFC 5, no. 1 (January-March 1930): 44-48; "El baile," AFC 5, no. 3 (July-September 1930): 246-55; Manuel A. Alonso, "Carreras de San Juan y San Pedro," AFC 5, no. 1 (October-December 1928): 371-76; and "La gallera," AFC 3, no. 4 (October-December 1928): 71-76; "Aguinaldos," AFC 5, no. 2 (April-June 1930): 164-69.

44. Irene A. Wright, "Nuestra Señora de la Caridad del Cobre," AFC 3, no. 1 (January-March 1928): 5-15; Antenor Nascentes, "Glosario de afronegrismos," AFC 4, no. 2 (April-June 1929): 157-60.

45. Aurelio M. Espinosa, "La ciencia del folklore," AFC 3, no. 4 (October-December 1928): 1-15; and "La trasmisión de los cuentos populares," AFC 4, no. 1 (January-March 1929): 39-52; "Una versión española del romance de Teresa," AFC 4, no. 2 (April-June 1929): 153-56; "El tema de Roncesvalle y Bernaldo del Carpio en la poesía popular de Cuba," AFC 5, no. 3 (July-September 1930): 193-95; Ramón A. Laval, "Nuevas variantes de romances populares," AFC 3, no. 4 (October-December 1928): 16-26; Elsie Parsons, "El culto de los espíritus en Haití," AFC 4, no. 3 (July-September 1929): 193-205; and "El culto de los espíritus en Haití," AFC 4, no. 4 (October-December 1929): 334-55.

46. "Noticias y comentarios," AFC 2, no. 2 (May 1926): 100-101; "Noticias y comentarios," AFC 2, no. 3 (October 1926): 274-75; "Notas del Folklore Cubano," AFC 3, no. 1 (January-March 1928): 95; "Los Archivos en el extranjero," AFC 3, no. 2 (April-June

1928): 192; "Noticias y Comentarios: Los Archivos en el extranjero," AFC 3, no. 3 (July–September 1928): 283–286.

47. "Notes on Cuban Folklore." "With this title we inaugurate a new Sunday section in Havana's *Diario de la Marina*, by the initiative of one of its directors, our collaborator, Dr. Ramiro Guerra." The paper declared itself "honored" to reproduce articles and notes from Collectanea and happy to acknowledge their origin (unlike other publications) and thanked Guerra for his "ardent work of recording the folkloric treasure of the Cuban people, which has languished forgotten and unknown." "Notas del Folklore Cubano," AFC 3, no. 1 (January–March 1928): 95.

48. Another figure who contributed to the presence of innovative work in the *Diario de la Marina* was José Antonio Fernández de Castro, a left-wing writer and journalist, member of the artistic vanguard of the time, and director of the paper's literary section between 1927 and 1929.

49. "Bases de la Sociedad del Folklore," AFC 1, no. 1 (January 1924): 81.

50. "Actas de la Sociedad del Folklore Cubano," AFC 1, no. 1 (January 1924): 85–86.

51. "De la Sociedad del Folklore Cubano," AFC 1, no. 2 (April 1924): 187.

52. "Actas de la Sociedad del Folklore Cubano," AFC 3, no. 1 (January–March 1928): 93–94.

53. "Actas de la Sociedad del Folklore Cubano," AFC 3, no. 1 (January–March 1928): 85.

54. Of the many examples, one could cite the notice of the editors of *Archivos*, appearing on the cover of vol. 3, no. 4 (October–December 1928), concerning the pagination error on the first eighty pages of the volume.

55. AFC 3, no. 1 (January–March 1928): 94, registers the fact that there were only forty subscribers in 1924, and a year later the number had dropped to thirty-two.

56. Only fifteen years after its founding did the academy accept the marketing of its publications, but not before exempting from payment those agencies or people that the secretary of publications has authorized. The refusal to commercialize the journal is evident in the response that the institution gave to the "Martí" circulating library, saying that they will not exempt the library from paying for its publications because "it is an establishment that lends its books in exchange for a fee from the reader." *Anales de la Academia de la Historia de Cuba* 8 (La Habana, January–December 1926): 39; *Anales de la Academia de la Historia de Cuba* 9 (January–December 1927): 60, *Anales de la Academia de la Historia de Cuba* 11 (January–December 1930): 85.

57. In Cuba's political cartoon culture, Liborio was a character representing the people, whose garb was that of a campesino.

58. According to announcements published in vol. 1 of *Archivos*, at the price of 47.50 pesos per issue, the Sociedad del Folklore Cubano received 190 pesos; but at a price of 77.50 pesos for each edition of 2, the institution received 310 pesos; "Reorganización del la Sociedad del Folklore Cubano," AFC 3, no. 1 (January–March 1928): 94.

59. "Actas de la Sociedad del Folklore Cubano," AFC 1, no. 1 (January 1924): 7.

60. Véase: Ortiz, "La música sagrada de los negros yoruba en Cuba," *Ultra* 3, no. 13 (July 1937): 77–86.

61. "Constitución de la república de Cuba 1940," 197.

CHAPTER II

Nation, State, and the Making of the Cuban Working Class, 1920–1940

Robert Whitney

The majority of persons participating in labor shall be Cubans by birth as much as regards to total amount of wages and salaries as in distinct categories of labor, in the form determined by law. Protection shall also be extended to naturalised Cubans with families born in the national territory, with preference over naturalized citizens who do not meet these conditions, and over aliens. The stipulations in the preceding paragraphs concerning aliens shall not be applied in the filling of indispensable technical positions, subject to the prior formalities of the law, and with provision that apprenticeship in the technical work in question be facilitated for native Cubans.
—CUBAN CONSTITUTION OF 1940, TITLE VI, SECTION I, ARTICLE 73

The law shall regulate immigration in keeping with the national economic system and with social necessities. The importation of contract labor, as well as all immigration tending to debase the condition of labor, is prohibited.
—CUBAN CONSTITUTION OF 1940, TITLE VI, SECTION I, ARTICLE 76

My parents did not return to Jamaica. My mother maintained contact with an aunt and my father with a brother [in the 1950s]. . . . Once, when I was working at the Base, an American lady told me something offensive. I told her, "Miss, I am Cuban because I was born here, I am Cuban by right." I am a Jamaican because both my parents are from Jamaica. I am like a ball, you hit it and it jumps from here to there.
—VIOLDA CAREY, *GUANTÁNAMO*, OCTOBER 10, 2001

Who Are the Cuban People?

The title of this opening section might seem odd given that historians and social scientists agree that most Cubans trace their ancestry to either Spain or Africa. We know that the indigenous inhabitants of Cuba were largely exterminated soon after the Spanish conquest.

Thereafter successive waves of Spanish immigrants and African slaves populated the island. There are many Cubans of Chinese origin, but most of the descendants of the indentured laborers who went to Cuba in the nineteenth century either left the island once their contracts finished or assimilated into Cuban society. And, while immigrants from central and Eastern Europe and the Middle East went to Cuba in the early twentieth century, they did so in much smaller numbers as compared with other Latin American countries. So, in terms of ethnic background, the answer to the question "Who are the Cuban people?" is clear: the large majority of Cubans are of Hispanic or African origin.

Ancestry, however, tells us little about cultural identity. "Culture," in the broadest sense, refers to sets of popular representations, symbols, traditions, and values that people use to organize social life and help them make sense of their actions and the world around them. Throughout the long colonial period (1511–1898) the formation of Cuban identity was shaped largely by highly localized struggles over the limits and degrees of slavery and freedom. By the middle of the nineteenth century segments of the white upper classes increasingly expressed nationalist (if not always separatist) sentiments against Spanish rule. Cuba had become the world's largest sugar producer and Spain's most important colony. Sugar production, in turn, was based on slavery, and by the 1850s blacks (both slave and free) almost outnumbered whites, which provoked racist fears about the "Africanization of Cuba" and a Haitian-like slave revolution. Consequently, despite tensions between the Cuban elite and Spain, economic prosperity and fear of slave revolt kept Cuba under Spanish rule. A white and Hispano-centric vision of a Cuban imagined community was certainly emerging at this time, but membership in that community did not include slaves, free blacks, and mulattos and much of rural Cuba that was outside the control of the Hispano-Cuban economic and intellectual elite.

As for slaves, former slaves, mulattos, and poor rural residents throughout Cuba, their exclusion from a white Hispanic Cuba did not mean they were not Cuban. Their subaltern nationalism, however, was more egalitarian and reflected their struggles for land, freedom, and equality. The day-to-day meaning of freedom for slaves and their descendants was shaped by localized struggles against those who tried to limit freedom based on a person's race, class, or gender. Local and regional conflicts, in turn, shaped people's notions of race, class, and nation. And when local struggles merged with islandwide movements (as they increasingly did by the mid-nineteenth century) they brought with them subaltern notions about rights and freedom that often clashed with those of the usually self-appointed white leaders of these movements. By the last half of the nineteenth century, for most black and mulatto Cubans, freedom from slavery and the struggle for independence were inseparable. Yet if many members of the Cuban elite resigned themselves to safe, if stifling, colonial rule, others could not. The antiracist and egalitarian nationalism of slaves, the freed colored, and their descendants would not accept anything less than the immediate abolition of slavery, political and racial equality, and total independence from Spain.

These tensions within Cuban nationalism became particularly acute between 1868 and 1902. Within a period of thirty years Cuba experienced two wars for independence (1868–78 and 1895–98), the abolition of slavery in 1886, the development of technologically advanced sugar production, and, between 1898 and 1902, the transition from Spanish colony to a semi-independent republic under American hegemony. The cornerstone of American power over Cuba was the Platt Amendment, which the United States imposed on the Cuban Constitution of 1901. According to this amendment, the United States had the right to intervene in Cuban affairs in order to protect private property and ensure political order: it would be semi-independence, or no independence at all. Elite Cuban political opinion supported American intervention because many believed that only American power could ensure Cuban stability. The backbone of Cuba's Liberation Army in both wars had been former slaves and poor peasants. By 1895 the need for political and military unity against Spain forged a viable, if tense, alliance that crossed the lines of race and class. Nationalist discourse, in turn, promised a future republic where all Cubans, regardless of race, would be equal. Yet the inclusiveness of nationalist discourse could not hide the fear of many white Cubans that blacks and mulattos were "culturally" ill-prepared for equal citizenship in an independent Cuba. War, the struggle against slavery and colonialism, and the fight for equal rights had forged a powerful—if divided and frustrated—popular nationalism. Despite these sharp political and cultural tensions, by the time Cuba became a semi-independent republic in 1902, there was a widespread consensus that "Cubans" were people of either Spanish or African origin who had fought for, or at least not actively opposed, independence.

So if we know that most Cubans are of Spanish or African heritage and that a strong, if highly contested, sense of national identity was firmly in place by the end of the nineteenth century, why ask the question "Who are the Cuban people?" at the beginning of a chapter about the formation of the Cuban working class in the twentieth century? I do so not to challenge accepted wisdom but to suggest that if we are not careful, apparently simple answers to simple questions might cause us to gloss over or ignore complex and historically unique moments of Cuban history. Cuba was the only Caribbean and Latin American nation in the twentieth century to receive large numbers of both white (mostly Spanish) and black (Haitian and West Indian) immigrants. By 1930, *half* of the island's four million inhabitants had arrived after independence. One of the ironies of Cuban history is that more Spaniards migrated to Cuba just before or after Spain lost the island in 1898 than during the entire colonial period. As of 1930, 800,000 Spaniards had entered Cuba.[1] The majority of Spaniards settled in or near the towns and cities of western Cuba. Meanwhile, between 1900 and 1930, 325,000 Afro-Caribbean workers went to Cuba legally, of which roughly 185,000 were Haitians and 140,000 were West Indians.[2] Approximately 80 percent of the West Indians were Jamaican, with the remainder from Barbados and the smaller Leeward and Windward Islands. The vast majority of Caribbeans arrived after 1916, when the Cuban government relaxed immigration regulations to facilitate the labor needs of the rapidly expanding sugar industry in eastern Cuba. The stark reality was that Cuba did not have enough native-born workers to bring in the annual sugar harvests in the east. Consequently, most Haitians and West Indians lived on or near sugar plantations and company towns in the eastern provinces. By the mid-1920s at least one in ten persons in the eastern provinces of Camagüey and Oriente were either Haitian or West Indian.[3] In 1940 there were 40,000 legal British West Indians in Cuba, with perhaps another 55,000 to 60,000 illegal residents.[4]

Yet despite the dramatic change in the size and composition of the Cuban population in the twentieth century, we know very little about how and why immigrants became Cuban. Was it "easier" for Spaniards to become Cuban than it was for Haitians and West Indians, and if so, how and why? Was the experience of Haitians in Cuba different from that of West Indians, and if so, how and why? Most new immigrants could be categorized broadly as "workers" or "peasants" of one kind or another. So once they arrived and settled in Cuba, did they simply become part of a Cuban working class? The answer to this question was by no means obvious because many Spanish and Caribbean immigrants went to Cuba with no guarantee that they would find a job or land or be able to live there permanently. There were simply too many economic, political, and personal uncertainties to make becoming Cuban a foregone conclusion. It was for this reason that Spaniards, West Indians, and Haitians did their best to stay connected with diaspora networks that might, if necessary, provide the means for people to return home or move elsewhere. In this sense, diaspora identities were inseparable from class identities. If social classes are identified by their relation to the means of production, few people in the Caribbean had secure access to any means of production for any length of time. Wage labor was one way to meet subsistence needs, and it was by no means the most reliable way to do so. Most working people were neither peasants nor proletarians but a complex combination of the two social classes. Frequently, peasantlike means of production coexisted with proletarianlike relations of production.[5] A person could be a wage laborer, cutting cane or working in a sugar mill for part of the year, and a peasant, domestic servant, shoemaker, carpenter, shopkeeper, street vendor, or any combination of occupations for the rest of the year. And when people lost their job, land, or workshop, as many invariably did, knowing they had the option to return home or leave for another country provided some measure of security in an otherwise uncertain world.

This essay cannot possibly provide answers to all the questions raised above. Much more research about the immigrant experience is required before we can make too many accurate generalizations about Cuba's population in the first half of the twentieth century. What I will try to do, however, is show how the Cuban state, under the watchful eye of Fulgencio Batista, implemented labor legislation that "nationalized" the Cuban working class between 1933 and 1940. This period in Cuban history was decisive because, once Batista consolidated power after the revolution of 1933, he and his allies in the police, army, judiciary, and labor movement used the power of the state to compel immigrant workers to either leave the country or become Cuban citizens—or, failing that, to remain in the country illegally and with the constant threat of expulsion. While Spanish and Caribbean immigrants alike were subject to these authoritarian measures, the labor legislation was implemented in such a way so as to make it much harder for Haitians and West Indians to become Cuban than it was for Spaniards. Some people wanted to become Cuban citizens, but were not allowed to because of their race and class; others wanted to leave, but could not because they did not have the money or contacts to do so. Of course many immigrants or migrant workers who had lived in Cuba for years, if not decades, regarded themselves as Cuban, no matter what their legal status or whether or not they ever got their citizen papers.[6] Whatever the case, what is clear is that in the 1920s, 1930s, and 1940s, there was nothing simple about becoming Cuban. Nor was the answer to the question "Who are the Cuban people?" as obvious then (or now) as we might think.

The Unmaking of a Cuban Working Class: Eastern Cuba, 1916–1933

By the 1920s, then, it was by no means clear how "Cuban" the island's working population was, especially in rural eastern Cuba. Nor was it clear what being "Cuban" meant to new immigrants. For Cuban nationalists whose sense of *cubanidad* (Cubanness) had been shaped by the country's fight for independence, the "problem" of immigration and the ethnic and racial makeup of the island's population became one of the defining issues of their time. There was widespread agreement among Cuba's political and economic elite that Cuba needed *immigrants*, preferably Spaniards; but Cuba also needed *workers*, especially in eastern Cuba. The practical problem was how could governments encourage Spaniards (and white immigrants generally) to become Cubans while discouraging black migrant workers from doing so. In theory, sugar companies were supposed to bring in the workers they needed for each harvest and then ship them back once it was over. In practice, of course, thousands of Haitians and West Indians remained in the country illegally, often with company connivance, and there was little Cuban authorities could do to prevent this. Immigration authorities, in fact, had at best only incomplete information about how many foreign workers were in the country at any given time or where they lived and worked.

The two articles from the Cuban Constitution of 1940 quoted above clearly indicate that that in the 1930s the "Cubanness"—or lack thereof—of the island's population was of great concern to state leaders. The articles also highlight how issues of national sovereignty, citizenship, immigration, and labor were entangled. The quotation from Violda Carey, however, shows that for some immigrants the meaning of being Cuban had less to do with what the state said it was and more to do with people's day-to-day lives and personal history. Especially in the Caribbean, where identities *are* diaspora identities, the ability of national or imperial states to supervise and control diaspora populations has been partial at best. Caribbean peoples have always forged their identities within the shifting cracks and spaces of plantation, island, empire, and nation.[7] National identities in the Caribbean are therefore decentered and fragmented.[8]

Nowhere is this observation more accurate than for eastern Cuba, where company-dominated enclave economies had far more control over people's lives than did the "national" state in Havana. Despite the claims of state leaders, Cuban sovereignty was not only limited by the Platt Amendment, it was also limited by the fact that large parts of the countryside in the east were effectively outside its control. And for workers in the east it was easier, cheaper, and faster to travel to Jamaica, Haiti, Barbados, or Central America than to Havana, where there was probably little reason to visit at all. Hundreds of thousands of people were in Cuba for one reason and one reason only: to get a job and save enough money to send or take home. Depending on an ever changing set of personal and economic circumstances, the decision to become Cuban (or not) was not the reason many people went to Cuba. On the contrary, given the cyclical and volatile nature of the Cuban and other regional economies, it made more sense for people to keep their options by *not* becoming a citizen in case they had to pick up and leave quickly to find a job elsewhere. Employers, too, and especially sugar companies, wanted access to a cheap and mobile labor force that could easily cross national borders with minimal interference from state bureaucracies. Before the 1930s companies (and Cuban governments) worried that too many immigration regulations would impede the "free" flow of labor, especially during the annual sugar harvests; they also were concerned that too many Cubans on the payroll would result in too many people claiming rights as both citizens and workers. Migrant workers, on the other hand, were easier to hire, fire, or deport and they were less likely (it was hoped) to demand rights and better wages and working conditions than would Cubans.

To one degree or another, this was the reality throughout the Caribbean (and in much of the world). Highly mobile multinational, multiethnic, and multiracial workforces were the norm, and in many ways Cuba was no exception to this general pattern, especially eastern Cuba. But given Cuba's unique history of anticolonial and nationalist struggle, combined with the international importance of its sugar economy, Cuba's lack of control over its own laboring population was a particularly sensitive point with nationalists. Of course, in the early twentieth century the idea that governments could or should interfere in how private capitalist recruited and deployed labor smacked of socialism and communism, so most politicians, no matter how nationalist they were, stayed away from such pronouncements. It would take a unique combination of political and economic conditions to create the conditions where Cuban state leaders could assert effective sovereignty over the entire working population of the island. Those conditions would arise, as we will see, between 1933 and 1940.

There were, then, understandable reasons why Cuban nationalists of all tendencies were "obsessed" with the problem of national identity.[9] While the threat of American military intervention had diminished by the 1920s, nationalists worried that the very existence of the "Cuban people" was threatened by the overwhelming power of foreign capital and a sea of foreign labor.[10] The popular saying, "Sin azúcar, no hay país" (Without sugar, there is no country) certainly rang true to most Cubans, but the conundrum was that without foreign labor, there would be no sugar harvests. Cuba had always depended upon foreign labor, whether it was slave, indentured, or wage labor. And it was not just any foreign labor that would do: the association of black labor with cutting and hauling cane was deeply engrained in the popular imagination, and it was unimaginable to many that sugar could be harvested any other way.[11] This reliance on black foreign labor had provoked two "Africanization of Cuba" scares: the first was in the 1850s when blacks threatened to outnumber whites, and the second was in the early 1920s when the "uncontrolled" importation of Haitians and West Indians threatened to undermine "civilized" Cuban society by increasing crime, disease, and racial tensions.[12] But as long as the logic of capital dictated the need to bring in cheap, foreign, and black labor, the logic of racism would take second place.

For the first thirty years of the twentieth century the racist anxieties of some nationalists were tempered somewhat by the fact that most Haitians and West Indians arrived and remained in the eastern provinces. Politicians based in Havana and the west certainly lamented their inability to assert complete sovereignty over significant portions of eastern Cuba, but in one sense this problem long predated the most recent sugar boom. Western and eastern Cuba had always been different societies. The western half of the island, and Havana in particular, was the historic center of economic and political power. More Spaniards settled in the west, and the east had a higher percentage of black and mulatto Cubans. In the nineteenth century, slave-based agricultural production was not as important in the east, and manumissions were relatively easier for slaves to obtain there. In the east, only about 6 percent of the population lived on sugar estates, whereas in the west the percentage was typically over 50 percent. Most rural people in the east had no title to their land. "Property" lines were usually ill-defined, and customary land tenure persisted well into the twentieth century.[13]

Prior to 1916 the east was relatively unpopulated. This made it easier for sugar companies, with government support, to purchase, if not simply expropriate, large tracts of land. In the process, peasants became proletarians or fled to more isolated and often mountainous regions where plantation owners or the Cuban state could not touch them. In order to survive, many of the dispossessed attached themselves to regional *caudillos* who might provide them with a job, a plot of land, or some other means to make a living.[14] What complicated matters was that people in the east had a long history of struggle against plantation labor of any kind and the fact that some of the new and largest plantations were American owned and run increased resentment against both foreign capitalists and the politicians in Havana who supported them. The sugar companies built massive sugar mills, railroads, private port facilities, workers' barracks at the mill itself, and company towns. Many of these mill towns had segregated neighborhoods for company managers, skilled foreign employees, Cuban workers, and, after 1916, foreign workers. As long as most of these foreign workers remained on isolated plantation enclaves in distant Camagüey and Oriente, political elites in Havana might complain, but were not too concerned, about how many foreigners were in the country.

The boom in sugar production, of course, would not last. By the late 1920s international agreements had placed restrictions on the size of Cuba's harvests, with the result that fewer workers were needed for the harvests. Even for those who found work, the harvests lasted three months instead of the usual ten.[15] Once the world depression hit with full force after 1929, the economic and political situation became far worse. In the 1930s, out of a national population of 4 million perhaps 300,000 were chronically unemployed.[16] Even though the massive importations of foreign workers declined after the peak years of 1916–21 and had virtually ended by 1927, the continued presence of hundreds of thousands of foreign workers in the country fueled popular resentment against foreign labor. Hunger marches were commonplace. Mass migration of the unemployed and landless from the county to the cities and towns became endemic. Unprecedented numbers of *orientales* (easterners) traveled to western Cuba and Havana in search of work, and many foreigners (especially Jamaicans) joined them. For many westerners, the intrusion of so many (mostly black) easterners into their world was a shock, both economically and culturally. The struggle to get and to keep a job—any job—became desperate, and many *habaneros* resented the presence of so many "uncultured" orientales in their city. The Cuban economy had been through many cyclical crises over the past thirty years, but none compared to the prolonged crisis of the 1930s.

One dramatic example of the vulnerability of migrant workers was the "Sabanaso crisis" in eastern Cuba from July 8 to 13, 1931.[17] Sabanaso, a small town in Oriente, was on the railway line between the large sugar mills at Delicias and Chaparra. The year 1931, of course, was a hard year in Cuba, and unemployment and poverty were endemic. Unemployed British West Indians and Haitians were trying to find work elsewhere on the island or, if possible, return to their home islands. On July 8 some five hundred British West Indians were "dumped" at the railway station at Sabanaso as they tried to get to Santiago to leave the island. The train to Santiago did not arrive, and the train station manager asked for the assistance of a Mr. Neil Hone, a well-known manager of the sugar *colonia* El Canada in Sabanaso. Hone provided some rice and food for the men, and he asked the general manager of the Chaparra mill to provide a cow and water for the stranded workers. Cuban immigration officials soon arrived, but they did nothing. When a train did arrive, it took thirty Haitian workers back to Chaparra where they were to go to a company dock at Cayo Juan Claro and board a ship for Haiti.

The British West Indians at the station, however, were determined to leave for Santiago, and they remained in Sabanaso. At nights they slept in boxcars or on the train platform. Hone continued to provide food, milk, and coffee for the women and children, and he eventually persuaded fifty workers to return to Chaparra. Meanwhile, the problem was compounded because more workers kept arriving at the station from other nearby mills. Matters neared the point of violence when Cuban authorities announced that only Haitians and Jamaicans would be repatriated to their islands if they returned to Chaparra and Delicias: most of the people trapped at the station, however, were from the Lesser Antilles, and they were told they were not eligible for repatriation. A district military chief based at Delicias wanted to take the Jamaicans and Haitians back to Chaparra, and he asked Hone to help persuade the workers to go. Hone agreed to help on the condition he was left alone to persuade the men that returning to Chaparra and Delicias was the lesser of two evils. Some workers did return to the mills, but 150 men said they would rather walk to Santiago than return to unbearable working conditions. Hone explained to the British authorities that the problem was caused because neither the sugar company at Chaparra and Delicias nor the Cuban authorities had arranged for transportation of these workers, and as a result no one would take responsibility for them once they were abandoned in Sabanaso.

Five years later, near the town of Sabanaso itself, conditions for local workers remained desperate. Workers who had jobs in the mills, in construction, or on the railroads were in a fairly good position compared with fieldworkers. Fieldworkers, however, were more vulnerable. There were thousands of men and women scattered about in small towns and hamlets, many of them squatters with no title to the land they lived on. Wages were so low that people survived by cultivating a small plot to supplement their wages. According to one report, "not one of these men can support their families from the small pieces of land they cultivate and always depend on the work during the crop together with what they can produce in the way of foodstuffs from their land to see them through."[18]

A similar situation took place in May 1931 when unemployed British West Indians in Camagüey tried to get to Santiago so they could return home or at least find work elsewhere. The British consul in Santiago estimated that there were over ten thousand Jamaicans in Camagüey "that want to go home right now." There were twenty-six sugar mills in the province, with an average of one thousand British West Indian workers on each estate. The largest estates included the Morón, Ciego de Avila, Nuevitas, and the Florida mills. The cost of train fare from Camagüey to Santiago was more than most workers could afford, with the average train ticket costing around $2.25 per person (which included their belongings, such as wash pans, bedding, and sewing machines). Bus fare from Camagüey City to Santiago was even more expensive, costing around $3.00 per person. Workers from the smaller centers found it difficult to get to a main town or city because there was no reliable transportation. Many West Indians complained to the consulate that they had no clothes for the trip and that numerous people were forced to beg for food and shelter. Meanwhile, in Santiago, the problem was that there were not enough facilities to take care of the large number of destitute people arriving in the city. The British consul in Santiago complained that too many West Indians were arriving at his office and he had to pay the bus drivers who had brought them there because people could not pay the fares. Hostels and hotels were usually full and expensive. It cost around $1.00 a day for a person to stay in Santiago, and since there was no assurance when or even if there would be an affordable boat ride back to their islands of origin, many hundreds of West Indians were trapped in the city with no work or shelter.[19]

Other West Indian workers, however, managed to remain in Cuba, despite their illegal status. Pantera, a Barbadian who arrived illegally in Cuba in 1916, said the key to survival was to stay single and keep on the move. His parents had wanted him to join the British army because that seemed the best way to find a better life away from a hopeless situation in Barbados. Pantera, however, went to Cuba instead. The docks at Bridgetown were full of labor recruiters tempting young men like Pantera to hop on a boat to Cuba, and since no one seemed to care if he had permission to leave or not, he boarded the ship. Once in Cuba, Pantera worked as a cane cutter, tobacco picker, and professional boxer, and in 1927 he joined the Communist Party. He claimed he never worried much about being legal in Cuba: he said the only proof he needed that he was Cuban was his 1927 Party membership card, which he pulled out of his pocket and proudly displayed.[20] Another Barbadian, Charles Yearwood, had no intention of going to Cuba at all. In 1924 he went to the dock at Bridgetown to see a friend off who was going to Cuba. He boarded the ship to chat with his friend before departure, but, Yearwood said, he and his friend "got into the rum a bit," and when he went back on deck to disembark, the ship had departed. He asked the captain to take him back to port, but he was told the ship would not turn around for one person. Yearwood arrived at the port of Cayo Juan Claro near the Chaparra and Delicias mills with nothing but his clothes and not a penny on him. He quickly found work cutting cane and never returned home.[21]

The Making of a Cuban Working Class, 1933–1940

It was the profound economic and political crisis of the 1930s that fueled unprecedented mass mobilization, nationalist sentiment, and, in 1933, social revolution. The story of the Cuban revolution has been told elsewhere.[22] It was fueled by a mixture of nationalist, anti-imperialist, sometimes anticapitalist, and frequently racist and antiforeign sentiment. Between September 1933 and January 1934, a loose coalition of students, middle-class intellectuals, and disgruntled lower-rank soldiers ruled Cuba. This coalition was directed by a popular university professor, Dr. Ramón Grau San Martín. The Grau government promised a "new Cuba" with social justice for all classes and the abrogation of the Platt Amendment. In addition to social and political reforms, the new government created a Ministry of Labor and passed "nationalization of labor laws." Popularly known as the "Fifty-Percent Law," this legislation stipulated that a 50 percent quota of employees in industry, agriculture, and commerce be native-born Cuban citizens, that another 30 percent be naturalized citizens, and that the remaining 20 percent could be foreign legal residents. Sometimes the same law was referred to as the Eighty-Percent Law when native-born and naturalized Cuban citizens were included in the same category.[23] Grau's government had promised "Cuba for Cubans," and the nationalization of labor law was the concrete expression of that promise.

Grau's government was overthrown in January 1934 by an equally loose but conservative coalition under Fulgencio Batista. Many people at the time wondered if Cuba would revert back to the old ways of doing politics, yet Batista understood that after 1933 governments could not afford to ignore nationalist sentiment and popular demands for jobs. While Grau's more radical laws were shelved, between 1936 and 1940 Batista oversaw the successful implementation of nationalization of labor laws. The most dramatic example of its implementation was the mass expulsion of thousands of Haitian and West Indian workers between 1937 and 1940.[24] By 1940 Cuba's sugar economy no longer depended upon foreign labor to cut and harvest cane.

There were two reasons why post-1933 governments successfully implemented the nationalization of labor laws. First, prior to 1933, state leaders had neither the political will nor the bureaucratic capacity to influence local labor markets. As long as companies brought in massive numbers of foreign workers, they had total control over whom they hired. But after 1927, and especially during the 1930s, the reduction in the size of Cuban sugar harvests meant that companies no longer needed to import foreign labor. There were enough workers within Cuba to bring in the harvests and maintain plantation infrastructure. In fact, while there was not exactly a shortage of labor during the 1930s, depending on local circumstances employers increasingly found themselves competing among themselves for the same workers. At the same time, workers competed with other workers for the same jobs, and sometimes workers could play off one employer against another. Companies were uncertain if they could find enough qualified workers when they needed them. In other words, the downturn in sugar production, combined with an uncertain labor supply, weakened employers' stranglehold over local labor markets, which in turn left those markets vulnerable to political interference from forces outside company control.

It was this conjuncture that explains why the nationalist labor laws were implemented successfully after 1933. Batista understood that Cuba had changed after 1933. Thereafter, to stay in power, governments had to respond (or at least appear to respond) to popular demands. No demand was more popular than "Cuba for Cubans." The practical problem was that the state had no reliable information about how many foreign workers were in the country (legally or illegally), where they lived, and what jobs they had. And even if the state had such information, it did not have the administrative or coercive power to implement labor legislation, especially in the eastern provinces. Once the flow of foreign labor had stopped, the effective "denationalization" of the workforce had come to end; the problem for Cuban nationalists, however, was that the population that remained in the country was still too multinational and multiethnic for their liking. It was this population that needed to be "nationalized." Under the watchful eye of Batista, after 1936 the state developed that power. Once Batista reorganized the army and police, he placed loyal followers in key administrative and supervisory positions, at both the national and local levels.[25] By 1937 Batista had entered his "populist phase," and his "redistributionist demagoguery" was accompanied by some real, if modest, reforms.[26] His most popular measure was the implementation of nationalist labor legislation. Backed by the army and police, and in alliance with the Communist Party and trade unions, Batista had both the political support and coercive power necessary to compel employers to hire Cubans before foreigners. Unemployed Cubans, of course, were delighted. Even if they did not get a job, the idea that a powerful man like Batista was on their side gave the unemployed some hope. Employers grumbled, but there was little else they could do.

According to the labor legislation, once employers reached the quotas for the percentage of Cuban workers, they were obliged by law to maintain the percentages or risk incremental fines for every violation discovered. The 20 percent of foreigners employed must be legal residents of Cuba, though "the President of the Republic is authorised to make exception to this provision . . . in the case of non-resident foreigners whom it is necessary to employ each year in the cleaning and cutting of cane"—a clear recognition of the high numbers of illegal immigrants cutting and hauling cane in Cuba. Exceptions were made for technical workers who could not be replaced by native Cubans. Even more important, exemptions were made for anyone employed as a single worker, for fathers and children who worked in their own homes, and for domestic servants employed in private homes. As we will see, many British West Indians, and especially Jamaicans, fell into this latter category because many arrived in Cuba on their own initiatives as individual workers and not through the mediation of labor recruiters or contactors. Dismissals of foreign workers were to be prioritized in the following order: single foreigners were to be let go first, followed by married foreigners, then married foreigners with children, and foreigners married to Cuban women. Foreigners married to Cuban women and with children were the last dismissed.[27]

The problem was that in Cuba, in the short term, there were simply too few "Cuban" workers to fill all the available positions. If economic activity was not to be disrupted, foreign labor could not be replaced too quickly. This situation was especially true in eastern Cuba, where the expansion of the sugar industry had been especially notable since 1914.[28] The seasonal nature of work, combined with frequent competition for skilled labor among sugar companies, meant that the demand for labor could be stiff, and skilled contract workers could choose between employers. Employers and employees alike used the ambiguous status of "contract worker" to claim exemptions from the law, thus retaining a higher percentage of foreign workers on the payroll bill than the law, as narrowly interpreted, permitted. Contract workers, whether skilled or unskilled, changed occupations frequently, and since their employment was seasonal, whether or not they were classified as "skilled" depended on the season, their occupation at the time, the decision of an individual employer, or the political context. An "unskilled" Barbadian cane cutter during the harvest was a skilled gardener, railroad worker, mechanic, or carpenter during the dead season; a skilled Jamaican mill worker could lose his job to a less skilled Cuban because state officials (including Batista's military men) at the local level might compel an employer to fire the Jamaican.

A further complication was that a "Jamaican" worker who might have lived in Cuba for many years was for all intents and purposes as Cuban as anyone else, at least as far as he or she was concerned. After years in Cuba, many West Indians spoke Spanish as well as "native" Cubans, and since few poor rural people, whether native-born or not, had birth certificates or legal documentation of any kind, there was no reliable way to determine who was or was not a "foreigner." Needless to say, the sugar companies and the workers themselves could exploit this situation to their own advantage, and laws passed in a distant Havana could easily be ignored. Since the sugar companies themselves could not be trusted to implement labor legislation that might hurt their immediate interests, the Cuban state needed to create institutions (backed up by Batista's police and soldiers) that would ensure that the labor laws were enforced. Prior to the 1930s it simply did not matter much to people in the west if people who worked in the far-off sugar plantations of eastern Cuba were Cuban citizens or not. But once severe economic crisis and mass unemployment gripped the entire nation, the issue of the "Cubanness" of the working class went to the very top of the national political agenda.

The Cuban nationalist labor laws were based on the simple conviction that in order for the nation to exist, there must be a national workforce. The problem, therefore, was how to create one. Information about how many foreigners were in the country and where they lived and worked was equally hard to come by. Government immigration data were useful up to a point, especially for the ports at Havana and Santiago de Cuba, but many sugar companies brought in thousands of foreign workers through private ports. Companies were under no obligation to provide the government with detailed information on how many workers they employed or their occupations. Government immigration figures would always fall short of the actual number of foreigners in the country.

Clearly, before Cuban governments could implement the nationalization of labor legislation, they had to establish a bureaucracy and local and regional offices to collect basic information about the Cuban labor force. The state needed information about how many "Cuban" and "foreign" workers were in the country, what their skills were, where they lived, and what the specific labor market needs of the sugar industry were at any given time and place. It was for this reason that between 1935 and 1940 the Cuban state established civil registries and labor exchanges throughout the country, but especially in the east. The Mendieta-Batista government of 1935–36 passed Law no. 148, which established labor exchanges in all five provinces. The law stated that exchanges were created for the "government to control the supply and demand of labor in order to improve the possibilities of employment and afford laborers professional orientation on a firm basis."[29] The law stipulated that employers must advise the provincial labor exchange of all hiring and discharging of workers. When taking on new workers, employers were to hire unemployed laborers whose names were supplied by local exchanges. Employers were required to submit lists of all their employees, their technical qualifications, and their nationality. These lists would go to the director general of the Ministry of Labor, and the ministry would then determine whether or not there were enough Cubans to fill positions held by foreigners. Unions were required to inform the labor exchanges which of their members were fired, hired, and rehired. Employers could not hire workers who did not possess a labor exchange registration card, and violators of this provision were subject to fines ranging as high as $500. By December 1935 the government claimed that a total of 94,346 unemployed workers had registered at the exchanges, with provincial breakdowns of 2,515 for Pinar del Rio, 6,990 for the Province of Havana, 11,370 for Matanzas, 17,849 for Santa Clara, 11,756 for Camagüey, and 43,866 for Oriente.[30]

With large numbers of foreign workers no longer entering the country, the sugar plantations had little choice but to use the labor exchanges to obtain the labor they needed. Mills constantly petitioned the labor exchanges for more labor, and managers often complained that they could not get enough workers. In Camagüey and Oriente, the Central Alto Cedro asked local exchanges for eight hundred workers, while the Central Boston requested five hundred laborers. The Tánamo mill asked for one hundred workers. On January 28, the Department of Labor declared that "a notice has been sent to all Labor Exchanges requesting them to speed measures to send any cane laborers they may have available to the mills. . . . The Labor Department is making every effort . . . to supply an adequate number of workers in its program to handle the crop exclusively with native Cubans and thereby reduce unemployment."[31] The Labor Ministry ordered that foreign workers should not be registered at the exchanges, and the local authorities were told in no uncertain terms that there were to be no exceptions.[32] Local politics, however, were very personal. Many exchange officials were friends of local mill managers or were former employees of sugar companies (or might want a job with one in the future). These personal ties were often more compelling than directives from a distant Havana. Some mills bribed labor exchange officials, paying them to overlook the regulations and to place foreigners on the exchanges' lists of available workers.[33]

Another purpose of the exchanges was to gather information about the number of foreigners in the country. Workers were required to register at the exchanges, and they had to show documents indicating their legal status as either Cuban citizens or as foreigners. If workers did not possess any documents proving their legal status (a very frequent occurrence), their employers were required to provide that information. In one case, the local inspector for the Registro de Extranjeros in Holguín wrote to the manager of the Chaparra and Delicias mills and warned him that the mill would be fined if it failed to inform the registry of all foreign workers on the company payroll.[34] Of course, there were many delays in the establishment of the labor exchanges: officials needed to be appointed for each exchange, employers frequently did not comply by registering their workers at the exchanges, and it was not possible to force all workers to register if they did not want to. Though corruption and bribery would be a constant problem in the labor exchanges, Batista placed loyal army and police officers in the exchanges to work alongside civilian officials and to ensure that fines against employers were issued.

By 1937 labor exchanges, along with the Cuban army and police, were present throughout the country, and in that year Haitian and British West Indian workers became the target of a campaign of mass repatriations to their islands of origin or to any British territory that would take them. On January 19, 1937, the Cuban government under Fulgencio Batista announced plans to expel British West Indian and Haitian workers, and the armed forces were to enforce this order.[35] By the end of February, three large resettlement camps in the eastern provinces of Camagüey and Oriente held several thousand Haitian and Jamaican workers.[36] The British embassy complained about the treatment of their Jamaican and Barbadian subjects in these camps, though it was "a debatable point whether the British West Indians would be worse off roaming the countryside without food or shelter, or in a camp, fed and sheltered, but more or less a prisoner and probably subject to deplorable sanitary conditions." The Cuban Ministry of Labor informed the British embassy that these camps were for Haitians only, but the embassy dispatch concluded, "If the camps . . . are really intended for Haytians only, there must inevitably be great delay in disposing of the British West Indians, which in itself constitutes a most thorny problem.... [G]iven the rough and ready army methods prevailing in the provinces, it is almost certain that if large numbers of Haytians are rounded up many British subjects will find themselves swept into the mob."[37] Batista ordered the Rural Guard to expel Haitian and Jamaican workers from the sugar estates, while "encouraging" mill managers to hire Cubans in their place. By March 1937, thirty thousand Haitians were repatriated from Cuba, with an expected fifty thousand to follow shortly.[38] Thousands of Jamaicans, Barbadians, and other West Indians were subject to the same measures.

One of the central challenges of implementing the nationalization of labor legislation was the problem of documenting who was a foreigner and who was a "Cuban." The cultural ambiguities, especially in the east, of determining who was "Cuban" were problem enough, but since very few poor people at all had any legal documentation whatsoever, it was nearly impossible for state authorities or employers to single out "Cubans" from "foreigners." Since the early twentieth century, Cuban immigration officials had provided foreign residents of Cuba with *carnets de extranjeros* (foreign residency cards). As indicated earlier, for years the large sugar companies had brought in hundreds of thousands of workers through private ports, and companies were not obligated to provide workers with carnets de extranjero. After 1936, however, Cuban authorities strengthened the regulations about how carnets would be issued and how immigration laws would be enforced. One way the state did this was by placing Batista's loyal followers in the army and police in the labor exchanges and municipal offices to oversee the distribution of the carnets. All foreigners were required to obtain a carnet at a cost of $1.45. These cards were valid for one year and could be renewed again for the same price. Thereafter a new carnet would be issued for a period of five years; this new document, however, had a photograph of the holder along with his or her fingerprints. Failure to register or to renew the carnet within thirty days of expiration resulted in a fine of $1.00. A similar fine was imposed for failure to notify authorities of a change of address. If a person did not pay these fines, they were to be deported. Destitute foreigners could obtain a free and temporary carnet if they could prove they were in fact destitute; if they managed to do this, they could remain in the country for six months with the possibility of a six-month extension if their condition had not improved. If after the second six months a person was still destitute, they were to be deported.[39]

One of the functions of the labor exchanges was to issue carnets to workers once they registered at the exchanges. Workers had to fill out a legal declaration stating their name, age, occupation, salary, employer, address, marital status, and nationality.[40] In addition to registering at the labor exchanges, all

Cubans and foreigners were to register at civil registry offices in the provincial capitals. The civil registries were the place where foreigners were to go to declare their intention of becoming Cuban citizens. A registration fee was charged to every person who registered at the civil registry offices. If migrant workers were caught without their carnet, they risked jail and deportation.

Of course, what people were supposed to do and what they did were frequently at odds. Two factors complicated matters when it came to issuing the carnets de extranjero. The nationalization of labor law stipulated that temporary carnets could be provided to newly arrived migrants who could not afford to pay the initial registration fee: the understanding was that they would pay the fee when they received their first paycheck. If workers stayed within the boundaries of the foreign enclaves, they did not need to have a carnet. But, of course, people rarely stayed in one place, especially when the "dead season" arrived. Before the more aggressive implementation of the nationalization of labor law in 1937, it was safer for both workers and employers to avoid the law altogether: for workers it made no sense to draw the attention of the police and army by requesting legal papers; for employers, their labor needs were too uncertain to worry about whether their employees were Cuban or not.

Provincial civil registries in Las Tunas, Puerto Padre, Delicias, Chaparra, Guantánamo, and Santiago for the years 1936 through 1940 provide some fascinating profiles about individual West Indian workers and how they lived in Cuba before they became Cuban citizens. One of the striking aspects of these profiles was how often people openly declared that they had been in the country illegally for years and that they possessed no legal documents of any kind. Fear of deportation did not seem to be a factor.[41] Many people brought witnesses with them to the registries who could corroborate that the claimants had regular employment and/or were respected members of their communities. It was not uncommon for claimants to highlight that they were married to "native" Cubans and that their children were Cuban. In terms of occupation, the majority of British West Indians who registered fell into the categories "contract laborer," "domestic worker," or small-scale traders of some kind.

As indicated above, the nationalization of labor legislation had identified certain kinds of contract labor that were not subject to the strict letter of the law. It appears that many British West Indian contract workers felt that their occupational status might permit them to remain in the country without becoming Cuban citizens. Another explanation for the willingness of undocumented British West Indians to come forward in late 1937 and 1938 was that the Cuban government's repatriation plans were stalled. An editorial in the influential sugar industry magazine *Revista Semanal Azucarera* wrote that "mass repatriations have struck a snag in the Cuban mill-owner's and planter's fear of a consequent scarcity of labor for the coming sugar crop. The plan, if carried out, will therefore be on a much smaller scale than originally conceived."[42] By 1938 the flow of migrant labor to Cuba had long stopped and sugar companies were uncertain if there were enough "Cubans" to supply their labor needs. Consequently, for a brief period both sugar companies and workers found ways to evade the labor laws, sometimes with the unofficial approval of local government officials.

An example of the complex situation faced by sugar workers in the east is provided by Charles Ray, who was employed at the huge Chaparra sugar mill in the late 1930s.

> I began to work in the mill . . . at age fourteen or fifteen. When they established the eight-hour work day, I was a cart driver, and I remained driving carts on the sugar floor carrying sacks of sugar, which were big sacks, not like now where the sacks are small. . . . Being a cart driver wasn't so lucky, and you earned $1.25. Then my father spoke with the American manager, and they took me from the sugar floor and sent me to work in the lab with the chemicals. . . . But when harvest time came, I don't remember which harvest it was, an American chemist came who did not speak Spanish. He was the chemical manager; the owners brought him from the United States. The lab was outside the mill in a large, two-story building where the overseer was below and the laboratory was on top. He chose one of the chemists who was working in the mill, a half Chinese. His father was Chinese, but he was Cuban because he was born in Cuba in the 1920s. Then he chose me to work with them there as an interpreter. . . . In 1937, when the English people went on their shift during crop time, as usual, a day went up to 6 P.M. The whistle would blow, and the English people would leave with their little bags over their shoulders. At each door there was a guard. "What are you, English? You cannot enter." So in 1937, they took out all English people, and there were only fifty left. They left to look for jobs in other parts. I continued because I was not working in the mill. . . . In 1937 and 1938 they were trying to identify who I was. Although they knew me since I was a boy, they were not sure if I was or wasn't born in Cuba, because I had been playing baseball and dominoes and all those things with them. They had to be sure before they said anything, and so they said nothing to me. But at the end of 1937, an American chemist called me and

said to me: "Listen to me, Charles, they are after you because the guard has already gone to tell the general manager that there is still an English person working at the mill, and that English person is you." The Cuban chemist told me: "To cover you, you are going with me to Puerto Padre. I have friends there. I am going to change your birth certificate from English to Cuban." . . . They only left the Cuban boys and the "Gallegos" or Spanish immigrants on the sugar plantation, because the "Gallegos" were Cubans. . . . But then they wanted to dismiss me, too, and then the American kept me on the job until the harvest ended. He told me: "I am going to keep you here until the harvest ends. When it ends, you cannot work here anymore because the general manager gave me the order to take away your job."[43]

Ray's mention of the Chinese workers in the mill indicates another set of tensions at the Chaparra mill. On April 4, 1936, Francisco Chiong wrote a letter of complaint to the mill's general manager. Chiong claimed to represent the Chinese workers at the mill, and he argued that many of them had been unjustly released from their jobs because they were not Cubans. Chiong pointed out that he had lived in Cuba for thirty years. He had worked for the company as a labor contractor, and he had traveled to China and to Jamaica to recruit workers for the Chaparra Sugar Company. He had been a loyal worker for years, and now he was out of a job. Chinese workers, Chiong argued, were being replaced "by other individuals just as foreign as we are." Chiong made a point of saying that he was not opposed to the Fifty-Percent Law in principle, but he felt that it was not applied consistently or fairly.[44]

Clearly the nationalization of labor laws had a serious impact on the lives of Haitian and British West Indian migrants. Haitians were the most vulnerable group of all: they had arrived in Cuba under the strict control of sugar companies, and they were employed almost exclusively as cane cutters and haulers. Workers' housing (*bateyes*) within the sugar company enclaves was often segregated, with Haitians, British West Indians, Spaniards, Chinese, and Americans each living in their own areas. When Haitians were no longer needed at the end of each harvest, they could easily be located and deported. Between February and the summer of 1937, some 25,000 Haitians were deported.[45] By January 1939, another 5,700 Haitians had been repatriated.[46]

One of the striking features of these years was that there was virtually no serious opposition to the nationalist labor laws. Even the Communist Party and its trade union cadre, for whom working-class solidarity and class-based politics were ideological mantras, supported the nationalization of labor laws and remained silent about the treatment of Haitians and West Indians in Cuba. The reasons for this silence are hard to identify with certainty. On the one hand, the party had a long history of antiracist struggle, and its membership included a high percentage of Afro-Cubans, so it is logical to assume that they could not support attacks on workers, Cuban or foreign. On the other hand, by 1938 the Communist Party was firmly allied with Batista, and as junior partners in his coalition it was not in their strategic interest to create divisions in what they regarded as an anti-oligarchic democratic alliance. To date, there is no hard evidence to suggest that the Party condoned the treatment of Haitians and West Indians or participated in excluding them from getting jobs. Yet there is also no evidence that party members, even at the local level, stood up for foreign workers. This silence is striking given that so many communists in the east had a long history of grassroots working-class organizing, and they were not known as timid people. Until more research is done, we can only surmise that the party's relative weakness within Batista's coalition, combined with its strict adherence to the principles of democratic centralism, kept its members silent.[47]

It is also important to note that by 1939 Batista felt secure enough to legalize the mainly communist Confederación de Trabajadores de Cuba. The CTC was a confederation of unions, many of which had functioned underground for years. Communist Party organizers had provided the experience and discipline required to get a union off the ground and running; as a consequence, party union activists enjoyed widespread support among working-class people in general. Communist organizers, especially at the local level, were typically regarded as hardworking, selfless, and usually uncorruptible—the latter characteristic being no small feat in mid-twentieth-century Cuba. Now that the union movement was legal, however, its leaders had access to the highest levels of state power (and resources), and being a union member no longer meant a person was automatically a revolutionary or subversive. On the contrary, the two mass-based political parties to emerge after 1939—the Auténticos and the communists—had strong trade union federations that not only served to gain working-class support for each party but also legitimized the link between class, state, and nation.[48]

What all these changes meant for foreign workers in Cuba—whether they regarded themselves as "foreign" or not—was clear. The pressure on people to assimilate into an intensely nationalistic society where there was a strong tendency for native-born Cubans to resent foreigners, especially if they competed for the same jobs, was intense. Haitians in Cuba were by far the most vulnerable because their weak governments could provide no support for its citizens abroad: they found some way to return to Haiti, were expelled from the country, or assimilated into society at large.[49] West Indians, however, were British subjects, and if they had not taken out Cuban citizenship, they were still nominally under the authority of the British Empire.[50] British imperial officials were keenly aware that the presence of so many of their colonial subjects in places like Cuba was both a problem for the empire and a source of tension with regional governments. In October 1943 the British ambassador to Cuba, Sir George Oglivie-Forbes, informed the Foreign Office that his embassy and consulates were inundated with West Indians seeking relief or financial help to return home.

> The time is approaching when an important decision of policy should be made. Is it the desire of His Majesty's Government that the British West Indians born in Cuba should remain British subjects, or are they to be told that as there is no prospect of settlement in the British Empire, it is in their best interests to allow their British nationality to lapse and to become Cuban citizens? Such is the strength of nationalism here that there is already ample evidence of discrimination against naturalised Cubans and Cuban citizens born of alien parents, and I accordingly fear that to urge British West Indians against their wills to become Cuban citizens would not be an honourable course of action. . . . My own view is that while we should continue to give all possible protection and assistance to any who remain British subjects in Cuba or elsewhere, it is definitely undesirable that we should encourage children born in the British West Indian community in Cuba (or Santo Domingo) to maintain their British nationality if their intention is to continue to live in Cuba (or Santo Domingo).[51]

The ambassador did not want to encourage West Indians in Cuba to renounce their nationality. But to encourage people to stay in Cuba only provoked the Cuban government.

Another British dispatch written four years later was more blunt:

> There is really no reason why a lot of these people should not merge with the people of the country [Cuba]. In Cuba there is little difference between the two standards of living [Jamaica and Cuba], nor need we be concerned very much about losing these people as British subjects—their loyalty to us is mainly sentimental, and personally I have found in practice they much prefer to serve Americans. They also cause a lot of unnecessary trouble by proclaiming their British allegiance in a manner that is offensive to the people of the country whom they despise.[52]

In 1950, according to Neil Hone, by this point British consul at Santiago, every West Indian on the relief list had been offered repatriation, "but very many prefer to remain in Cuba even without relief." Able-bodied young men hoped to find work during the next sugar crop to save money for the trip home, but employers were even more reluctant to hire them and trade unions advocated for native-born workers to be employed first. Others simply did not have the money to leave the country, while many were too old to travel or had been away for so long they had no family to return to. Repatriation by sea was less feasible than before because the one line that took deck passengers—the Standard Fruit Company—had stopped its Santiago-Kingston run.[53] There were still many Haitians and West Indians who were illegal residents of the country, but that status now meant that a person would be subject to systematic job discrimination and, depending on the community, racism. By 1940, for Caribbean immigrants and their descendants the best way to get a secure job or access to land was to become a citizen.

So who are the Cuban people? Again, we know the answer to this question, at least in terms of the ethnic background of most Cubans. Perhaps the more meaningful, interesting, and difficult questions to answer are how, when, why, and under what conditions people become Cuban. Grand national (and nationalist) narratives tend to lead to equally grand conclusions. However correct those conclusions might be, in our hurry to make sweeping observations about national identity and state formation, we can forget to tell the stories (especially local ones) of people who do not always fit easily into those grand narratives. Clearly, given the dramatic change in both the size and composition of Cuba's population, any answer to the question "Who are the Cuban people?" could not possibly be the same in 1940 as it was in 1900. Ancestry and ethnic background might tell us *where* people came from, but they do not tell us *who* people are.

Nationalism of all kinds tends to reduce "the people" to a homogeneous body with the same ethnic roots. In the Cuban case (as with so many others), reducing the Cuban people to a single ethnic background was always complicated by issues of race, class, region, and the struggles against slavery and colonialism. After independence, the story got even more complicated thanks to the political economy of sugar and labor migration. As much as Cuban nationalists wanted to ground Cuban identity in past struggles for nationhood and, more problematically, in a nonracial sense of cubanidad, the reality they faced was that the island's population was too multiracial, multiethnic, and multinational for their liking. As long as Cuba depended on sugar, and as long as harvesting sugar depended on foreign labor, there was little nationalists could do to alleviate their anxiety about the future of "the Cuban nation." While there were a few radical labor organizers and intellectuals who argued against racist and ethno-centric nationalism, their voices were drowned out by those who saw foreign capital—but especially foreign black labor—as the greatest threat to "the Cuban people."

Thanks to the world depression and the downturn in sugar production in the late 1920s and 1930s, nationalist state leaders could realize their dream of "nationalizing" the Cuban working class. Once sugar companies, especially in the east, no longer needed foreign labor to cut and haul cane, post-1933 governments were no longer under the same intense pressure to make immigration policy conform to company needs. After the revolutionary mass mobilizations of the early 1930s, Cuban politics would never be the same. Thereafter, political leaders of almost every stripe—including many communists and otherwise revolutionary figures—either supported or turned a blind eye to the state-sponsored attack on Haitians and West Indians. What had started as a series of "revolutionary" laws to nationalize the Cuban labor force became, by 1940, constitutional edicts. The state now had the power to grant or deny citizenship by enforcing who could get a job and who could not. Being—or at least claiming to be—a "native" Cuban now mattered a great deal. To what degree people were actually free to become Cuban or not very much depended on a combination of local circumstances, personal history, and ultimately state power.

The significance of the Constitution of 1940 was that Cuba became, judicially speaking, a nation-state.[54] Equally significant was that in the years leading up to the passing of the constitution, the coercive power of the state reached almost every corner of the country. Nominally national governments in Havana could pass, and enforce, legislation throughout the entire country. The abrogation of the Platt Amendment in 1934 symbolized the formal end to American neocolonial power in Cuba. Informally, of course, a strong argument can be made that Cuba remained a neocolony up to the revolution of 1959. But nation-states can still be neocolonies of one kind or another.[55] And nationalism, no matter how radical in either discourse or practice, can still accommodate itself to powerful external forces, be they political, cultural, or economic. The real and symbolic importance of the constitutional consensus of 1940 was that for the first time in its history the Cuban nation was sovereign, at least over its own population. How state leaders used and abused that sovereignty was the central political bone of contention for the next twenty years.

What is indisputable, however, is that in the six years leading up to 1940 and afterward, Cuban governments exercised the coercive power of the state to help make a Cuban working class. By making this argument, I in no way want to diminish or deny that Cuban and foreign workers themselves created their own class identities through struggle and sacrifice. I am not suggesting that some kind of Foucauldian repressive state discourse took hold in Cuba between 1933 and 1940 and molded a Cuban working class from on high. Cuba's long history of subaltern rebellion and militant class struggle was too powerful to be smothered or co-opted by any single nationalist discourse. We also have some—but not enough—information about the role Haitian and West Indian workers played in the class and revolutionary struggles of the 1920s and 1930s. What I hope to have shown in this chapter, though, is that in order to better understand what it meant to be Cuban during the republican period, we need to appreciate the complex interplay between population history, class, and state formation.

Notes

This chapter stems from research that also resulted in Robert Whitney and Graciela Chailloux, *Subjects or Citizens: British Caribbean Workers in Cuba, 1900-1960* (Gainesville: University Press of Florida, 2013). I would like to thank Dr. Graciela Chailloux from the Casa de Altos Estudios Fernando Ortiz for her collaboration on the research for this chapter and for the forthcoming book. She is, of course, not responsible for any of the arguments or conclusions in either.

1. On Spanish migration to Cuba, see Sánchez Alonso, *Las causas de la emigración española*, 116-17, 142-51; Moya, "Spanish Emigration to Cuba and Argentina," 7.

2. For the published work on British West Indian migration to Cuba, see Pérez de la Riva, "Cuba y la migración antillana, 1900-1931," 3-75; Knight, "Jamaican Migrants and the Cuban Sugar Industry, 1900-1934," 94-114. Fortunately, recent and pioneering doctoral dissertations by Jorge Giovannetti, Marc Mcleod, and Cadence Wynter have provided a more complete and nuanced picture of British West Indian life in Cuba. See Giovannetti, "Black British Subjects in Cuba: Race, Ethnicity, Nation, and Identity in the Migration Experience"; Mcleod, "Undesirable Aliens: Haitian and British West Indian Workers in Cuba, 1898-1940"; Wynter, "Jamaican Labor Migration to Cuba, 1885-1930 in the Caribbean Context." The published works are Giovannetti, "The Elusive Organization of 'Identity,'" 1-27, 231; Chailloux Laffita and Whitney, "British Subjects y Pichones en Cuba"; and Whitney and Chailloux Laffita, "West Indian Migrants to Cuba and Their Descendants," 133-54.

3. Mcleod, "Undesirable Aliens: Haitian and British West Indian Immigrant Workers in Cuba, 1898-1940," 7.

4. The first figure is taken from McLean Petras, *Jamaican Labour Migration*, 68. The figure on illegal British West Indian residents is from "Repatriation of British West

Indians: British West Indian Relief in Cuba, Santo Domingo, and Hayti," by M. E. Vibert, Consular Department, Foreign Office, January 14, 1948, National Archives of the United Kingdom (hereafter NA), /FO/369/3962/117907. These figures do not include the children of first-generation immigrants. There are, to our knowledge, no reliable figures on the number of Haitians who remained in Cuba after 1940.

5. The phrase "neither peasants nor proletarians" is taken from Frucht, "A Caribbean Social Type."

6. It is still possible today to meet people who arrived in Cuba between 1916 and the 1950s who never got citizenship papers. In effect, before they were provided with proper identification papers from the revolutionary government after 1959, they had lived illegally in Cuba and were not legally Cuban.

7. Holt, "Slavery and Freedom in the Atlantic World," 33–44; Trouillot, "Caribbean: Sociocultural Aspects," 1484–88.

8. The notion of "fragmented nationalism," of course, is borrowed from Knight, *The Caribbean: The Genesis of a Fragmented Nationalism*.

9. On the issue of Cuban national identity, see Pérez, *On Becoming Cuban*; Kapcia, *Cuba: Island of Dreams*; Ibarra, *Un análisis psicosocial del cubano, 1898–1925*; Torres-Cuevas, "En busca de la cubanidad."

10. For some representative works expressing these views, see Carrión, "El desenvolvimiento social de Cuba en los últimos veinte años"; Trelles, "El progreso (1902 a 1905) y el retroceso (1906 a 1922) de la República de Cuba"; Guerra y Sánchez, *Sugar and Society in the Caribbean*; Ortiz, *Cuban Counterpoint*; Maestri, *Capitalismo y anticapitalismo*; Maestri, *Latifundismo en la economía cubana*; Arrendondo, *Cuba, tierra indefensa*.

11. Andrews, "Black Workers in the Export Years: Latin America, 1880–1930," 7–29.

12. Bronfman, *Measures of Equality*; Chomsky, "'Barbados or Canada?,'" 415–62; Chomsky, "The Aftermath of Repression: Race and Nation in Cuba after 1912."

13. Swanger, "Lands of Rebellion: Oriente and Escambray Encountering Cuban State Formation, 1934–1974."

14. Hoernel, "Sugar and Social Change in Oriente, 1898–1946"; Pérez, *Lords of the Mountain: Social Banditry and Peasant Protest in Cuba, 1878–1919*.

15. An excellent analysis of the Cuban sugar industry during this period is Dye, *Cuban Sugar in the Age of Mass Production*.

16. For economic and social conditions in the late 1920s and 1930s, see Buell et al., *Problems of the New Cuba*, and República de Cuba, *Adaptación de Cuba a las condiciones económicas actuales*.

17. The information in this and the following paragraph is summarized from British Legation to Neil Hone, Colonia "El Canada," Sabanaso, Oriente, July 16, 1931: Enclosure, "Detailed account of the happenings from the 8th to the 13th of July (1931) with reference to the dumping of some 500 men in Sabanaso from Chaparra," NA/FO/1001/1.

18. Enclosure No. 2: Letter from Mr. Neil Hone, Sabanazo, Oriente to Mr. T. I. Rees, British Consul General, Havana, October 28, 1936, Despatch No. 158, from the British Legation, Havana, to the Right Honourable Sr. Anthony Eden, November 9, 1936. NA/CO/318/424/4.

19. F. E. Kezar, British Vice-Consulate, Camagüey, to the British Legation, Havana, May 5, 1931, Jamaican Archives (hereafter JA), 1B/5/77/55/1931.

20. Chailloux and Whitney, interview with Pantera, Chaparra, June 13, 2002. When Pantera discovered that I was Canadian, he asked if he could speak English with me. He spoke with a strong Barbadian accent. There was considerable debate about Pantera's age. He claimed he was 103, but some of the nurses said he was "only" around 98. What is certain is that several of the other residents in the home who were in their eighties said they knew "Pantera" when they were children.

21. Chailloux and Whitney, interview with Charles Yearwood, Delicias, June 12, 2002.

22. The main works on the Cuban revolution of 1933 are Lumen, *La revolución cubana*; Roa García, *La revolución del 30 se fue a bolina*; Aguilar, *Cuba 1933: Prologue to Revolution*; Tabares del Real, *La revolución del 30: Sus dos últimos años*; Raby, *The Cuban Pre-Revolution of 1933: An Analysis*; Soto, *La revolución del 33*; Osa, *Crónica del año 33*; Carrillo, *Cuba 1933: Students, Yankees, and Soldiers*; and Whitney, *State and Revolution in Cuba*.

23. The full text of the law can be found in "Nationalization of Labor in Cuba," Enclosure 8 to Dispatch 224, November 14, 1933, from the embassy in Cuba to the secretary of state, in Confidential U.S. Diplomatic Post Records, 1930–39 (hereafter CUSDPR), RG 84, reel 11, 1933. According to a U.S. embassy report on the nationalization of labor law in Cuba, the Cuban decrees were part of a wave of nationalist legislation throughout Latin America. The report gave the following percentages: El Salvador, 80, Guatemala, 75, Venezuela, 75, Brazil, 66, Chile, 85, Mexico, 90, Nicaragua, 75, Uruguay, 80, Peru, 80, Dominican Republic, 70, Haiti, retail trade restricted to Haitian citizens, Panama, 75, Ecuador, 80, Bolivia, 85, and Cuba, 50. See Memorandum to the Ambassador, Havana, January 19, 1938, in CUSDPR, RG 84, reel 50. For an academic analysis of Latin America in the 1930s and 1940s, see Rock, ed., *Latin America in the 1940s*; Bethell and Roxborough, eds., *Latin America between the Second World War and the Cold War, 1944–1948*.

24. Whitney, *State and Revolution*, 155.

25. Pérez, *Army and Politics in Cuba, 1898–1958*.

26. The phrase "redistributionist demagoguery" is taken from Vilas, "Latin American Populism: A Structural Approach," 389–420. On Batista's populist phase, see Whitney, *State and Revolution*, chapters 6 and 7.

27. "Nationalization of Labor in Cuba," Enclosure 8 to Dispatch 224, November 14, 1933, from the Embassy in Cuba to the Secretary of State, in CUSDPR, RG 84, reel 11, 1933.

28. Hoernel, "Sugar and Social Change in Oriente, 1898–1946."

29. Hoernel, "Sugar and Social Change in Oriente, 1898–1946."

30. H. Freeman Mathews, First Secretary of the Embassy to the Department of State, "94,346 unemployed workers registered at the Bolsas de Trabajo as of November 30, 1936," Dispatch No. 7786, December 9, 1936, in CUSDPR, RG 84, reel 34.

31. "Sugar Mills Ask Labor Exchanges for Field Help," *Havana Post*, January 28, 1937, 12.

32. "Idle in Camagüey Forced to Work," *Havana Post*, February 11, 1937, 1.

33. "Labor Situation in Cuba and Repatriation of British West Indians." February 11, 1937, NA/CO/318/424/4.

34. Luis Rodríguez to the General Administration of the Chaparra and Delicias Mills, Holguín, May 16, 1936, in Archivo Histórico Provincial de Las Tunas, Fondo 5: Cuban American Sugar Mills Company, Exp. 456, Leg. 39.

35. *Havana Post*, January 20, 1937, 1; *Havana Post*, January 28, 1937, 12.

36. British Vice-Consul at Santiago (Haydock-Wilson) to the Consul General at Havana, February 10, 1937, NA/CO/318/424/4; "The Labor Situation in Cuba"; *Havana Post*, February 23, 1937, 1; *Havana Post*, April 6, 1937, 1.

37. Mr. Rees to Mr. Eden, Havana, February 20, 1937, Enclosure Document 21, "The Labor Situation in Cuba and the British West Indies," NA/FO/A/1864/65/14.

38. Grant Watson (Havana) to the Foreign Office, July 7, 1937, NA/CO/318/424/5.

39. This information is summarized from "Report on the Present Condition of the British West Indian Community in Cuba," by F. A. Stockdale, July 21, 1943, NA/CO/318/453/14/119685.

40. A large collection of these legal declarations are located in the Archivo Histórico Provincial de Las Tunas, Fondo 5: Cuban-American Sugar Mills Company.

41. It is interesting to note that Haitian names rarely appear in the civil registry volumes, whereas English names are very common.

42. "Los antillanos," *Revista Semanal Azucarera*, October 22, 1937, 59.

43. Interview with Charles Ray (born in Saint Lucia in 1919 and in Cuba since 1924), interviewed in Guantánamo, October 8, 2001.

44. Francisco Chiong to the General Manager, Chaparra, April 4, 1936, in Archivo Histórico Provincial de Las Tunas, Fondo 5: Cuban-American Sugar Mills Company, Exp. 456, Leg. 39.

45. Mathews to the Secretary of State, "Repatriation of Haitians and Jamaicans," Havana, August 18, 1937, in CUSDPR, reel 43.

46. Mcleod, "Undesirable Aliens," 266.

47. On the alliance between Batista and the Communist Party of Cuba, see Whitney, *State and Revolution in Cuba*, chapter 7; Argote-Freyre, *Fulgencio Batista*, chapter 13; Simms, "Cuban Labor and the Communist Party, 1937–1958: An Interpretation," 43–58; García Montes and Alonso Ávila, *Historia del partido comunista de Cuba*; Goldenberg, "The Rise and Fall of a Party: The Cuban CP (1925–59)," 61–80. On the Communist Party's justification of its position, as well as its silence on the treatment of foreign labor, see Roca, *Por la igualdad de todos los cubanos*, and Roca, *Las experiencias de Cuba*.

48. For an informative contemporary analysis of the Cuban labor movement, see United States Office of Strategic Services, *The Political Significance and Influence of the Labor Movement in Latin America: A Preliminary Survey: Cuba*, Washington, D.C., September 18, 1945, R&A, no. 3,076.1. For a contemporary communist perspective, see Roca and Peña, *La colaboración entre obreros y patrones*. Also see Riera Hernández, *Historial obrero cubano, 1574–1965*; Sims, "Cuban Labor and the Communist Party, 1937–1958: An Interpretation," 43–58; and Sims, "Collapse of the House of Labor: Ideological Divisions in the Cuban Labor Movement," 123–47.

49. This is not to say that Haitians and their descendants have not had a large impact on Cuban—and especially eastern Cuban—society. We certainly know that many local religious ceremonies, patterns of dress, musical forms, and colloquial expressions have their origins in Haitian culture. But much more research is required if we are going to get a better picture of the Haitian influence in Cuba. An excellent, if short, study is Espronceda Amor, *Parentesco, inmigración y comunidad: Una visión del caso haitiano*. Also see Gómez Navia, "Lo Haitiano en lo Cubano."

50. The question of the relationship between West Indians as British subjects and the British Empire will be dealt with at length in Whitney, *Caribbean Connections*.

51. Questions for Discussion with the Foreign Office at Meeting on the 20th of October, 1943, NA/CO/318/453/14.

52. Repatriation of British West Indians: "British West Indian Relief in Cuba, Santo Domingo, and Hayti," by M. E. Vibert, Consular Department, Foreign Office, January 14, 1948, NA/FO/369/3962/117907.

53. British Vice-Consulate (Neil Hone), Santiago de Cuba, to the British Embassy, Havana, April 20, 1950, NA/FO/369/4363.

54. For some observations on this issue, see Álvarez Martens, "La Constitución de 1940 es una lección de madurez nacional"; International Bank for Reconstruction and Development, *Report on Cuba*; Pérez-Stable, *The Cuban Revolution: Origins, Course, and Legacy*.

55. For some observations on this theme, see Cooper, "Empire Multiplied," 247–72; Cooper and Stoler, eds., *Tensions of Empire: Colonial Cultures in a Bourgeois World*; and Calhoun, Cooper, and Moore, eds., *Lessons of Empire: Imperial Histories and American Power*.

BIBLIOGRAPHY

Abdala Franco, Jorge. "El club rotario de Santiago de Cuba (1950–1960)." MA thesis, Universidad de Oriente, 2003.
Academia de la Historia de Cuba. *Constituciones de la República de Cuba*. Havana: Artes Gráficas S.A., 1952.
Acevedo Laborde, René. *Manual Rotario*. Havana: Rambla Bouza, 1925.
Agramonte, Arístedes. "Notas acerca de la pasteurización de la leche." *Anales*, t. 50 (1913–14): 903–11.
Aguilar, Luis E. "Cuba, 1860–1934." In *The Cambridge History of Latin America*. Edited by Leslie Bethel. Vol. 5. New York: Cambridge University Press, 1984–2008.
Aguilar, Luis E. *Cuba 1933: Prologue to Revolution*. Ithaca, NY: Cornell University Press, 1972.
Alienes y Urosa, Julián. *Características fundamentales de la economía cubana*. Havana: Banco Nacional de Cuba, 1950.
Alienes y Urosa, Julián. *La economía nacional de Cuba*. Havana: Cámara de Comercio, 1943.
Almodóvar Muñoz, Carmen. *Antología crítica de la historiografía cubana (período neocolonial)*. Havana: Pueblo y Educación, 1989.
Altshuler, José, and Roberto Díaz, eds. *El teléfono en Cuba, 1849–1959*. Havana: Sociedad Cubana de Historia de la Ciencia y la Tecnología, 2004.
Alvarez, Manuel A. "A History of Cuban Broadcasting." http://www.oldradio.com/archives/international/cuban.html, accessed April 20, 2010.
Álvarez Estévez, Rolando. *Azúcar e inmigración, 1900–1940*. Havana: Ciencias Sociales, 1988.
Álvarez Estévez, Rolando. *Isla de Pinos y el tratado Hay-Quesada*. Havana: Editorial de Ciencias Sociales, 1973.
Álvarez Martens, Berta. "La Constitución de 1940 es una lección de madurez nacional: El período 1935–1940 en la historia de Cuba." In *La imaginación contra la norma: Ocho enfoces sobre la república de 1902*. Edited by Julio César Guanche. Havana: Editorial L Memoria, Centro Cultural Pablo de la Torriente Brau, 2001.

Anderson, Benedict. *Imagined Communities: Reflections on the Origins and Spread of Nationalism.* New York: Verso, 1991.

Anderson, Benedict. *Under Three Flags: Anarchism and the Anti-colonial Imagination.* New York: Verso, 2005.

Anderson, Warwick. *Colonial Pathologies: American Tropical Medicine, Race, and Hygiene in the Philippines.* Durham, NC: Duke University Press, 2006.

Andrews, George Reid. "Black Workers in the Export Years: Latin America, 1880–1930." *International Labor and Working-Class History* 51 (spring 1997): 7–29.

Añorga, Joaquín. "El rotarismo en Cuba: Su origen, sus características y sus obras." In *Libro de Cuba* [Talleres litográficos de Artes Gráficas], 1954: 951–52.

Arencibia, Roberto Luis. "Emeterio Santovenia: El historiador pinareño olvidado por la historia." *Revista Vitral* 12, no. 71 (January/February 2006): 7–8.

Argote-Freyre, Frank. *Fulgencio Batista.* New Brunswick, NJ: Rutgers University Press, 2006.

Armas, Ramón de. *La revolución pospuesta.* Havana: Ciencias Sociales, 1975.

Arnheim, Rudolf. *Radio.* London: Faber and Faber, 1936.

Arrendondo, Alberto. *Cuba, tierra indefensa.* Havana: Editorial Lex, 1945.

Atkins, Edwin F. *Sixty Years in Cuba.* New York: Arno Press, 1980.

Averill, Gage. "Ballad Hunting in the Black Republic: Alan Lomax in Haiti, 1936–37." *Caribbean Studies* 36, no. 2 (July–December 2008): 3–22.

Ayala, César J. *American Sugar Kingdom: The Plantation Economy of the Spanish Caribbean, 1898–1934.* Chapel Hill: University of North Carolina Press, 1999.

Baily, Samuel L., and Eduardo José Míguez, eds. *Mass Migration to Modern Latin America.* Willimington, DE: Scholarly Resources, 2003.

Balboa, Imilcy. "La herencia de la tierra: Antiguos y nuevos conflictos en torno a la propiedad. Cuba 1898–1920." *Op. Cit.* 15 (Puerto Rico, 2004): 123–54.

Balboa, Imilcy. *Los brazos necesarios: Inmigración, colonización y trabajo libre en Cuba, 1878–1898.* Valencia, Spain: Biblioteca de Historia Social, 2000.

Barcia, María del Carmen. *Capas populares y modernidad en Cuba (1878–1930).* Havana: La Fuente Viva, Fundación Fernando Ortiz, 2005.

Barickman, Bert. *Bahian Counterpoint: Sugar, Tobacco, Cassava, and Slavery in the Recôncavo, 1780–1860.* Palo Alto, CA: Stanford University Press, 1998.

Barkley Brown, Elsa. "Negotiating and Transforming the Public Sphere: African American Political Life in the Transition from Slavery to Freedom." *Public Culture* 7, no. 1 (1994) 107–46.

Benchimol, Jaime. *Dos micróbios aos mosquitos: Febre amarela e a revoluçao pasteuriana no Brasil.* Rio de Janeiro: Editora Fiocruz, 1999.

Bergad, Laird W., Fe Iglesias García, and María del Carmen Barcia. *The Cuban Slave Market, 1790–1880.* New York: Cambridge University Press, 1995.

Berlin, Ira, et al. *Slaves No More: Three Essays on Emancipation and the Civil War.* Cambridge: Cambridge University Press, 1992.

Bethell, Leslie, and Ian Roxborough, eds. *Latin America between the Second World War and the Cold War, 1944–1948.* Cambridge: Cambridge University Press, 1992.

Bogart, Michele H. "Maine Memorial and Pulitzer Fountain: A Study in Patronage and Process." *Winterthur Portfolio* 21, no. 1 (spring 1986): 41–63.

Bordería, Enric, Antonio Laguna, and Francesc A. Martínez Gallego. *Historia de la comunicación social: Voces, registros y consciencias*. Madrid: Síntesis, 1996.

Bourdieu, Pierre. "Intellectual Field and Creative Project." *Journal of Social Science Information* 8, no. 2 (1969): 89–119.

Brady, Erika. *A Spiral Way: How the Phonograph Changed Ethnography*. Jackson: University Press of Mississippi, 1999.

Bronfman, Alejandra. "Clientelismo y represión: La 'Guerrita del 12' en Cienfuegos." In *Espacios, silencios y los sentidos de la libertad: Cuba, 1878–1912*. Edited by Fernando Martínez Heredia, Orlando García Martínez, and Rebecca J. Scott. Havana: Ediciones Unión, 2001.

Bronfman, Alejandra. *Measures of Equality: Social Science, Citizenship, and Race in Cuba, 1902–1940*. Chapel Hill: University of North Carolina Press, 2004.

Brown, Karen, and Daniel Gilfoyle, eds. *Healing the Herds: Disease, Livestock Economies, and the Globalization of Veterinary Medicine*. Athens: Ohio University Press.

Buell, Leslie Raymond, et al. *Problems of the New Cuba*. New York: Foreign Policy Association, 1935.

Butler, Frank. "How Radio Came to Cuba." *Radio Broadcast*, March 1925, 916–25. http://earlyradiohistory.us/cuba.htm, accessed April 29, 2010.

Cabrera, Olga. *Los que viven por sus manos*. Havana: Ciencias Sociales, 1985.

Cabrera, Raimundo. *¡Vapor correo! A comical-lyrical revue in one act and four scenes*. Music by D. Rafael Palau. Havana: Impr. El Retiro, 1888.

Cabrera, Raimundo. *Viaje a la luna. A comedy in two scenes*. Music by D. M. I. Mauri. Güines, Cuba: Impr. El Demócrata, 1885.

Cairo, Ana. *La revolución del 30 en la narrativa y el testimonio cubanos*. Havana: Editorial de Ciencias Sociales, 1993.

Calhoun, Craig, Frederick Cooper, and Kevin W. Moore, eds. *Lessons of Empire: Imperial Histories and American Power*. New York: New Press, 2006.

Cambra, Jordi de. *Anarquismo y positivismo: El caso Ferrer*. Madrid: Centro de Investigaciones Sociológicas, 1981.

Campbell, W. Joseph. *Yellow Journalism: Puncturing the Myths, Defining the Legacies*. Westport, CT: Praeger, 2003.

Cancio, Leopoldo. "Haciendas comuneras." *Cuba y América*, no. 6 (Havana, 1902): 227–36.

Cantón Blanco, Luis. *Conferencias de derecho de propiedad*. Havana: Ministerio de Educación, 1992.

Carpentier, Alejo. "Conciencia e identidad de América." In *Razón de ser*. Havana: Letras Cubanas, 2007.

Carr, Barry. "Identity, Class, and Nation: Black Immigrant Workers, Cuban Communism, and the Sugar Insurgency, 1925–1934." *Hispanic American Historical Review* 78, no. 1 (February 1998): 63–116.

Carr, Barry. "Mill Occupations and Soviets: The Mobilization of Sugar Workers in

Cuba, 1917–1933." *Journal of Latin American Studies* 28, no. 1 (February 1996): 129–58.

Carrillo, Justo. *Cuba 1933: Students, Yankees, and Soldiers*. New Brunswick, NJ: Transaction, 1994.

Carrión, Miguel. "El desenvolvimiento social de Cuba en los últimos veinte años." *Cuba Contemporánea* 27 (September 1921): 5–27.

Casanovas, Joan. "El movimiento obrero y la política colonial española en la Cuba de finales del XIX." In *La nación soñada: Cuba, Puerto Rico y Filipinas ante el 98*. Edited by Consuelo Naranjo, Miguel A. Puig Samper, and Luis García Mora, 363–75. Aranjuez, Spain: Doce Calles, 1996.

Casanovas, Joan. "La prensa obrera y la evolución ideológico-táctica del obrerismo cubano del siglo XIX." *Signos históricos*, no. 9 (January–June 2003): 13–42.

Casanovas, Joan. *¡O pan o plomo! Los trabajadores urbanos y el colonialismo español en Cuba, 1850–1898*. Madrid: Siglo XXI, 2000.

Casimir, Enver. "Champion of the *Patria*: Kid Chocolate, Athletic Achievement, and the Significance of Race for Cuban National Aspiration." PhD diss., University of North Carolina, 2010.

Caveda Romaní, Edita. *Las sociedades filarmónicas habaneras (1824–1844)*. Havana: Instituto Cubano de Investigación Cultural Juan Marinello, 2009.

Celorio, Benito. *La refacción: Comentarios a la Ley de Refacción Agrícola de Colonato y de Molienda de Cañas*. Havana: Librería Cervantes de Ricardo Veloso, 1922.

Celorio, Benito. *Las haciendas comuneras*. Havana: Imprenta de Rambla y Bouza, 1914.

Censo de la República de Cuba, año de 1919. Havana: Maza, Arroyo y Caso Impresores, 1919.

Censo de la República de Cuba bajo la administración provisional de los Estados Unidos, 1907. Washington, DC: Office of the Census, 1908.

Chailloux, Graciela, and Robert Whitney, "British Subjects y Pichones en Cuba." In *¿De Dónde son los cubanos?* Edited by Graciela Chailloux Laffita. Havana: Editorial de Ciencias Sociales, 2007.

Chailloux Carmona, Juan M. *Los horrores del solar habanero* [1945]. Havana: Ciencias Sociales, 2005.

Chamber of Representatives. *Compendio legislativo, 1902 a 1950*. Havana: Impr. Modelo, 1950.

Chanan, Michael. *Cuban Cinema*. Minneapolis: University of Minnesota Press, 2004.

Chang, Federico. *El Ejército Nacional en la República neocolonial, 1899–1933*. Havana: Ciencias Sociales, 1981.

Chang, Federico. "Reajustes para la estabilización del sistema neocolonial." In Instituto de Historia de Cuba, *Historia de Cuba: La neocolonia*, 3:337–38. Havana: Editora Política, 1994–98.

Chapman, Charles. *A History of the Cuban Republic: A Study in Hispanic American Politics*. New York: Macmillan, 1927.

Chomsky, Aviva. "The Aftermath of Repression: Race and Nation in Cuba after 1912." *Journal of Iberian and Latin American Studies* 4, no. 2 (December 1998): 1–40.

Chomsky, Aviva. "'Barbados or Canada?' Race, Immigration, and Nation in Early Twentieth-Century Cuba." *Hispanic American Historical Review* 80, no. 3 (August 2000): 415–62.

Clark, Lombillo. "Obras públicas." In *Impresiones de la República de Cuba en el siglo xx. Historia, gente, comercio, industria y riqueza*. London: Lloyd's Greater Britain, 1913.

Clark, Victor S. "Labor Conditions in Cuba." *Bulletin of the Department of Labor* 41 (July 1902): 780.

Club Rotario de la Habana. *Actividades desarrolladas durante el presente año por el Club Rotario de La Habana en conjunción con otras entidades para la solución del problema del abasto de agua a la ciudad*. Havana: Imp. Otero Hnos., 1924.

Club Rotario de la Habana. *Haciendo patria: Conferencias sobre nuestros problemas educacionales, pronunciadas en el Club Rotario de La Habana durante el período social de 1924 a 1925*. Havana: Imp. Otero Hnos., 1925.

Collins, George R. "The Transfer of Thin Masonry Vaulting from Spain to America." *Journal of the Society of Architectural Historians* 27, no. 3 (October 1968): 176–201.

Commission on Cuban Affairs. *Problems of the New Cuba*. New York: Foreign Policy Association, 1935.

Cooper, Frederick. "Empire Multiplied." *Comparative Studies in Society and History* 46 (2004): 247–72.

Cooper, Frederick, Thomas Holt, and Rebecca J. Scott. *Beyond Slavery: Explorations of Race, Labor, and Citizenship in Postemancipation Societies*. Chapel Hill: University of North Carolina Press, 2000.

Cooper, Frederick, and Ann Stoler, eds. *Tensions of Empire: Colonial Cultures in a Bourgeois World*. Berkeley: University of California Press, 1997.

Cosculluela, Juan A. *La Salubridad Urbana: Con especial referencia a la ciudad de La Habana*. Havana: Imp. Compostela y Chacón, 1925.

Dacal, Ramón, and M. Rivero de la Calle. *Arqueología aborigen en Cuba*. Havana: Editorial de Ciencias Sociales, 1986.

Danielson, Ross. *Cuban Medicine*. Rutgers, NJ: Transaction, 1978.

Deerr, Noel. *The History of Sugar*. London: Chapman and Hall, 1950.

Delaporte, François. *The History of Yellow Fever: An Essay on the Birth of Tropical Medicine*. Cambridge, MA: MIT Press, 1991.

Delfín, Manuel. *Treinta años de médico*. Havana: Imprenta La Propagandista, 1909–1910.

Delgado, Buenaventura. *La escuela moderna de Ferrer i Guardia*. Barcelona: Ediciones CEAC, 1979.

Díaz-Arguelles, Nancy. *El Laboratorio Histobacteriológico e Instituto de Vacunación Antirrábica*. Havana: Centro de Estudios de Historia y Organización de la Ciencia "Carlos J. Finlay," 1988.

Díaz del Moral, Juan. *Historia de las agitaciones campesinas andaluzas: Córdoba (Antecedentes para una reforma agraria)*. Madrid: Alianza Editorial, 1984.

Díaz Quiñones, Arcadio. "El enemigo íntimo: Cultura nacional y autoridad en Ramiro Guerra y Sánchez y Antonio S. Pedreira." *Op. Cit. Boletín del Centro de Investigaciones Históricas* 7 (1992): 9–65.

Diccionario Enciclopédico UTEHA. Mexico City: Unión Tipográfica Editorial Hispano-Americana [1952] 1968.

Dorta, Manuel. *Curso de legislación hipotecaria*. Havana: Ed. Verdugo, 1938.

Dumoulin, John. "El primer desarrollo del movimiento obrero y la formación del proletariado en el sector azucarero: Cruces, 1886–1902." *Islas: Revista de la Universidad de las Villas* 48 (1974).

Dye, Alan. *Cuban Sugar in the Age of Mass Production: Technology and the Economics of the Sugar Central, 1899–1929*. Palo Alto, CA: Stanford University Press, 1998.

Edo, Enrique. *Memoria histórica de Cienfuegos y su jurisdicción*. 3rd ed. Havana: Ucar, García, 1943.

Eggert, Gerald G. "Our Man in Havana: Fitzhugh Lee." *Hispanic American Historical Review* 47, no. 4 (November 1967).

Eiss, Paul. "A Share in the Land: Freedpeople and the Government of Labor in Southern Louisiana, 1862–1865." *Slavery and Abolition* 19, no. 1 (1998): 46–89.

Ely, Roland T. *Cuando reinaba su majestad el azúcar*. Buenos Aires: Editorial Sudamericana, 1963.

Enciclopedia Universal Ilustrada Europeo-Americana. Barcelona: Espasa-Calpe, 1925.

Espinosa, Mariola. *Epidemic Invasions: Yellow Fever and the Limits of Cuban Independence*. Chicago: University of Chicago Press, 2009.

Espronceda Amor, María Eugenia. *Parentesco, inmigración y comunidad: Una visión del caso haitiano*. Guantánamo: Editorial El Mar y la Montaña, 2001.

Estrade, Paul. *La colonia cubana de París, 1895–98: El combate patriótico de Betances y la solidaridad de los revolucionarios franceses*. Havana: Editorial de Ciencias Sociales, 1984.

Fariñas Borrego, Maikel. "El asociacionismo náutico en La Habana: Las prácticas socioculturales observadas desde las élites hasta las capas populares (1886–1958)." *Revista Esboços, Revista do Programa de Pós-Graduação em História da UFSC* 16, no. 21 (Florianópolis, Brazil: UFSC, 2009): 137–57.

Fariñas Borrego, Maikel. *Sociabilidad y cultura del ocio: Las élites habaneras y sus clubes de recreo (1902–1930)*. Havana: La Fuente Viva, Fundación Fernando Ortiz, 2009.

Farley, John. *Bilharzia: A History of Imperial Tropical Medicine*. London: Cambridge University Press, 1991.

Fernández Benítez, José A. "Instituciones científicas creadas en Cuba con posterioridad a la guerra de independencia: Datos históricos." *Anales de la Academia de Ciencias Médicas, Físicas y Naturales de la Habana* 51 (1914–1915).

Fernández, Frank. *El anarquismo en Cuba*. Madrid: Fundación de Estudios Libertarios Anselmo Lorenzo, 2000.

Fernández Losada, Cesáreo. *Consideraciones higiénicas sobre la ciudad de La Habana.* Havana: Imprenta El Fígaro, 1896.
Fernández Prieto, Leída, and Armando García González. "Ciencia." In *Historia de Cuba.* Edited by Consuelo Naranjo Orovio, 475–504. Madrid: Consejo Superior de Investigaciones Científicas, 2009.
Fernández Robaina, Tomás. *El negro en Cuba, 1902–1958: Apuntes para la historia de la lucha contra la discriminación racial.* Havana: Editorial de las Ciencias Sociales, 1990.
Ferrer, Ada. *Insurgent Cuba: Race, Nation, and Revolution, 1868–98.* Chapel Hill: University of North Carolina Press, 1999.
Ferrer, Ada. "Rustic Men, Civilized Nation: Race, Culture, and Convention on the Eve of Cuban Independence." *Hispanic American Historical Review* 78, no. 4 (November 1998): 663–86.
Figarola, Joel James. *Cuba, 1900–1928: La república dividida contra sí misma.* Havana: Universidad de Oriente, 1996.
Foner, Eric. *Reconstruction: America's Unfinished Revolution, 1863–1877.* New York: Harper and Row, 1988.
Fox, Jon E., and Cynthia Miller-Idriss. "Everyday Nationhood." *Ethnicities* 8, no. 4 (April 2008): 536–63.
Fradera, Josep María. "Quiebra imperial y reorganización política en las Antillas españolas, 1810–1868." In *El Caribe entre imperios: Op. Cit.: Revista del Centro de Investigaciones Históricas* 9. Edited by Arcadio Díaz Quiñones, 189–316. Río Piedras: 1997.
Fraga Filho, Walter. *Encruzilhadas da Liberdade: Histórias de Escravos e Libertos na Bahia (1870–1910).* Campinas, Brazil: Editora Unicamp, 2006.
Franqui, Carlos. *Retrato de familia con Fidel.* Barcelona: Seix Barral, 1981.
Frucht, Richard. "A Caribbean Social Type: Neither 'Peasant' nor 'Proletarian.'" *Social and Economic Studies* 13, no. 3 (1967): 295–300.
Fuente, Alejandro de la. "Los mitos de la democracia racial, Cuba 1900–1912." In *Espacios, silencios y los sentidos de la libertad: Cuba, 1878–1912.* Edited by Fernando Martínez Heredia, Orlando García Martínez, and Rebecca J. Scott. Havana: Ediciones Unión, 2001.
Fuente, Alejandro de la. "Myths of Racial Democracy: Cuba, 1900–1912." *Latin American Research Review* 34, no. 3 (1999): 39–73.
Fuente, Alejandro de la. *A Nation for All: Race, Inequality, and Politics in Twentieth-Century Cuba.* Chapel Hill: University of North Carolina Press, 2001.
Fuente, Alejandro de la. "Negros y electores: desigualdad y políticas raciales en Cuba, 1900–1930." In *La nación soñada: Cuba, Puerto Rico y Filipinas ante el 98.* Edited by Consuelo Naranjo, Miguel A. Puig Samper, and Luis García Mora. Aranjuez, Spain: Doce Calles, 1996.
Funes, Reinaldo. "El *boom* azucarero durante la Primera Guerra Mundial y su impacto sobre zonas boscosas de Cuba." In *Cuba: de colonia a república.* Edited by Martín Rodrigo, 225–45. Madrid: Biblioteca Nueva, 2006.

Funes, Reinaldo. *Despertar del asociacionismo científico en Cuba, 1876–1920*. Havana: Centro de Investigación y Desarrollo de la Cultura Juan Marinello, 2005.
Funes, Reinaldo, coord. *Naturaleza en declive*. Valencia, Spain: UNED, 2008.
Gallini, Stefania. "De razas y de carne: Veterinarios y discursos expertos en la historia de la producción y consumo de carne en Colombia de la primera mitad del siglo XX." In *El poder de la carne: Historias de ganaderías en la primera mitad del siglo XX*. Edited by Alberto G. Flórez-Malagón, 290–337. Bogotá: Editorial Pontificia Universidad Javeriana, 2008.
García, Afrânio, Jr. *Libres et assujettis: Marché du travail et modes de domination au Nordeste*. Paris: Editions de la Maison des Sciences de l'Homme, 1989.
García Alvarez, Alejandro. "Estructuras de una economía colonial en transición." In *La nación soñada: Cuba, Puerto Rico y Filipinas*. Edited by Consuelo Naranjo, Miguel A. Puig-Samper, and Luis Miguel García, 195–210. Madrid: Doce Calles, 1996.
García Blanco, Rolando, et al. *Cien figuras de la ciencia en Cuba*. Havana: Editorial Científico-Técnica, 2002.
García Carranza, Araceli. *Bio-bibliografía de Don Fernando Ortiz*. Havana: Instituto del Libro, 1976.
García Carranza, Araceli. "Breve Biobibliografía del doctor Ramiro Guerra." *Revista de la Biblioteca Nacional "José Martí"* 14, no. 1 (January–April 1972): 141–99.
García del Real, Eduardo. *Historia de la medicina en España*. Madrid: Editorial Reus, 1921.
García González, Armando, and Raquel Álvarez Peláez. *En busca de la raza perfecta: Eugenesia e higiene en Cuba (1898–1958)*. Madrid: CSIC, 1999.
García Martínez, Orlando. "La Brigada de Cienfuegos: Un análisis social de su formación." In *Espacios, silencios y los sentidos de la libertad: Cuba, 1878–1912*. Edited by Fernando Martínez Heredia, Orlando García Martínez, and Rebecca J. Scott. Havana: Ediciones Unión, 2001.
García Martínez, Orlando, and Irán Millán Cuétara. "Estudio de la economía cienfueguera desde la fundación de la colonia Fernandina de Jagua hasta mediados del siglo XIX." *Islas* 55–56 (September 1976–April 1977).
García Martínez, Orlando, and Irán Millán Cuétara. "Testimonios del quehacer constructivo en la industria azucarera cienfueguera." Paper presented to the I Coloquio Internacional: El Patrimonio Cultural de la Ciudad Iberoamericana del Siglo XIX, Cienfuegos, 1996.
García Montes, Jorge, and Antonio Alonso Ávila. *Historia del partido comunista de Cuba*. Miami: Editorial Universal, 1970.
García Mora, Luis Miguel, and Consuelo Naranjo Orovio. "Intelectualidad criolla y nación en Cuba, 1878–1898." *Studia Histórica; Historia contemporánea* 15 (1997): 115–34.
Gelfand, Toby. "11 January 1887, the Day Medicine Changed: Joseph Grancher's Defense of Pasteur's Treatment for Rabies." *Bulletin of the History of Medicine* 76, no. 4 (2002): 698–718.

Giovannetti, Jorge L. "Black British Subjects in Cuba: Race, Ethnicity, Nation, and Identity in the Migration Experience." PhD diss., University of London, 2001.

Giovannetti, Jorge L. "The Elusive Organization of 'Identity': Race, Religion, and Empire among Caribbean Migrants in Cuba." *Small Axe* 10, no. 1 (February 2006): 1–27.

Gitelman, Lisa, and Geoffrey Pingree. "Introduction: What's New about New Media?" In *New Media, 1740–1915*. Edited by Lisa Gitelman and Geoffrey Pingree. Cambridge, MA: MIT Press, 2003.

Goldenberg, Bonnie. "Imperial Culture and National Conscience: The Role of the Press in the United States and Spain during the Crisis of 1898." *Bulletin of Hispanic Studies* 77 (July 2000): 169–91.

Goldenberg, Boris. "The Rise and Fall of a Party: The Cuban CP (1925–59)." *Problems of Communism* 19, no. 4 (July–August 1970): 61–80.

Gómez, José R. *Historia, deslinde y reparto de haciendas comuneras*. Santa Clara, Cuba: Imprenta J. Berenguer, 1910.

Gómez Navia, Raimundo. "Lo Haitiano en lo Cubano." In *¿De Dónde son los cubanos?* Edited by Graciela Chailloux Laffita. Havana: Editorial de Ciencias Sociales, 2007.

Gonzalez, Joseph J. "The Cause of Civilization: The United States Experience with Nation-Building in Cuba, 1898–1909." PhD diss., University of Michigan, 2002.

González, Reynaldo. *La Fiesta de los Tiburones*. Havana: Editorial de Ciencias Sociales, 1978.

González, Reynaldo. *Llorar es un placer*. Havana: Editorial Letras Cubanas, 2002.

Gorin, George. *History of Ophthalmology*. Wilmington, DE: Publish or Perish, 1982.

Graham, Richard. *Patronage and Politics in Nineteenth-Century Brazil*. Palo Alto, CA: Stanford University Press, 1990.

Gramsci, Antonio. *Selections from the Prison Notebooks*. London: Lawrence and Wishart, 1971.

Guerra López, Dolores. *El legado social de los españoles en Cuba*. Vigo, Spain: Grupo de Comunicación Galicia en el Mundo, 2008.

Guerra y Sánchez, Ramiro. *Azúcar y población en las Antillas*. Havana: Cultural, 1927; reprint, Ciencias Sociales, 1976.

Guerra y Sánchez, Ramiro. *Un cuarto de siglo de evolución cubana*. Havana: Librería Cervantes, 1924.

Guerra y Sánchez, Ramiro. *La Defensa nacional y la escuela*. Havana: Librería Cervantes, 1923.

Guerra y Sánchez, Ramiro. *En el camino de la independencia*. Havana: Cultural, 1930.

Guerra y Sánchez, Ramiro. *La expansión territorial de los Estados Unidos a expensas de España y de los países hispanoamericanos*. Havana: Cultural, 1935; reprint, Ciencias Sociales, 1975.

Guerra y Sánchez, Ramiro. *Guerra de los Diez Años, 1868–1878*. Havana: Cultural, 1950–1952.

Guerra y Sánchez, Ramiro. *Historia de la Nación Cubana*. Havana: Editorial Historia de la Nación Cubana, 1952.

Guerra y Sánchez, Ramiro. *Historia Elemental de Cuba (Escuelas Primarias Superiores, Preparatorias y Normales)*. Havana: Librería Cervantes, 1922.

Guerra y Sánchez, Ramiro. *La industria azucarera de Cuba, su importancia nacional su organización, sus mercados y su situación actual*. Havana: Cultural S.A., 1935.

Guerra y Sánchez, Ramiro. *Introducción a la historia de la colonización española en América: Fascículo primero*. Havana: Cultural, 1930.

Guerra y Sánchez, Ramiro. *La lección en la Escuela Primaria*. Havana: Imprenta Cuba Pedagógica, 1913.

Guerra y Sánchez, Ramiro. *Manual de Historia de Cuba*. Havana: Cultural, 1938.

Guerra y Sánchez, Ramiro. *Sugar and Society in the Caribbean: An Economic History of Cuban Agriculture*. New Haven, CT: Yale University Press, 1964.

Guiteras, Juan. "Consideraciones generales." *Revista de Medicina Tropical* 1, no. 1 (1900): 3–4.

Guiteras, Juan. "Estudios demográficos." *Revista bimestre cubana* 8, no. 6 (November/December 1913): 405–21.

Guiteras, Juan. "Prefacio." *Revista de Medicina Tropical* 1, no. 1 (1900): 1.

Gutiérrez Lanza, Mariano. *El mago del siglo veinte*. Havana, 1936.

Gutiérrez Vega, Zenaida. *José María Chacón y Calvo, hispanista cubano*. Madrid: Ediciones de Cultura Hispánica, 1969.

Hahn, Emily. *Eve and the Apes*. New York: Weidenfeld and Nicolson, 1988.

Haraway, Donna. *Primate Visions: Gender, Race, and Nature in the World of Modern Science*. New York: Routledge, 1989.

Haring, Kristen. *Ham Radio's Technical Culture*. Cambridge, MA: MIT Press, 2006.

Harvey, David. *Spaces of Hope*. Berkeley: University of California Press, 2000.

Helg, Aline. *Our Rightful Share: The Afro-Cuban Struggle for Equality, 1886–1912*. Chapel Hill: University of North Carolina Press, 1995.

Hernández Godoy, Silvia Teresita. "Arqueología e historiografía aborigen de Cuba en el siglo XIX." *Anales del Museo de América*, no. 11 (2003): 177–96.

Hernández Godoy, Silvia Teresita. "La primera década del siglo XX y el desarrollo de la Arqueología en la Isla." *El Caribe Arqueológico*, no. 9 (2006): 2–8.

Hevia Lanier, Oilda. *El directorio central de las sociedades negras de Cuba, 1886–1894*. Havana: Ed. de Ciencias Sociales, 1996.

Hilmes, Michele. *Network Nations: A Transnational History of British and American Broadcasting*. New York: Routledge, 2011.

Hirschberg, Julius. Geschichte der augenheilkunde. Bonn: n.p., 1982–94.

Hirschkind, Charles. *The Ethical Soundscape: Cassette Sermons and Islamic Counterpublics*. New York: Columbia University Press, 2006.

Hirschman, Albert O. *Exit, Voice, and Loyalty: Responses to Decline in Firms, Organizations, and States*. Cambridge, MA: Harvard University Press, 1970.

Hirschman, Albert O. *A Propensity to Self-Subversion*. Cambridge, MA: Harvard University Press, 1995.

Hoernel, Robert. "Sugar and Social Change in Oriente, 1898–1946." *Journal of Latin American Studies* 8, no. 2 (1976): 215–48.

Holt, Thomas. "Slavery and Freedom in the Atlantic World: Reflections on the Diasporan Framework." In *Crossing Boundaries: Comparative History of Black People in Diaspora*. Edited by Darlene Clark Hine and Jacqueline McLeod, 33–44. Bloomington: Indiana University Press, 1999.
Ibarra Cuesta, Jorge. "Caciquismo, racismos y actitudes con relación al status político de la República, 1906–1909." In *Espacios, silencios y los sentidos de la libertad: Cuba, 1878–1912*. Edited by Fernando Martínez Heredia, Orlando García Martínez, and Rebecca J. Scott. Havana: Ediciones Unión, 2001.
Ibarra Cuesta, Jorge. *Cuba, 1898–1921: Partidos políticos y clases sociales*. Havana: Ciencias Sociales, 1992.
Ibarra Cuesta, Jorge. *Cuba, 1898–1958: Estructura y procesos sociales*. Havana: Ciencias Sociales, 1995.
Ibarra Cuesta, Jorge. *Ideología mambisa*. Havana: Instituto Cubano del Libro, 1972.
Ibarra Cuesta, Jorge. *Nación y cultura nacional*. Havana: Letras Cubanas, 1981.
Ibarra Cuesta, Jorge. "La Sociedad cubana en las tres primeras décadas del siglo XX." In Instituto de Historia de Cuba, *Historia de Cuba: La neocolonia*, 3:164–66. Havana: Editora Política, 1994–98.
Ibarra Cuesta, Jorge. *Un análisis psicosocial del cubano, 1898–1925*. Havana: Editorial de Ciencias Sociales, 1985.
Ibarra Guitart, Jorge Renato. *El fracaso de los moderados en Cuba: Las alternativas reformistas de 1957 a 1958*. Havana: Editorial Política, 2000.
Ibarra Guitart, Jorge Renato. *Sociedad de Amigos de la República: Historia de una mediación*. Havana: Editorial Ciencias Sociales, 2003.
Iglesias García, Fe. "La concentración azucarera y la comarca de Cienfuegos." In *Espacios, silencios y los sentidos de la libertad: Cuba, 1878–1912*. Edited by Fernando Martínez Heredia, Orlando García Martínez, and Rebecca J. Scott. Havana: Ediciones Unión, 2001.
Iglesias Utset, Marial. *A Cultural History of Cuba during the U.S. Occupation, 1898–1902*. Chapel Hill: University of North Carolina Press, 2011.
Iglesias Utset, Marial. *Las metáforas del cambio en la vida cotidiana: Cuba 1898–1902*. Havana: Editorial Unión, 2003.
Informe sobre el Censo de Cuba, 1899: Cuba Gobernador Militar, 1899–1902 (Civil Report 1899–1900). Vol. 7. Havana, 1901.
Instituto de Historia de Cuba. *Historia de Cuba: La neocolonia. Organización y crisis, desde 1899 hasta 1940*. Vol. 3. Havana: Editora Política, 1998.
Instituto de Historia del Movimiento Comunista y la Revolución Socialista de Cuba. *Historia de movimiento obrero cubano, 1865–1958*. 2 vols. Havana: Editora Política, 1985.
Instituto de Literatura y Lingüística de la Academia de Ciencias de Cuba. *Diccionario de la Literatura Cubana*. Vol. 1. Havana: Letras Cubanas, 1980.
International Association of Rotary Clubs. *Seventh Annual Convention of the International Association of Rotary Clubs*. Chicago, 1916.

International Bank for Reconstruction and Development. *Report on Cuba*. Washington, DC: International Bank for Reconstruction and Development, 1951.
Jenks, Leland H. *Nuestra colonia de Cuba*. Havana: Ediciones Revolucionarias, 1966.
Jenks, Leland H. *Our Cuban Colony: A Study in Sugar*. New York: Vanguard Press, 1928.
Jiménez, Juan Bautista. *Los esclavos blancos por un colono de Las Villas*. Havana: Impr. de A. Alvarez y Cía., 1893.
Jones, Maldwyn A. *Historia de Estados Unidos, 1607–1992*. Madrid: Cátedra, 1995.
Kapcia, Antoni. *Cuba: Island of Dreams*. New York: Berg, 2000.
Klein, John-Marshall. "Spaniards and the Politics of Memory in Cuba, 1898–1934." PhD diss., University of Texas, 2002.
Knight, Franklin W. *The Caribbean: The Genesis of a Fragmented Nationalism*. Oxford: Oxford University Press, 1990.
Knight, Franklin W. "Jamaican Migrants and the Cuban Sugar Industry, 1900–1934." In *Between Slavery and Free Labor: The Spanish-Speaking Caribbean in the Nineteenth Century*. Edited by Manuel Moreno Fraginals, Frank Moya Pons, and Stanley L. Engerman, 94–114. Baltimore: Johns Hopkins University Press, 1985.
Laboratorio de la Isla de Cuba. *Informe de los trabajos realizados en la isla de Cuba*. Havana: Imprenta de Rambla y Bouza, 1905.
Lara, María Julia de. "Laura Martínez de Carvajal y del Camino." *Cuadernos de Historia de la Salud* 28 (1964).
Latour, Bruno. *Reassembling the Social: An Introduction to Actor-Network-Theory*. New York: Oxford University Press, 2005.
Lázaro, Luis M. *Las escuelas racionalistas en el País Valenciano (1906–1931)*. Valencia, Spain: Nau, 1992.
Lázaro, Luis M. *Prensa racionalista y educación en España (1901–1932)*. Valencia, Spain: Universidad de Valencia, 1995.
Lee, Paula Young, ed. *Meat, Modernity, and the Rise of the Slaughterhouse*. Durham: University of New Hampshire Press, 2008.
Legout, Sandra. *La famille pasteurienne: Le personnel scientifique permanent de l'Institut Pasteur de Paris entre 1889 et 1914*. Memoire de DEA, 1999.
Legueu, Félix. *Albarran, Joachin (1860–1912)*. Paris: J.-B. Baillière et Fils, 1938.
Lejeune, Jean-Francois, John Beusterien, and Narciso G. Menocal. "The City as Landscape: Jean Claude Nicolas Forestier and the Great Urban Works of Havana, 1925–1930." *Journal of Decorative and Propaganda Arts* 22, Cuba Theme Issue (1996): 174–76.
Le Roy y Cassá, Jorge. "Homenaje al Dr. Juan Santos Fernández." *Anales de la Academia de Ciencias Médicas, Físicas y Naturales* 54 (1917): 194–95.
Le Roy y Cassá, Jorge. "Sanidad pública." In *Impresiones de la República de Cuba en el siglo XX: Historia, gente, comercio, industria y riqueza*, 139–41. London: Lloyd's Greater Britain, 1913.
Le Roy y Cassá, Jorge. "Ubicación social de los ocho estudiantes fusilados en 1871."

In *Dos conferencias sobre el 27 de noviembre de 1871*. Havana: Centro de Información Científica y Técnica, Universidad de la Habana, 1975.

Le Roy y Gálvez, Jorge F. *La inocencia de los estudiantes fusilados en 1871*. Havana: Centro de Información Científica y Técnica, Universidad de la Habana, 1971.

Lévi-Strauss, Claude. *Tristes trópicos*. 2nd ed. Buenos Aires: Eudeba, 1973.

Lida, Clara. *Anarquismo y revolución en la España del XIX*. Madrid: Siglo XXI, 1972.

Litvak, Lily. "La prensa anarquista." In *El anarquismo español y sus tradiciones culturales*. Edited by Bert Hofmann, Joan Pere, and Manfred Tietz, 215–36. Madrid: Vervuert-Iberoamericana, 1995.

Lloyd, Reginald. *Impresiones de la República de Cuba en el siglo XX: Historia, gente, comercio, industria y riqueza*. London: Lloyd's Greater Britain, 1913.

López, Oscar Luis. *La radio en Cuba*. Havana: Editorial Letras Cubanas, 1998.

López Civeira, Francisca. *Cuba entre 1899 y 1959: Seis décadas de historia*. Havana: Editorial Pueblo y Educación, 2007.

López Denis, Adrián. "Disease and Society in Colonial Cuba, 1790–1840." PhD diss., University of California, Los Angeles, 2007.

López Rivero, Sergio, and Francisco Ibarra. "En torno a 1898: Una exploración en el curso de la aprobación de la Enmienda Platt en la Convención Constituyente cubana durante el año 1901." *Millars: Espai i Història* 18 (1995): 55–66.

López Sánchez, José. *Carlos J. Finlay: His Life and His Work*. Havana: Editorial José Martí, 1999.

López Segrera, Francisco. *Raíces históricas de la revolución cubana (1868–1959)*. Havana: Ediciones Unión, 1980.

Loveira, Carlos. *Los ciegos*. Havana: Letras Cubanas, 1980.

Loveira, Carlos. *De los 26 a los 35: Lecciones de la experiencia en la lucha obrera (1908–1917)*. Washington, DC: Law Reporter Printing, 1917.

Luis, William. *Lunes de Revolución: Literatura y cultura en los primeros años de la Revolución Cubana*. Madrid: Verbum, 2003.

Lumen, Enrique. *La revolución cubana, 1902–1934*. Mexico City: Ediciones Bota, 1934.

Maceo, Antonio. *Antonio Maceo: Ideología política; Cartas y otros documentos; Edición nacional del centenario de su nacimiento, 1845–14 de junio 1945*, vol. 2: *1895–1896*. Havana: Sociedad Cubana de Estudios Históricos e Internacionales, 1952.

Maderos, Tomás. *La gestión municipal en los mataderos de La Habana*.

Maestri, Raúl. *Capitalismo y anticapitalismo*. Havana: Editorial Atalaya, 1939.

Maestri, Raúl. *El latifundismo en la economía cubana*. Havana: Ed. Hermes, 1929.

Magoon, Charles Edward. *Reports on the Law of Civil Government in Territory Subject to Military Occupation by the Military Forces of the United States*. Washington, DC: Government Printing Office, 1902.

Maluquer de Motes, Jordi. "La inmigración española en Cuba: elementos de un debate histórico." In *Cuba: La Perla de las Antillas*. Edited by Consuelo Naranjo and Tomás Mallo, 137–47. Aranjuez, Spain: Doce Calles, 1994.

Maluquer de Motes, Jordi. *Nación e inmigración: Los españoles en Cuba (ss. XIX y XX)*. Oviedo: Ediciones Júcar, 1992.

Marqués Dolz, María Antonia. *Las industrias menores: Empresarios y empresas en Cuba (1880–1920)*. Havana: Ciencias Sociales, 2006.

Marrero, Leví. *Geografía de Cuba*. 3rd ed. Havana: Editorial Selecta, 1957.

Martínez Alier, Juan and Verena. *Cuba: Economía y sociedad*. París: Ruedo Ibérico, 1972.

Martínez Ortiz, Rafael. *Cuba: Los primeros años de independencia*. 3rd ed. París: Le Livre Libre, 1929.

Martínez Viera, Rafael. *La Estación Experimental Agronómica de Santiago de las Vegas: 100 años de historia al servicio de la agricultura cubana (1904–2004)*. Havana: Editorial INIFAT, 2004.

Martínez Viera, Rafael. *Juan Tomás Roig: Hacedor del futuro*. Havana: Editorial Científico-técnica, 2009.

Marvin, Carolyn. *When Old Technologies Were New: Thinking about Electric Communication in the Late Nineteenth Century*. New York: Oxford University Press, 1988.

Marx, Leo. "Technology: The Emergence of a Hazardous Concept." *Social Research* 64, no. 3 (fall 1997): 965–88.

Mattos de Castro, Hebe Maria. "El color inexistente: Relaciones raciales y trabajo rural en Rio de Janeiro tras la abolición de la esclavitud." *Historia Social* 22 (Valencia, Spain, 1995).

Mattos de Castro, Hebe Maria. *Das cores do silêncio: os significados da liberdade no sudeste escravista–Brasil século xix*. Rio de Janeiro: Arquivo Nacional, 1995.

Mayo, James M. *War Memorials as Political Landscape: The American Experience and Beyond*. New York: Praeger, 1988.

McCook, Stuart. *States of Nature: Science, Agriculture, and Environment in the Spanish Caribbean, 1760–1940*. Austin: University of Texas Press, 2002.

McGillivray, Gillian. *Blazing Cane: Sugar Communities, Class, and State Formation in Cuba, 1868–1959*. Durham, NC: Duke University Press, 2009.

Mcleod, Marc. "Undesirable Aliens: Haitian and British West Indian Workers in Cuba, 1898–1940." PhD diss., University of Texas at Austin, 2000.

Mcleod, Marc. "Undesirable Aliens: Race, Ethnicity, and Nationalism in the Comparison of Haitian and British West Indian Workers in Cuba, 1912–1939." *Journal of Social History* 31, no. 3 (spring 1998): 599–623.

Mederos, Tomás. *La gestión municipal en los mataderos de La Habana*. Havana: El Arte, 1899.

Mena, César A. *Historia de la medicina en Cuba: Ejercicio y enseñanza de las ciencias médicas época colonial*. Miami: Ediciones Universal, 1993.

Mena Múgica, Mayra, and Severiano Hernández Vicente. *Fuentes documentales de la administración española en el Archivo Nacional de Cuba: La administración autonómica española de Cuba en 1898*. Salamanca, Spain: Ediciones University de Salamanca, 1994.

Mestre, Antonio. "La antropología en Cuba." *Catauro*, no. 1 (Fundación Fernando Ortiz, Havana, 1999): 9–15.

Miller, Bonnie. "The Spectacle of War: A Study of Spanish-American War Visual and Popular Culture." PhD diss., Johns Hopkins University, 2006.
Miller, Daniel. *Material Culture and Mass Consumption*. Oxford: Blackwell, 1987.
Miller, Daniel. *A Theory of Shopping*. Cambridge: Polity Press, 1998.
Ministerio de Ultramar, Spain. *Spanish Rule in Cuba: Laws Governing the Island*. New York, 1896.
Miró Argenter, José. *Cuba: Crónicas de la guerra: Las campañas de invasión y de Occidente, 1895-96*. 4th ed. Havana: Ed. Lex, 1945.
Montané, Louis. "A Cuban Chimpanzee." *Journal of Animal Behavior* 6, no. 4 (July-August 1916): 330-33.
Moore, Robin D. *Nationalizing Blackness: Afrocubanismo and Artistic Revolution in Havana, 1920-1940*. Pittsburgh: University of Pittsburgh Press, 1997.
Moreno Fraginals, Manuel. *El ingenio: Complejo socio-económico cubano*. Havana, 1964.
Moreno Fraginals, Manuel. *El ingenio*. Havana: Ciencias Sociales, 1978.
Moreno Fraginals, Manuel. "Sugar in the Caribbean, 1870-1930." In *The Cambridge History of Latin America*, vol. 5. Edited by Leslie Bethell. New York: Cambridge University Press, 1984-2008.
Motola, Patricia, and Marialys Perdomo. "La Academia Cubana de la Lengua: Notas para una historia de la corporación." *Opus Habana*, no. 38 (September 2009-January 2010): 6-7.
Mott, Frank Luther. *American Journalism: A History, 1690-1960*. New York: Macmillan, 1962.
Moya, Jose C. "Spanish Emigration to Cuba and Argentina." In *Mass Migration to Modern Latin America*. Edited by Samuel L. Baily and Eduardo José Miguez. Wilmington, DE: Scholarly Resources, 2003.
Najarro Pujol, Lázaro David. "Luis Casas Romero: Iniciador de la era de la radio en Cuba." http://www.upec.cu/baul/27.html, accessed April 21, 2010.
Naranjo Orovio, Consuelo, and Josef Opatrny. *Del campo a la bodega: Recuerdos de gallegos en Cuba*. A Coruña, Spain: Ediciós do Castro, 1988.
Naranjo Orovio, Consuelo, and Josef Opatrny. "En busca de lo nacional: Migraciones y racismo en Cuba (1880-1910)." In *La Nación Soñada: Cuba, Puerto Rico y Filipinas en torno al 9.*, Edited by Consuelo Naranjo, Miguel Ángel Puig-Samper, and Luis Miguel García, 149-62. Aranjuez, Spain: Doce Calles, 1996.
Naranjo Orovio, Consuelo, and Josef Opatrny. "Estudios cubanos a fines del milenio." In *Visitando la isla: Temas de historia de Cuba*. Edited by Josef Opatrny and Consuelo Naranjo Orovio, 11-22. Madrid: AHILA-Iberoamericana-Vervuert, 2002.
Naranjo Orovio, Consuelo, Josef Opatrny, and Armando García. *Medicina y Racismo en Cuba: La ciencia ante la inmigración canaria en el siglo XX*. Tenerife, Canary Islands: Centro de la Cultura Popular Canaria, 1996.
Nora, Pierre. "Between Memory and History: Les Lieux de Mémoire." *Representations*, no. 26 (spring 1989): 7-24.

Núñez Jover, Jorge. "Aproximación a la sociología cubana." *Papers*, no. 52 (1997): 187–203.

O'Brien, Thomas. *The Revolutionary Mission: American Enterprise in Latin America, 1940–1945*. New York: Cambridge University Press, 1996.

Olmsted, Victor H., dir. *Censo de la República de Cuba bajo la administración provisional de los Estado Unidos 1907*. Washington, DC: U.S. Census Bureau, 1908.

Ortiz, Fernando. *Cuban Counterpoint: Tobacco and Sugar*. New York: Random House, 1970; reprint, Durham, NC: Duke University Press, 1995.

Ortiz, Fernando. "La música sagrada de los negros yoruba en Cuba." *Ultra* 3, no. 13 (July 1937): 77–86.

Ortiz, Fernando. "La poesía mulata: Presencia de Eusebia Cosme, la recitadora." *Revista Bimestre Cubana* 24, nos. 2–3 (September–December 1934): 209–10.

Ortiz García, Carmen. "Cultura popular y construcción nacional: La institucionalización de los estudios del folklore en Cuba." *Revista de Indias* 63, no. 229 (2003): 704.

Osa, Enrique de la. *Crónica del año 33*. Havana: Editorial de Ciencias Sociales, 1989.

Pacyga, Dominic A., "Chicago: Slaughterhouse to the World." In *Meat, Modernity, and the Rise of the Slaughterhouse*. Edited by Paula Young Lee, 153–66. Durham: University of New Hampshire Press, 2008.

Palmer, Steven. "Beginnings of Cuban Bacteriology: Juan Santos Fernández, Medical Research, and the Search for Scientific Sovereignty, 1880–1920." *Hispanic American Historical Review* 91, no. 3 (2011): 445–68.

Palmer, Steven. "A Cuban Scientist between Empires: Peripheral Vision on Race and Tropical Medicine." *Canadian Journal of Latin American and Caribbean Studies* 35, no. 69 (2010): 110–17.

Palmié, Stephan. *Wizards and Scientists: Explorations in Afrocuban Modernity and Tradition*. Durham, NC: Duke University Press, 2002.

Pardo Llada, José. "La voladura del Maine: 15 de febrero de 1898." *Instituto Nacional de Reforma Agraria*, no. 4 (April 1960).

Pavez Ojeda, Jorge. *El Vedado: De monte a reparto (1860–1940); Territorio e identidades de una barrio habanero*. Havana: Centro Juan Marinello-Clacso, 2002.

Pemberton, Rita. "Animal Disease and Veterinary Administration in Trinidad and Tobago, 1879–1962." In *Healing the Herds: Disease, Livestock Economies, and the Globalization of Veterinary Medicine*. Edited by Karen Brown and Daniel Gilfoyle, 163–79. Athens: Ohio University Press, 2010.

Pérez, Echazábal L., et al. "Escuelas Nacionales de Arte de Cubanacán: Diagnóstico y proyecto de restauración de artes plásticas." *Informes de la Construcción* 55 (May/June 2003): 45–51.

Pérez, Louis A., Jr. "Approaching Martí: Text and Context." In *Imagining a Free Cuba: Carlos Manuel de Céspedes and José Martí*. Edited by José Amor y Vázquez. Providence, RI: Thomas J. Watson Jr. Institute for International Studies, Brown University, 1996.

Pérez, Louis A., Jr. *Army and Politics in Cuba, 1898–1958*. Pittsburgh: Pittsburgh University Press, 1976.

Pérez, Louis A., Jr. *Cuba between Empires, 1878–1902*. Pittsburgh: University of Pittsburgh Press, 1983.

Pérez, Louis A., Jr. *Cuba: Between Reform and Revolution*. 4th ed. New York: Oxford University Press, 2011.

Pérez, Louis A., Jr. *Cuba under the Platt Amendment, 1902–1934*. Pittsburgh: University of Pittsburgh Press, 1986.

Pérez, Louis A., Jr. "Incurring a Debt of Gratitude: 1898 and the Moral Sources of United States Hegemony in Cuba." *American Historical Review* 104, no. 2 (April 1999): 356–98.

Pérez, Louis A., Jr. *Lords of the Mountain: Social Banditry and Peasant Protest in Cuba, 1878–1919*. Pittsburgh: University of Pittsburgh Press, 1989.

Pérez, Louis A., Jr. "The Meaning of the *Maine*: Causation and the Historiography of the Spanish-American War." *Pacific Historical Review* 58 (1989): 293–322.

Pérez, Louis A., Jr. *On Becoming Cuban: Identity, Nationality, and Culture*. Chapel Hill: University of North Carolina Press, 1999.

Pérez, Louis A., Jr. "Reminiscences of a *Lector*: Cuban Cigar Workers in Tampa." *Florida Historical Quarterly* 53 (1975).

Pérez, Louis A., Jr. *Ser cubano: Identidad, nacionalidad y cultura*. Havana: Ciencias Sociales, 2006.

Pérez, Louis A., Jr. *To Die in Cuba: Suicide and Society*. Chapel Hill: University of North Carolina Press, 2007.

Pérez, Louis A., Jr. *The War of 1898: The United States and Cuba in History and Historiography*. Chapel Hill: University of North Carolina Press, 1998.

Pérez, Louis A., Jr. *Winds of Change: Hurricanes and the Transformation of Cuba in the Nineteenth Century*. Chapel Hill: University of North Carolina Press, 2001.

Pérez de la Riva, Juan. "Cuba y la migración antillana, 1900–1931." In *La República Neocolonial: Anuario de Estudios Cubanos*, 3–75. Havana: Editorial de Ciencias Sociales, 1979.

Pérez de la Riva, Juan. "Los recursos humanos de Cuba al comenzar el siglo." In *La República Neocolonial: Anuario de Estudios Cubanos*, 1:7–44. Havana: Ciencias Sociales, 1979.

Pérez Salomón, Omar. *Cuba: 125 años de telefonía*. Havana: Editora Política, 2009.

Pérez-Stable, Marifeli. *The Cuban Revolution: Origins, Course, and Legacy*. New York: Oxford University Press, 1993.

Pérez Vigueras, Ildefonso. "Funciones del veterinario en la higiene pública y en la industria pecuaria nacional." *Anales de la Academia de Ciencias Médicas, Físicas y Naturales de La Habana*, t. 74 (1938): 528–536.

Peris Mencheta, F. *De Madrid a Panamá* [1886]. Valencia, Spain: Generalitat Valenciana, 1993.

Petras, Elizabeth McLean. *Jamaican Labor Migration: White Capital and Black Labor, 1850–1930*. Boulder, CO: Westview Press, 1988.

Pichardo, Esteban. *Agrimensura legal en la Isla de Cuba: Segunda edición corregida y aumentad*. Havana: Imprenta y Librería Antigua de Valdepares, 1902.

Pichardo, Hortensia. *Documentos para la historia de Cuba, tomos II y III.* Havana: Editorial de Ciencias Sociales, 1973.

Pilcher, Jeffrey M. *The Sausage Rebellion: Public Health, Private Enterprise, and Meat in Mexico City, 1890–1917.* Albuquerque: University of New Mexico Press, 2006.

Pino-Santos, Oscar. *El asalto a Cuba por la oligarquía financiera yanqui.* Havana: Casa de las Américas, 1973.

Pino-Santos, Oscar. "Lo que fue aquella República: Protectorado y neocolonia." *Contracorriente* 5 (2002).

Piqueras, José Antonio. "Ciudadanía y cultura cívica en la construcción de la República." *Op. Cit.*, no. 15 (2004): 24–53.

Piqueras, José Antonio. *Cuba, emporio y colonia: La disputa de un mercado interferido (1878–1895).* Madrid: Fondo de Cultura Económica, 2003.

Piqueras, José Antonio. "La individualización de la propiedad agraria en la transición al capitalismo." In *Desposeer y custodiar: Transformaciones agrarias y guardería rural en la provincia de Valencia, 1844–1874.* Edited by Vicent R. Mir Montalt, 7–24. Valencia, Spain: Edicions Alfons el Magnànim, 1997.

Piqueras, José Antonio. *Sociedad civil y poder en Cuba: Colonia y poscolonia.* Madrid: Siglo XXI, 2005.

Plá, Eduardo. "Memoria anual de los trabajos del Laboratorio Histo-bacteriológico e Instituto Anti-rábico de la Crónica Médico-Quirúrgica de la Habana." *Crónica Médico-Quirúrgica* 14 (1888): 294.

Portuondo, José Antonio. *La historia y las generaciones.* Havana: Editorial Letras Cubanas, 1981.

Primelles, León. *Crónica Cubana, 1919–1922.* Havana: Editorial Lex, 1957.

Pruna, Pedro M. *Ciencia y científicos en Cuba colonial: La Real Academia de Ciencias de La Habana, 1861–1898.* Havana: Editorial Academia, 2001.

Pruna, Pedro M. "National Science in a Colonial Context: The Royal Academy of Sciences of Havana, 1861–1898." *Isis* 85, no. 3 (1994): 412–26.

Pruna, Pedro M. *La Real Academia de Ciencias de la Habana, 1861–1898.* Madrid: CSIC, 2002.

Pruna, Pedro M., and Armando García González. *Darwinismo y sociedad en Cuba, siglo XIX.* Madrid: CSIC, 1989.

Puig-Samper, Miguel-Ángel, and Consuelo Naranjo. "Fernando Ortiz: Herencias culturales y forja de la nacionalidad." In *Imágenes e imaginarios nacionales en el Ultramar español.* Edited by Consuelo Naranjo Orovio and Carlos Serrano, 197–226. Madrid: CSIC, 1999.

Pulido Fernández, Antonio. "Pedro González Velasco." In *Médicos ilustres del siglo XIX: Conferencias leídas en el Ateneo de Madrid por los doctores Cortezo, Pulido, Pinilla y Luís y Yague,* 35–65. Madrid: Imprenta del Sucursal de E. Teodoro, 1926.

Quiza Moreno, Ricardo. *El cuento al revés: Historia, nacionalismo y poder en Cuba (1902–1930).* Havana: Editorial Unicornio, 2003.

Raby, David. *The Cuban Pre-Revolution of 1933: An Analysis.* Glasgow: Institute of Latin American Studies, 1975.

Radick, Gregory. "R. L. Garner and the Rise of the Edison Phonograph in Evolutionary Philology." In *New Media, 1740–1915*. Edited by Lisa Gitelman and Geoffrey Pingrees. Cambridge, MA: MIT Press, 2003.

Ramos, José Antonio. *Manual del perfecto fulanista*. Havana, 1916.

Rebello, Carlos. *Estados relativos a la producción azucarera de la Isla de Cuba formados competentemente y con autorización de la Intendencia de Ejército y Hacienda*. Havana, 1860.

Reig Romero, Carlos E. *YMCA de La Habana. Memorias Deportivas (1905–1910)*. Quito: Consejo Latinoamericano de Iglesias, 2003.

Reis, João José. *Slave Rebellion in Brazil: The Muslim Uprising of 1835 in Bahia*. Baltimore: Johns Hopkins University Press, 1993.

República de Cuba. *Adaptación de Cuba a las condiciones económicas actuales*. Havana: Imprenta Rambla y Bouza, 1930.

República de Cuba. *El libro de Cuba*. Havana: Artes Gráficas, 1925.

Riera Hernández, Mario. *Historial obrero cubano, 1574–1965*. Miami: Rema Press, 1965.

Rionda, C. M. *El Club Rotario de Pinar del Río: En sus 4 primeros años*. Havana: Imprenta Montalvo y Cárdenas, /s. f. /.

Riverend, Julio Le. "La década de los años 30 y las Ciencias Sociales." In *La revolución del 30 en la narrativa y el testimonio cubanos*. Edited by Ana Cairo. Havana: Editorial de Ciencias Sociales, 1993.

Riverend, Julio Le. *Historia Económica de Cuba*. Havana: Instituto Cubano del Libro, 1971.

Riverend, Julio Le. *La República: Dependencia y revolución*. Havana: Ciencias Sociales, 1975.

Rivero, Yeidy M. "Havana as a 1940s–1950s Latin American Media Capital." *Critical Studies in Media Communication* 26, no. 3 (August 2009): 275–93.

Rivero Muñiz, José. *El movimiento obrero durante la primera intervención: Apuntes para la historia del proletariado en Cuba*. Santa Clara, Cuba: Universidad Central Las Villas, 1961.

Rivero Muñiz, José. "La Primera Huelga General Obrera en Cuba Republicana." *Islas* 3, no. 3 (May–August 1961): 281–330.

Rivero Muñiz, José. "Los orígenes de la prensa obrera en Cuba." *Revista de la biblioteca Nacional José Martí* 2, nos. 1–4 (1960): 67–89.

Roa García, Raúl. *La revolución del 30 se fue a bolina*. Havana: Instituto Cubano del Libro, 1969.

Roca, Blas. *Las experiencias de Cuba*. Mexico City: Editorial Popular, 1939.

Roca, Blas. *Por la igualdad de todos los cubanos*. Havana: Ediciones Sociales, 1939.

Roca, Blas, and Lázaro Peña. *La colaboración entre obreros y patronos*. Havana: Ediciones Sociales, 1945.

Rock, David, ed. *Latin America in the 1940s: War and Postwar Transitions*. Berkeley: University of California Press, 1994.

Rodrigue, John C. *Reconstruction in the Cane Fields: From Slavery to Free Labor in*

Louisiana's Sugar Parishes, 1862–1880. Baton Rouge: Louisiana State University Press, 2001.

Rodríguez García, Rolando. *Cuba, las Máscaras y las sombras: La primera ocupación.* Havana: Ciencias Sociales, 2007.

Roig de Leuchsenring, Emilio. *Cuba no debe su independencia a los Estados Unidos.* Santiago de Cuba: Editorial Oriente, 1975.

Roig de Leuchsenring, Emilio. "El Grupo Minorista de intelectuales y artistas habaneros." *Cuadernos de Historia Habanera*, no. 73 (1961): 10–12.

Roig de Leuchsenring, Emilio. *Las calles de La Habana: Bases para su denominación; Restitución de nombres antiguos, tradicionales y populares.* Havana: Municipio de La Habana, 1936.

Roig de Leuchsenring, Emilio. *Por su propio esfuerzo conquistó el pueblo cubano su independencia.* Havana: Oficina del Historiador de la ciudad, 1957.

Rojas, Rafael. "Otro gallo cantaría: Ensayo sobre el primer republicanismo cubano." In *El republicanismo en Hispanoamérica: Ensayos de historia intelectual y política.* Edited by José Antonio Aguilar and Rafael Rojas. Mexica City: Fondo de Cultura Económica-CIDE, 2002.

Rojas, Ursinio. *Las luchas obreras en el central "Tacajo."* Havana: Editora Política, 1979.

Roldán de Montaud, Inés. "Cuba entre Romero Robledo y Maura (1891–1894)." In *La nación soñada: Cuba, Puerto Rico y Filipinas ante el 98.* Edited by Consuelo Naranjo, Miguel A. Puig Samper, and Luis García Mora, 377–89. Aranjuez, Spain: Doce Calles, 1996.

Rosenthal, Anton Benjamin. "Spectacle, Fear, and Protest: A Guide to the History of Urban Public Space in Latin America." *Social Science History* 24, no. 1 (spring 2000): 33–73.

Rossiianov, Kirrill. "Beyond Species: Il'ya Ivanov and His Experiments on Cross-Breeding Humans with Anthropoid Apes." *Science in Context* 15, no. 2 (2002): 277–316.

Rotary Club de Matanzas. *Ocho años de rotarismo en Matanzas, 14 de julio de 1918, 14 de julio de 1926.* Matanzas: Impr. A. Barani, 1926.

Rotary Internacional. Distrito 25. *Memoria del año oficial de 1939 a 1940.* Havana: Imp. El lápiz rojo, 1941.

Rotary International. *¡Bienvenido a Rotary! Una explicación de Rotary al Nuevo Socio.* Chicago: Publicado por Rotary International, 194?.

Rotary International. *Conferencia del Distrito 25, 19ª. Camagüey, Cuba, 1929: Programa de la XIX Conferencia del Distrito 25 de Rotary International mayo 5, 6 y 7 de 1939.* Camagüey: Imprenta Cía. El Camagüeyano, 1939.

Roussillat, Jacques. *La vie et l'oeuvre du Professeur Jacques-Joseph Grancher.* Guéret, France: Les Presses du Massif Central, 1964.

Saco, José Antonio. "Análisis de don José Antonio Saco de una obra sobre el Brasil intitulada, Notices of Brazil in 1828 and 1829 by Rev. Walsh, author of a Journey from Constantinople, etc." In *José Antonio Saco: Acerca de la esclavitud y su histo-*

ria. Edited by Eduardo Torres-Cuevas and Arturo Sorhegui, 203-4. Havana: Ciencias Sociales, 1982.

Saco, José Antonio. *Mi primera pregunta: ¿La abolición del comercio de esclavos africanos arruinará o atrasará la agricultura cubana? Dedicada a los hacendados de la isla de Cuba por su compatriota José Antonio Saco*. Madrid: Imp. de Marcelino Calero, 1837.

Sagra, Ramón de la. *Cuba, 1860*. Havana: Comisión Nacional Cubana de la UNESCO, 1963.

Salas y Quiroga, Jacinto. *Viages: Isla de Cuba*. Madrid: Boix, 1840.

Sánchez Alonso, Blanca. *Las causas de la emigración española, 1880-1930*. Madrid: Alianza, 1995.

Sánchez Cobos, Amparo. "Extranjeros perniciosos: El orden público y la expulsión de anarquistas españoles de Cuba (1899-1930)." *Historia Social*, no. 59 (2007): 171-88.

Sánchez Cobos, Amparo. "La última frontera: Los anarquistas españoles y la independencia de Cuba." In *El Caribe hispano de los siglos XIX y XX: Viajeros y testimonios*. Edited by Josef Opatrny, 247-54. Prague: Ed. Karolinum, 2010.

Sánchez Cobos, Amparo. "Los anarquistas españoles y la formación de la clase trabajadora cubana: La educación racionalista." In *Cuba in the World, the World in Cuba: Essays on Cuban History, Politics, and Culture*. Edited by Alessandra Lorini and Duccio Basosi, 125-38. Florence: Firenze University Press, 2009.

Sánchez Cobos, Amparo. *Sembrando ideales Anarquistas españoles en Cuba*. Seville: CSICE, 2008.

Sánchez Cobos, Amparo. "Una educación alternativa: Las escuelas racionalistas en Cuba, 1902-1925." In *Nación y cultura nacional en el Caribe hispano*. Edited by Josef Opatrny, 143-52. Prague: Ed. Karolinum, 2006.

Sanger, J. P., dir. *Informe sobre el Censo de Cuba, 1899*. Washington, DC: Government Printing Office, 1900.

Sanjurio D'Arellano J. *Inauguration du Pavillon Albarran a l'Hôpital Cochin*. Paris: Masson, 1926.

Santamaría, Antonio. *Sin azúcar no hay país: La industria azucarera y la economía cubana (1919-1939)*. Seville: CSIC-Escuela de Estudios Hispano-americanos, 2001.

Santamaría, Antonio, and Luis Miguel García Mora. "Colonos: Agricultores cañeros, ¿clase media rural en Cuba? 1880-1898." *Revista de Indias* 58, no. 212 (1998): 131-61.

Santí, Enrico Mario. "Fernando Ortiz, o la crítica de la caña." In *Bienes del siglo: Sobre cultura cubana*, 138-44. Mexica City: Fondo de Cultura Económica, 2002.

Santí, Enrico Mario. "Primera República." In *Bienes del siglo: Sobre cultura cubana*. Mexica City: Fondo de Cultura Económica, 2002.

Santí, Enrico Mario. *Recuerdos de mi vida*. Havana: Imprenta Libredo, 1918.

Santos Fernández, Juan. *Enfermedades de los Ojos en los Negros y Mulatos*. Havana, 1901.

Santovenia, Emeterio. *Libro conmemorativo de la inauguración de la Plaza del Maine en la Habana*. Havana: Secretaría de Obras Públicas, 1928.

Sartorius, David. "Conucos y subsistencia: El caso de Santa Rosalía." In *Espacios, silencios y los sentidos de la libertad: Cuba, 1878–1912*. Edited by Fernando Martínez Heredia, Orlando García Martínez, and Rebecca J. Scott. Havana: Ediciones Unión.

Sauvy, Alfredo. "Lobbys y grupos de presión." *Revista de Estudios Políticos*, no. 89 (September/October 1956).

Saville, Julie. *The Work of Reconstruction: From Slave to Wage Laborer in South Carolina, 1860–1870*. Cambridge: Cambridge University Press, 1994.

Scarpaci, Joseph L., Roberto Segre, and Mario Coyula. *Havana: Two Faces of the Antillean Metropolis*. Chapel Hill: University of North Carolina Press, 2002.

Schafer, R. Murray. *Tuning of the World*. New York: Knopf, 1977.

Schwartz, Stuart B. *Slaves, Peasants, and Rebels: Reconsidering Brazilian Slavery*. Urbana: University of Illinois Press, 1996.

Scott, Rebecca J. "Defining the Boundaries of Freedom in the World of Cane: Cuba, Brazil, and Louisiana after Emancipation." *American Historical Review* 99 (1994).

Scott, Rebecca J. *Degrees of Freedom: Louisiana and Cuba after Slavery*. Cambridge, MA: Harvard University Press, 2005.

Scott, Rebecca J. "El sistema monumental en la Ciudad de La Habana, 1900–1930." *Universidad de La Habana* 222 (1984): 187–200.

Scott, Rebecca J. "'The Lower Class of Whites' and 'the Negro Element': Race, Social Identity, and Politics in Central Cuba, 1899–1909." In *La nación soñada: Cuba, Puerto Rico y Filipinas ante el 98*. Edited by Consuelo Naranjo, Miguel A. Puig Samper, and Luis García Mora. Aranjuez, Spain: Doce Calles, 1996.

Scott, Rebecca J. "Raza, clase y acción colectiva en Cuba, 1895–1912: La formación de alianzas interraciales en el mundo de la caña." In Arcadio Díaz Quiñones, ed. *El Caribe entre imperios. Op. Cit.: Revista del Centro de Investigaciones Históricas* 9 (Río Piedras, 1997): 131–63.

Scott, Rebecca J. "Reclaiming Gregoria's Mule: The Meanings of Freedom in the Arimao and Caunao Valleys, Cienfuegos, Cuba, 1880–1899." *Past and Present* 170 (February 2001): 181–216.

Scott, Rebecca J. "Relaciones de clase e ideologías raciales: Acción rural colectiva en Louisiana y Cuba, 1865–1912." *Historia Social*, no. 22 (1995): 139–49.

Scott, Rebecca J. *Slave Emancipation in Cuba: The Transition to Free Labor, 1860–1899*. Princeton, NJ: Princeton University Press, 1985.

Scott, Rebecca J. "'Stubborn and Disposed to Stand Their Ground': Black Militia, Sugar Workers, and the Dynamics of Collective Action in the Louisiana Sugar Bowl, 1863–1887." *Slavery and Abolition* 20 (1999): 103–26.

Scott, Rebecca J., and Michael Zeuske. "Property in Writing, Property on the Ground: Pigs, Horses, Land, and Citizenship in the Aftermath of Slavery, Cuba, 1880–1909." *Comparative Studies in Society and History* 44, no. 4 (October 2002): 669–97.

Segre, Roberto. *Arquitectura antillana del siglo xx*. Havana-Bogotá: Editorial Arte y Literatura-Universidad Nacional de Colombia, 2003.

Shaffer, Kirwin. *Anarchism and Countercultural Politics in Early Twentieth-Century Cuba*. Gainesville: University Press of Florida, 2005.

Shaffer, Kirwin. "Havana Hub: Cuban Anarchism, Radical Media, and the Trans-Caribbean Anarchist Network, 1902–1915." *Caribbean Studies* 37, no. 2 (July/December 2009): 45–81.

Shaffer, Kirwin. "The Radical Muse: Anarchism and Women in Early Twentieth-Century Cuba." *Cuban Studies* 34 (2003): 130–53.

Sigsbee, Charles D. *The "Maine": An Account of Her Destruction in Havana Harbor*. New York: Century, 1899.

Simpson, José A. "La leche en Cuba." *Anales* (1922): 34–73.

Sims, Harold. "Collapse of the House of Labor: Ideological Divisions in the Cuban Labor Movement." *Cuban Studies* 21 (1991): 123–47.

Sims, Harold. "Cuban Labor and the Communist Party, 1937–1958: An Interpretation." *Cuban Studies* 15, no. 1 (winter 1985): 43–58.

Solá, Pere. *Las escuelas racionalistas en Cataluña (1909–1939)*. Barcelona: Tusquets, 1978.

Soto, Lionel. *La revolución del 33*. 3 vols. Havana: Editorial de Ciencias Sociales, 1977.

Stein, Stanley J. *Vassouras: A Brazilian Coffee County, 1850–1900*. Princeton, NJ: Princeton University Press, 1985.

Stein, Stanley J., and Barbara H. Stein. *The Colonial Heritage of Latin America: Essays on Economic Dependence in Perspective*. New York: Oxford University Press, 1970.

Stepan, Nancy. "The Interplay between Socio-Economic Factors and Medical Science: Yellow Fever Research, Cuba, and the United States." *Social Studies of Science* 8, no. 4 (1978).

Stern, Alexandra Minna. "Yellow Fever Crusade: U.S. Colonialism, Tropical Medicine, and the International Politics of Mosquito Control, 1900–1920." In *Medicine at the Border: Disease, Globalization, and Security, 1850 to the Present*. Edited by Alison Bashford. London: Palgrave, 2006.

Sterne, Jonathan. *The Audible Past: Cultural Origins of Sound Reproduction*. Durham, NC: Duke University Press, 2003.

Stoner, K. Lynn. *From the House to the Streets: The Cuban Women's Movement for Legal Reform, 1898–1940*. Durham, NC: Duke University Press, 1991.

Stubbs, Jean. *Tobacco on the Periphery: A Case Study in Cuban Labour History, 1860–1958*. Cambridge: Cambridge University Press, 1985.

Suriano, Juan. *Anarquistas: Cultura y política libertaria en Buenos Aires, 1890–1910*. Buenos Aires: Manantial, 2001.

Swanger, Joanna Beth. "Lands of Rebellion: Oriente and Escambray Encountering Cuban State Formation, 1934–1974." PhD diss., University of Texas at Austin, 1999.

Tabares del Real, José. *La revolución del 30: Sus dos últimos años*. Havana: Editorial de Ciencias Sociales, 1973.

Tamayo, Diego. "Correspondencia de París." *Crónica Médico-Quirúrgica* 12 (1886): 475–79, 539–46, 606–9.

Tamayo, Diego. *Les microbes de la fievre jaune*. Havana: Imprimerie de Soler, Álvarez, 1888.

Tanco Armero, Nicolás. *Viaje de Nueva Granada a China y de China a Francia* [1861]. In Juan Pérez de la Riva, *La isla de Cuba en el siglo XIX vista por los extranjeros*. Havana: Editorial de Ciencias Sociales, 1981.

Tannenbaum, Frank. *Slave and Citizen*. Boston: Beacon Press, 1992.

Tavera, Susana. "Revolucionarios, publicistas y bohemios: Los periodistas anarquistas (1918–1936)." In *El anarquismo español y sus tradiciones culturales*. Edited by Bert Hofmann, Pere Joan, and Manfred Tietz, 377–92. Madrid: Vervuert-Iberoamericana, 1995.

Tavera, Susana, and Enric Ucelay. "Grupos de afinidad, disciplina bélica y periodismo libertario, 1936–1938." *Historia Contemporánea*, no. 9 (1993): 167–90.

Tellería, Evelio. *Los Congresos Obreros en Cuba*. Havana: Editorial de Arte y Literatura, Instituto Cubano del Libro, 1973.

Thomas, Hugh. *Cuba: The Pursuit of Freedom*. New York: Harper and Row, 1971.

Thompson, Edward P. *La formación de la clase obrera en Inglaterra*. Barcelona: Crítica, 1989.

Tinajero, Araceli. *El Lector: A History of the Cigar Factory Reader*. Austin: University of Texas Press, 2010.

Topp, Michael Miller. "The Transnationalism of the Italian-American Left: The Lawrence Strike of 1912 and the Italian Chamber of Labor of New York City." *Journal of American Ethnic History* 17, no. 1 (fall 1997): 39–63.

Toro, Carlos del. *La alta burguesía cubana, 1920–1958*. Havana: Ciencias Sociales, 2003.

Toro, Carlos del, and Enrique Collazo. "Primeras manifestaciones de la crisis del sistema colonial." In Instituto de Historia de Cuba, *Historia de Cuba: La neocolonia*, 3:194–208. Havana: Editora Política, 1994–98.

Torre, Mildred de la, et al. *La sociedad cubana en los albores de la República*. Havana: Ciencia Sociales, 2002.

Torres-Cuevas, Eduardo. "En busca de la cubanidad." *Debates Americanos* 1 (1995): 2–17.

Torres-Cuevas, Eduardo. *Historia de la masonería en Cuba: Seis ensayos*. Havana: Imagen Contemporánea, 2004.

Trelles, Carlos M. "El progreso (1902 a 1905) y el retroceso (1906 a 1922) de la República de Cuba." *Revista Bimestre Cubana* 18 (1924): 313–19.

Trouillot, M. R. "Caribbean: Sociocultural Aspects." In *International Encyclopaedia of the Social & Behavioural Sciences*. Edited by N. J. Smelse and P. B. Baltes, 1484–88. New York: Cambridge University Press, 2004.

Turcato, Davide. "European Anarchism in the 1890s: Why Labor Matters in Categorizing Anarchism." *Working USA: The Journal of Labor and Society* 12 (September 2009): 451–66.

Turcato, Davide. "Italian Anarchism as a Transnational Movement, 1885–1915." *International Review of Social History* 52, no. 3 (December 2009): 407–44.

United States Office of Strategic Services. *The Political Significance and Influence of the*

Labor Movement in Latin America; A Preliminary Survey: Cuba. Washington, DC, September 18, 1945.

Uralde, Marilú. "La Guardia Rural: Un instrumento de dominación neocolonial (1898–1902)." In *La sociedad cubana en los albores de la República*. Edited by Mildred de La Torre et al., 255–82. Havana: Ciencia Sociales, 2002.

Van Der Linden, Marcel. "The 'Globalization' of Labor and Working-Class History and Its Consequences." *International Labor and Working-Class History*, no. 65 (spring 2004): 136–56.

Van Der Linden, Marcel. *Transnational Labor History*. Aldershot, UK: Ashgate, 2002.

Van Der Linden, Marcel, and Wayne Thorpe, eds. *Revolutionary Syndicalism: An International Perspective*. Aldershot, UK: Scolar Press, 1990.

Varona, Enrique J. "Recepción en la Academia Nacional." In *Política y sociedad*. Havana: Ciencias Sociales, 1999.

Vega Suñol, José. *Norteamericanos en Cuba: Estudio etnohistórico*. Havana: La Fuente Viva, Fundación Fernando Ortiz, 2004.

Venegas Fornias, Carlos. *La urbanización de las murallas: Dependencia y modernidad*. Havana: Letras Cubanas, 1990.

Verdery, Katherine. *The Political Lives of Dead Bodies: Reburial and Postsocialist Change*. New York: Columbia University Press, 1999.

Vilas, Carlos M. "Latin American Populism: A Structural Approach." *Science and Society* 56, no. 4 (winter 1992–93): 389–420.

Viotti da Costa, Emilia. *Da Monarquia à República: Momentos decisivos*. 3rd ed. São Paulo: Brasiliense, 1985.

Warner, Michael. *Publics and Counterpublics*. Cambridge, MA: MIT Press, 2002.

Weitz, Eric D. *Weimar Germany: Promise and Tragedy*. Princeton, NJ: Princeton University Press, 2007.

Whitbeck, R. H. "Geographical Relations in the Development of Cuban Agriculture." *Geographical Review* 12, no. 2 (1911): 222–40.

Whitney, Robert. *State and Revolution in Cuba: Mass Mobilization and Political Change, 1920–1940*. Chapel Hill: University of North Carolina Press, 2001.

Whitney, Robert, and Graciela Chailloux. *Subjects or Citizens: British Caribbean Workers in Cuba, 1900–1960*. Gainesville: University Press of Florida, 2013.

Whitney, Robert, and Graciela Chailloux. "West Indian Migrants to Cuba and Their Descendants." In *Regional Footprints: The Travels and Travails of Early Caribbean Migrants*. Edited by Annette Insanally, Mark Clifford, and Sean Sheriff, 133–54. Kingston, Jamaica: University Press of the West Indies, 2006.

Wisan, Josef. *The Cuban Crisis as Reflected in the New York Press, 1895–1898*. New York: Columbia University Press, 1934.

Wolfe, Joel. *Autos and Progress: The Brazilian Search for Modernity*. New York: Oxford University Press, 2010.

Wolfe, Joel. *Working Women, Working Men: São Paulo and the Rise of Brazil's Industrial Working Class, 1900–1955*. Durham, NC: Duke University Press, 1993.

Worboys, Michael. "Germs, Malaria, and the Invention of Mansonian Tropical Medicine: From 'Diseases in the Tropics' to 'Tropical Diseases.'" In *Warm Climates and Western Medicine: The Emergence of Tropical Medicine, 1500–1900*. Edited by David Arnold. Amsterdam: Rodopi, 1996.

Wurtzler, Steve. *Electric Sounds: Technological Change and the Rise of Corporate Mass Media*. New York: Columbia University Press, 2007.

Wynne, Clive. "Rosalía Abreu and the Apes of Havana." *International Journal of Primatology* 29 (2008): 289–302.

Wynter, Cadence A. "Jamaican Labor Migration to Cuba, 1885–1930, in the Caribbean Context." PhD diss., University of Illinois, Chicago, 2001.

Yerkes, Robert M. *Almost Human*. New York: Century, 1925.

Yglesia Martínez, Teresita. *Cuba, primera república, segunda ocupación*. Havana: Ciencias Sociales, 1976.

Zanetti, Oscar. *Los cautivos de la reciprocidad*. 2nd ed. Havana: Ciencias Sociales, 2003. [*Los cautivos de la reciprocidad: La burguesía cubana y la dependencia comercial*. Havana: Ministerio de Educación Superior, 1989.]

Zanetti, Oscar. "El comercio exterior de la república neocolonial." In *La República Neocolonial: Anuario de Estudios Cubanos*, 1:76–78. Havana: Ciencias Sociales, 1979.

Zanetti, Oscar, and Alejandro García. *Caminos para el azúcar*. Havana: Ciencias Sociales, 1987.

Zanetti, Oscar, and Alejandro García. *United Fruit Company: Un caso del dominio imperialista en Cuba*. Havana: Ciencias Sociales, 1976.

Zapata, Felipe. "Esquema y notas para una historia de la organización obrera en Cuba." *Justicia Social Cristiana* 1, nos. 1–4 (1951): 64–65.

Zardoya, María Victoria. "Ciudad, imagen y memoria: El río Almendares y la ciudad de La Habana." *Urbano* 17 (2008): 63–75.

Zeuske, Michael. "1898: Cuba y el problema de la 'transición pactada': Prolegómenos a una historia de la cultura política en Cuba (1898–1920)." In *La nación soñada: Cuba, Puerto Rico y Filipinas*. Edited by Consuelo Naranjo, Miguel A. Puig-Samper, and Luis M. García, 131–47. Madrid: Doce Calles, 1996.

Zeuske, Michael. "Die diskrete Macht der Sklaven: Zur politischen Partizipation von Afrokubanern während des kubanischen Unabhängigkeitskrieges und der ersten Jahre der Republik (1895–1908) — eine regionale Perspektive." *Comparativ* 1 (1997).

Zeuske, Michael. "Estructuras, movilización afrocubana y clientelas en un hinterland cubano: Cienfuegos 1895–1906." *Tiempos de América*, no. 2 (1998): 93–116.

Zeuske, Michael. "Movilización afrocubana y clientelas en un hinterland cubano: Cienfuegos entre colonia y república (1895–1912)." In *Espacios, silencios y los sentidos de la libertad: Cuba, 1878–1912*. Edited by Fernando Martínez Heredia, Orlando García Martínez, and Rebecca J. Scott. Havana: Ediciones Unión, 2001.

CONTRIBUTORS

Imilcy Balboa Navarro is associate professor at Universitat Jaume I, Castellón, Spain. She is the author of *Los brazos necesarios: Inmigración, colonización y trabajo libre en Cuba, 1878–1898* (2000) and *La protesta rural en Cuba: Resistencia cotidiana, bandolerismo y revolución, 1878–1902* (2003), coeditor with José Antonio Piqueras of *La excepción americana: Cuba en el ocaso del imperio continental* (2006), and coauthor with María del Carmen Barcia, Gloria García, Mildred de la Torre, and Raquel Vinat of *La Turbulencia del Reposo, Cuba, 1878–1895* (1998).

Alejandra Bronfman is associate professor at the University of British Columbia. She is the author of *On the Move: A Recent History of the Caribbean since 1989* (2007) and *Measures of Equality: Social Science, Citizenship, and Race in Cuba, 1902–1940* (2004), and coeditor of *Media, Sound, and Culture in Latin America and the Caribbean* (2012). She is currently involved in the book project *Talking Machines: Caribbean Media and Publics*, which explores the perambulations of objects in empires in the early twentieth century, with particular attention to new media including telegraph, telephone, and broadcasting and their relationships to capital flows, imperial projects, and regional political mobilizations.

Maikel Fariñas Borrego is a PhD student at the University of North Carolina at Chapel Hill and a former researcher at the Instituto de Historia de Cuba. Author of *Sociabilidad y cultura del ocio: Las élites habaneras y sus clubes de recreo (1902–1930)* (2010), he has also published several articles focused on sociability and leisure in Cuba, including "El asociacionismo náutico en La Habana: Desde las élites hasta las capas populares (1886–1958)" (2010), and "Las asociaciones de recreo del tipo 'yacht club' y su papel en el trazado socio-urbanístico de La Habana (1920–1958)" (2008).

Reinaldo Funes Monzote is research director at the Fundación Antonio Núñez Jiménez de la Naturaleza y el Hombre, Havana, and assistant professor at the University of Havana. He is the author of *El despertar del asociacionismo científico en Cuba, 1876–1920* (2004), and *From Rainforest to Cane Field in Cuba: An Environmental His-*

tory since 1492 (2008), the Spanish version of which won Cuba's Premio Catauro and Premio de la Crítica and the UNESCO Prize for Caribbean Environmental Thought.

Marial Iglesias Utset is an independent scholar and former associate professor at the University of Havana. The Spanish edition of her book, recently published in English as *A Cultural History of Cuba during the U.S. Occupation, 1898–1902* (2011), was awarded the Clarence H. Haring Prize of the American Historical Association, the Annual Prize of the Cuban Academy of Sciences and the Instituto del Libro, and the Essay Prize of the Union of Artists and Writers of Cuba (UNEAC).

Steven Palmer is Canada Research Chair in History of International Health and associate professor at the University of Windsor, Canada. He is the author of *Launching Global Health: The Caribbean Odyssey of the Rockefeller Foundation* (2010) and *From Popular Medicine to Medical Populism: Doctors, Healers, and Public Power in Costa Rica, 1800–1940* (Duke University Press, 2003). He has coedited with Iván Molina *The Costa Rica Reader: History, Culture, Politics* (Duke University Press, 2005), with María Silvia Di Liscia and Gilberto Hochman *Patologías de la Patria: Enfermedades, Enfermos, y Nación en América Latina* (2012), and with Juanita De Barros and David Wright *Health and Medicine in the Circum-Caribbean, 1800–1968* (2009).

José Antonio Piqueras Arenas is chair of contemporary history at the Universitat Jaume I, Castellón, Spain. He is the author of several books focused on Cuban and Caribbean history, including *Trabajo libre y coactivo en sociedades de plantación* (2009), *Félix Varela y la prosperidad de la patria criolla* (2007), *Sociedad civil y poder en Cuba: Colonia y poscolonia* (2006), and *Cuba, colonia y emporio: La disputa de un mercado interferido (1878–1895)* (2003), and has coedited with Imilcy Balboa *La excepción americana: Cuba en el ocaso del imperio continental* (2006).

Ricardo Quiza Moreno is a professor of history at the Casa Fernando Ortíz in Havana and a former researcher at the Instituto de Historia de Cuba. He is author of *El cuento al revés: historia, nacionalismo y poder en Cuba (1902–1930)* (2003), *Embajada de España en La Habana, Antiguo Palacio Velasco Sarrá* (2008), and *Imaginarios al ruedo: Cuba y los Estados Unidos en las exposiciones internacionales (1876–1904)* (2011).

Amparo Sánchez Cobos is assistant professor at Universitat Jaume I, Castellón, Spain. She is author of *Sembrando ideales: Anarquistas españoles en Cuba* (2008) and several articles on the history of anarchism in Spain and Cuba published in refereed books and international journals, including "La reorganización del trabajo libre: Los anarquistas españoles y la difusión del ideal libertario en Cuba" (2010) and "Extranjeros perniciosos: El orden público y la expulsion de anarquistas españoles de Cuba (1899–1930)" (2007).

Rebecca J. Scott is Charles Gibson Distinguished University Professor of History and Professor of Law at the University of Michigan. She was awarded the MacArthur Fellowship and is a recent recipient of the Guggenheim Fellowship and a member of the American Academy of Arts and Sciences. She is the author of *Degrees of Freedom:*

Louisiana and Cuba after Slavery (2005), which received the Frederick Douglass Prize and the John Hope Franklin Prize, and *Slave Emancipation in Cuba: The Transition to Free Labor* (1985), and coauthor with Frederick Cooper and Thomas Holt of *Beyond Slavery: Explorations of Race, Labor, and Citizenship in Postemancipation Societies* (2003). She has also edited with Fernando Martínez Heredia and Orlando García *Espacios, silencios y los sentidos de la libertad: Cuba, 1878–1912* (2001).

Robert Whitney is associate professor at the University of New Brunswick, Saint John. He is author of *State and Revolution in Cuba: Mass Mobilization and Political Change, 1920–1940* (2001), as well as several articles focused on diaspora studies, cultural identity, and transnational history, including "Observaciones sobre el Estado y la Revolución en Cuba, 1920 a 1940" (2001), "History or Teleology: Recent Publications on Pre-1959 Cuba" (2001), and "The Architect of the Cuban State: Fulgencio Batista and Cuban Populism, 1937–1940" (2000). He is coauthor, with Graciela Chailloux Laffita, of *Subjects or Citizens: British Caribbean Workers in Cuba, 1900–1960* (2013).

INDEX

Numbers in italics indicate illustrations.

Abad, Miguel Angel, 97
Abreu, Rosalía, 55, 59, 72–75, 80n63
Abreu, Sixto, 142
Academia Cubana de la Lengua, 277, 286n8, 287n24
Academia de la Historia de Cuba, 271–72, 276, 283, 286n8, 287n24
Academia Nacional de Artes y Letras, 272, 276, 286n8, 287n24
Acción Libertaria (newspaper), 193
Achón, Francisco, 105
Acosta, Enrique, 134
advertising, 261–65, 282–85
Afro Cubans: anthropology and, 279–80, 286n19, 288n36, 289n37; citizenship concerns of, 2–3, 13–14, 102–9, 220–25, 255, 292–316; labor conditions and, 210, 220–25, 294–303; science discourses and, 68–70, 72–75, 176; wars of independence and, 83–85, 94–102, 116n61, 117n69, 279, 294. *See also* citizenship; class; Cuba; labor activism and policies; race; sugar
Agramonte, Aristides, 67, 70, 138–39
agronomy, 13, 55, 71–75. *See also* science discourses; sugar; United States
Agrupación racionalista Ferrer, 201

La Alarma, 198
Albarrán, Joaquín, 59
Albear, Francisco, 166
Aldama, Domingo, 150, 164
Alfonso XIII Spanish military hospital, 170–71
Aller, Juan, 184, 198
Alonso, Manuel A., 281
Alonso, Mercedes, 90, 92
Alvarado, Cipriano, 260
Alvarez, Manuel, 257
American Club, 232
American Medical Congress, 258
American Sugar Refining Company, 213
American Tobacco Co., 161
anarchism, 30, 108, 181–207, 220, 228n46. *See also* Atlantic community (of circulation); labor activism and policies; Spain; transnationality
anarcho-syndicalism, 197–98
The Antebellum State of Mind (sculpture group), 42
anthropology, 72, 75, 260–61, 269–91. *See also* science discourses; Sociedad del Folklore Cubano; *specific people and publications*

Antilles and Antilleans, 18, 127–28, 214–23, 301–3
Apprentices' Strike of 1902, 184, 187–88, 191, 193
Archivos del Folklore Cubano, 272–73, 275, 278–79, 281–84, 288n36, 289n37
Argentine Regional Workers Federation, 198
Arlington National Cemetery, 35, 38, 40, 51n46
Arteaga, Emilio, 220
Asociación de Almacenistas y Cosecheros, 241
Asociación de Colonos de Cuba, 222
Asociación de Dependientes del Comercio, 159
Asociación de Veteranos de la Independencia de Cuba, 42
Asociación para el Fomento de la Inmigración, 215
Atkins, Edwin, 72, 88, 91, 94–96, 103, 114n23
Atkins Garden, 72–73
Atlanta Constitution, 50n10
Atlantic community (of circulation), 15, 56, 182–95, 205n33, 294–303
Auténticos (party), 313
Autonomism, 2, 19n2, 57–58, 62, 92–93, 100–101, 108–9, 168–69, 175
Azúcar y población en las Antillas (Guerra), 209, 221, 271

Bachiller y Morales, Antonio, 281
Balboa Navarro, Imilcy, 15–16, 208–30
Baliño, Carlos, 204n15
Bances y López, 161
Banco Español, 171
Banco Nacional de Cuba, 154
Bandera, Quintín, 98
Baquero, J. M., 257–58
Barcia, Luís, 184
Barnet, Enrique, 126, 131, 138
Barton, Clara, 28

bateyes, 215–30, 312. See also *centrales*; class; sugar
Batista, Fulgencio, 5, 18, 46–47, 151, 157, 161, 276, 296, 306, 309, 313
Bay of Pigs, 23, 47
Beal, P. M., 98
Behn, Hernand and Sosthenes, 256
Belau, Paul, 154
Berchon, Charles, 146n23
Berger, Ernest, 234
Betancourt, Luis Adrián, 137
Betancourt, Luis Victoriano, 281
Biblioteca Nacional, 161
Blanco, Manuel, 87, 103–5, 111
Boas, Franz, 281
El Boletín de la Escuela Moderna, 193
Bolívar, Simón, 157
Borglum, Gutzom, 44
Bourdieu, Pierre, 271, 284
Brazil, 9, 83, 109–10, 176, 193
Britain, 67, 301–3, 305, 308–10, 313–14
broadcasting, 251–68
Broca, Pierre, 56
Bronfman, Alejandra, 17, 72, 115n44, 251–68
Brooke, John R., 171, 211–12
Broussé, María, 192
Búa Palacios, Juan, 185
Bulletin of the Panamerican Union, 138
Butler, Frank, 257

Caballero, Gaspar, 95
Cabarrocas, Félix, 43
Cabrera, Raimundo, 168–69
Las calles de la Habana (Roig), 155
Calvino, Mario, 71
Campos, Pedro Albizu, 10
Capitólio Nacional, 172
Carballo, Roberto, 201
Carbonell, Néstor, 286n8
Carey, Violda, 292, 297
Carmona, Rómulo S., 192
Carpentier, Alejo, 156, 162

Carteles (magazine), 258, 260–61
casas de salud, 159
Casas Romero, Luis, 257
Casino Español, 174
Castillo, Andrés, 184
Castro, Fidel, 47–49
Catalá, Ramón, 286n8
caudillismo, 14, 33
Ceci, Enrique, 185
Cedulario Cubano (Chacón), 275
Cementerio de Colón, 29, 33, 38, 41
Center for Artisan Instruction and Recreation, 185
Center for Social Studies, 201
centrales, 16, 86–90, 211, 300. *See also* labor activism and policies; sugar
Central Labor Union, 30
Centro Asturiano, 155, 162
Centro Gallego, 154–55
CGT (French General Workers Confederation), 197–98
Chacón y Calvo, José María, 274–75, 277, 280, 283
Chailloux, Juan Manuel, 160, 164
Chaparra Sugar Company, 218, 223, 300–303, 308, 310–12
Charter of Amiens, 197
Chibás Guerra, Eduardo Justo, 236
Chidwick, John, 28, 41
Chinese laborers, 84, 86, 105, 149, 228n51, 293, 312
Los ciegos (Loveira), 208–9, 224
Cienfuegos, 14, 82–120, *84*
Circo-Teatro Jané, 159
Círculo de Hacendados, 212
Círculo Militar y Naval, 232
citizenship: class concerns and labor activism and, 14, 82–120, 220–25, 292–315; definitions of, 82–83, 112n8; gender and, 13–14, 92, 109–11; racialization and, 3, 14, 18, 68–69, 92–97, 100–111, 169, 255, 292–303
La ciudad de las columnas (Carpentier), 156

Civil War (U.S.), 13, 260
Clark, Victor, 82, 111
class: citizenship concerns and, 294–315; consumerism and, 261–65; Cuba's creole elite and, 2–3, 148–51, 292–321; folklore and, 269–91; immigration and, 15–16, 18, 202–3, 292–303; labor activism and policies and, 14–15, 181–207, 303–15; listening practices and, 255–61, 264–67; race's intersections with, 8, 90–91, 93–94, 159, 176, 292–315, 317; urbanization and, 157–58, 163–64, 171
clientelism, 109–11, 112n5
Club Atenas, 233
Club Atlético de Cuba, 232
Club de Leones de la Habana, 233
Club Rotario de la Habana, 233
Colegio de Médicos Cubanos, 76–77
Colonial Medical Service (British), 67
colonos, 208–30
Columbia Triumphant (Piccirilli), 41–42
Comisión Revisora de Aranceles, 241
Communist Committee of Havana, 270
Communist Confederación de Trabajadores de Cuba (CTC), 313
Conservative Party, 3, 33, 109, 303
Constancia (*central*), 87
Constitutional Union Party, 92–93
Constitution of 1901, 294
Constitution of 1940, 285, 292, 316
Coolidge, Calvin, 45
Córdova, Sofía, 274
Coronado, Tomás, 68, 138
Cortina, José Antonio, 58
Cosculluela, Juan Antonio, 127–29
cosmopolitanism, 15, 181–207, 205n33, 275, 294–303
Costigan-Jones Law, 228n42
Country Club de la Habana, 232–33
creole elite (of Cuba): agrarian class politics and, 16, 208–30; colonial politics and, 19n2, 56–61, 150–51; racial anxieties of, 11, 102–9, 220–25; science dis-

Index | 355

creole elite (of Cuba) (*continued*)
   courses and, 54–81; sociability organizations, 233–50; U.S. cooperation with, 2, 4, 8, 12, 62, 71, 108
Crónica Médico-Quirúgica de la Habana, 56–60, 76
Crowder, Enoch H., 4, 44
Cuadrado, Alonso, 138
Cuba: citizenship concerns and, 13, 68–69, 82–120, 151, 164, 169, 220–25, 255, 292–316; class interests and, 3, 16–17, 90–94, 159–60, 163–64, 176, 181–207, 212–30, 242, 292–321; constitutions of, 3–4, 10, 125–26, 285, 294, 316; cosmopolitanism and, 15, 181–207, 231–50, 275, 294–303; decadence of, 126–30, 144; independence wars of, 1–2, 5, 8–9, 11–13, 20n18, 22, 31–33, 35, 42, 47–49, 54, 56–61, 71, 83–85, 94–102, 116n61, 117n69, 160, 185, 211–16, 227n30, 257; labor laws and practices of, 18, 84, 86, 105, 149, 216–23, 228n51, 292–316; *Maine*'s symbolism and, 11–12, 31–49; nationalism and, 17–18, 47–49, 62, 75–76, 210, 220–25, 231–50, 255, 271–73, 280–81, 292–316; political corruption in, 8, 33, 46, 108, 129, 254, 270, 308; racial identity and, 15, 18, 68–69, 129, 186, 228n51, 292–315, 321n49; sanitation discourses and, 14, 18, 62, 64–66, 121–47, 169–77; science discourses in, 12–13, 18, 54–81, 144; slavery and, 14, 82–92, 166, 186, 211–16, 279, 292–303; sovereignty and, 1–2, 4–7, 10, 12–13, 17, 19n1, 22–24, 33, 38, 44, 54–55, 62, 71–75, 125, 129, 244, 294, 316; Spain's colonial presence and, 6, 56–61, 64, 67, 84, 92–97, 103, 108–9, 124, 129–31, 133, 144, 148–50, 160, 162–69, 174, 216, 232, 239–42, 292–303; tourism industry and, 46, 155, 159–69, 245–46; U.S. financial interests in, 33–34, 49n2, 87, 148–49, 151–56, 167–69, 171–77, 187, 211–25, 226n17, 227n27, 250n50; U.S. military interventions and occupations and, 1–6, 10, 13–14, 22–53, 61–65, 71, 101–9, 122, 124–25, 129, 132, 152–56, 169–77, 179n40, 195–200. *See also* class; labor activism and policies; race; sovereignty; sugar; *specific organizations, people, and publications*
Cuba Contemporánea, 121
Cuban American Sugar Company, 213, 218
Cuban Anthropological Society, 57
Cuban Communist Party, 15, 182, 242, 302, 304–5, 312–13
Cuban Council for National Renovation, 244
Cuban Folklore Society, 17–18, 269–91, 286n8
Cuban Humanitarian Society, 134
Cuban League of Mental Hygiene, 76
Cuban League of Railway Workers, 181
Cuban Medical Federation (FMC), 77
Cuban Society for the Protection of Animals, 76
Cuban Society of Natural History, 73
Cuban Telephone Company, 254, 256–57
Cuesta, Ángel, 234
Cultura Obrera (newspaper), 193
Cusidó i Baró, Rafael, 184

dairy production, 136–44
Dairy Supply Inspection Service, 140
Danielson, Ross, 77
Daughters of the American Revolution, 35
Dávalos, Juan, 62, 64, 65, 68, 134
Day, William R., 24
De Cárdenas Echarte, Raúl, 245
De Céspedes, Carlos Miguel, 44, 172
Decree no. 1,158, 219
Decree no. 1,331, 220
Decree no. 1,404, 219
De Forest, Lee, 257, 261
De Jesús Monteagudo, José, 99
De la Cruz Senmanat, María, 22–23, 38

De la Fuente, Alejandro, 13, 69, 120n101
De la Huerta, Moisés, 43
De la Sagra, Ramón, 221
De la Torre y de la Huerta, Carlos, 235
De la Torriente, Cosme, 246
Del Carrión, Miguel, 121, 129–30
Delgado Jugo, Francisco, 56
Del Valle, Adrián, 184, 187, 195
De Maeztu, Ramiro, 194
De Paula Coronado, Francisco, 278
El Dependiente (newspaper), 202
De Solá, Fermin, 87
El Despertar (newspaper), 184
Diario de la Marina (newspaper), 165, 209, 271, 282
Díaz, Enrique, 41
Díaz del Moral, Juan, 188
Diccionario botánico de nombres vulgares cubanos, 72
Dihígo, Juan Miguel, 286n8
La Discusión (newspaper), 39
Douglas, Albert, 34–35
Dupuis, Melanie, 136

Educación del Porvenir (group), 201
education, 200–202, 207n56, 274
Enfermedades de los Ojos en los Negros y Mulatos (Santos Fernández), 69
Entrialgo Bolado, Aquilino, 236
epidemic diseases, 54–55, 61–70, 121, 123–30, 170
Espinosa, Aurelio, 281
Esquerra, Higinio, 99, *99*, 109
Estación Experimental Agronómica de Santiago de las Vegas, 71
Estación Villanueva, 158
Estrada Palma, Tomás, 1–4, 107–8, 172, 174–75, 214
ethnography. *See* anthropology
eugenics, 13, 55, 69, 72–76, 80n42, 122. *See also* race; science discourses

Fábrica Partagás, 161
Fariñas, Maikel, 16–17, 231–50

Federación de Sociedades Económicas, 241
Federation of Anarchist Groups, 196
Federation of University Students, 270
Federation of Workers of the Spanish Region, 185
Fernández, Cesáreo, 124
Fernández, Francisco María, 76–77
Fernández, Maximino, 185
Fernández, Nicolás, 108–9
Fernández de Castro, J., 92–93
Fernández Estéves, Andrés, 278
Ferrara, Orestes, 243
Ferreiro del Monte, Paulino, 185
Ferrer, Ada, 85, 100, 116n61
Ferrer i Guardia, Francisco, 200–201, 207n53
field theory, 284–85
"Fifty-Percent Law," 303–5, 307–9. *See also* labor activism and policies
El Figaro (magazine), 135
Figueroa, Anselmo L., 192
Finlay, Carlos, 61–62, *63*, 66, 68
"First Landing Monument," 32
First World War, 127, 176, 216–17, 254, 256, 269–70
Fitzgerald, John J., 37
Flores Magón, Ricardo and Enrique, 192
"The Folklore of Cuban Children" (Córdova), 274
Fonseca García, Manuela, 274
Foreign Policy Association, 220, 224
Forestier, Jean-Claude, 45, 151, 175
Foucault, Michel, 317
Fraginals, Moreno, 58
Franqui, Carlos, 46–47, 52n66
freemasonry, 233, 248n5
French Labor Exchange, 197
French Society for Anthropology, 75
From 26 to 35 (Loveira), 181
Funes Monzote, Reinaldo, 14, 71, 77n1, 121–47

Galezowski, Xavier, 56
Gallini, Stefania, 123

Index | 357

Gárate Brú, Carlos, 245
García, Vicente, 189
García Blanco, Manuel, 103
García Blanco, Rolando, 72
García Menocal, Mario, 3–4, 13, 43, 73, 170, 175, 177, 218, 220, 223
García Purón, Gervasio, 185
Gates, William, 260
Geats Botet, Juan, 236
gender: citizenship concerns and, 13–14, 92, 109–11; consumerism and, 261–64; labor activism and, 88–90, 188, 192, 196; scientific work and, 17, 72–75, 274
General Electric, 257, 260–61, 263
Giquel, Humberto, 257–58, 264
Gitelman, Lisa, 252
glanders, 60, 63, 125
"Glanders and the Intervention" (article), 63
Godoy Sayán, Enrique, 236
Gómez, José Miguel, 4, 35, 40, 108, 115n44, 154, 175, 215, 223
Gómez, Juan Gualberto, 93
Gómez, Máximo, 96–97, 103
Gómez de Avellaneda, Gertudis, 281
Gómez Murillo, Ricardo, 136
González, Jorge, 259
González Bobés, Eduardo, 185
González Curquejo, Antonio, 127
González de Aguilar, Teresa, 58
González del Valle, Ambrosio, 131
González Planas, José, 99, *102*
González Sola, Francisco, 194, 199, 201–2
Grancher, Joseph, 59, 74
Grau San Martín, Ramón, 77, 222, 245, 303
Guantánamo Bay, 3
Guardiola, José, 184, 190
Guastavino, Rafael, 154, 178n3
Guerra Chiquita, 85
Guerra y Sánchez, Ramiro, 16, 209, 217–25, 271, 275–76, 282, 286n19, 288n25
Guigou, Alberto, 265, *266*
Guillén, Nicólas, 282, 289n37, 289n39

Guirao, Ramón, 289n39
Guiteras, John/Juan, 67–70

Habana Yacht Club, 232
Haitian laborers, 18, 216–23, 228n45, 229n54, 295–316, 321n49
Haraway, Donna, 74
Harrington, John, 260
Harris, Paul, 233
Harvey, David, 157
Havana: architecture and urban landscape of, 14–15, 38–39, 42–49, 148–80; *Maine*'s display and, 10–12, 22–53; maps of, *150*, *158*, *165*; sanitation and, 121–47
Havana Biltmore Yacht & Country Club, 233
Havana Cigar and Tobacco Factories, Limited, 161
Havana Dairy Supply Company, 141
Havana Workers Federation, 198
Hay-Quesada treaty, 246
Hearst, William Randolph, 26, 29–30, 41
Helg, Aline, 100
Hernández, Gregorio, 185
Herrera Clavería, Julio Blanco, 236, 246
La Higiene, 63, *64*, 65, 124
Hone, Neil, 301–3, 315
Hospital Calixto García, 170–71
Hospital Nacional, 171
Hotel America (Roma), 165
Hotel Inglaterra, 162
Hotel Pasaje, 165
Hotel Plaza, 165
Hotel Saratoga, 165
Hotel Sevilla Biltmore, 154, 165
Hotel Telégrafo, 165
Hoxie, Charles, 260
hygiene. *See* sanitation discourses

Ibarra, Jorge, 223, 228n35
Iglesias Utset, Marial, 5, 10–12, 22–53, 149, 255
immigration (to Cuba): racialized

laborers and, 18, 84, 86, 105, 149, 228n51, 293, 312; Spanish desirability and, 18, 69, 151, 166, 183, 186, 202–3, 214, 229n51, 295–303. *See also* class; Cuba; labor activism and policies; race; slavery; sugar
Industrial Workers of the World (IWW), 197–98
infant mortality rates, 14, 128, 137
Institute for Hispano-Cuban Culture, 154
Instituto Histo-bacteriológico, 65, 68, 70
Insurgent Cuba (Ferrer), 116n61
internationalism, 181–207, 205n33
International League for the Rational Education of Children, 200
International Telephone and Telegraph, 254, 256

Jagüeyal strike, 194
Jamaican laborers, 219, 222–23, 229n54, 294–303
Jones, Frank, 257
"José Martí" Popular University, 270
journalism: anarchism and, 181–207; *Maine* sinking and, 24–30, 35–36, 39–40, 42–43, 49n8, 50n10; modernity and, 167–68. See also *specific newspapers and publications*
Journal of African Society, 282
Journal of American Folklore, 282
Journal of Animal Behavior, 73
Juvanet, Arturo, 184, 187

King, Leland W., 46

labor activism and policies, 14–15, 18, 30, 83–92, 181–207, 212–31, 303–15
Lago Tacón, Manuel, 105
Lainé, Eduardo, 68
Landa, Evaristo, 108
Latifundia and the Cuban Economy (Maestri), 220
latifundia system, 209–10, 212–20
Latour, Bruno, 252, 266–67

Laval, Ramón A., 281
Law no. 148, 307
Lawn Tennis Club, 233
Law on Espionage, 228n46
League of Cuban Workers, 185
Leal, Eusebio, 48
Lee, Fitzhugh, 24, 28
Le Roy y Cassá, Jorge, 70, 171
Lévi-Strauss, Claude, 156–57
La Ley Arteaga, 214
La Ley de Inmigración, Colonización y Trabajo, 214–15
Leyva, Herminio, 124–25
Liberal Party, 8, 33, 56, 76, 108–9, 236, 244
Liberal period (of Latin American history), 8–9, 20n17
listening spaces and practices, 255–61
Litvak, Lily, 195
Lodge, Henry Cabot, 31
Lonja de Víveres, 154
López, Enrique, 68, 73
López Sánchez, José, 58
Losada, Fernández, 137
Loveira, Carlos, 10, 181, 199–200, 208–9, 217, 224, 285n1
Lozano Ariza, Miguel, 185
Lucena, Joaquín, 185
Luís, Washington, 176
Luyanó Slaughterhouse, 134
Lyceum, 233

Macbeath, Mario, 239
Maceo, Antonio, 11, 95–97, 116n50
Machado, Gerardo, 5, 44–47, 76, 155–57, 172–75, 220–23, 236–44, 272–76
Macon, Robert B., 36–37
Madan, Cristóbal, 168
Madrid Ophthalmic Institute, 56
Maestri, Raúl, 220
Magonigle, Harold Van Buren, 41
Magoon, Charles, 33–35, 170
Maine, the, 10–12, 22–53, 25, 27, 36, 40
malaria, 67–68, 127–28
Mann, James R., 37

Index | 359

Manson, Patrick, 67
La Manzana de Gómez, 162–63
Marinello, Juan, 234, 236, 274–75
Marrero, Leví, 163
Martí, José, 2, 43, 46, 101, 161, 173, 281
Martínez, Emilio, 68
Martínez, Miguel, 201
Martínez, Oscar, 184
Martínez Abello, Manuel, 184, 187–88, 198
Martínez Campos, Arsenio, 96
Martínez de Carvajal, Laura, 73
Maruri, Rodolfo, 155
Marvin, Carolyn, 252
Massaguer, Conrado W., 235
Mattos de Castro, Hebe, 83
McGillivray, Gillian, 254
McKinley, William, 44, 49n2
Mederos, Tomás, 132–33
media, 251–68. *See also* journalism
medicine, 54–70, 121, 123–27, 130–36
Mella, Julio Antonio, 242
Mencheta, Peris, 158–59
Mendieta, Carlos, 223
Menéndez Pidal, Ramón, 275
Mercado de Colón, 159
Mercado de Tacón, 159
La Meridiana, 161
Mesonier, Enrique, 185–86
Mexican Revolution, 192
Mexico, 4, 8–9, 153, 191, 193
Military Order no. 62, 212–13
Military Order no. 139, 212
Military Order no. 155, 214–15, 221
Military Order no. 213, 214
milk production, 136–44, *137*, *142*, *143*
Miramar Yacht Club, 233
Miranda, Consuelo, 274
Mir Durich, Domingo, 184, 190
modernity, 148–62, 169–77, 253–55, 261–64. *See also* sanitation discourses; science discourses; United States
Modesto Suárez y Hno, 142, *143*
Moncada, Guillermo, 116n50
Moncaleano, Juan Francisco, 185, 192

Montané, Luis, 56–57, 72–73, 75
Monte, Rafael, 97
Montoro, Rafael, 169, 175
Mora, Tomás, 90, 92
Moreno Fraginals, Manuel, 114n35, 178n3
Moret Law (1870), 84
Morgan, Charles, 30
Morton, F. W., 257
Motola, Patricia, 277
Movimiento Minorista, 274–75, 282, 286n19, 287n20
El Mundo (newspaper), 282
Mur, Tomás, 154
Mussolini, Benito, 270
mutual aid societies, 92–93, 120n101, 146n23, 196, 231–32

Najarro, Benigno, 96–97
Najarro Pujol, Lázaro David, 257
Nascentes, Antenor, 281
National Association of Rotary Clubs, 233
nationalism and nationalist movements, 17–18, 47–49, 62, 75–76, 220–25, 231–50, 271–73, 292–316. *See also* class; Cuba; race; sovereignty; Spain
National Movement of Veterans and Patriots, 270
National Workers Central of Cuba, 198
National Workers Confederation, 198
El negro esclavo (Ortiz), 169
Nettlau, Max, 192
New York Journal, 26, 29–30
The New York Times, 40, 42
La Noche (newspaper), 43
Nora, Pierre, 24
Nuestra Señora de las Mercedes Hospital, 159, 170–71
Nuevo Ideal (newspaper), 184, 195

El Obrero Industrial (newspaper), 193
Oglivie-Forbes, George, 314
O'Rourke, John, 34
Orsi, Peter, 48

Ortiz, Fernando, 17, 69, 144–45, 169, 176, 274–75, 277–79, 282–83, 286n8, 286n19

Palacio Aldama, 150, 161
Palacio Balboa, 162
Palacio de Bellas Artes, 161
Palacio de Gobierno, 155, 175
Palacio de Justicia, 161
Palacio de la Asociación de Dependientes, 152
Palacio de la Leche, 142
Palacio de la Música, 156
Palacio de los Capitanes Generales, 155, 174–75
Palacio del Segundo Cabo, 174–75
Palacio Presidencial, 155, 162
Palmer, Steven, 1–21, 54–81
Panama Canal Zone, 33, 67, 192
Parsons, Elsie Clews, 281
Partido Cubano Revolucionario, 245
Partido Independiente de Color, 110, 279
Partido Revolucionario Cubano, 2
Partido Socialista Popular, 236
Pasteur, Louis, 58–60, 62, 74, 80n63
patronato system, 85–86, 93, 184
Perdomo, Marialys, 277
Pérez, Bárbara, 89, 91, 106–8, 111
Pérez, Constantino, 103–5
Pérez, Louis A., 6, 118n74, 168, 179n40
Pérez Beato, Manuel, 280
Pérez Galdós plantation, 105–7
Pérez Moreno, Olga Lidia, 77n1
Pérez Vigueras, Idelfonso, 143
Pérez y Pérez, Tomás, 88–89, 91, 105–6, 106, 114n35
Pershing, John J., 44
Philippines, 23, 67
PIC (Independent Party of Color), 3
Piccirilli, Attilio, 41
Pingree, Geoffrey, 252
Piqueras Arenas, José Antonio, 1–21, 148–80, 225n2, 226n13
Plá, Eduardo, 131
Plasencia, Leonel, 139, 147n49

Platt, Orville, 3
Platt Amendment, 3–5, 7, 9, 23–24, 33, 54–55, 61–75, 125, 129, 244, 294, 316. *See also* Cuba; sovereignty; United States
Plaza de la Catedral, 155
Poey, Felipe, 281
Pogolotti, Dino, 179n22
The Political Lives of Dead Bodies (Verdery), 41
Poncet y de Cárdenas, Carolina, 274, 280, 286n17
Power, Julian, 258–59, 265
Prieto, Feliciano, 184, 187–88
El Productor (newspaper), 185, 193
La Protesta (newspaper), 193, 195
"Protesta de los Trece," 270, 286n19
proyecto batistiano, 151
Pruna, Pedro, 57
public health, 55, 64, 67–68, 73–75, 124, 128, 138, 141. *See also* epidemic diseases; sanitation discourses; *specific ailments*
Puerto Rico, 23, 67, 192
Pulitzer, Joseph, 26
Purdy & Henderson (company), 154
PWX broadcasts, 17, 253–68

Quesada, Caridad, 118n79
Quesada, Ciriaco and Cayetano, 96, 100, 104–5, 111
Quesada, Fermín, 109
Quesada, Gabriel, 93, 115n44
Quesada, José, 87
Quinta Palatino, 59, 73, 75, 80n63
Quiza Moreno, Ricardo, 17, 269–91

race: citizenship and, 2–3, 18, 68–69, 92–97, 100–111, 164, 169, 214, 220–25, 255, 292–316; class intersections and, 90–91, 93–94, 159–60, 176, 295–317; creole elite's anxieties and, 11, 220–25, 303–16; Cuban identity and, 3, 129, 186, 210, 214–15, 228n51, 292–315; epidemiology and, 68–69, 80n42; Folklore

race (*continued*)
  Society and, 17, 279–80, 289n37; labor activism and, 83–94, 102–9, 119n90, 210, 214, 219–20, 303–16; Spanish immigration and, 15, 18, 69, 151, 166, 183, 186, 202–3, 214, 229n51, 295–303; wars of independence and, 83–85, 92–93, 97–102, 116n61, 117n69. *See also* Cuba; eugenics; labor activism and policies; slavery
radio, 17, 251–68
"Radio and Love" (Guigou), 266
railway workers' strike (1911), 181, 199
Ramírez Olivera, Juan, 96
Ramos, Domingo, 140
rationalist movement (in education), 200–201
Ray, Charles, 311
RCA (corporation), 262–63
El Rebelde (newspaper), 193
reconcentración (policy), 38, 103, 124, 160, 169
Reed, Walter, 61–62, 67–68
Rego, Alfredo, 96
Regueiferos, Erasmos, 43
Regulation of Slaughterhouses, 132
Reis, João, 83
Renovación (faction), 77
Renovación (newspaper), 193
Reparto Las Murallas, 162, 166
La Revista Blanca (newspaper), 193
Revista de Cuba, 57–58
Revista de Medicina Tropical, 68
Revista Semanal Azucarera, 311
revolution of 1933, 5, 15
Rivera, Librado, 192
Rivero, Yeidy, 251
Rivero Muñiz, José, 185
Robledo, Pilar A., 192
Rockefeller Foundation, 70, 74
Rodríguez, Pedro, 185
Rodríguez y Lacret, Mayía, 175
Roig de Leuchsenring, Emilio, 49n4, 155, 282, 286n19
Roig San Martín, Enrique, 185

Roig y Mesa, Juan Tomás, 71
Roosevelt, Theodore, 44
Ros Planas, Francisco, 187–88, 191
Ross, Ronald, 67
Rotarian (publication), 233
Rotary clubs, 16, 231–50
Royal Academy of Sciences, 57
Ruiz Casabó, Manuel, 134–35
Rural Guard, 216, 220, 309

Saavedra, Abelardo, 194, 198–202
Sabatés Pérez, Juan, 236
Saco, José Antonio, 221, 288n27
Salamanca, Manuel, 131
Salinas, Marcelo, 185, 191
Salvochea, Fermí, 199
Sánchez Cobos, Amparo, 1–21, 181–207, 228n46
Sánchez Rosa, José, 192, 199
Sánchez Toledo, Domingo, 74
Sánchez y Murillo, Lino, 95
Sanguily, Manuel, 220
Sanitary Ordinances of 1906, 137
sanitation discourses, 14, 18, 62, 65–66, 121–47, 169–77
San Juan Hill, 32
Santa Clara (province), 82–120
Santa Rosalía estate, 87–88, 91, 95–96, 103
Santos Fernández y Hernández, Juan, 55–65, 68–77, 126, 288n25
Santovenia, Emeterio, 275, 287n24
Sarría, Claudio, 96–97, 100, 105
Schafer, R. Murray, 266
science discourses: anti-colonialist purposes of, 54–61, 64–65, 270; folklore and, 269–91; racialization and, 72–76, 80n42, 279–80, 288n36, 289n37; sanitation and, 121–47, 260; U.S. interests and, 55, 61–65, 71–75
Scott, Rebecca, 13–14, 82–120
Second World War, 164
Segre, Roberto, 153, 155, 157, 161–62, 175
Ser cubano (Pérez), 168
Shaffer, Kirwin, 182, 189, 192

Shafter, William R., 102
Sigsbee, Charles D., 28, 41
Simpson, José, 139–41
Sisson, Thomas, 36–37
slaughterhouses, 123, 125, 130–36, *135*, *136*
Slave and Citizen (Tannenbaum), 82
slavery: Brazil and, 9, 83; citizenship issues and, 82–92; Cuban emancipation and, 14, 22–23, 93, 102–9, 111, 166, 186, 211–16, 279, 292–303; sugar economy and, 56–58, 292–303; U.S. experiences with, 87, 102–3
smallholders, 90, 92, 211–16, 224–25
Social (magazine), 260–61
Sociedad del Folklore Cubano, 269–91, 286n8
Sociedad Económica Amigos del País, 272, 276, 282, 286n8, 287n24
Sociedad Gallega, 159
Sociedad Minerva, 93
Sociedad Racionalista, 201
Society of Cigarmakers, 184
Society of Geography of Paris, 146n23
Soledad (*central*), 86, 87–92, 94–96, 98, *104*, 105, 108, 113n16, 114n24
Soteras, Pedro, 184
sound studies, 251–68
sovereignty: *Maine* and, 11–12; radio technology and, 17, 251–68; rural elite and, 297–303; science discourses and, 12, 62, 125–26, 129–36; tutelage relationship and, 38, 40, 44, 152, 174, 244–46, 261–64; U.S. occupations and, 1, 10, 22–24, 33, 61–65, 102–9, 244. *See also* Cuba; Platt Amendment; sugar; United States
Spain: anarchism and, 182–85, 189–202, 207n53, 220; architecture of, 14–15, 38–43, 148–50; citizenship requirements of, 100–102; commercial agreements with, 239–42; Cuba's colonial status and, 1, 6, 9, 12, 19n2, 23–24, 56–61, 64, 67, 84–85, 88, 92–94, 96–103, 108–9, 129–31, 133, 144, 148–51, 160, 168–69, 174, 216, 232, 292–94; emigration to Cuba and, 15, 18, 69, 151, 166, 183, 186, 202–3, 214, 229n51, 295–303; *Maine* disaster and, 24–28, 31, 35–36
Spanish-American War, 5–6, 10, 22, 24–28, 31, 35–40
Spanish Anthropological Society, 56
Spanish style (architecture), 152–56
Special Commission for the Extinction of Glanders, 63–64
Spengler, Oswald, 270
Standard Fruit Company, 315
Stein, Stanley, 82
Sternberg, George, 60, 62, 67–68
Sterne, Jonathan, 260
Stoner, Lynn, 13
sugar: boom period of, 3–4, 87, 166–67, 172–73, 176, 216–20, 300; bust period of, 16, 121, 209, 316; *centrales* and, 16, 86–90, 92–98, 211, 300; labor activism and policies and, 102–9, 186, 194, 208–30, 292–316; Rotary clubs and, 236–37; scientific research and, 13, 55, 60, 71–75; slavery and, 56, 82–92. *See also* labor activism and policies; latifundia system
Sulzer, William, 34
"Superstitions and Cuban Children" (Miranda), 274
"Superstitions and Cuban Schoolchildren" (Fonseca García), 274

El Tabaco (journal), 241
Taft, William H., 3, 35, 42
Tallet, José Zacarías, 289n39
Tamayo y Figueredo, Diego, 55, 59–65, 75–76, 124–25
Tanco, Nicolás, 149, 162
Tannenbaum, Frank, 82
Teatro Albisu, 159
Teatro Alhambra, 159
Teatro Irijoa, 159, 165
Teatro Martí, 159
Teatro Nacional, 174
Teatro Payret, 159, 165

Teatro Tacón, 150, 154, 159
Tejara, Vicente, 204n15
El Templete, 155
Tenorio Fernández, Juan, 185
Ten Years' War, 57, 85, 95, 162, 166
Thompson, E. P., 204n7
¡Tierra!, 15, 181–207
Tierra y Libertad (newspaper), 193, 198
Tinajero, Araceli, 255
Tomé, Pedro, 162
Toraya, José, 154
tourism, 46, 155, 159–69, 245–46
La Tramontana (newspaper), 185
transnationality, 15, 181–207, 205n33, 275, 294–303
Tratado de Reciprocidad Comercial, 215
Treaty of Paris, 149
Treaty of Zanjón, 163
Trelles, Carlos, 122
La Tropical (beer), 283, 284
Tropical Diseases (Manson), 67
tuberculosis, 55, 64, 73–75, 124, 128, 138, 141
Tur i Tur, Juan, 185
Turner, John, 234
typhoid fever, 121, 124, 128, 138

Ugarte, Bernabé, 184
Unión Club de La Habana, 232
Unión de Fabricantes de Tabacos y Cigarros, 241
United Fruit, 8, 213
United States: agricultural research and, 12–13, 71–75; civil religion of, 35–38, 41–47; class politics and, 182, 189–95; Cuban interventions and occupations by, 1–3, 5, 9–10, 13–14, 19n1, 22–53, 61–65, 71, 101–9, 122, 124–25, 129, 132, 152–56, 169–77, 179n40, 195–200, 216–25; economic dealings with Cuba of, 4, 33–35, 49n2, 87, 148–49, 151–56, 162–69, 171–77, 187, 211–25, 226n17, 227n27, 250n50; epidemiological interests of, 54–55, 61–70, 144; imperialism of, 1–3, 5–6, 8–10, 13–14, 26–28, 42, 44, 47–49, 129; modernity's relation to, 148–62, 167–77, 253–55, 261–64; public imagination of Cuba and, 23–28, 35–41, 46, 167–68, 245, 251–68; Revolution of 1959 and, 47–49; Rotary clubs and, 16–17, 231–50; sanitation discourses and, 14, 121–47, 169–77; Spanish-American War and, 5–6, 10, 24–28, 31–35, 39–40
Urrutia, Gustavo, 282, 289n37
USS Birmingham, 40
USS Maine, 10–12, 22–53, 25, 27
USS New York, 30
USS North Carolina, 40

Vallina, Pedro, 199
¡Vapor correo! (Cabrera), 168–69
Varona, José Enrique, 12
Vasconcelos, Ramón, 289n37
Vassouras (Stein), 82
Vedado (neighborhood), 164–65, 168, 177
Vedado Tennis Club, 232
Velasco, Pedro, 56
Venegas, Carlos, 166
Venetian Renaissance, 152
Verdery, Katherine, 41
Versailles Treaty, 7
veterinarians, 14, 121–47
Viaje a la luna (Cabrera), 168
Vida Nueva (journal), 121, 193
Vildósola, Francisco, 59
Villamisar, Nicolás, 192
Volktam und Kultur der Romanan, 282
La Voz del Dependiente (newspaper), 202

Walker, William, 8
Wallace, Henry A., 145
WEAF (radio station), 254
Weimar Germany, 7–8
West Indian laborers, 18, 295–316
Westinghouse, 257, 260–63
Weyler, Valeriano, 103, 124, 160
Whitney, Robert, 18, 254, 292–321
Wilson, James Grant, 41
Wizards and Scientists (Palmié), 80n42

Wood, Leonard, 44, 62–65, 75, 79n28, 107, 125, 152, 170–71, 211–12
Workers Solidarity, 198
The World, 26
Wurtzler, Steve, 261
Wynne, Clive, 74

Yearwood, Charles, 302–3
yellow fever, 61–70, 123–27, 144, 146n23, 170, 245

Yerkes, Robert, 73–74, 80n63
YMCA (Young Men's Christian Association), 232
Young, Samuel B. M., 33

Zaldivar, Miguel, 133
Zayas, Alfredo, 4, 17, 19n9, 35, 43, 73, 175, 244, 253–54
Zulueta, Julián, 162

www.ingramcontent.com/pod-product-compliance
Lightning Source LLC
Chambersburg PA
CBHW061343300426
44116CB00011B/1966